Economic transformation in Eastern Europe and the distribution of income

Who gains and who loses from economic transformation in Eastern Europe is a key question, but one which is too rarely discussed. This book examines the evidence about the distribution of income and poverty under Communism in Eastern Europe. Contrary to popular impressions, a great deal of information exists about the distribution of earnings and household incomes in Czechoslovakia, Hungary and Poland. With *glasnost'* much material previously kept secret in the USSR became available. The book contains extensive statistical evidence that has not previously been assembled on a comparative basis, and takes the story right up to the end of Communism. The findings bring out the differences in experience between countries under Communism: between Central Europe and the former Union, between Czechoslovakia, Hungary and Poland, and between the newly independent states of the the former Soviet Union.

Economic transformation in Eastern Europe and the distribution of income

ANTHONY B. ATKINSON

and

JOHN MICKLEWRIGHT

Published by the Press Syndicate of the University of Cambridge
The Pitt Building, Trumpington Street, Cambridge CB2 1RP
40 West 20th Street, New York, NY 10011-4211, USA
10 Stamford Road, Oakleigh, Victoria 3166, Australia

First published 1992

Printed in Great Britain at the University Press, Cambridge

A catalogue record for this book is available from the British Library

Library of Congress cataloguing in publication data

Atkinson, A. B. (Anthony Barnes)
Economic transformation in Eastern Europe and the distribution of
income/Anthony B. Atkinson and John Micklewright.
p.   cm.
Includes bibliographical references and index.
ISBN 0-521-43329-0. – ISBN 0-521-43882-9 (pbk.)
1. Income distribution – Europe, Eastern. 2. Income distribution – Central
Europe. 3. Europe, Eastern – Economic conditions – 1945–1989. 4. Central
Europe – Economic conditions. I. Micklewright, John. II. Title.
HC244.Z91514   1992
339.2′0947 – dc20   92-17601 CIP

ISBN 0 521 43329 0 hardback
ISBN 0 521 43882 9 paperback

SE

To all those who have helped us and
especially Judith and Tina

Contents

Figures

Tables

Acknowledgements

This book would not have been possible without the help of a great many people. First, we must thank the government statisticians and ministry officials from Eastern Europe who provided us with much of the data and other information on which we draw in the book. Without their patient help, often involving substantial amounts of their time, we would have had much less material and would have understood far less about its significance.

In the course of the research for the book we corresponded with and visited the central statistical offices and other relevant government offices of the four Eastern European countries which we cover. Our correspondance and discussions, often involving translation and interpretation provided by the offices concerned, were based around a standard questionnaire which we prepared. The response to this was most generous and the exchanges were, for our part, enjoyable as well as informative. A number of those we met were later kind enough to comment on parts of the manuscript.

We hope we have done justice to what we were told or were given. However, we would like to stress that none of those thanked below are to be held in any way responsible for errors we have made or for the views expressed in this book:

Jaroslav Berka   Federal Statistical Office, Prague
Eda Dabrowska   Institute of Labour and Social Affairs,Warsaw
Jiří Dlouhý   Federal Statistical Office, Prague
Ödön Éltető   Central Statistical Office, Budapest
Gáspár Fajth   Central Statistical Office, Budapest
Jiří Fremr   Federal Statistical Office, Prague
G. Gennikovna   Goskomstat, Moscow
V. Guriev   Goskomstat, Moscow
Miroslav Hiršl   Federal Ministry of Labour, Prague
Ondřej Huslar   Federal Ministry of Finance, Prague

Małgorzata Kalaska   Central Statistical Office, Warsaw
András Keleti   Central Statistical Office, Budapest
L. Khakhulina   VTsIOM, Moscow
N. Kovaleva   VTsIOM, Moscow
Jan Kordos   Central Statistical Office, Warsaw
A. Krakovsky   Goskomstat, Moscow
Alena Kroupová   Federal Ministry of Labour and Social Affairs, Prague
Antoni Kubiczek   Central Statistical Office, Warsaw
Jaroslav Kux   Federal Statistical Office, Prague
Iraida Manykina   Goskomstat, Moscow
M. Mozhina   Institute of Social-Economic Problems of the Population, Moscow
Elzbieta Rawicz   Central Statistical Office, Warsaw
Jan Rutkowski   Central Statistical Office, Warsaw
Zosia Rutkowska   Institute of Labour and Social Affairs, Warsaw
Judit Salamin   Central Statistical Office, Budapest
Adam Szulc   Central Statistical Office, Warsaw
Janina Szumlicz   Institute of Labour and Social Affairs, Warsaw
L. Zubova   VTsIOM, Moscow

Secondly, we owe much to those who helped us with the research in STICERD at the London School of Economics and in the European University Institute, Florence (EUI).

At EUI, two persons worked with us throughout the course of the book, and we are grateful to the Institute for providing funds which made this possible. Sheila Marnie's knowledge of the Soviet literature and of the Russian language were invaluable. Without her help we could not have included the USSR in our study. She suggested numerous sources, was responsible for the collection of all the data from the USSR, and visited Moscow on our behalf for discussions with the statistical authorities and other officials. Gianna Giannelli carried out much of the analysis of the data for the tables in the Statistical Appendix. This she did with great efficiency and cheerfulness. By taking responsibility for this considerable task she provided a firm anchor in a turbulent sea of data, thus significantly shortening the amount of time we needed to write the book.

Several other persons at STICERD and EUI provided invaluable assistance. Joanna Gomulka greatly aided our understanding of information we had collected in Warsaw. Following this, she undertook a visit on our behalf to the Polish central statistical office to obtain much of the household income data we eventually used and to clarify a number of aspects with those responsible for these data. Her comments on the manuscript were particularly useful. Jiří Večerník of the Academy of

Sciences, Prague, spent a month at EUI as a visitor under the PHARE programme during which time he spent long hours explaining Czechoslovak data to us. He provided us with all our other contacts in the CSFR, helped in many ways during our visit to Prague, and supplied us with a substantial amount of the data from his country. Without his generous help, our analysis of Czechoslovakia would have been seriously restricted.

At STICERD, the work came under the umbrella of the Welfare State Programme. Denise Marchant helped by collecting and processing data for the Appendix. Holly Sutherland prepared and analysed the British microdata which we use in comparisons. Our statistical work was made much easier by use of the INEQ programme written by Frank Cowell (details of which are given in the Sources and Methods section of the book) and we are grateful to him for the helpful responses he gave to our queries and suggestions. At an early stage of the work, M. Zukowski helped identify the relevant Polish sources and Karen Gardiner assisted us by uncovering and collecting material present in the LSE Library.

At EUI, Milica Uvalic drew our attention to a number of most useful references in the Institute's Library. Agnes and Arpád Szakolczai and Agnes Hochberg translated Hungarian material for us, as did Theresa Gericke who also found a valuable source of data in Budapest. Sarah Jarvis collected data for us while in Hungary. Paula Adam helped with the index. Jane Dickson, in London, and Marcia Gastaldo, in Florence, did much to reduce the difficulties of our being based in different countries; they copied, faxed and posted large amounts of material between England and Italy. Marcia helped organise our travel to work with each other and to visit Eastern Europe. Jane took responsibility for producing the Statistical Appendix in camera-ready form. She did this with great skill under considerable pressure of time.

Thirdly, there are the people who helped us by providing names of possible contacts in Eastern Europe, by drawing our attention to sources, by commenting on our ideas, by answering our questions, by reading draft chapters, or who helped in a number of other ways. We thank: Charles Atkinson, Judith Atkinson, Nicholas Barr, Andrea Brandolini, Pat Brown, Shelley Buckwalter, Sandrine Cazes, Giovanni Andrea Cornia, Jean-Yves Duclos, Gosta Esping-Andersen, Zsuzsa Ferge, John Hills, Stephen Jenkins, Stanislaw Gomulka, Björn Gustafsson, Jacques Le Cacheux, Katarina Katz, Christine Kessides, Alan Kirman, George Kopits, Alastair McAuley, Branco Milanovic, Christian Morrisson, Gyula Nagy, Ludmila Nivorozhkina, James Owen, Tim Smeeding, Sándor Sipos, Eva Souskova, Julia Szalai, Catherine Tausz, Irena Topińska, David Winter, Simon Wood, and the anonymous readers of our original book proposal.

Finally, we would like to thank Patrick McCartan and his colleagues at Cambridge University Press, notably Anne Rix, for their work on the production of the book.

And last, but by no means least, we thank our long-suffering families for continued support and encouragement. Because of Judith and Tina's contribution, we dedicate the book to them.

Brightlingsea and Scarperia

1 Introduction and summary

It is everyone's hope that the present economic and political reforms in Eastern Europe will lead to marked rises in the national incomes of these countries, narrowing the gap between their standard of living and that found in Western Europe. At the same time, it seems clear that the reforms will do much more than change average income in the countries concerned – they will also change its *distribution*. There will be losers as well as gainers from the transition to a market economy. Privatisation will benefit some people more than others. Macro-economic adjustments will bear more heavily on some groups than on others.

The distributional aspects of economic transformation have not been at the centre of popular and academic discussion of change in Eastern Europe. The socialist ideal of economic justice is widely regarded as discredited. The emergence with the transition of new inequalities is regarded as an irrelevance. The focus is on other concerns, such as stimulating the growth of the economy, dealing with macro-economic imbalance, the opening up of markets, and the privatisation of state enterprises. Economic success is to be judged in aggregate terms or by the extent to which the economy approaches a free market.

To give an example of the lack of attention paid to distributional issues, the impressive *Journal of Economic Perspectives* Symposium on 'Economic Transition in the Soviet Union and Eastern Europe' (Fall 1991) makes only passing references to earnings and income differentials. It is noteworthy that recently published Western statistical handbooks on the former USSR, valuable though they are, do not cover in any detail the distribution of income. Ryan (1990) gives data on *average* pensions; Pockney (1991) provides information on average wages but not on the distribution of earnings. The handbook *Comecon Data 1990* (Vienna Institute for Comparative Economic Studies, 1991), covering the whole former Soviet bloc, contains no information on the distribution of income.

Why, then, do we devote this book to the distribution of earnings and income in Eastern Europe as it was before 1990?

1

1.1 The distribution of income and economic transformation

People hold very different views with regard to the role of distributional issues in post-transition Eastern Europe. First, there are those who conclude from the rejection of Communism that the distribution of income has become a matter of indifference – that we should not be concerned with who benefits from the introduction of a market economy and who bears the costs. Such a view may be justified on the grounds that it is the *process* rather than the *consequences* by which economic organisation is to be judged. Free exchange on the market is seen as a morally acceptable process and income differences are justifiable providing that the initial point of departure is regarded as 'fair'. If the market economy leads to inequality of outcomes, then such inequality has no ethical implications. This argument is often accompanied by suggestions that, in any case, inequality was no less under Communism than under capitalism – that the idea of greater equity under socialism was a mirage.

Indifference with regard to outcomes is justified, on this argument, by the fairness of the starting point. Concern is with equality of opportunity, not of results, as illustrated by the 1991 manifesto of Civic Forum in Czechoslovakia:

Our approach to the establishment of social justice stems from the belief that equity and justice mean equal opportunities, not equal outcomes. (quoted by Brada, 1991, p. 173)

The precise meaning of equality of opportunity is less easily determined, but the initial opportunities of the new market economies of Eastern Europe are inevitably heavily influenced by the pre-1990 situation. It is not as though the market economy is being established by settlers newly arrived in a previously unpopulated land. The slate is not being wiped completely clean and the state of distribution under Communism is of relevance. If, for example, the former political elite enjoyed substantial economic benefits under Communism, they may have been well placed to take advantage of the move to a market economy. This then is the first reason for being interested in the pre-1990 distribution.

A different position with regard to distributional outcomes is held by those concerned to set in place an adequate *social safety net*. This has been the focus of many policy-makers. The study of the Soviet economy by the IMF, World Bank, OECD and EBRD predicted that the move to a market economy and removal of existing government intervention will 'impose substantial hardship on many groups of the population during the transition' (IMF *et al.*, 1991, p. 331) and went on to argue that 'to minimize this hardship and to assure political support for economic restructuring, it is necessary to design policies that cushion the less well-off from excessive burdens'. The need for a safety net has been emphasised in other countries. The account given by Charap and Dyba (Minister in the Czech government) of the transition in Czechoslovakia lists as one of the six key points of the reform 'the creation of an adequate social safety net' (1991, p. 581). In his book on *The Road to a Free Economy*, Kornai advocates that in Hungary 'aid must be given to all whom the stabilization lands in trouble until they are able to adapt to the new situation' (1990, p. 198).

This position regarding distributional issues during transition may therefore be summarised as concern that there be an effective safety net. What exactly is meant by a 'safety net' is not always clear, but, in general, it is contrasted with the more far-reaching redistributive ambitions of a socialist society. A not untypical view is expressed in the study of the Soviet economy by the IMF *et al.* quoted earlier:

While there is likely to be some increase in inequality in the transition period, it is important from a policy point of view to be concerned about minimum living standards of the poor rather than inequality per se. (IMF *et al.*, 1991, p. 154)

On this basis, the transition to a market economy may be justified on the grounds that, even if the better-off gain most, the poor will enjoy an absolute improvement in their income. This is often referred to as the *trickle-down* defence of economic growth. In order to judge whether or not this has been achieved, evidence about the position of the poor under Communism is obviously necessary. If the bottom groups enjoyed a larger share in the pre-1990 distribution, then a corresponding increase in average per capita income is required to justify the economic transition.

The arguments listed so far attach either no weight to the distributional outcome or are concerned only with the absolute position of the poor. A third position takes a wider view of the distributional objective, being concerned with the *relative* distribution of income. This recognises that, as in the welfare economics of Western market economies, social welfare depends on both total income and its distribution, a position that is described in textbook accounts of policy as an equity/efficiency trade-off. This trade-off between equity and efficiency has been seen as the central dilemma of economic policy-making in Western countries. Okun, Chairman of the US Council of Economic Advisers under President Johnson, wrote a book called *Equality and Efficiency: the Big Trade-Off*, in which he described it as:

our biggest socioeconomic tradeoff, and [one which] plagues us in dozens of dimensions of social policy. (1975, p. 2)

It is this quotation that heads the relevant chapter in Samuelson's *Economics*, one of the best-known student texts in the US (Samuelson and Nordhaus, 1989). The authors associate the institutions of modern capitalism with the pursuit of efficiency, but see this as being tempered by democratic ideals of equal rights:

If a democratic society does not like the distribution of dollar votes under a laissez-faire market system, it can take steps to change the distribution of income. (1989, p. 466)

This quotation envisages the capitalist system moving round the equity/efficiency frontier in the direction of greater equity; the transition from Communism in Eastern Europe may be interpreted as a move in the opposite direction, with greater efficiency being chosen at the expense of less equality. In this context, it is helpful, at least for understanding, to place the choices made pre-1990 in Eastern Europe relative to those in their Western counterparts. Was it the case that earnings differentials in Eastern Europe were compressed relative to the West (with associated costs in terms of incentives)? How far did a different balance between wages and social benefits lead to a less unequal distribution of household incomes under Communism?

The distributional outcome of economic transformation may be of interest not just in its own right but also as a means to other objectives. Concern for distributional equity may be justified not just intrinsically but also on account of its contribution to the securing of effective liberty and democracy. Even though the Communist regimes had undisputed costs in terms of the loss of personal liberty and democratic freedom, this does not mean that *all* redistribution is in conflict with liberty and democracy. While some people hold that liberty only requires the absence of restrictions, others hold that the effective enjoyment of liberty depends on the guarantee of a basic minimum of resources for all. On this latter view, the provision of a safety net may underwrite freedom in legal, political and other spheres. One of the most fully articulated justifications is that of Hayek, who in his *Constitution of Liberty* argued that:

in the Western world some provision for those threatened by the extremes of indigence or starvation due to circumstances beyond their control has long been accepted as a duty of the community ... The necessity of some such arrangement in an industrial society is unquestioned – be it only in the interest of those who require protection against acts of desperation on the part of the needy. (1960, p. 285)

The IMF *et al.* in their report referred to the need to ensure political support for restructuring, and questions of political stability must be to the forefront in Eastern Europe and the republics which formed the USSR. The distribution of political power is affected by the extent of economic inequality. The legitimacy of governments may be called into question if too large a gap opens between rich and poor.

In considering these distributional issues, one recurring consideration is the state of distribution in Eastern Europe before 1990. The argument for rejecting concern with distributional outcomes is often accompanied by assertions that empirically inequality was no less under Communism. The provision of a safety net is related to the improvement or protection of the position of the least advantaged relative to the starting point in 1990. Support for a move towards greater efficiency at the cost of less equity derives from the presumption that equality had received too much weight under Communist governments, a comparison being made implicitly or explicitly with Western societies. Earnings differentials are considered to have been too compressed. Considerations of political stability are concerned with changes relative to the past.

It is for this reason that we have concentrated in this book on describing the position *before reform* regarding the distribution of income in Eastern Europe. Was the earnings distribution in fact more compressed than that in Western market economies? Was there less overall income inequality? How had inequality been changing over time? How much regional inequality was there in the Soviet Union and were the different republics similar in their income distributions? Was there poverty under Communism and what support mechanisms existed to combat low incomes? It is our hope that, by describing the situation under Communism, we can provide a base of evidence against which the economic transition of the 1990s can be assessed.

1.2 Scope and contribution of the book

The extent of inequality of incomes under Communism is a subject about which a great deal has already been written, and we would like to acknowledge at the outset our very considerable debt to the earlier literature. What do we add that is new? First of all, much of that literature is rather dated and we want to bring the analysis forward right up to the end of the Communist period. The 1980s was a decade of considerable economic change. One of the reasons commonly stated for the collapse of the Communist regimes was a decline in real living standards. Was it also a period of rising inequality? In considering the results of economic transformation, does it make any difference whether we take the 1970s or the 1980s as the point of reference?

Secondly, notwithstanding the earlier literature, it was clear that many economists in the West were unaware – as were we – of the *extent* of the data collected in pre-reform Eastern Europe on distributional issues. Impressions are dominated by the situation in the Soviet Union, where until recently almost no data were available, but the position in countries such as Hungary and Poland was quite different. In these countries the Central

Statistical Offices have an impressive record of publications concerning the distribution of earnings and income. Some of this information is contained in publications readily available in libraries in the West, but its existence is not widely known. This led us to collect and make available data for analysis by others. To this purpose, we have put together a Statistical Appendix containing all the raw data which we have used. For each country we have assembled as long a time-series as we could for the post-war period on the distribution of earnings and of household income.

Thirdly, we consider evidence for several countries in Eastern Europe: Czechoslovakia, Hungary, Poland and the Soviet Union. We have found relatively few surveys which had brought together material covering a number of countries. This seemed an important omission to us. Without some comparison across the different countries it is easy to fall into the trap of treating them as a homogenous bloc. The evidence from one country on the extent of inequality under Communism may be quite inapplicable to other countries. Just to give one example, the changes in income inequality in Poland during the 1980s, following the advent of Solidarity, may be quite different from those in other countries.

Our work is comparative in another sense, in that we seek to compare the evidence available for these four countries with that for the United Kingdom. This is important for the obvious reason that a comparison of the distribution of incomes in Communist and market economies provides valuable insights into the working of different economic systems. The extent of inequality under Communism compared with that under capitalism has been of enduring interest, and this has been heightened by the move of the command economies of Eastern European countries to the pattern of economic organisation seen in the West. Moreover, the evolution of the distribution of income over time is of particular interest in view of the evidence of rising inequality in some, but not all, Western market economies during the 1980s.

Our concern is, however, not only with the substantive questions. Equally important in our view is the light that the comparison can cast on the *quality of evidence* available in Communist countries. It is common to hear statistics on earnings or incomes in Eastern Europe being dismissed as incomplete or unrepresentative, without regard either to any variations in quality within the region or to the fact that statistics in Western countries are also incomplete and unrepresentative. The quality of data found in different Eastern European countries should be compared, not with an unattainable ideal, but with that found in OECD countries. The qualifications which surround estimates of the distribution of income in countries such as the United Kingdom help put in perspective the doubts which have been expressed with regard to the statistics available for Communist countries.

When attempting to make such a comparison, we were indeed struck by the fact that there have been relatively few attempts in the Western literature to discuss systematically the methodology of the Eastern European sources. An exception is the USSR where the lack of almost any published data for many years forced researchers to consider in some detail the methodology behind what information was available. For other countries, with richer sources of data, it is rare to find in the Western literature any adequate account of the methods used to collect the data. It is hard to find any discussion of basic issues such as the sampling frames and response rates in household surveys. Yet, we know from analysis of Western data that such detail is vital to a clear understanding of what the data can reveal. This is doubly important when comparing data across countries. Are the income distribution data from country X comparable with those from country Y? In what direction are the known limitations of the sources likely to affect the comparison?

The development of methods for comparing distributional outcomes is relevant not just for the historical question of comparing Communism with capitalism. The comparison of the distribution in years after 1990 with that prevailing under the Communist regime is going to raise many of the same problems as the comparison of East and West pre-1990. What are the available data from Eastern Europe pre-1990, how were they collected, and how should they be interpreted? Without an assessment of the quantity and quality of data pre-1990, we lack a reference point from which to appraise information on what is happening as a result of the process of transformation. As it was put by Heston and Summers in a different context:

[it is] our strong view that documentation of recent Eastern European economic experience is a statistical task that should rank in importance with and be a part of any revisions in currently collected economic statistics. (1990, p. 1)

It therefore seemed important to collect together information on statistical methods relating to distributional issues in pre-reform Eastern Europe and to provide some assessment of the reliability of the data and of the information they contain. This is why we devote to these issues the whole of Chapter 3 and a lengthy section at the end of the book entitled 'Sources and Methods'. Our discussion is undoubtedly incomplete but we feel that the information provided in these sections has helped us to improve our own understanding of Eastern European data.

Choice of countries

The countries from Eastern Europe that we consider are Czechoslovakia, Hungary, Poland and the former USSR. For convenience we include the former USSR in 'Eastern Europe'; on occasion, we refer to the first three countries as 'Central European'. The three Central European countries are fairly obvious choices. They are the countries which are most advanced in terms of economic and political reform; they are countries for which considerable amounts of data on the distribution of earnings and income are available from the pre-1990 period. The former USSR is too big and too important to be ignored; its population of 286 million is some four and a half times that of the three Central European countries taken together. It is the country where the Communist experiment had the longest trial, although it should be emphasised that our concern here is with the period after the Second World War. And there is a rich seam of Western literature on distributional issues in the Soviet economy which has proved invaluable to us as newcomers to the study of the region.

It is evident that the situation in the USSR is different from that in the other three countries, just as there are large differences between the different independent states which made up the former Union. One of our aims is to bring out these differences. In the case of the USSR we consider the state of distribution at the level of the individual republics as well as that of the Union. Given the events which have taken place in the USSR since we began writing, it is evidently of interest to treat the republics on a par with the Central European countries. Not only Russia but also the Ukraine, Uzbekistan and Kazakhstan have larger populations than Czechoslovakia. Belarus has the same population as Hungary. These population figures are given in Table 1.1, in decreasing order of size, where we also show the populations of the two republics in Czechoslovakia, of England, Scotland, Wales and Northern Ireland (virtually the same size as Estonia). For those whose geographical knowledge is as shaky as was ours, we include in Figure 1.1 a map identifying the different countries and republics. Among other things, it serves to bring out how far removed geographically much of the former Soviet Union is from Europe.

The three Central European countries of Czechoslovakia, Hungary and Poland are, as a group, different from the Soviet Union, but it is equally important to stress the differences between them – especially in the period which led up to 1990. These differences are one of the principal reasons for selecting a number of countries for analysis. Czechoslovakia was, right up until November 1989, a 'hardline' Communist state committed to the centrally planned command economy system and with an almost complete absence of legalised private employment. In Poland and Hungary, the end of Communist Party rule was less dramatic and in both cases came after periods in which there had been some decentralisation of the economic system, since 1981 in the case of Poland and since as long ago as 1968 in Hungary. In Hungary the Communist Party appeared simply to run out of steam and gave up power quietly. In Poland the change from Communist

Table 1.1 *Population of countries at end of 1980s*

	Population (000's)
USSR	286,731
Russia	147,400
UNITED KINGDOM	57,236
Ukraine	51,707
England	47,689
POLAND	38,038
Uzbekistan	19,905
Kazakhstan	16,536
CZECHOSLOVAKIA	15,639
HUNGARY	10,375
Czech Republic	10,364
Belarus	10,200
Azerbaidzhan	7,038
Georgia	5,443
Slovak Republic	5,275
Tadzhikistan	5,109
Scotland	5,091
Moldavia	4,338
Kirgizia	4,290
Armenia	3,288
Lithuania	3,690
Turkmenia	3,534
Wales	2,873
Latvia	2,680
Northern Ireland	1,583
Estonia	1,573

Note:
The dates to which these figures refer are as follows:
Czechoslovakia (1989), Hungary (January 1990),
Poland (December 1989), USSR (1989), UK (mid-
year estimate of resident population, 1989).
Sources: (see Sources and Methods for definition of
abbreviations used for statistical yearbooks.)
Czechoslovakia: SR 1990, Table 1-1, p. 21, Table 1-
2, p. 41, Table 1-3, p. 57.
Hungary: SY 1989, Table 3.1, p. 37.
Poland: RS 1990, Table 4(62), p. 39.
USSR: NK 1989, p. 17.
UK: AAS 1991, Table 2.1, p. 6.

Figure 1.1 Country map 1992.

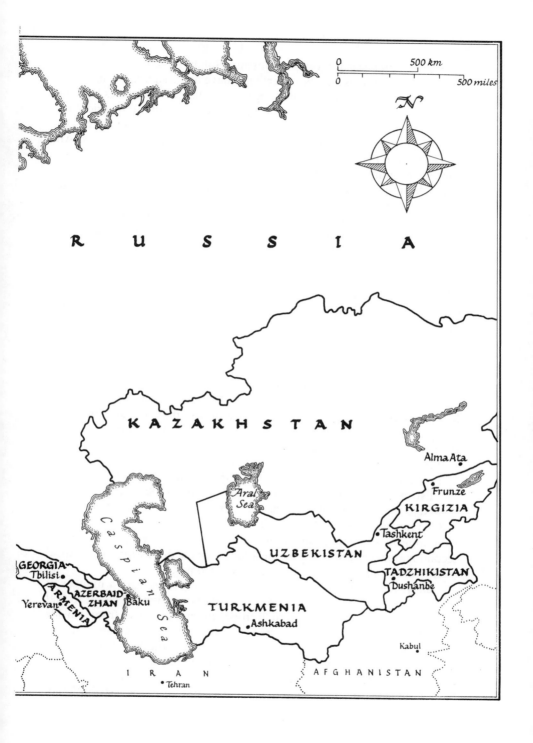

rule came after several years of intense Solidarity-led pressure which, amongst other things, can be expected to have had a significant impact on the distribution of earnings. In Hungary private sector ventures had been legalised since the early 1980s; while in Poland the substantial agricultural sector had always been largely in private hands. Both these factors can again be expected to be reflected in the income distribution figures. And there are the differences in macro-economic experience in the three Central European countries and the USSR.

In selecting these four countries we have had to ignore others which could put forward equally good claims for attention. An obvious choice would have been East Germany. A relatively affluent country with a 'hardline' regime, its transformation 'by merger' gives it special interest. Yugoslavia would have been interesting in view of its unique form of economic organisation within the Communist bloc. The other Balkan countries offer examples of less developed economies which would have provided useful comparisons. In the end, however, we had to restrict ourselves to the four – Czechoslovakia, Hungary, Poland and the USSR – in order to keep the book within manageable length.

A view from Britain

It will be evident to the reader that we are not experts on any of the four Eastern European countries we cover. Nor do we speak any of the languages concerned. This undoubtedly means that we have in places misunderstood the significance of certain statistics and institutions despite the patient help of many people with more knowledge than ourselves.

What the book offers is a view from outside, or more specifically a view from Britain. The evidence assembled is that available to outsiders about the distribution of income in Eastern Europe pre-1990, and it is in turn related to that for the United Kingdom. As we have already indicated, this is done for two reasons. The comparison of inequality and poverty under Communism and capitalism is an important substantive question, but a second major concern is to provide a focus for the discussion of statistical methodology and the meaning of data on incomes.

Ideally, we would take for these purposes of comparison a number of Western countries, including those at a level of development closer to that found in the four from Eastern Europe, or indeed those from outside OECD. By showing results for a range of Western countries we would be able to exhibit the diversity to be found within the group of market economies, a diversity which is often forgotten in debate about alternative economic systems. However, to do this on anything other than a superficial basis would have involved a major comparative study of the distribution of income in the West. This in turn would have seriously delayed the appearance of the book. We have therefore chosen to focus primarily from the point of view of comparison on the United Kingdom, the country whose data and institutions we know best and where we can draw best on our experience of problems of methodology. (On occasion we refer loosely to 'Britain'; technically 'Great Britain' refers to England, Wales and Scotland, whereas the 'United Kingdom' includes in addition Northern Ireland. Where it is important, we make the distinction precise.)

In making this choice, we are in no way suggesting that the United Kingdom is typical. The extent of inequality in Britain has undoubtedly been influenced by the Conservative government which came to power in 1979. The period since this date has seen a significant attempt to change much of the ideology behind the political and economic organisation of British society. Successive administrations under Mrs Thatcher sought to reduce the role of the government and to increase the emphasis on individual responsibility and economic freedom. This led to cuts in direct taxation, rising real wages for those in employment, a growth of self-employment, against which must be set a declining overall proportion in work, a reduction in the relative level of state cash transfers, and concern about the services provided for health, public transport and education. People may argue about the extent to which fundamental changes did actually occur, but the government's intentions were undoubtedly more radical than those of most governments on the mainland of Europe. It is certainly not the case that what happened in Britain in the 1980s was representative of Western countries. At the same time, the experience of Britain has attracted considerable attention in Eastern Europe, the 'export' of information and advice on privatisation being an example.

In terms of methodological comparison, Britain is again not typical. There has been a long tradition of the collection of household survey data which can be used to analyse the distribution of income and the extent of poverty, the latter dating back to the pioneering studies of Charles Booth and Seebohm Rowntree at the end of the last century. The existence of a continuing household survey, the Family Expenditure Survey, provides regular information, in contrast to the situation in countries where such surveys are only carried out periodically (as, for example, in France). At the same time, while in most countries the quantity and quality of distributional data has been improving over time, the overall availability of information on the distribution of income in the United Kingdom did in certain crucial respects worsen over the 1980s. As part of its efforts to cut public expenditure and reduce state intrusion, the first Thatcher administration undertook a review of government statistical services which significantly diminished the work carried out in this area. In particular, the official estimates of the distribution of income, which used to be included in the national accounts publication, are now only produced at three-yearly intervals and with considerable delay.

It is for these reasons that we would like to emphasise that we view the subject from a distinct perspective – a perspective which no doubt leads us to view some aspects more clearly than others.

1.3 Plan of the book and summary of main conclusions

The book ranges widely in terms of its subject matter, from ethical judgments to sample survey methodology, from economic theory to labour market institutions, from the measurement of subsistence to the valuation of the privileges of the elite. At the same time, each of the chapters tends to focus on a particular set of issues, and the reader can select those parts of special interest. The aim of this section is to describe the contents of each chapter and to summarise the conclusions.

Chapter 2

Chapter 2 aims to answer the question – why should we be interested in the distribution of income before 1990? How is study of this topic related to the economic transformation now underway? Is what happened in Eastern Europe under Communism now only of historical interest?

To begin with, we should make clear that it is not our belief that the distribution of income is the sole, or even the major, criterion for evaluating the historical experience of Communism. It is not our intention to provide such an evaluation, which would undoubtedly give priority to issues of civil and democratic rights. However, we do feel that an understanding of the state of economic justice under Communism is necessary in assessing the consequences of economic transformation. Once basic liberties have been achieved in the new democracies of Eastern Europe, the distribution of economic advantage becomes a legitimate issue for concern. As we have already argued, there are different forms that such concern might take – with equality of opportunities, with an adequate safety net, with relative disparities – but the distribution pre-1990 is in each case an important point of reference.

In describing the project to write this book, we have encountered two main critical reactions. The first is from those who believe that the basic facts about the distribution of income under Communism are well known. If we then asked *what* is well known, we found that people tended to hold one of two very different views. According to one set of views, the distribution of income was significantly less unequal than in comparable market economies, and earnings differentials had been definitely compressed; according to the second set of views, inequality in the Communist countries of Eastern Europe was in fact no lower than under capitalism.

Those who hold the view that inequality was less under Communism tend also to believe that inequality will rise with economic transformation. Whether this in fact follows depends on the underlying economic system, and in Chapter 2 we provide a brief sketch of the main features which distinguish the earlier type of economy, notably the state ownership of productive capital, the provision of social benefits, centralised wage determination and maintenance of employment. Those who hold the alternative view that inequality was no less than under capitalism argue that this analysis ignores important features of real-world Communist economies, such as the holding down of wage levels, the dominance of incentive considerations in wage-setting, and the appropriation by the political elite of the income received by the state. It is not our aim to explore in depth these theoretical aspects, but differing views appear to arise not just from different views of the empirical evidence but also from differing perceptions as to how the system operated.

Chapter 3

The second set of doubts that we encountered when describing our plan to write this book were those concerning the availability of data. *But where will you get your data from?* was a question often posed. In Chapter 3, we describe the distributional information available from the pre-reform period in the four Eastern European countries and compare the position with that in Britain. Common impressions are dominated by the position with regard to the Soviet Union, where the distribution of income appeared next to alcoholism and drug addiction in the censor's list of prohibited subjects, but – as we have tried to bring out – the position in other Eastern European countries has been quite different. In the case of the earnings distribution, not only is information available for Czechoslovakia, Hungary and Poland, but its similarities with the corresponding survey in Britain (the New Earnings Survey) are more striking than the differences. Insofar as the earnings data are different, there are certain respects in which they are superior to those in Britain: for example, there appears to be less of a problem of non-response, and the series goes back to the 1950s rather than just to 1968.

The USSR *is* different and the information which became available with *glasnost'* is less detailed than that available for many years in the other Eastern European countries. As far as the distribution of income is concerned, the USSR Family Budget Survey is a less satisfactory source, given the unrepresentative nature of its sample, than the income and budget surveys in the other three countries studied here. The latter do indeed compare favourably with the information available for Britain. The surveys in Eastern Europe typically have had larger samples, have had higher response rates, have been able to substantiate earnings data from employers, have considered the deviations of survey results from macro aggregates, and have set out to collect information on annual income. The Eastern European sources have significant deficiencies, and there are undoubtedly aspects which are not adequately covered, such as private incomes, legal or illegal, which may well have been a growing feature of the 1980s. It is important to bear these in mind when interpreting the data, but it must be remembered that data from *all* countries are deficient in some respect whether they come from market or socialist economies.

Chapter 4

The findings with regard to the distribution of earnings are the subject of Chapter 4. The most evident conclusion is that there is considerable diversity across countries and across time. Among the Eastern European countries, Czechoslovakia stands out. The low recorded degree of earnings dispersion in Czechoslovakia is indeed remarkable, as is the relative stability of the distribution over a period of three decades. This may be explicable by the historical development of the country, but it would be interesting to know more. Within Czechoslovakia, the inter-republic difference in average earnings is small, but the gender differential is wider than in the other Central European countries.

In Hungary, too, the difference in the earnings distribution from that in Britain is clear in all years studied. The changes over time exhibit somewhat the same pattern as in Britain, with a decline in dispersion up to 1980 and then a rise over the 1980s. The ratio of median female to male earnings is rather higher than in Britain. The position in Poland is an intermediate one. In the mid 1980s the degree of dispersion was undoubtedly less than in Britain, but there has been considerable change over time. The 1980s saw an apparent fall, then a rise, and finally a fall, in earnings differentials. In the 1970s inequality had risen, taking the inequality indicators above those in Britain. Of particular interest are the relative earnings of men and women. Not only is the female disadvantage on average smaller than in other countries, except for Hungary, but there is distinctly less earnings dispersion among women. As a consequence, the distribution of earnings *among women* in Poland is much closer to that in Czechoslovakia.

Finally, we turn to the Soviet Union, which has attracted the most attention. We show that it is possible, by choosing different dates, to arrive at the conclusion that earnings dispersion was greater, less, or the same as in Britain. The degree of dispersion, after apparently falling sharply from 1956 to a low point in 1968, varied over the 1970s with the protracted wage reform of that decade. The coincidence of the rise in inequality over the 1980s with that in Britain is striking, although no more than coincidence. There is considerable difference in average money earnings between the constituent republics, and there is no clear evidence that this has become smaller over time. Indeed in the late 1980s, there was a marked widening of the gap with Russia. What happens within the individual republics is now of great interest. There are considerable differences in the degree of dispersion, but the least unequal still exhibits greater inequality than the countries of Central Europe.

Chapter 5

In Chapter 5, we move to the distribution of household income, taking into account all sources of income, not just earnings, and covering the whole population, not just those in employment. We typically expect household incomes to exhibit greater inequality than earnings, and for the United Kingdom this appears to be the case. In contrast, in the Eastern European countries the extent of inequality in incomes is similar to that in earnings. The gap between East and West becomes larger therefore when we consider total income. The ranking of the Eastern European countries is the same as for earnings – Czechoslovakia is the least unequal, followed by Hungary, Poland and the USSR – but now the former USSR is clearly ahead of the United Kingdom. Of particular interest are the findings for individual republics of the former Soviet Union. Ukraine and Belarus turn out to have less income inequality than Hungary, and Armenia and Moldavia come before Poland.

In comparing the distribution in Eastern Europe with that in Britain, it is important to bear in mind that both have seen changes over time in the degree of inequality. In the UK the degree of income inequality has undoubtedly increased between the 1970s and the 1980s. In Hungary and Poland the tendency over the 1980s has been for inequality to rise, and the same appears to be true in the USSR. The picture in Czechoslovakia is again different and our results show the degree of inequality as falling over the entire period since 1958, first sharply and then gradually. This was associated in part with a marked narrowing of the difference in average incomes between the Czech Lands and Slovakia.

The fact that inequality in incomes is of the same order as that of earnings does not imply that the latter is the sole determinant of income inequality. The discussion of the trends in different countries shows that the two distributions do not always move together and the income distribution, while heavily influenced by that of earnings, also reflects other determinants, notably the contribution of social incomes.

Chapter 6

The reader used to newspaper reports of queues and shortages in Eastern Europe may well wonder about the significance of money incomes in those countries. The *interpretation* of the data on incomes and earnings is the subject of Chapter 6. It is clear that the concepts of 'earnings' and 'income' may have had different meaning in Communist societies. The distribution of money income may not reflect the distribution of the standard of living. In all countries we have to allow for differences in prices generated by subsidies and for the provision of public goods, but in the pre-reform economies of Eastern Europe, the interpretation of money income was rendered even more difficult by the system of pricing and rationing of goods.

In the first part of Chapter 6, we examine the role of social benefits in kind, which are widely believed to play a major role in the socialist distribution system. Public spending on such services as education and health is of course also important in Western countries, and we compare the distributional incidence of such social provision revealed in official studies for the UK, Hungary, Poland and Czechoslovakia. The results show that in both the UK and Central Europe social benefits in general have a substantial equalising impact on the overall degree of inequality. At the same time there are differences in the effect of individual benefits, and allowance must be made for the dispersion of benefits within income groups (which is not taken into account in the statistical results cited). The calculation of the incidence and value of social benefits raises a number of problems, and a variety of alternative approaches could be adopted.

A second major form of social provision in Eastern Europe took the form of consumer subsidies, and much policy advice has focused on the reduction or elimination of such subsidies. Although such subsidies are not unknown in Western countries, it is on their impact in Eastern Europe, and particularly Hungary and Poland, that we concentrate. Official studies of the incidence of consumer subsidies show that overall they contribute to reducing inequality, although they are less progressive than social benefits in kind. Again, the valuation of the impact of state intervention raises methodological issues, not least because there may be a limited supply of goods at the subsidised prices. The existence of secondary private markets, and the resulting price differential, have to be taken into account.

Where goods were scarce, the principle by which they were allocated may have an important distributional impact. In Chapter 6, we examine the question of the privileged position of the political elite and the role of enterprises in securing supplies of goods in short supply. It is impossible to make any very precise quantitative assessment, but we indicate the possible impact of inequality at the top that is not recorded in the income distribution statistics. It should also be noted at this point that we do not give explicit consideration to the distribution of *wealth*. This is important as regards the pre-reform situation in Eastern Europe, where housing wealth and stocks of foreign currency were of considerable significance in determining living standards, and as regards the debate about different modes of privatisation of state enterprises.

Chapter 7

Concern for the least advantaged in the course of transformation means that considerable importance attaches to the extent of poverty at the outset of the process. How many people were living in poverty before 1990, and who were they?

The existence of poverty was a sensitive issue in Communist societies and it was only in the 1980s that there was significant public discussion. This does not mean that the subject was not investigated, and social or subsistence minima had been calculated in all of the four countries studied. In the USSR, when Prime Minister Ryzhkov told the first Congress of People's Deputies that nearly 40 million people lived below the poverty line, he could draw on a tradition of work on minimum budgets. This figure is strikingly similar to that officially reported for the European Community – an area with a broadly similar population. But such figures depend on what one means by poverty, and we devote Chapter 7 to a discussion of the methodological problems of poverty measurement.

This methodological discussion starts with an account of the different issues which have arisen in Western attempts to measure poverty, the purpose being to provide a framework in which to understand the choices that have been made, explicitly or implicitly, in the design of social minimum standards in Eastern Europe. We then consider the poverty lines developed in Eastern Europe and some of the special problems which arise on account of the different economic and social context. Particular attention is given to the relative treatment of different types of household. Eastern European scales tend to give a higher allowance to persons of active age than to pensioners, in contrast to the UK, and give more weight to the needs of larger households. The procedures for adjusting the social minima over time have also differed, a matter which is of great importance during the process of economic transition. There could be a significant difference between an adjustment related to prices and an adjustment related to average, or minimum, wages.

Chapter 8

The existence of poverty in pre-1990 Eastern Europe conflicts with the widely held perception of Communist states providing social welfare from 'cradle to grave'. However, the experience of Western countries has shown that it is quite possible for problems of poverty to persist despite the existence of elaborate social transfers. In the first section of Chapter 8, we provide a brief summary of some of the features of social support in Eastern Europe, with the aim of indicating how gaps may have arisen in the safety net, giving rise to the poverty which is the subject of the rest of the chapter.

It would be possible to apply a range of different poverty measures to the original data on incomes in Eastern Europe, and to arrive at new substantive conclusions. Our purpose in Chapter 8 is more modest, in that we rely solely on existing studies of poverty in the four countries. We review in turn the evidence from Czechoslovakia, Hungary and Poland about the extent of poverty measured by the official social or subsistence minima, paying particular attention to the changes in poverty over time and to the composition of the poor. In Czechoslovakia, where the poverty standard is adjusted in line with average incomes, the poverty rate has nonetheless fallen over the past decades. The decline is especially marked for pensioners and in Slovakia, reflecting the reduction in income disparities between republics. At the same time, increased attention has focused on child poverty, and the poverty rate among active households rose from 1985 to 1988.

In Hungary and Poland, the incidence of poverty in the 1980s has to be seen against a macro-economic background of falling real wages and, in the case of Poland, of considerable turbulence. It is not surprising that different groups fared differently. In Hungary, as in Czechoslovakia, the position of low-income pensioners appears to have improved, and the active population came to represent a larger proportion of those below the poverty line. In Poland, pensioners experienced higher poverty rates throughout the period, but there was a great deal of variation.

The information available to us about poverty in the USSR is much less detailed. We are unable to present a breakdown of the 40 million figure, nor a series of comparable estimates of the extent of poverty at different dates. Of particular interest is the variation in poverty across republics, and we present evidence on the picture revealed by the 1989 Family Budget Survey. The interpretation of these figures however raises many problems, and the final reference to the life of the Uzbek shepherd is intended to remind the reader that throughout the book we have been telling a story 'as seen from Britain'.

The conclusions reached in each chapter have been summarised above. There is no final concluding chapter. As far as Eastern Europe is concerned, it is too early to draw conclusions.

2 Why study the distribution pre-1990?

The aim of this chapter is to examine why we should study the distribution of income in Eastern Europe before 1990. Is the record of Communism in these countries purely of historical interest? How is it relevant to the economic transformation which appears in the title of this book?

At the outset, we should make it clear that we do not believe that the distribution of income is the sole, or major, criterion for evaluating the historical experience of Communism. There are other features of these societies which are more important, notably the curtailment of civil and democratic rights. Readers may feel – and it is a view with which we have considerable sympathy – that *no* lessening of inequality could justify the violations of individual freedom that characterised the worst aspects of totalitarian Communist regimes. Just as in the theory of justice of Rawls (1971), economic equality can only be pursued subject to the *prior* condition of a basic set of liberties for individual citizens. There are certain fundamental freedoms – which we do not attempt to define here – that cannot be put in the balance with economic equality.

However, once these basic liberties have been achieved, then the distribution of economic advantage becomes a legitimate issue for concern. It is a matter for personal judgment how much weight is given to distributional objectives, but the issue is on the agenda. As explained in the introductory chapter, many people have argued that economic transformation should be accompanied by an adequate safety net. This may be on grounds of social justice, or it may be seen as essential to secure the effective liberty of the individual. More generally, the effective working of democracy, and the avoidance of a return to a totalitarian regime, may be seen to depend on the extent of economic disparities that emerge during the process of transformation.

In the newly democratic societies of Eastern Europe, therefore, the balance between equity and efficiency is one that will be debated, and we begin by considering how the issue can be formulated in terms of standard economic analysis.

22

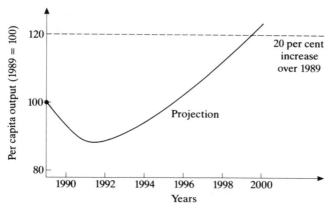

Figure 2.1 Projections of growth in per capita output in Central Europe
1990–2000

Source: Based on Gelb and Gray (1991, Figure 1, p. 7), projection for Hungary,
Poland and Czechoslovakia combined.

2.1 Economic transformation and the distribution of income

The widely held macro-economic view of the prospects for Eastern Europe
is that there will be an initial decline in per capita income, followed, once the
reforms are working, by strong upward growth. In Figure 2.1, we reproduce the World Bank projections of output per capita for Hungary, Poland
and Czechoslovakia (combined) over the decade 1990–2000. Output per
capita is not projected to attain its 1989 level until the middle of the 1990s.
At this point, these countries, which the World Bank considers better
placed than others in Eastern Europe, are assumed to be enjoying rapid
growth. By the year 2000, output per capita is projected to be more than 20
percent higher than in 1989.

This growth in total income per head may be accompanied by widening
income differentials. If the incomes of the better-off grow faster than those
lower down the income scale, then measures of relative inequality will show
a worsening. The situation is a dynamic version of the textbook trade-off
between equity and efficiency referred to in Chapter 1. In these terms, the
move to a market economy in Eastern Europe can be seen as a move round
the frontier of policy choices, with greater (dynamic) efficiency being
obtained at the cost of greater inequality. A rise in living standards is being
obtained at the cost of a rise in relative inequality.

We do not attempt to consider here the extent to which an increase in
inequality is the necessary price of a rise in living standards. It is not our
personal view that economic transformation *necessarily* involves a sacrifice
of equity for efficiency, but we accept that many people see the trade-off as

inevitable. What we are concerned with here is the evaluation of the particular combination of equity and efficiency that has been chosen. According to standard welfare economics, it is social welfare which is our ultimate concern, and this should form the basis for our evaluation. The level of social welfare in turn depends on both the *distribution* of income and on its *level*. A rise in the level of income can compensate for a rise in inequality. Thus, if our concern is with the standard of living of the lowest income group, we may find that their absolute position is improving even if their relative share is falling. This *trickle-down* defence of economic growth, already referred to in Chapter 1, is in effect based on evaluating social welfare according to:

per capita income *times* share of lowest group.

If, to take a hypothetical example, the share of the bottom 20 percent of the population were to fall from 12 percent of total income to 10 percent, then a rise of 20 percent in per capita income would be necessary to achieve the same level of welfare (10 percent of 120 is the same as 12 percent of 100). If the rise in inequality were once-and-for-all, and the faster growth were to be permanent, then of course ultimately the rise in per capita income would be sufficient. The only question then is how long it will be before the growth curve reaches the level necessary to compensate for the increased relative inequality, as illustrated in Figure 2.1 for a 20 percent 'target'.

Such a welfare economic perspective of the distributional issue does not need to be confined to the position of the least advantaged. Suppose that concern extends to the range of incomes as a whole, as is expressed commonly in terms of the *Lorenz curve* of the distribution. The Lorenz curve is a graphic device for representing the degree of inequality. It is constructed by imagining everyone lined up in order of their income, the lowest incomes first, and then calculating their cumulative share of total income, as in the hypothetical example in Figure 2.2 (see Cowell, 1977, and Atkinson, 1983, for an exposition). The curve shows the share of the bottom 10 percent, then the share of the bottom 20 percent (which includes the bottom 10 percent), and so on. If all incomes were equal, the Lorenz curve would follow the diagonal.

In showing the *shares* of total income, the Lorenz curve is concerned with the relative distribution, but it may be converted to an absolute basis by the simple process of multiplying the share by the level of per capita income, as in the discussion of the position of the lowest income group. The resulting curve then shows the *total* income received by the bottom 10 percent, 20 percent, and so on. This is referred to as a *generalised Lorenz curve* (Shorrocks, 1983). In what follows, we do not draw the multiplied-up curves as such, but the comparison with income growth is one that underlies

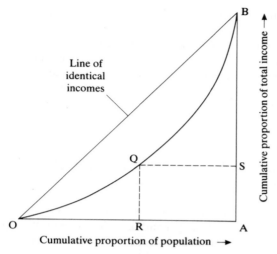

Figure 2.2 Illustrative Lorenz curve

Note: The Lorenz curve may be interpreted as follows: the point Q shows that a proportion OR of the population receive a proportion AS of total income.

much of the discussion. To take again a hypothetical example, suppose that the shares before and after economic transformation were as follows:

share of bottom	before	after
25%	15%	10%
50%	36%	30%
75%	60%	54%

(from which information a simple Lorenz curve can be constructed). If per capita income were to rise by a fifth, then in absolute terms the bottom 50 percent would be in the same position as before (30 percent of 120 is the same as 36 percent of 100). The bottom 75 percent would be better off (since 54 percent of 120 is higher than 60 percent of 100), but the bottom 25 percent would be worse off in absolute terms. In the case of this hypothetical situation, there is no unambiguous statement that can be made as to the desirability of the change.

Where there are conflicting conclusions regarding the distributional impact, it is tempting to seek to combine them in a single *summary measure*. One measure which is widely used, at least in Western countries, is the *Gini coefficient*. This measure has the following mathematical interpretation: twice the Gini coefficient is equal to the expected absolute difference in incomes, relative to the mean, between any two persons drawn at random from the population (Kendall and Stuart, 1969, p. 47). A Gini coefficient of

20 percent, for example, implies that the absolute difference, on average, between the incomes of two persons is equal to 40 percent of mean income in the population. Better known is the simple geometric interpretation of the Gini coefficient in terms of the area between the Lorenz curve and the diagonal line of equal incomes: the coefficient is equal to the ratio of this area to the area of the whole triangle OAB (see Figure 2.2). Combined with changes in per capita income, the level of social welfare may be evaluated in terms of:

per capita income *times* $(1 - \text{Gini})$.

The Gini coefficient represents a *subtraction* on account of the welfare loss from unequal distribution. (The relation of this measure to more conventional national accounting is discussed by Sen, 1976.) The question to be asked of the economic transformation is then whether the percentage increase in per capita income exceeds the percentage fall in $(1 - \text{Gini})$. If, hypothetically, the Gini were to rise from 20 percent to 30 percent, a rise of 14 percent in per capita income would be needed to compensate.

The adoption of a summary measure like the Gini coefficient is convenient, and in what follows we make use of this measure, but it should not obscure the fact that different people make different distributional judgments. Any single statistic involves weighting changes at different points in the distribution, and people may disagree about the more appropriate choice of weights. A person concerned, for example, about the position of the lowest income group, as in our earlier discussion, would not accept that the Gini coefficient necessarily provided a good summary of distributional change. To accommodate such diversity of judgments, we make use, in summarising the empirical evidence in this book, of a variety of ways of describing the distribution.

More fundamentally, the whole approach in terms of social welfare may be questioned as a representation of social objectives. People may legitimately feel that multiplying per capita income by (1 minus the Gini coefficient) gives too little, or too much, weight to distributional as opposed to aggregate concerns. Some people after all attach no weight to distributional objectives. Indeed, as we have seen in Chapter 1, there are those who argue that the *outcome* of economic transformation is not a matter for concern, providing that there is equality of opportunity. Others may feel that the social welfare formulation fails to express adequately distributional objectives, such as those focusing on the *gap* between the poor and the rich. Relative inequality may be a concern in its own right, as with theories of justice that start from an explicitly egalitarian perspective.

Of particular interest in the present context is the view that the distribution of income in post-transformation Eastern Europe has to be viewed by *historical* standards. Such a perspective has been clearly enunciated by Kornai, who, in the context of concern for the least advantaged, has advanced a *dynamic criterion of justice*: 'a distribution system is fair only if it ensures continuous improvement in the material situation of the least well-off strata of society in the long run' (1990, p. 124). The distribution cannot, on this basis, be seen independently of the point of departure.

This last observation brings us to the contribution of the present book. There are many different views about the criteria to evaluate the distributional impact of economic transformation, but one common element is the need for information about the state of distribution in Eastern Europe before 1990. We have given above some hypothetical examples of the change in the distribution. As far as the ultimate post-transformation situation is concerned, the exact state of the distribution must at present remain hypothetical, but the pre-transformation situation is one about which something can be said, and this is the rationale for the present book.

2.2 Different views about the distribution under Communism

Why is it necessary to examine the evidence about the distribution of income in Eastern Europe prior to 1990? Are not the basic facts well known? In fact it turns out that people hold very different views about the extent of inequality under Communism.

According to one set of views, the distribution was indeed less unequal than in comparable market economies. After a careful review of the information available about the distribution of earnings, Lydall concluded that:

The communist countries are, in relation to level of economic development, all more equal than the non-communist countries. (1968, p. 157)

Analysing similar data on earnings for Eastern Europe, Pryor found that:

if we calculate the Gini coefficients of inequality, we find that the coefficients are about [6 percentage points] greater in the Western nations than in the Eastern nations, which is a considerable and important difference. (1973, p. 84)

Phelps Brown reached the conclusion that:

the three Soviet-type distributions that we have sampled are much more egalitarian than the Western-type. (1988, p. 303)

On this view, there was less inequality under Communism.

The second – quite different – view is that the difference in the economic system was not in fact associated with greater equity. Empirically, inequality was no less under Communism than under capitalism. In Chapter 1, we referred to one of the best-known introductory textbooks in economics, that by Samuelson and Nordhaus. In this, they tell readers that:

one of the major complaints levied by Marx and many socialists and radicals has been that capitalism [is] a very unequal, class-ridden society. By contrast, a socialist society would share the return to capital among the workers, thereby allowing much greater equality than a market economy. (Samuelson and Nordhaus, 1989, p. 842)

However, the authors go on to say that:

in practice, communist planners have allowed sizable but declining wage differentials. And the privileges of the capitalist class have been replaced by generous benefits for the ruling party elites. Recent estimates of income distribution indicate that, except for the absence of a super-rich class, the income distribution in the Soviet Union and Eastern Europe shows a striking similarity to that in Western countries.

After a review of this evidence, a recent text on comparative economic systems confirms that:

in general, one would have to say that the differences in the distribution of income between the planned socialist economies and the capitalist welfare states are relatively minor. (Gregory and Stuart, 1989, p. 434)

There is, therefore, a marked difference of opinion as to the empirical facts. In the rest of this chapter, we examine some of the *a priori* reasoning that might lead to these different assessments, but, before doing so, we note three reasons why such differences in view may arise.

First, it is obvious that the distribution of income under Communism is not the same in all countries. In this study we are not examining the situation in China, nor in Cuba, nor in Yugoslavia, but even between the four countries considered there is important variation. One of the themes that recurs throughout the book is that of the differences between the former USSR and the three countries of Central Europe. Nor can Czechoslovakia, Hungary and Poland be treated as one. Viewed from the West, it is easy to focus on the similarities in economic systems to the neglect of the important historical and cultural differences of which the citizens of these countries are well aware. Just to give one example, the situation in Czechoslovakia after the Second World War was different from that in other Central European countries. According to Teichova, 'the desire for greater equality had deep historical roots in the social consciousness of broad segments of society' (1988, p. 101). Differences in starting point may well be expected to have led to differing degrees of inequality, just as there will be differences in the evolution of the post-transformation societies.

Secondly, there has been considerable change over time within the countries. The USSR of Khrushchev was not the same as that under Stalin, nor did it remain unchanged under Brezhnev. A comparison with the West at one date may lead to different conclusions from one made earlier or later. The process of economic reform, however limited, in Central Europe meant that the distribution of earnings and income may have been changing over time in these countries. In Czechoslovakia, there was the campaign for 'de-levelling' in the 1960s. In Hungary there was the New Economic Mechanism introduced in 1968. As described by Berend:

as incomes grew more rapidly, so did income differentials, which could not have been allowed to happen until general living standards were rising. Earlier measures to equalize incomes had been a way to improve the wretched condition of the poor strata in society. Now differentials were encouraged so as to provide more incentive to better and more highly qualified work – to speed up progress. (1990, p. 192)

What was true in the 1960s (the date of much of the evidence on earnings cited above) may therefore no longer hold in the 1980s. The trends over time will be one of the subjects that we shall explore in Chapters 4 and 5.

Thirdly, it hardly needs to be pointed out that there may be a large gap between aspirations and realities, a gap which may be more evident in the case of Communist states in view of their explicit adherence to an ideological position. Views about the difference between Communism and capitalism may see the former in terms of its stated objectives, which may bear little relation to what happens in reality. Critics of Communism, and supporters of socialism, may combine in arguing that the real-world experience of Communism in Eastern Europe had little to do with egalitarianism.

2.3 Communism and socialism in theory

In this book, our concern is with the empirical evidence, not with ideological principles, but the latter have certainly affected people's perceptions as to the possible impact of Communism on the degree of inequality in Eastern Europe. In the *Critique of the Gotha Programme*, and elsewhere, Marx set out his view of the principles of distribution, distinguishing two successive stages of development, the first of which came to be referred to by Marxist economists as 'socialism' as distinct from 'communism' (we use a lower case 'c', to distinguish it from real-world Communist regimes). With the attainment of the higher stage of communism, the problem of production would have been solved, so that incentive issues could be left on one side and income distributed according to the famous phrase 'each according to his needs'. But in the prior stage of socialism, achieving production remains an over-riding concern and incentives require that income be distributed according to the rule 'from each according to his ability, to each according to his labour', or what has been called *the socialist principle of distribution*.

Capital income

At the stage of socialism, as opposed to communism, there are therefore no grounds to expect that income would be distributed solely in line with need. What reason, then, is there to expect less inequality under socialism? The most evident contribution to the reduction in inequality is that resulting from the abolition of the private ownership of the means of production. In terms of factor incomes, that part of national income received by capitalists as profit and rent (both referred to here as 'capital income') in a pure market economy accrues under socialism to the state. Even if none of the spending by the state benefits individual citizens, this elimination of private capital income can in itself be expected to reduce substantially relative inequality.

It is the role of capital income that is referred to in the earlier quotation from Samuelson and Nordhaus (1989) and many people seem to have this in mind. When asked about the difference between socialism and capitalism, people tend to think of a situation where in a capitalist economy all profit income accrues to a 'capitalist class' but in a socialist economy it accrues to the state. To make concrete this simple *class* model, let us assume that in a capitalist society a proportion α of the population receive income only from capital and they are all better off than the remainder who receive only income from work. The share of capital in total income is denoted by β, this being considerably greater than α. For example, α equal to 0.05 and β equal to 0.25 would imply that the capitalists make up 5 percent of the population but receive 25 percent of total income in the economy. We emphasise that we do not believe that this model is a realistic description of any actual economy; it is intended only as an expositional device.

In this theoretical class model of the determination of the distribution of income, the elimination of private ownership will assuredly reduce inequality. The situation is depicted in Figure 2.3, where we draw the Lorenz curve for the capitalist economy. This consists of the curved segment OP corresponding to the working population and then of the segment PB which brings in the capitalist class. The degree of inequality is indicated by the distance of the Lorenz curve from the diagonal. It may be seen that the larger the share of capital, β, the greater the degree of inequality. Let the value of the Gini coefficient be G in a socialist society where there are only workers and all capital income accrues to the state (and is not redistributed to the workers). In contrast, in the capitalist society the contribution of wage income to inequality will be proportionately smaller, by a factor (1–

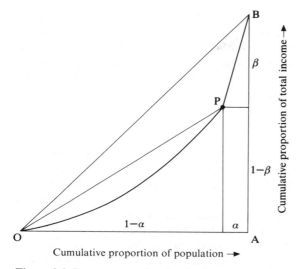

Figure 2.3 Lorenz curve for simple class model of income distribution in capitalist economy

Notes: α denotes the proportion of the population who are capitalists; β denotes the share of capitalists in total income.

The Gini coefficient is equal to twice the sum of the area of the triangle OPB and the area between the curve and OP. The area of the triangle may be calculated as $(\beta-\alpha)/2$. The area between the curve and the straight line OP is equal to $(1-\alpha)(1-\beta)$ times half the Gini coefficient for an economy consisting solely of workers, since the population (horizontal axis) is reduced by a factor $(1-\alpha)$ and the mean income (vertical axis) by a factor $(1-\beta)$.

$\beta)(1-\alpha)$, but the contribution of capital income will now add a term $(\beta-\alpha)$ to the Gini coefficient (see the note to Figure 2.3). This means that if the share of capital is 25 percent of total national income, and capitalists make up 5 percent of the population (which means that they have 5 times the average income), then the Gini coefficient in the capitalist society is, as a percentage:

G times 0.95 times 0.75 plus 20

If *G* were 20 percent, then the capitalist country would have a Gini coefficient of 34.25 percent.

This comparison assumes that the profits accruing to the state provide no direct benefit to individual citizens. If profits accruing to the state were equally distributed to all workers, as referred to in the earlier quotation from Samuelson and Nordhaus, the difference between the two systems would be still wider. This would reduce the Gini coefficient among a society of pure workers by a factor of $(1-\beta)$, and, with the numbers used earlier, would mean a Gini coefficient for incomes of 15 percent. The combination of the abolition of private ownership, and the use of profits to finance social programmes (such as education, pensions, health care), has, on this basis, a substantial redistributive impact. (The reader is invited to consider the implications of different values for the parameters.)

Wage differentials and employment

The impact of socialism on the production side of the economy has been treated so far simply in terms of the beneficial ownership of capital by the state. But the difference between the economic systems goes much further than this – it is a matter of control over the economy and not just the ownership of capital. Wide-ranging state intervention in socialist economies, and the operation of central planning, with the centralised determination of wage scales and of prices, mean that the distributional outcome may be quite different from that where the state is simply the recipient of capital income.

Socialism could in this way have an egalitarian influence on the distribution of earnings (assumed in the above hypothetical calculations to be unaffected by the change in economic system). Centralised determination of wages may allow the narrowing of differentials, such as those between manual and non-manual workers. A structure of industrial employment in which large enterprises are dominant may ensure greater wage uniformity. The distribution may be affected by 'equal pay for equal work' for men and women, and by the existence of an official minimum wage. The latter has been explicitly related to socialist theory in the USSR. According to Chapman, the large increase in the minimum wage in 1968 'was hailed as implementing the Party's policy of eliminating the gap between the incomes of the low-paid and highly paid workers and creating the conditions for securing the material well-being of the families of all workers' (1991, p. 180).

Control over the economy can also be claimed to have produced a major difference between socialist and capitalist labour markets in that the former avoid large-scale unemployment. If there is assumed to be a trade-off between high employment at the cost of low productivity and low wages, on the one hand, and, on the other, increased efficiency, with higher wages for those in work at the cost of unemployment, then a socialist economy could make a different choice from that made by the government of a capitalist economy. This choice in turn has distributional implications which depend on the degree of protection provided to the unemployed and to other groups such as pensioners, a subject which brings us to the welfare state.

2.4 Choice of counter-factual: modern mixed economies and welfare states

The analysis just given suggests that socialism could in theory secure greater equality than a capitalist economy through the state ownership of capital, payment of social benefits, centralised wage determination and avoidance of unemployment. The objection that this analysis ignores many real-world features of Communist countries is taken up in the next section. Here we consider the problem that the comparison we need to make is with the counter-factual position of *what would have happened in the absence of a Communist regime*. The critics of Communism can argue that this counter-factual position is better represented by a modern mixed economy with a substantial welfare state than by the hypothetical class model, and that the differences in the distribution of income would disappear.

Property and net worth of the state

In terms of the distribution of wealth, the class model may have been a reasonable approximation when discussing nineteenth-century Britain, but over the course of this century there has been a significant move towards reduced concentration of wealth (Atkinson and Harrison, 1978, Chapter 6). Property is more widely dispersed, via home ownership, via individual share-holdings and via intermediate institutions such as pension funds and life assurance companies. While we are probably equally far removed from pure 'people's capitalism', where everyone has an equal share in capital income, the difference in inequality between socialism and capitalism is less than the simple class example suggests.

The difference between the two systems has been further attenuated in the course of much of the past century by the acquisition of productive capital by the state. Governments in Western Europe have nationalised important sectors of the economy. These countries have been described as *mixed economies*, with a combination of private and public ownership, although this term has been less in vogue in recent years, and a number of countries have pursued policies of privatisation.

There has also been a rise in the net worth of the state, defined as the difference between the value of assets owned by the state and its liabilities (the national debt). In the case of Britain, the net worth of the state has moved from negative to positive in the post-war period, to the extent that by 1979 it was broadly equal in size to the national income (Hills, 1989, Table 1). (Over the 1980s the net worth of the state has fallen, not least on account of privatisation.) The existence of a positive net worth to the state affects the relation between the distribution of factor income and the distribution of *personal* income, that is the income received by persons. The way in which the personal distribution is changed depends in turn on the fiscal policy pursued.

Progressive taxation

It can reasonably be argued that the earlier comparison of socialist and capitalist distributions ignored the contribution of progressive personal taxation, and of taxes on corporate profits, to reducing the inequality in the after-tax distribution in market economies. However, the real-world significance can be debated, since the extent of effective progression of taxation in Western countries has been called into question. The studies by Pechman for the United States, for example, have found that the combined effect of all US taxes is:

either moderately progressive or slightly progressive, depending on the incidence assumptions for the major taxes ... The tax system has relatively little effect on the distribution of income. (1985, p. 10)

Moreover, the past decade has seen, particularly in Britain, movement in the direction of dismantling the progressive tax structure (Hills, 1988). This calls into question the effectiveness of taxation in reducing the difference in the distributions between capitalist and socialist countries; and, in any case, socialist countries themselves have made use of progressive taxation.

Welfare state

State intervention in a mixed market economy also takes the form of public spending. The quotation earlier from Gregory and Stuart referred explicitly to capitalist *welfare states* as the basis for comparison. The payment of social security benefits is one of the most progressive activities of the British government when measured in terms of the reduction achieved in the Gini coefficient (Central Statistical Office, 1991, p. 110). At the same time, Western countries differ in the form of their welfare state (see, for example, Esping-Andersen and Micklewright, 1991). It makes a considerable difference whether we suppose, as our counter-factual, that Eastern Europe would have developed like the USA or like Sweden. And within these countries there is debate as to the extent of redistribution which is achieved by the welfare state. While cash transfers, for example, may reduce inequality in current income, they may be closer to neutral when seen from a lifetime perspective.

These differences affect any comparison between the Communist states of Eastern Europe and Western Europe. They also affect any conclusions drawn for the consequences of economic transformation. If inequality is reduced in Western welfare states by the provision of a social safety net, will the new societies of Eastern Europe be equally successful in reducing inequality if they follow the model of these states in social as well as economic policy? The moderating effect of the state ownership of property will only apply if a sizeable part of the nation's assets remains in the hands of the state. The reduction of income differentials in a market economy through progressive taxation presupposes that such a tax system will be put into effect and will be made to operate efficiently.

Development over time and the counter-factual

The choice of counter-factual has also to take account of possible links between the stage of development and the degree of income inequality. In the literature on income distribution there has been extensive discussion of the hypothesis of Kuznets (1955) that inequality first rises and then falls with the process of development: i.e. there is an inverse U-shaped relation between inequality and income per head. The conversion of the economy from one which is largely agricultural to one containing a large industrial sector may operate in this direction, but such an outcome is not inevitable (Robinson, 1976).

In empirical terms, the support for the Kuznets curve deduced from cross-country comparisons (plotting income inequality against per capita income for different countries) appears to have been the result of country-specific differences, notably that the Latin American countries tended to have both high inequality and intermediate levels of income. Empirical investigations of the Kuznets hypothesis which use longitudinal data and take account of systematic differences between countries (such as the work of Fields and Jakubson, 1990) do not suggest that any such generalisation can be sustained. While the long-run development of Britain is character-ised by Williamson (1985) in terms of a rise in inequality accompanying industrialisation, associated particularly with a widening premium for skill, followed by a fall after 1867, this historical evidence for Britain is disputed (see Feinstein, 1988). The controversy surrounding this whole issue in capitalist countries provides a warning of the difficulties in trying to predict what would have been the course of inequality in Eastern Europe if these countries had retained a capitalist system. Certainly, there is no widely accepted empirical relationship between the degree of income inequality and the level of income per capita which we can use to 'correct' for differences in the level of development between East and West.

2.5 Why socialism may not have achieved greater equality

What do people have in mind when they say that in practice Communism failed to bring about greater economic justice? The expectations about socialism based on the earlier theoretical analysis (of Section 2.3) may be criticised for having failed to take account of the way in which inequalities were perpetuated in Communist societies and new inequalities were created. On this view, it would not be surprising to find empirically that there was little difference in the distributions of income between East and West. Poverty was to be found under Communism just as much as under capitalism. The degree of inequality, although not necessarily the position of individuals within the distribution, is independent of the choice of economic system.

Level of wages and social benefits

Three main components of this argument may be identified. First, it is argued that Communist states held down the proportion of output distributed to workers via the wage fund (the size of $(1-\beta)$ in our earlier notation). With non-pecuniary instruments to ensure a high level of participation, and restrictions on emigration, it was possible within the framework of a planned economy for Communist governments to reduce the general level of wages below that which would have obtained in a pure market economy where the government only participated as the (monopoly) owner of capital. The wage share would be lower than under capitalism, and thus reduce the level of social welfare.

The distributional implications of such a smaller wage share would depend on how the state determined its budget, in particular the extent to which lower wages were compensated for by social benefits, under which families receive cash transfers or social service benefits in kind. To the extent that the total paid was less, then the absolute standard of living of the lower income groups may have been lower than under capitalism.

As has been emphasised in Western economies by the public choice school, the behaviour of the state in this, and other, respects needs to be treated as something to be explained. There is little doubt that Communist governments were subject to conflicting pressures. Adam has described the situation regarding the balance between wages and social benefits in the three Central European countries:

usually when the economy is faltering and there is a desire to improve its performance by intensifying incentives, greater stress is put on wage increases and the widening of wage differentials. When dissatisfaction builds up with the state of wage differentials, or when lower income groups press for a betterment of their material situation, the planners may provide redress by expanding social benefits. (1984, p. 70)

We would for example expect the pattern of distributional change in Poland to reflect, at least to some degree, the rise of Solidarity at the beginning of the 1980s and the associated pressure on the Communist government for more egalitarian wage settlements and for improved social benefits.

Wage differentials and incentives

Communist governments also failed, on this view, to pursue egalitarian objectives when determining how the total wages were to be distributed, giving priority to production incentives. Whatever the ultimate aims of communism, the economies of the Soviet Union and Eastern Europe have been guided by a principle of distribution according to contribution, not need. As is well known, in 1931 Stalin launched an attack on 'egalitarianism', which he described as 'petty-bourgeois' (Nove, 1972, p. 208), and sought to reward those who chose to acquire skills. Skilled labour was extremely scarce and this dominated labour policy. The reduction of earnings differentials as such was not part of the socialist project:

no particular ethical claims are made for the socialist principle of distribution, it is forced upon society by the 'level of productive forces', and by individual attitudes to work ... it is universally asserted that any attempt to eliminate earnings differentials or even to reduce them prematurely would undermine the main objective of socialist society – the building of communism. (McAuley, 1980, p. 241)

Wage differentials have been set with regard to incentives to invest in human capital, to enter occupations with unpleasant conditions, to bear responsibility, to work hard on the job and to move to industries or areas selected for an expansion of employment.

The reason why considerations of incentives were so influential is that, despite the state intervention described earlier, there was an active labour market in the Communist countries considered here. As has been noted by Marnie, 'the image of labour allocation under "communism" tends to be associated with the planned allocation of production inputs and goods, and in the case of manpower, workers are assumed to be allocated by planners to a job, enterprise, region, and obliged to stay there' (1992, p. 38). This image is derived from memories of the 1930s, and she goes on to explain that it does not characterise the post-war USSR:

Although the Soviet literature never referred to a 'labour market', labour allocation was in fact predominantly achieved through market mechanisms. Since the mid 1950s workers in the Soviet Union have been free to quit their jobs at will. Only a small share of jobs are centrally allocated; otherwise employees are free to choose their job, skill, or profession, as well as the region where they work... Employers have always been legally permitted to make redundancies, and, although a state employment service has existed since the 1960s, it has never had a monopoly over the allocation of labour. (1992, pp. 38–39)

Advantages to the elite

The third reason why, it is argued, Communist governments cannot be seen as egalitarian is that they provided significant economic advantages to the *nomenklatura*, or political elite. In place of the owners of capital came a new class, whose privileged position originated with Stalin, who 'encouraged a policy of higher pay and privileges for industrial cadres, and abandoned the old rule, established by Lenin, that party members should not earn more than a skilled worker' (Nove, 1972, p. 208). That this dimension of inequality under Communism has remained important is shown by the speech to the Twenty-Seventh Party Congress in 1986 by B.N. El'tsin, then a candidate for membership of the Politburo, who said that:

You feel uncomfortable when you hear of the indignation caused by any manifestation of injustice ... But it becomes especially painful when people speak bluntly about the special goods for leaders ... it is my opinion that where goods available to leaders at all levels are not justified, they must be taken away. (quoted by Rogovin, 1989, p. 140)

The existence of such benefits, which may take the form of the ability to purchase goods and services not otherwise available on the market, as well as free provision, has attracted considerable attention in the West (for example, Matthews, 1978). In his 1985 Tanner Lectures, under the subheading 'Failures of both liberal capitalism and socialism', Moore concludes that:

the system of inequality under prevailing forms of socialism has turned out to be not very different from that under liberal capitalism. At the apex of the system there is a tiny élite whose official position gives them access to most of the material goods of this life: luxurious housing, fine food, chauffeured automobiles, in some cases an airplane for private use, special access to health care and vacation resorts, etc., etc. All that seems to be missing are fancy yachts ... at the bottom of the social pyramid we find large numbers of people who are forced to make do at the margin of subsistence. (1987, p. 118)

Conclusions

Our aim in this chapter has been to explain why study of the distribution in Eastern Europe before 1990 is relevant to the analysis of economic transformation. While there are different criteria to evaluate the distributional impact of economic transformation, one common element is the need for information about the state of distribution in Eastern Europe before 1990. Opinions differ about the degree of inequality under Communism. One school of thought holds that the distribution was indeed less unequal than in comparable market economies, there being *a priori* reasons to expect this to be the case in view of the state ownership of capital, provision of social benefits, and centralised wage determination. The alternative view of the historical record sees the Communist countries of Eastern Europe as characterised by no less inequality, with wages and social provision having been held down, wage differentials dominated by incentive considerations, and an elite group appropriating the income received by the state.

In order to establish the position before 1990, it is therefore necessary to examine the empirical evidence. This is the primary subject of the book. As we have emphasised, the degree of inequality may well vary across countries and across time, and these comparisons will be a major focus of our research. In examining the evidence, our concern will be with the reality of the distribution of income, but it is worth stressing that it is *perceptions* about the degree of inequality that affect people's behaviour and judgments. These perceptions are in turn affected by the *availability* of evidence, and this has been particularly relevant to Eastern Europe. It is with the subject of data availability and reliability that we begin.

3 Data: availability, quality and comparability

Many people believe that under the Communist regimes of Eastern Europe little or no information was made available about the distribution of income. According to this view, the claims of Communism to have reduced income differentials or to have abolished poverty could not be assessed because of the absence of statistical data. State censorship, and the suppression of independent academic enquiry, meant that any information collected was not available to the outside world. Summarising the situation in his 1984 survey article, Bergson concluded that 'the Soviet government apparently prefers to withhold rather than to release information' (1984, p. 1091).

It would however be wrong to suppose that the situation in the USSR was representative of Eastern Europe as a whole. As we describe in Section 3.1, the position in the Central European countries – Czechoslovakia, Hungary and Poland – was quite different. In these countries there has been a long tradition of collecting and publishing data on the distribution of earnings and incomes. Our examination of the data from the pre-reform period in Eastern Europe suggests that in a number of respects the availability of data in these countries compares favourably with that in Britain. And the situation has changed dramatically with *glasnost'* in the Soviet Union, where information is now available about the distribution of earnings back to the 1950s and about household incomes in the 1980s.

The second common belief about data on the distribution of income in Eastern Europe is that they are of poor quality. It is thought that the low priority attached to distributional issues led to inadequate resources being allocated to statistical activities. It is alleged that the relation between Communist governments and individual enterprises, and that between the state and its citizens, was not such as to induce accurate reporting. But it is important to judge the quality of data, not by some ideal standard, but by the standard of what can realistically be achieved in any society. All data are imperfect to some degree. Even the best designed survey has problems of incomplete coverage, of non-response or partial response, and of ambiguity in the interpretation of definitions. There are bound to be respondents whose particular circumstances do not fit tidily within the categories of the statistical enquiry or whose circumstances at the time of the enquiry are atypical. There are, even with best-practice statistical techniques, difficulties in grossing-up survey data to be representative of the population as a whole and of reconciling the findings with aggregate statistics.

For these reasons, we believe that it is important to judge the quality of Eastern European income distribution data with reference to the actual practice of Western countries – not to some unattainable ideal. This is one of the major reasons why we have included Britain in our study. In Sections 3.2 and 3.3, we contrast the quality of earnings and income information for Eastern Europe with that in Britain. In doing so, we are making no claims for the achievements of Britain; indeed, as soon will become clear, we regard the statistical data for Britain as far from ideal. Nor do we regard Britain as representative of OECD countries, which differ greatly with regard to information on the distribution of income, and we doubt whether any country could be regarded as representative.

The third question addressed in this chapter – in Sections 3.2 and 3.4 – is the *comparability* of income distribution data. The degree of comparability of data for Eastern and Western Europe has been discussed in a number of earlier comparative studies, such as those of Pryor (1973), Morrisson (1984), Bruinooge *et al.* (1990), and it is evident that there are significant differences in the scope and content of the data collected. Information on earnings may, for instance, be limited in Eastern European countries to the state sector of the economy. Moreover, it should be remembered that it is not just *differences* in methods of collecting data that may cause problems. It is also the case that statistical deficiencies which are common to East and West may have different implications on account of the social and economic differences. Household budget surveys exclude the homeless, an omission which is more important in some countries than others. Inadequate coverage of income from the underground economy may have a different effect on the estimated distribution of income. The omission from income data of capital gains is more significant in Western countries with substantial private ownership of capital and land.

This chapter summarises a large quantity of material which we have assembled on the five countries. This material is presented for each country in the section at the end of the book called 'Sources and Methods'. The reader requiring further information about the statistical sources should refer to Sources and Methods. At the same time, it should be emphasised that our discussion of sources is selective. It concentrates on those sources that we use. This means that, for example, we discuss the Czechoslovak

Microcensus, which is our source of information on the income distribution in that country, but do not discuss the Czechoslovak budget survey or social stratification survey, either of which could give information on the distribution of income. Nor do we attempt to provide an exhaustive account of the data sources on which we do draw. Our aim is to give a broad overview of statistical practice in the Eastern European countries and to set the data concerned in context in relation to those from Britain.

3.1 The availability of data

When seeking to assess the extent of inequality in Communist countries, the problem of the availability of data may seem insuperable. This impression seems to be borne out, in the case of the USSR, by statements from both Western and Soviet writers who for years have been frustrated by lack of data:

published statistics on the distribution of earnings in the Soviet Union are almost nonexistent. (McAuley, 1979, p. 218)

or:

The average wage in 1986 was 195.5 rubles a month. But what share of the population receives this amount? How many receive more? How many receive less? In vain did we try to learn this. (Dmitriev, 1989, p. 60)

The topic of income distribution in the USSR was subject to censorship:

Extracts from a censor's handbook published for closed distribution, probably in 1970, listed many relevant prohibitions. They applied to such topics as the distribution of wages and incomes, the purchasing power of the ruble, alcoholism, drug addiction, occupational injuries, the incidence of crime, vagrancy, prison populations, illiteracy, and mass accidents. (Matthews, 1989, p. 113)

The effect of this censorship has been described by Wiles:

They clearly dispose of innumerable surveys and a rich store of data, but scarcely any absolute figure has been published. All numerical data are drawn from unspecified areas rather than the whole country, or are marked 'stipulated' (*uslovni*). All diagrams are given without absolute numbers on the axes. (1974, p. 1)

Some information was made available: estimates of the decile ratio of earnings for a number of years were reported in Russian publications, thus providing an important source for Western writers, but it was extremely limited. (The decile ratio is the ratio of the ninetieth percentile in the distribution to the tenth, counting from the bottom.)

This censorship was a challenge that scholars from outside the Soviet Union found hard to resist, and they exhibited remarkable ingenuity in making deductions from the limited information that was released. Perhaps

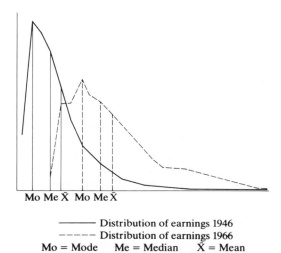

Mo Me X̄ Mo Me X̄

———— Distribution of earnings 1946
– – – – Distribution of earnings 1966
Mo = Mode   Me = Median   X̄ = Mean

Figure 3.1 USSR earnings distribution as originally published without numbering of axes

Source: Wiles and Markowski (1971, Figure 6, p. 501).

the best known is the reconstruction of the Soviet earnings distribution by Wiles and Markowski (1971) from a graph published with no scale. All that they had to go on is the graph reproduced in Figure 3.1, which comes from an article by Loznevaya (1968). As they note:

The axes have not been numbered off. This is therefore the maximum that the censors are prepared to let out. (Wiles and Markowski, 1971, p. 501)

However, using other information contained in the article (which includes the decile ratio), they provide a plausible interpretation of the graph which allows them to reconstruct the scale on the horizontal axis within some 5 percent. A more recent attempt to fill in the missing information is the work by Braithwaite and Heleniak (1989) who construct a 'synthetic' distribution of income using information on employment totals and average earnings by branch, skill level and republic, together with other average income information. Vinokur and Ofer (1987), Matthews (1989) and others have provided insights using sample survey data collected from Soviet emigrés to the US and Israel in the 1970s.

The situation in the Soviet Union with regard to the publication of data on income distribution changed completely with *glasnost'*. We now have a much richer basis to assess the performance of the USSR over the post-war period and to examine the situation in individual republics. In the late 1980s there was a marked change in publication policy by Goskomstat (the USSR central statistical office). The 1988 statistical yearbook contained figures for the distribution of earnings, not only for a recent year but retrospectively for a number of years back to 1956, and figures for the individual distribution of per capita household income in the 1980s (although information from earlier years remained unpublished). As a result of this and subsequent publications, we can now examine the evolution of the distribution of earnings over the period 1956–1989 (Table UE1 in the Statistical Appendix), the distribution of earnings for males and females in 1989 (Table UE3), the distribution of earnings by republics (Tables UE5–UE8), the distribution of household income per capita 1980–1989 (Table UI1), and the distribution of household income by republic (Table UI3).

Czechoslovakia, Hungary and Poland

The main features of the sources of earnings and income data in the former Soviet Union are summarised in Tables 3.1 and 3.2. The same tables show the position in the other Eastern European countries which we consider – Czechoslovakia, Hungary and Poland. As already noted, the position regarding the availability of income distribution data is completely different in these Central European countries. In general, data have been readily available in these countries, as is evident from a browse through their annual statistical yearbooks.

Indeed, a rough yardstick of a government's openness on the issue of economic inequality is whether or not information on the distribution of earnings and income is published in the official annual statistical yearbook. Hungary and Poland have scored well on this measure for most of the post-war period. Evidence about the distribution of earnings began to be published regularly in the statistical yearbooks in the late 1950s/early 1960s. The same was true in Czechoslovakia, although the publication of the earnings data in the yearbook was discontinued in the 1980s. Moreover, efforts were made to ensure that the information was accessible to outsiders. In Czechoslovakia, the yearbook had in the past English translations of the contents pages and a useful dictionary of statistical terms was made available in 1973. The Hungarian yearbook has been available in a combined English–Russian version for many years and, more recently, the basic table for Poland has been published in English (*Poland Statistical Data 1988*).

Published information relating to the distribution of household income in the Communist period may be found for Czechoslovakia, Hungary and Poland in the annual statistical yearbooks. Again, the information has often been published for many years. For example, a quinquennial house-

Table 3.1 *Main sources of data on the distribution of earnings at end of 1980s*

	Type of source (last year prior to 1990)	Coverage	Definition of earnings	Presentation of results in statistical yearbook
Czechoslovakia	Periodic census of employers (1989)	Full-month, full-time employees in state sector	Gross monthly earnings and bonuses excluding monthly value of annual bonuses	Not in annual yearbook in 1980s
Hungary	Two-yearly census of employers (1988)	Full-month, full-time employees in all sectors	Gross monthly earnings including monthly value of all bonuses	Summary table in yearbook (e.g. SY, 1988, p. 70)
Poland	Annual sample survey of employers (1989)	Full-month full-time, employees in socialised sector	Gross monthly earnings including monthly value of all bonuses	Summary table in yearbook (e.g. RS, 1989, p. 225)
USSR	Five-yearly census of employers (1986)	Full-month employees in state sector (full-time employees can be separately identified)	Gross monthly earnings including monthly value of quarterly bonuses	Summary table in yearbook (e.g. NK, 1988, p. 79)
Great Britain	Annual sample survey of employees (1989)	Employees in all sectors (full-time employees can be separately identified)	Gross weekly earnings including weekly value of all bonuses	Summary table in yearbook (e.g. AAS, 1991, Table 6.17)

Notes:

(a) See Sources and Methods for more detailed information, and for the definition of abbreviations used for the statistical yearbooks.

(b) The 'socialised sector' includes co-operative employment (excluded from the 'state sector'), although the definitions vary from country to country.

(c) Earnings information is also available from household surveys described in Table 3.2.

Table 3.2 *Main sources of data on the distribution of income at end of 1980s*

	Type of source (last year prior to 1990)	Response in last year prior to 1990 and achieved sample size	Income concept	Presentation of results in statistical yearbook
Czechoslovakia	Periodic microcensus of non-institutional population (1988)	96.6% in 1989 (1988 incomes) About 100,000 households	Annual net per capita income excluding agricultural income in kind	Summary table in yearbook (e.g. SR, 1990, p. 558)
Hungary	Five-yearly income survey of non-institutional population (1987)	83.1% in 1988 (1987 incomes) About 20,000 households	Annual net income (total household, per capita, or equivalised) including agricultural income in kind	Summary table in yearbook (e.g. SY, 1988, pp. 433–5)
Poland	Annual budget survey of non-institutional population (excluding households of non-agricultural private sector workers) (1989)	58.4% in 1989 among households selected for first participation (substitution of non-respondents) About 30,000 households	Annual net per capita income including income in kind	Summary table in yearbook for 4 household types (e.g. RS, 1989, Table 19(233) p. 162)
USSR	Annual budget survey of households of workers in socialised sector (1989)	Response unknown About 92,000 families in 1989	Annual gross per capita income including agricultural income in kind	Summary table in yearbook (e.g. NK, 1989, p. 89)
Britain	(a) Annual budget survey of non-institutional population (FES) (1989) (b) Annual sample of administrative register of income tax records (SPI) (1987/8)	(a) 73% in 1989 About 7,500 households (b) Not applicable About 120,000 tax units	(a) Gross and net income collected for a variety of periods (b) Taxable income in the tax year	(a) No summary table of distribution in yearbook (b) Summary table in yearbook (e.g. AAS, 1987, Table 15.2)

Note:
(a) See Sources and Methods for more detailed information.

hold income survey was first held in Hungary in 1963 with some limited results published in the 1964 yearbook. A special English language publication was produced giving results of the 1973 survey (Hungarian Central Statistical Office, 1975). The Czechoslovak yearbook has since the early 1960s given information on the distribution of income drawn from a periodic population microcensus. The Polish income distribution data derived from the household budget survey are summarised for four types of household in the statistical yearbook.

Depth of detail

The situation by the end of the 1980s was that all four Eastern European countries which we consider were making data available on distributional issues in official statistical yearbooks and three of them had done so for many years. It is important to distinguish, however, the act of making *any* data available from that of publishing data in a form which is sufficiently detailed to allow the information to be used for worthwhile research.

Here again there is a significant difference between the Soviet Union and the other Eastern European countries studied here. The level of detail of published data for the USSR is less than for the other countries. The earnings data finally made available in the yearbook in 1988 were presented with only a few (eight) ruble classes and with the same class intervals for each year. This renders the data for 1956 of limited use, since 71 percent of the distribution falls in the lowest range. The income distribution data published by Goskomstat in 1989 took the form of nine income classes, two of which each contain more than 15 percent of the population.

In contrast, the published sources are much richer in the other Eastern European countries considered here. The annual yearbooks have at times presented very detailed information (although not consistently throughout the post-war period) and often contain valuable summary statistics. The Polish yearbook has published the decile values of the earnings distribution going back to 1970. The 1988 Hungarian yearbook gave the individual distribution of household per capita income in 1987 in a form which includes class means, summary inequality measures, and the incidence of 'social income in kind' across the income distribution.

More detailed information than that in the countries' yearbooks has typically been available in other official publications, for example the reports on the Hungarian income surveys and the Polish budget surveys. Not unnaturally, these have rarely been published in English. We have drawn on some of these sources for our tables in the Statistical Appendix, and fuller references are given in the Sources and Methods section. It should also be noted that in some instances we have been able to use unpublished analyses made by the statistical offices or by other persons in the country in question.

The degree of detail is important when it comes to *interpolation* of size distributions in order to calculate summary statistics. The decile ratio is an example. Where the bottom range contains, say 7 percent of the population and the next range contains 9 percent, then it is necessary to interpolate. The tenth percentile comes part way into the second range, and some assumption has to be made about the distribution within that range. The results depend on the assumption made (see Sources and Methods). The extent of such interpolation – and hence the potential error – depends on the fineness of the income ranges and on their location in relation to the required percentiles. The problem is particularly severe when the required percentile falls in an open-ended upper interval or in the bottom interval. The accuracy of interpolation may be improved by the availability of information on the class means, as is illustrated in the Sources and Methods section using Hungarian income data for 1987. Where this information is available, we have used it in our analysis.

The issue of interpolation is important in that different amounts of detail are available for different countries, and within countries across time. This means that the accuracy of the estimates is not the same in each case. We have therefore placed more emphasis in our analysis on those summary measures which are likely to be less affected by errors of interpolation. In general, the tenth and ninetieth percentiles require less extrapolation than the fifth and ninety-fifth; for this reason we prefer the decile ratio to the semi-decile ratio advocated by Wiles (1974). We also tend to use the percentiles and the decile shares rather than summary measures such as the Gini coefficient which require full information about the distribution.

The need for interpolation arises because we are using grouped data; access to the raw micro-data, that is observations for individual house-holds, would obviate the need for interpolation. In this study, we have in general focused on the inferences that can be drawn from the published tables, but household micro-data from Czechoslovakia, Hungary and Poland relating to the pre-reform period are now available for secondary analysis through the Luxembourg Income Study (LIS), which also holds household micro-data from a range of Western countries including Britain. (The Luxembourg Income Study is described in Smeeding *et al.*, 1990.) The data from Britain are from the Family Expenditure Survey, to which we have direct access and have used in constructing Tables BI3, BI6 and BI7.

We have relied mainly on published tabulations, rather than using the micro-data, for three reasons. First, at the time the research was carried out, Poland was the only Eastern European country for which data were available in LIS. Secondly, we are interested in data covering as long a period as possible and micro-data are not typically available for the earlier years. Thirdly, the earnings data for Eastern Europe are aggregated at the level of the responding enterprise, and so are not available as individual micro-data.

Published data from Britain

How does the situation we have described for the Eastern European countries compare with that in Britain? In the case of earnings, there have been wage censuses in Britain since 1886, but these were infrequent (none between 1938 and 1960) and covered only part of the employed labour force. The regular collection of information about the earnings distribution in Britain only began in 1968, or some ten years after the starting point for our series in Eastern Europe (which go back to 1955 in the case of Hungary and 1956 for Poland and the USSR). The New Earnings Survey, initially held in September 1968, and carried out annually in April since 1970, provides a wealth of detail in the form of tabulations and summary statistics in the published reports and a summary table is given in the *Annual Abstract of Statistics*.

Turning to the distribution of income, we may note that, in contrast with Hungary, Britain has not to date had a regular purpose-built household survey specifically designed to produce information on the distribution of income in the population as a whole. Evidence about the distribution of household income has been obtained from sources whose main purpose is different. The first of these is the income tax records, which are the basis for the Survey of Personal Income (SPI) carried out each year by the Inland Revenue. The SPI does however exclude a substantial part of the non-tax-paying population – several million pensioners and others not at work – and does not cover non-taxable income, particularly certain social security benefits, such as child benefit. It does not therefore on its own provide a satisfactory source. For this reason, the official estimates of the overall distribution have been based on a combination of information from the SPI and the annual household budget survey – the Family Expenditure Survey (FES). These estimates are referred to as the Blue Book estimates, since they used to be published in the National Income Blue Book (*National Income and Expenditure*).

The official Blue Book series in the UK has had a rather chequered history. After being produced for many years, the series was halted by the government in 1970 on grounds of 'the increasing amount of estimation required' (Atkinson, 1983, p. 10). Five years later, the Royal Commission on the Distribution of Income and Wealth was responsible for the reintroduction, and improvement, of the series. In effect, a new government allocated more resources to this area of official statistics. But this in turn was reversed when Mrs Thatcher came to power. The review of the Government Statistical Service reduced the frequency of production of estimates of the distribution of personal income from every year to every three years. As a consequence, the most recent Blue Book distribution data available in the Spring of 1992 related to the year 1984/5. In other words, they were some seven years out of date. As this illustrates, political factors play a role in the availability of statistics in market as well as in Communist economies.

The reduced frequency of the Blue Book estimates has resulted in more attention being paid to one of the elements used in their construction: the information on the distribution of income provided by the Family Expenditure Survey (FES). The main reason why the Department of Employment commissions this survey is 'to provide a source of the weighting pattern of the Index of Retail Prices and so it is primarily concerned with household expenditure' (*Annual Abstract of Statistics*, 1987, p. 255). At the same time, the income information is collected in considerable detail, and the FES provides the basis for analysis of the distribution by other government departments (Tables BI4 and BI5 in the Statistical Appendix). The coverage is less complete, for reasons explained in the Sources and Methods section, but it provides more current information (up to 1989). The FES is also available as micro-data and these have been used in constructing Tables BI3, BI6 and BI7.

To sum up, there is a significant difference in terms of the publication of distributional information between the Soviet Union and the other countries of Eastern Europe. The situation in the latter does not in fact appear to be very different from that in Britain.

3.2 Data quality and comparability: earnings

The quality of data on the distribution of earnings by size is compared here, not with an unattainable ideal, but with what can realistically be achieved in the real world. For this purpose, we take the New Earnings Survey in Great Britain as the point of comparison – a source which, as we shall see, has both advantages and disadvantages in relation to the sources in Eastern Europe. We have chosen the British earnings survey as that with which we are most familiar, but there are alternative choices, such as the Déclarations Annuelles de Salaires (DAS) in France. The DAS is based on the documents supplied annually by employers for the use of the fiscal authorities and the social security administration (for a brief comparison with the NES in Britain, see Atkinson and Bazen, 1984).

The New Earnings Survey in Britain (and the DAS in France) is similar to the Eastern European sources in that it is a survey of *employers*. The earnings data are supplied by firms or enterprises, and the individual is not required to respond. Just as the worker in the URSUS tractor plant in Warsaw is probably unaware that the data are being reported, so too is the typical person with a National Insurance number ending in 14 unaware that he or she forms part of the NES sample. This should be stressed, since this situation is different from that where earnings data are obtained from household surveys or censuses. In the United States, for example, the principal source of earnings data are the annual earnings reported to the Census Bureau by members of a sample of households (the March Current Population Survey) – see Henle and Ryscavage (1980), Burtless (1990) and Levy and Murnane (forthcoming). In the case of the Soviet Union, we have also used data from the March Household Survey, in addition to that obtained from the enterprise sources. In this respect, the information for the USSR for certain years is different. (Data on earnings are also contained in household surveys in the Central European countries but we have not drawn on them.)

There are differences in how the earnings surveys operate. The NES in Britain is a sample of *employees* (as is the DAS in France, which takes those workers born in October of even-numbered years), so that the returns by the employer cover only those in the NES sample, of whom there may be none in the firm. In contrast, enterprises in the Eastern European countries were requested to make a return covering all their employees at that date. The NES employee approach has both advantages and drawbacks. On the one hand, the survey collects detailed micro-data on the sample members, and, since the survey attempts to include the same individuals each year (it has a panel design), considerably richer information about earnings changes is obtained. On the other hand, it is necessary to ensure that the person's current employer is included in the survey and in 1990 about one in eight of the NES questionnaires were returned with the statement that the employee cannot be traced or has left the firm (see Sources and Methods).

A second difference is that in four of the Eastern European countries the data came from a *census* of all employers of workers in the defined categories. This is an example of the emphasis put by statistical offices in command economies on 'exhaustive surveying' (Olenski, 1991). The exception is Poland; here a survey of enterprises was held but with a very high sampling fraction (around 20 percent).

The sources of earnings data are, with these exceptions, relatively similar. We now consider the quality of the data collected, under the headings of *coverage, response* and *definition of earnings*.

Coverage

It is common for earnings data in Western countries to exclude certain groups by design. The NES in Britain excludes the self-employed, as do all the earnings surveys considered here. It also excludes employees who are non-salaried directors, working for their spouse, or working outside the UK. In addition the NES exempts, for example, members of the armed forces, employees of the Territorial Army Association, certain clergymen, and employees of the Royal Household. Finally, persons employed within 'enterprise zones' are excluded from the survey, these being areas introduced by the Thatcher government in which employers are free from certain regulations (information on exemptions is given by Adams and Owen, 1989). (This last exemption illustrates how sample definitions are influenced by the ideology of the prevailing economic and political organisation.) These exclusions are quantitatively unimportant (see Sources and Methods), but the exclusions in other countries may be more significant. In France, the DAS excluded agricultural employees, those in domestic service or working at home, and employees of state and local authorities. As a result, the French data were estimated to cover in 1982 only some 11.9 million out of 16.3 million full-time workers (Bourit *et al.*, 1983, p. 29).

In the case of Eastern Europe, there are similarly exclusions. Some categories of workers were excluded in all Eastern European countries such as the armed forces, and full-time employees of the Communist Party were certainly excluded from the earnings enquiries in Czechoslovakia, Poland and the USSR. In other cases, the coverage differed from country to country. Those working in the private sector were excluded in Czechoslovakia and Poland, but in Hungary, where private ventures were permitted from 1982, we understand that those ventures which had a legal identity were included in the earnings enquiry. Enterprises operating outside the legal economy are unlikely to be fully covered in Hungary or any other economy.

Of particular importance, in view of its size in Eastern European countries, is the treatment of the agricultural sector. In Britain, all employees in the – much smaller – agricultural sector are covered by the NES. In Poland, much of the labour force in agriculture was self-employed, and hence is excluded; in Czechoslovakia, those working in agricultural co-operatives, about two-thirds of total employment in that sector, were excluded. In Hungary employees of agricultural co-operatives were included in the 'socialised sector', and employees of state farms were included in the narrower 'state sector'. In the earnings census of the former USSR, state farm workers were included, but those working on collective farms or private agricultural plots, were excluded. This difference in coverage of agriculture affects the comparison of republics in the USSR, since the proportion of the agricultural labour force on collective farms varied considerably.

Such differences in coverage may change over time, and their significance may change with the evolution of the economy. Agricultural employment has fallen. In the USSR there was at the same time a move from collective to state farms, which has an offsetting effect on state farm employment (which is covered by the earnings data). In the case of Hungary, there was an explicit extension of coverage. The figures prior to 1970 related to the state sector, defined as state-owned enterprises and farms, but after 1970 there are more extensive statistics covering the socialised sector, defined as the state sector plus co-operatives (agricultural and non-agricultural).

In one important respect the coverage in all the Eastern European countries was identical: the earnings enquiries were restricted to persons working a *full month*. This had the effect of excluding all those workers leaving or joining the employer part way through the month. Turnover in Eastern European labour markets was quite considerable, much of it due to voluntary quits. The 1–2 percent of employees per month excluded on grounds of turnover would not have been a random sample of all employees. The impact on the measured distribution can be expected to be a slight reduction in dispersion.

In general, the earnings data relate to full-time workers and to their main job. Part-time and second jobs are not covered. There are certain exceptions, as are described in more detail in Sources and Methods.

Response

Employer compliance with the earnings enquiries in Eastern Europe was obligatory and seems to all intents and purposes to have been complete. In Britain, too, employers are obliged to supply the requested information, although there is nonetheless a small element of non-compliance (about 4 percent – see Sources and Methods). Taken together with the larger proportion of employees who cannot be traced or who have left their employer, the response rate for full-time male employees is some 85 percent and around the same or less for full-time female employees (see Sources and Methods).

The shortfall in coverage in the NES may be expected to affect the distributional conclusions to the extent that the 15 + percent not 'responding' are concentrated at particular points in the distribution. The implications of non-response have been examined by Micklewright and Trinder (1981). Although there is little firm evidence, it seems plausible that non-compliance by employers may be commoner with small firms, and it seems possible that this would differentially affect the relatively low paid. The absence from the NES sample of recent job-changers (even though they worked the whole of the pay period and hence are eligible for inclusion) may also be expected to affect differentially the low paid for two reasons. Low pay tends to go together with shorter job durations and precarious employment; whereas the information supplied directly by large employers is more likely to be up-to-date (NES Report 1990, Part A, para. 3.4) and hence allow their employees who have recently changed jobs to be included in the survey.

Definition of earnings

The definition of earnings may appear to be a straightforward matter: what we are seeking is the amount paid to individual workers, recorded in their payslips. However, there are a number of questions which arise. What exactly is included? What allowance is made for taxes and other deductions? What time period do they cover?

First, we want to measure the total amount paid, and not just the basic wage or salary. The earnings figures in the five countries do indeed include any overtime payments, premia (such as those for unhealthy or hazardous working conditions), bonuses, and payment by results. They are, however, in general limited to *cash* payments and exclude income in kind from the employer. Income in kind is important in Britain, where the term 'fringe benefits' gives a misleading impression of their potential quantitative significance; in Eastern Europe it is clearly a major issue. We return to this question in Chapter 6.

Secondly, the earnings information relates to *gross* earnings before any deduction of income tax or employee social security contributions.

Thirdly, there are differences in the time period. This could refer to the rate per *unit of time*. The NES in Britain collects information on hours of work and the distribution may be expressed in terms of *hourly earnings*. As far as we are aware, information on hours is not contained in the sources of earnings data from Eastern Europe which we use.

The time period could, alternatively, refer to that over which earnings are *averaged*. Britain retains weekly payment for some, mostly manual, workers and the NES relates in their case to earnings in the specified *week*. (In the case of monthly paid workers, the NES takes the weekly equivalent of the monthly pay.) Insofar as there is some smoothing of weekly earnings over a month, as where there is a shift-cycle, we may expect to observe increased dispersion relative to the monthly period adopted in the Eastern European countries.

It is equally possible that *monthly* earnings may exhibit greater variation than the annual earnings recorded in some sources (such as the US Current Population Survey or the French DAS). This may particularly apply where there are bonus payments at less than monthly intervals (such as a Christmas bonus), or where holiday pay is different from that in work periods. Here there is a variety of practice. In Britain, employers are told to 'include the appropriate fraction of the bonus payments ... calculated by dividing the last payment (or the next payment if known) by the number of pay-periods it covers' (NES Report 1990, Appendix 3). In Poland and Hungary the monthly equivalents of bonuses were similarly included, but in the USSR this was only true of any bonuses relating to a period of up to three months, and in Czechoslovakia all bonuses other than for the month in question were excluded. The implications of this difference in treatment of bonuses depends on their incidence. If bonuses as a whole were distributionally neutral, but were paid in different months in different enterprises, then their exclusion would cause dispersion to be overstated. But if bonuses were more common (or proportionately larger) for persons higher up the distribution, then their omission in Czechoslovakia and the USSR would have the effect of reducing the relative inequality of earnings in those countries compared with Hungary and Poland.

The months in which the survey took place (March in the USSR, April in Britain, May or November in Czechoslovakia, September in Hungary and Poland) were undoubtedly chosen to avoid the main holiday period. But, in any estimate of annual earnings, allowance would have to be made for the treatment of holiday pay.

Conclusions

To summarise, our comparison of the earnings surveys for Eastern Europe and the New Earnings Survey in Britain suggests that the similarities are more striking than the differences. Information is obtained from employers; it covers a large part of the (non-agricultural) employed labour force; it relates in general to those working full-time and for a full period; and it encompasses a broad measure of cash earnings. In all cases, the survey information needs to be interpreted carefully in the light of significant non-cash remuneration which does not appear in the statistics.

Differences there certainly are. Agriculture is less well covered in the Eastern European data, although it should be noted that some of this is self-employment, which would also be excluded in the NES. In Britain, the NES has a non-response rate, on account of employer non-compliance or lack of up-to-date records, of some 15 percent, with some reason to believe that the low-paid are differentially under-represented. The NES data relate to a weekly pay period for a sizeable fraction of workers. Nor are the differences purely between Britain and Eastern Europe. There are also differences between Czechoslovakia (which for example only includes bonus payments in the current month), Hungary (where the socialised sector includes certain private ventures), Poland (where figures for earlier years were published on a different basis), and the USSR (which publishes estimates of the size distribution of earnings based both on censuses of enterprises and on a household survey). These differences need to be borne in mind in Chapter 4 where we look at the results of the earnings surveys.

3.3 Income data: quality

The methodology of collecting household income data is more complicated than that of individual earnings data. Household income may involve several sources and several recipients. There is no natural sampling frame in terms of lists of workers and no immediate point of contact such as the enterprise. The methods employed may appear mysterious – even to those from the country in question. One Soviet writer has said of the Family Budget Survey (FBS) carried out by Goskomstat in the USSR:

One gets the impression from the very beginning that Goskomstat does its utmost to keep us from learning from the truth. It would be interesting to know how these families were selected: from which regions, from which branches of the national economy, from which age groups, etc. What are these families incomes? Why was this number chosen? What is the make-up of these families? And, finally, what constitutes a family in the eyes of Goskomstat? Can these indicators be compared with the data of family budgets for previous years? According to what methods were the budgets calculated? A hundred 'why's and how's' and not one answer. (Dmitriev, 1989, p. 60)

The difficulty of working on distributional issues with Soviet Family Budget Survey data has equally been stressed by Western writers, who have severely criticised the methods used to collect the data.

Again it must be remembered that the Soviet Union is not typical of Eastern Europe. For other Eastern European countries, the sources of household income data are much better documented – a fact that does not seem sufficiently appreciated in much of the Western literature which focuses on the shortcomings of the Soviet data. Those responsible for collecting data in Czechoslovakia, Hungary and Poland have, for example, published papers in the English language in international journals describing their methods. Other descriptions are given in the publications of international agencies (United Nations, 1981); and there are in addition descriptions given in the original language in published survey reports.

At the same time, there are many potential pitfalls in the use of household survey data. The Family Expenditure Survey in Britain has an excellent handbook discussing methods (Kemsley *et al.*, 1980), and the annual report is documented at length, but the significance of various qualifications may well not be apparent, particularly to readers without local knowledge. There is, for instance, a table in the 1989 Report (Table 25) showing the quantiles of the household distribution of household disposable income. It is tempting to compare these results with those from the table with the same heading in the 1979 Report (Table 49), in order to see the change in the distribution of income over the decade. The user who has not read the 1989 report from cover to cover may well regard this as a consistent series, not least because there are no footnotes to these particular tables to warn the reader, and because there is a graph only three pages earlier in the 1989 report showing the changes over time (1968–1989) in the sources of income. However, as the Annex to the report makes clear, changes in 1982 and 1983 in the form of cash benefits for housing (Housing Benefit), and in the way in which income tax relief is given for those borrowing for house purchase (Mortgage Interest Relief At Source), mean that the figures cannot be compared. Part at least of the observed change in the distribution is due to these institutional changes.

We have described this example to highlight the risks in using data for countries with which one is not fully familiar. There is a risk that in the case of the Eastern European data we have made similar errors of interpretation. Even though we have established many of the details of the Eastern European surveys through direct contact with the officials responsible for collecting the data, there are undoubtedly aspects whose significance we have not fully appreciated. Specialists on individual countries will, at the very least, be able to provide greater detail. Nevertheless, we hope that the material assembled here is of some value in that it provides a *comparative* perspective.

The comparative perspective is of particular importance when assessing the reliability of Eastern European data. In the case of the USSR, Alexeev and Gaddy (1991) draw on work by Treml (1990) who compared the aggregate incomes of several types recorded in the Family Budget Survey (FBS) with those shown in national accounts. The percentage differences between the two were as follows:

apparent over (+) or under (−)
statement in the Soviet FBS

State wages and salaries	+ 11.2%
Collective farm pay	+ 6.5%
State transfers	− 9.8%

On the basis of these figures, Alexeev and Gaddy argue that Treml 'conclusively demonstrated the unrepresentativeness' of the FBS, and label the differences between the totals as 'quite substantial' (1991, p. 22).

It is however relevant to ask how these discrepancies compare with those found in Western sources. In the case of the Family Expenditure Survey (FES) data from the UK, we have investigated the divergence between income aggregates recorded in the survey for the years 1970–1977 and those shown in the national accounts (Atkinson and Micklewright, 1983). The results from this exercise for 1977 show a shortfall for earnings in the FES of 6.3 percent (see Sources and Methods), a figure which is described in the official FES Report (1989, p. v) as indicating that earnings in the survey are 'slightly deficient'. For social security benefits, the deficiency was 9.1 percent – a figure very similar to that quoted for state transfers in the USSR Family Budget Survey. When we come to income from self-employment and occupational pensions, we find that there is a shortfall of around one quarter, and for investment income as much as one half of total income appears to be missing from the FES.

The fact that such large income shortfalls should be observed in the UK FES, a survey which is widely recognised within the UK and elsewhere to be of a high standard, leads us to be cautious in reaching critical conclusions about the data for Eastern Europe. We find relatively reassuring the finding that per capita personal income recorded in the 1987 Hungarian Income Survey was 96.4 percent of that indicated by aggregate sources (*Statistical Yearbook*, 1988, p. 427) and 94.1 percent in 1972 (Hungarian Central Statistical Office, 1975, p. 10). Similarly, we were told that per capita money income in the 1988 Czechoslovak Microcensus was 85.9 percent of that suggested by aggregate data but that at least half the shortfall could be attributed to differences in definition, something which we found to be important in the comparison of the UK FES with the national accounts. (About half the apparent shortfall in the 1972 Hungarian Income Survey could also be explained in this way.)

At the same time, there are clearly weaknesses in the available household income data. In the case of the USSR, our appraisal (see below) of the Family Budget Survey from the USSR supports the conclusion of Alexeev and Gaddy that it is 'systematically biased' (1991, p. 22). There was significant non-response to the Polish Budget Survey. However, this does not mean that we should reject all household income data out of hand. What is necessary is a careful examination of how the surveys of household income were carried out in Eastern Europe and of the implications of the methodology for the quality of data. This involves investigation of the reasons for any income shortfall. The under-recording of income from self-employment in surveys compared with national aggregates could be because self-employed persons are deliberately excluded from the survey, or because their response rate is lower, or because they understate their incomes, or any combination of the three. Moreover, omitted from the earlier comparisons was consideration of income which is unrecorded in *both* the survey in question *and* national accounts figures. When this is taken into account the true understatement of income in household surveys will be greater than the comparisons above suggest. In all these cases the recorded distribution of income is likely as a result to depart from the true distribution in the population as a whole, but the direction of the departure may depend on the reason for the shortfall.

In what follows, we consider in more detail the data from household surveys, dealing in turn with *coverage, response rates* and *substantiation of the data.*

Coverage

Anyone familiar with the UK Family Expenditure Survey would, like us, be somewhat taken aback when reading about the methodology in the Soviet FBS. In contrast to standard household survey methodology in the West, which samples on a geographic basis, the point of departure for household income data collection in the FBS has been the enterprise: the sampling unit has been employees at their place of work. The survey has been a quota sample of families of persons working in state enterprises and collective farms. This meant that households without employed members were not normally included (although some 'pure' pensioner households have in fact been covered in recent years). Moreover, the quotas in the sampling process have not even been set so as to achieve a representative sample of employees in the covered enterprises (although changes in 1988 are said to have improved this situation – see Sources and Methods): employees in heavy industry, and hence the urban population, appear to be over-represented. The survey is a panel, respondents being pressured to co-operate indefinitely, until they leave their enterprise through retirement or some other reason, and this has further implications for the representativeness of the data. Even when viewed as a sample of families of working people, the FBS cannot be seen as adequate, although the use of the data on this basis would allow for greater comparability with the data for families of employed persons in other countries. (We discuss the problems with the FBS at more length in the Sources and Methods section.)

The sampling design is one important reason why the Family Budget Survey has attracted substantial criticism both inside and outside the Soviet Union. Shenfield (1983) argues that Soviet planners and academic researchers where possible avoid the FBS. He himself concludes that:

the sample is subject to a great many different biases, often severe and cumulative in effect, and that the survey is highly unrepresentative of the population as a whole. (1984, p. 3)

McAuley (1979) argues that 'statistics from this source have been rejected by many, perhaps a majority, of Soviet economists and statisticians as worthless' (p. 51) but goes on to note that it represents the only source of information on a number of questions.

The position is quite different in the other Eastern European countries. In contrast to the methodology described in the USSR, the household surveys used in this book from Czechoslovakia and Hungary, and from Poland since 1973, were all conducted on a geographic basis: in these countries the dwelling, and not the worker, was the sampling unit. For example, the sampling frame for the Czechoslovak Microcensus in 1988 was a centralised administrative register used to record addresses of all dwellings so as to collect a combined payment for gas, electricity and other utilities. This seems not dissimilar in conception to the Postcode Address File used since 1986 in the UK FES.

Broadly speaking, the theoretical coverage of the population by these surveys was reasonably complete, but certain categories of households were specifically excluded from the household surveys. This applied in Czechoslovakia and Poland to households with members in the army or the police. Our understanding is that households of members of the government or senior Communist Party officials were not in general excluded deliberately. (In the case of Poland it was strongly denied to us that this had happened and we were told that any problem that existed with these groups stemmed more from establishing contact with household members; we were told of one instance in which a government minister's household had been 'model' respondents!) In Poland a significant exclusion was of all households in which the main employment was the private non-agricultural sector, about 10 percent of the labour force. This does represent a serious omission. The reason for it is revealing: it was argued to us that these households were excluded on account of concerns regarding the reliability of income data they would provide rather than for ideological reasons. As we have seen, data on self-employment income in the UK FES appears too to be subject to significant understatement.

Both the Eastern European income surveys and the FES in the UK exclude persons living in institutions. The quantitative importance of omitting this section of the population may vary from country to country. We estimate that about 2–2.5 percent of the population was not covered by the Family Expenditure Survey for this reason (Atkinson and Micklewright, 1983, p. 35). In the USSR, Bergson (1984, p. 1057) estimated that 'in recent years, some 2.0 million persons or 1.6 percent of all Soviet workers' were in penal labour camps.

The achieved samples in the household surveys have been large: about 20,000 households in Hungary, 30,000 in Poland, 60,000 in the USSR

(90,000 from 1988) and 100,000 in Czechoslovakia. These may be compared with a sample size in the UK of only 7,000 in the FES (and 12,000 in the General Household Survey which also contains income data). It is true that the other main source of data used to give information in the UK on the distribution of income, the Survey of Personal Incomes (SPI) has a sample size of about 125,000 but this is based on a sample of tax records and is not a household survey. Sample size has to be judged in relation to the size and heterogeneity of the population. This applies particularly to the former USSR where the sample sizes for the individual republics may be quite small (see Sources and Methods).

The sample size, and the sample design, are relevant to calculations of standard errors for the survey results. The UK FES gives a simple calculation, and a more elaborate calculation which takes account of the stratified nature of the sample design: in 1989 the percentage standard error for gross household income was 1.0 percent on the former basis and 1.3 percent with the more elaborate calculation.

Response

The definition of the sampling frame is not the only factor determining a survey's coverage. The response to the survey by sampled households is also critical. To put the Eastern European surveys in perspective, it is useful to note that the overall level of response in Britain to the FES in 1985 (the year used in Tables BI3, BI6 and BI7) was 67 percent of the effective sample. Over the long-run, after two initial years with response rates of 59 percent (1957) and 61 percent (1958), the rate in the FES has varied between 65 and 75 percent. By this yardstick, the success of the periodic Czechoslovak Microcensus and the quinquennial Hungarian Income Survey was excellent: response to the former in 1988 was 97 percent and to the latter 91 percent in 1982 and 83 percent in 1987. Response rates of over 90 percent in a household survey must be considered outstanding by any standard. In contrast, response in the 1980s by households first selected for the Polish Budget Survey (the survey has a rotating panel design) was at or below the level of the British FES, averaging 65 percent during 1982–1989, but with much more variability, ranging from 71 percent in 1983 to only 58 percent in 1989. We have been unable to establish the extent of non-response to the Soviet Family Budget Survey. Goskomstat officials denied to us that non-response was a problem, but Boldyreva argues that it is difficult to get 'deviant' families to participate and that Goskomstat recognises this (1989, p. 91).

The more onerous burden involved in participation in *budget* surveys, involving keeping diary records of expenditure, as opposed to income surveys, seems an important explanation for the lower figures for response in British and Polish surveys; indeed, response to the four Hungarian Budget Surveys in the 1980s averaged 77 percent, ten percentage points beneath the average for the 1982 and 1987 Hungarian Income Surveys. (Similarly, response to the General Household Survey in Britain, which requires no expenditure diary to be collected, is about ten percentage points higher than response to the FES, although it should be noted that the definition of satisfactory response to income questions is more exacting in the latter.) The 'master survey' from which the Polish Budget Survey sample is drawn (see Sources and Methods) had a response rate in 1986 of 92 percent.

In terms of aggregate response rates, the surveys from three of the four Eastern European countries appear to be somewhat worse (Poland), considerably better (Hungary), or dramatically better (Czechoslovakia), than those in the British FES. Although the importance of outright refusal by households as a cause of non-response grew in several of the Eastern European countries during the 1980s, which may indicate a decreasing willingness to co-operate with official bodies, refusal remained significantly less common than in the UK. Even in 1989 when the overall response rate for the Polish Budget Survey was below 60 percent, the proportion of selected households which refused to take part in the survey was only 21 percent. In contrast, almost all the non-response in the FES is due to refusals (FES Report 1989, p. v).

If non-response were purely random, it would reduce the achieved sample size, thus increasing standard errors and affecting the precision with which estimates can be obtained of inequality measures such as the decile ratio or Gini coefficient. However, non-response of this type does not lead to biased results. It is *differential* non-response which is of a concern in this respect, that is non-response systematically related to income or to other variables. In the UK, differential response has been investigated in a number of ways. These include monitoring response by region during the course of surveying (with response being for instance consistently lower in Greater London – see Kemsley *et al.*, 1980, Table 10.4.1), comparing achieved totals of certain household types with those indicated by other sources, and inspection of the obligatory decennial population census returns of non-responding households. The evidence, described more fully in the Sources and Methods section, leads to the conclusion that 'older households, households where the head is self-employed, those without children and higher income households, are less likely to co-operate than others' (*Economic Trends*, December, 1988, p. 115). This is likely to affect the estimated level and distribution of income. In our comparison of income aggregates in the FES and the national accounts we concluded that lower response rates for the elderly was one important reason for the apparent shortfall in the FES of income from occupational pensions. Re-weighting the FES data on basis of the non-response rates by age estimated for 1971, the FES total rose from 75 percent of the national accounts figure to 84 percent (and the figure for investment income rose from 51 to 55 percent). Similarly, a lower response to the survey from the self-employed appeared to be an important reason for the shortfall in self-employment income (we estimated that a third was due to this cause).

The extent of differential non-response to the FES is such as to indicate that some adjustment of the data is advisable before estimating the distribution of income. This is done for the figures given in the Statistical Appendix, with the exception of Table BI4 which is taken from an official series where no adjustment is made. However, it should be noted that this should not be seen as solving the problem. Adjustment by a single set of characteristics (here family composition and age of head) may result in the data remaining (or becoming) unrepresentative in respect of other population characteristics. The existence of differential non-response must be seen as qualifying the conclusions which can be drawn from the UK FES.

In the Eastern European surveys there is some evidence of differential non-response. In Hungary response to the quinquennial Income Survey is substantially lower in Budapest, as is the case in Prague with the Czechoslovak Microcensus. This suggests that securing response in large cities may be a problem which is common to East and West. Response to the Hungarian Budget Survey (as opposed to Income Survey – see Sources and Methods) is known to be lower for the self-employed (a group included for the first time in 1989), as in the UK. We have noted a more severe problem of non-response to the Polish Budget Survey. The evidence indicates that it is not random. The average response rate by pensioner households at first selection during 1982–1989 was 60 percent compared with 65 percent for worker households. The Polish statistical office counters differential non-response by systematically substituting non-responding households with other households of similar characteristics, something which does not occur in the FES.

Substantiation of the data

Considerable effort in Eastern European surveys went into the collection of income data. Indeed the standards of data collection here seem very high. In all four countries, earnings data provided by respondents were verified with their employers. A great deal of care appears to have been taken: for instance, in the Hungarian Income Survey where job changes had taken place during the year, the information was requested from each employer. In the Czechoslovak Microcensus, information on pensions was collected from post-offices (and the employers were asked to give information about benefits they paid as well as well as earnings). There can be little doubt that this led to these sources of earnings and transfers being established with a high degree of accuracy.

In the UK, where the FES relies solely on information supplied by the respondents themselves, OPCS does not ask respondents to give the names of their employers so that earnings data can be verified, nor has OPCS had access to administrative records on social security payments. In the case of earnings, respondents are asked to verify their replies from wage slips and 70–80 percent of them do so. Earnings from main employment are among the best recorded items of income in the FES, not just in terms of the aggregate but also in comparison with the distribution recorded in the New Earnings Survey (Atkinson et al., 1988). On the other hand, coverage of income from subsidiary employment may not be so good (OPCS, 1982, p. 152).

Second economy

This brings us to the question of the 'second economy', a term loaded with ambiguity (see Wiles, 1987, for useful clarification of the possible interpretations). A significant amount of income from second economy jobs and other activities, legal or otherwise, may be missing from household surveys, and this may be much more important in Eastern Europe than in the UK. Anecdotal evidence suggests that incomes from outside the socialised sector was a growing phenomenon in the 1980s. The growth of the second economy in Hungary has been referred to by many authors (for example, Éltető and Vita, 1989). There are reports of large increases in the USSR (Alexeev and Gaddy, 1991, p. 20). In Poland, an important source of income for many households appears to have been transfers of hard currency from relatives working abroad. As one observer put to us, with the purchasing power of foreign currency in Poland in the 1980s, two months of washing dishes in London could mean the equivalent of two years of full-time work in Warsaw.

The coverage in household surveys of income from outside the official economy is a contentious subject. Writers on Eastern Europe often express concern that the recorded incomes refer only to 'official' income and that 'black economy income' does not enter the data concerned:

Needless to say, illegal income (from the black market, unauthorised moonlighting etc.) are not captured by official distribution statistics. (Michal, 1978, p. 210)

The notion that black economy income is *by definition* missing from data on income distribution from Eastern European household surveys is in our view incorrect. To begin with, the distinction between legal and illegal income is not a particularly useful one. From the statistician's point of view the problem is one of recording *all* income, legal or otherwise. As far as we can gather this is what the surveys in Eastern European countries in general tried to do. Our interpretation of the relevant questionnaires, based on discussions with the statistical offices concerned, indicate that a respondent wishing to report all income, legally or illegally obtained, in general had the opportunity to do so without penalty. In the case of the Family Budget Survey in the USSR, according to Boldyreva:

the study is anonymous so that people would reply without fear of sanctions. Every family is assigned a number, and their names are no longer used. Goskomstat can only give 'individual information' to the leadership of an oblast or city, for example, about the scale of moonshining or speculation without naming names. (1989, p. 89)

Of course, the *success* achieved in soliciting information about second economy income, legal or illegal, is a matter for real debate. In pointing to attempts by statistical offices to collect adequate data on 'illegal' income, we are not arguing that this was carried out in full and officials we spoke with who were responsible for the data fully recognised the problem. In the case of the USSR, a former member of the Soviet statistical service reported that:

people with considerable concealed income refuse to take part in the survey. They are afraid that the rule of confidentiality will not be respected, and justifiably so, because survey staff are not in a position to guarantee confidentiality. If, say, the KGB asks then for information, TsSU [the forerunner to Goskomstat] has no right to refuse. (Quoted in Shenfield and Hanson, 1986, p. 64)

Boldyreva reports how in 1988 the aggregate expenditures of those households in survey data (presumably FBS) involved in 'trade' exceeded their 'official' incomes by 60 percent. Official estimates put aggregate illegal income in the USSR at some 9 percent of GDP with about 40 percent of this being derived from the illicit production of alcohol but almost none coming from unlicensed work, which hardly seems credible (*Vestnik statistiki*, 1990, no. 6). Other estimates are significantly higher. Estimates based on a sample of Soviet emigrés suggest that up to a third of the urban population's income came from illegal sources (Grossman, 1987).

The under-reporting of second economy income is a serious qualification of the distributional estimates for Eastern Europe. In Chapter 5, we consider some of the attempts which have been made to allow for its effect. It should however be noted that the problem is not absent in the UK where there is concern about the under-reporting of self-employment income.

Assessment of the UK income data

In comparing the problems of collecting income data in Eastern Europe and Western countries, it is important to note that the differences in the types and sources of income affect the ease with which information can be collected. The income from self-employment is notoriously hard to define. In contrast to the lesser importance of income from savings in Eastern Europe, or its exclusion from the survey, as in Czechoslovakia, in the UK there may be considerable problems in obtaining details of bank and other accounts. The existence in the UK of a complex system of income-tested benefits, such as housing benefit, poorly understood by recipients, means that it may not be easy to frame questions that elicit correct responses as to the amount received under different headings. The measurement of income in a market economy such as the UK may be more difficult than in a planned economy at an earlier stage of development.

While the information on earnings appears to be relatively accurately reported in the UK FES, there can be little doubt that the FES responses on investment income and self-employment income are open to question. In the case of the self-employed, significant numbers of respondents cannot report income figures and OPCS have concluded that self-employment and investment income are 'quite clearly, the least reliable topic areas [on the income questionnaire]' (Kemsley et al., 1980, p. 50). In both cases a 'genuine lack of knowledge' by respondents appears to be part of the problem. The effect of missing income from self-employment and investments on the distribution of income recorded in the FES seems likely to be that the true dispersion of incomes is understated. On the basis of a comparison of the FES with the Survey of Personal Incomes (based on income tax records), the Central Statistical Office concluded that 'income recipients in the top one per cent of taxable incomes are under-represented in the FES by about 30–50 percent' (Central Statistical Office, 1979, p. 12). This conclusion relates to the situation in the 1970s and the growth in investment income in the 1980s may have exacerbated the problem.

The Blue Book estimates of the income distribution in Britain, which take the tax records as their starting point, are less subject to under-representation, although they fail to record income not declared for tax purposes. In fact, the national accounts figures with which we compared the FES include a substantial allowance for 'concealed income' which increased from 8 percent of self-employment income in 1972 to 21 percent in 1978. In Tables BI3, BI6 and BI7, our estimates make a correction for under-reporting of self-employment income, but this is not done in the official estimates in Tables BI4 and BI5 which are less sophisticated than those for Hungary, where reported agricultural production and self-employment income (in 1987) are brought into line with macro estimates.

Time period

In comparing the different surveys, account needs to be taken of the period over which income was measured – in theory and practice. In general, the

Eastern European surveys attempted to collect information on *annual* income. How did the statistical offices concerned go about this? In the case of the Budget Survey in the USSR, there were interviews twice a month with responding households throughout the year. In the surveys on which we draw from Czechoslovakia and Hungary, however, there was a single interview held in the Spring at which data were requested for the previous calendar year. The Polish Budget Survey is an intermediate case; households were surveyed throughout one quarter and then had a further interview at the end of the year.

Even for the respondent with good intentions there is a potential problem of recall error if the survey is requesting information about incomes in the past. This may be expected to lead to under-reporting of both legal and illegal incomes. In certain cases, such as family allowance and pensions in Hungary, information was requested for just the last payment and this could be combined with information on up-ratings during the year, timing of births and retirement, to impute annual income from these sources. But for other sources there was no alternative but to ask respondents to recall their entire annual income or to report an average monthly figure.

The problem was aggravated where the questionnaire was of a simple design, without detailed questions prompting responses for a range of named sources. For example, in the Czechoslovak Microcensus there were two questions relating to other cash income during the year from 'organised' and 'unorganised' sources (the former referring to the socialised sector, the latter not) which seem to have been 'catch-alls' for a range of sources not specifically enquired about elsewhere. The questionnaire of the Hungarian Income Survey, on the other hand, was much more detailed. There was an explicit question on the monthly average of tips and gratuities associated with the main job. Instead of asking direct questions about certain forms of income, the central statistical office enquired about the average time devoted to such activities, distinguishing various types of work. Income was then imputed on the basis of local average wage rates in the second and third economies for such work, as established by enquiries by the interviewer. This may have been a less than fully satisfactory method of trying to measure other cash income but it represented a creditable attempt to get to grips with the problem. In 1988, the self-employment income reported by respondents was inflated by the statistical office in line with totals in national accounts, something that had previously been done only in the case of farm incomes.

The UK FES does not attempt to collect annual income data; instead it sets itself the easier task of collecting data for those periods which are most readily available, taking different periods for different types of income (see Sources and Methods). It is easier to collect reliable data for a shorter than for a longer period of time, and the statistical agency decided on the basis of a feasibility study that the collection of income data on an annual basis for all sources 'would not be feasible if consultation of records was an important assurance of accuracy' (Kemsley *et al.*, 1980, p. 72). It may be noted that the income tax system in the UK requires an annual declaration of income from only a minority of tax-payers and many respondents in households interviewed by the FES have no need to keep annual income records.

3.4 Income data: comparability

There are several respects in which household income distribution data are not comparable between Eastern Europe and the West. The role of non-cash remuneration – the advantages of the nomenklatura – is a prominent example. The extent of price subsidies and social provision of goods such as housing or medical care is a second. These will be the subject of discussion in Chapter 6 on the interpretation of income data. Here we concentrate on a number of issues on which we may hope to approach comparability and which must be clarified in any comparative inequality analysis. The same issues also arise if we wish to use the survey data for the measurement of poverty.

The issues are largely conceptual and relate to the data which are collected and analysed. First, there is the definition of the income unit; what is the meaning of 'household' in each country? Secondly, we need to establish the treatment of different-sized units and the role of equivalence scales. Thirdly, how should different households be weighted? Fourthly, there is the period for which income is measured. Finally, the definition of income used in the data must be spelt out. In all these areas the question we are asking is – are we comparing like with like?

Income unit

The definition of the income unit is vital when comparing survey data across countries. Suppose that we were to treat each *individual* as a separate unit. We would then find a substantial number of individuals with virtually no recorded income, notably children and wives who are not in paid work. The share of the bottom quintile could well be zero. These people may however be enjoying a high standard of living as a result of sharing the income of their parents or husbands. In view of this income-sharing, we may decide to take the *nuclear family* (parent(s) and dependent children) as the unit of analysis. Adopting this unit would be equivalent to assuming that all income received by members of the family is shared, and for any given distribution of individual incomes the amalgamation into family incomes reduces the overall degree of dispersion. Income-sharing may extend beyond the nuclear family, and this may be a justification for taking the wider *household*, including others who live in the same household. By the same argument as before, this may be expected to reduce still further the observed degree of dispersion. The decision regarding the unit of analysis is therefore likely to affect the measured degree of dispersion. This is particularly important when comparing pre-reform Eastern European countries with those from the West; in view of the housing shortages in the former we could expect to find a higher proportion of multi-generation families living at the same address.

The choice between different units depends in part on the empirical question as to how far incomes are in fact shared, a question about which there is relatively little evidence. Moreover, it is possible that the degree of sharing varies significantly across countries, which would affect any comparisons made. (It may also vary within countries and across time.) The choice depends also on the ethical question as to how far we regard it as acceptable that individuals should be dependent on such within-household transfers. Should the elderly be forced to rely on their children or should they have an independent income?

In this book, we have chosen to concentrate on the *household* as the unit, solely for the reason that the data are mostly available in this form. (The only exception is the Blue Book income data for the UK, which are based on the tax unit, defined as a married couple or a single person aged 16 or over who has left school.) This raises the question as to how precisely 'household' is defined. Commenting on the definition of the household in the budget surveys of the European Community countries, Barreiros notes that:

Conditions and traditions are not identical among the Member States... Some countries use a broader definition of household ... in terms of co-residence only; others use a more restricted definition requiring pooling of resources or even family and emotional ties among the members. (1991, p. 2)

The Hungarian Income Survey referred to a group of individuals at the same address who partly or entirely share living expenses. The definitions in the Czechoslovak Microcensus and the Polish Budget Survey appear to have been similar (the former used a number of definitions but those for the income distribution data refer to 'common budget' households). The UK FES refers to 'common housekeeping' but adds the further condition of 'having meals prepared together', and therefore appears to be more restrictive.

The treatment of household size

Since households vary in composition, we have to ask how each unit's income (Y) is adjusted to take account of differences in unit size (H). The standard practice in Eastern Europe is to calculate *income per capita*, Y/H. This practice is easy to carry out and to explain. It is however different from that in the UK, where no official statistics have been published on a per capita basis. (In the Statistical Appendix we present tables that we have calculated ourselves on this basis.) Indeed the main official figures, the Blue Book estimates, make no adjustment for the size of the income unit. Each tax unit is attributed an income Y, with no adjustment for the number of members. That this can make an important difference is shown by the work of Bruinooge *et al.* (1990) who used micro-data from Hungary (the Income Survey for 1982) and the Netherlands to compare the distribution of income in the two countries. They conclude that 'most of the results are rather different depending on whether per household or per capita income is considered' (1990, p. 43). On a per capita basis, the Lorenz curve for Hungary lies inside that for the Netherlands, but on a household basis the curves intersect, with the share of the bottom 20 percent being less in Hungary.

An alternative approach is to adjust total household income by dividing by an equivalence scale to give *equivalent income*. In Britain, this is adopted in the ET series (in Table BI4) and the HBAI series (Table BI5), where the equivalence scale, denoted by S, varies with the number and age of household members: in 1988, it was 1.00 for a couple, and 0.61 for a single person. This means that income of £10,000 for a couple would be regarded as equivalent to £6,100 for a single person.

The use of an equivalence scale may be seen as preferable to taking household income per capita, since the latter makes no allowance for economies of scale in the household. Housing and heating may be relatively fixed costs, and not increase proportionately with the household size. The choice of equivalence scales to adjust for household composition has however been a matter of considerable debate, and a wide variety of scales have been advocated. The differences have been summarised by Buhmann *et al.* (1988) by expressing the number of equivalent adults as H^γ where H is the number of persons in the income unit and γ is a parameter measuring the elasticity of household 'needs' with respect to household size. So that $\gamma = 0.5$ corresponds to treating a household of four persons as equivalent to two single-person households. The measure of income which then enters the distribution is Y/H^γ. Setting $\gamma = 1$ (income per capita) represents the opposite extreme from making no adjustment ($\gamma = 0$). Between values of 0 and 1 for the parameter γ there are a number of intermediate possibilities.

Much of the debate about different equivalence scales has been relatively technical, but three points seem clear. First, at heart the choice of scale is a matter for social judgment, reflecting the weight attached to the needs of different groups in the population. Second, the choice of scale may vary across countries on account of differences in national objectives. Eastern

European countries may have adopted a per capita approach because they gave more weight to the needs of children. Alternatively, it may be seen as a 'democratic' approach in which everyone is treated as having equal needs, rather than the wife being treated as equivalent, say, to only 60 percent of the household head. Thirdly, the choice of scale may differ across countries on account of differences in the economic and social organisation. If the aim of the scale is to compare standards of living, then the appropriate scale depends on the mix of fixed and variable costs. If in Eastern European countries housing and heating were relatively cheap, then the fixed costs might have been smaller, so that a per capita adjustment may have been more appropriate than in a Western country where housing and heating were a large part of the household budget.

Weighting

When households have been ranked by equivalent (or per capita) income, do they count as 1 unit or H units? The two UK distributions of equivalent income referred to earlier give different answers. In the ET series, each household is treated as one unit with income (Y/S), but in the HBAI series each individual is attributed an income (Y/S). In neither case does the sum of incomes across households add up to total household income. In contrast, the Eastern European statistics of per capita income tend to treat each household as having H individuals each with income Y/H. The total income taken into account is then equal to the sum of household incomes.

These differences in weighting may affect the conclusions drawn. If, for example, there is a higher incidence of poverty among large households, then giving each household a weight of unity will lead to a lower overall poverty estimate than if each household receives a weight equal to the number of members. The possible quantitative importance of the difference may be illustrated by the figures for the distribution of per capita income given on two bases for Czechoslovakia for 1988 (Table CSI3). Giving each household a weight of unity, or what we refer to as the *household distribution*, the ratio of the top to bottom decile is 2.65, whereas giving each household a weight equal to the number of individuals, or what we refer to as the *individual distribution*, the decile ratio is 2.43.

The role of weighting is stressed because it is rarely given explicit attention in income distribution analysis; nor is it always evident from published tables what weighting has been applied. This adds a further dimension to the issue of availability of data: one of clarity of presentation.

Income period

All four Eastern European countries we consider collected information on *annual* incomes. This common time period is a significant aid to the analysis. On the other hand, a variety of periods are used for income distribution data in Britain. As we have seen, the UK FES does not attempt to collect annual income data; the user has to combine information from a number of different reference periods (see Sources and Methods). The estimates in the HBAI series (Table BI4), and those we have made ourselves (Tables BI3, BI6 and BI7), relate to current income, with investment and self-employment income assumed to accrue equally over the year and all amounts brought to a common date. On the other hand, the ET series (Table BI4) attempts to adjust the data to an annual basis by taking account of reported periods of absence from work in the previous twelve months and of past receipt of benefits, so as to reconstruct the respondent's history over this period. These figures may therefore be closer to an annual basis. Finally, the income tax data which underlie the Blue Book series in Tables BI1 and BI2 relate to annual incomes.

The distinction between annual income and that for any shorter period, such as a month or a week, is important since the latter can be expected to be more variable owing to changes in family status, wages and employment over the year. We would expect incomes recorded in the British FES to indicate more dispersion *ceteris paribus* than shown in the annual income data from the Eastern European surveys. On the other hand, an important source of income variability in Britain, that stemming from unemployment, was largely missing in the pre-reform period in Eastern Europe. This means in turn that, if we were to seek to standardise the time period, it would make a difference whether we took the week/month or the year as the common basis. If there were less monthly variation in Eastern Europe, then the move to a monthly assessment period would not greatly change the measured inequality; but standardisation on a year could significantly reduce the measured inequality in the UK. For this reason the choice of income period may be important even if there was less variation over time in incomes in Eastern Europe.

Definition of income

It is not uncommon to see cross-country comparisons of household income without any clear definition of this concept. To some extent, a failure to give all the details is inevitable since income has many forms and an exact description would take a great deal of space. Here we do not attempt to give full definitions, but it is necessary to describe the treatment of certain key categories of income. The importance of these may vary significantly across country and economic system. In Eastern Europe the treatment of the value of agricultural production for own-consumption is a major issue due to the bigger share of the labour force in agricultural employment than in many

Western countries, including Britain, and the importance of small private plots. Other issues are important in both East and West: for example whether income from rent is imputed for owner-occupiers (these make up a significant proportion of households in Eastern Europe as well as in Britain).

In discussing the Soviet statistics, McAuley (1979, pp. 9–12) distinguishes between:

Money income
> cash income received (earnings, self-employment income, transfer payments from the state or private institutions, income from savings), after deduction of direct tax and social security contributions.

Personal income
> Money income *plus* the value of agricultural production for own-consumption, receipts in kind from collective farms, income in kind from employment (fringe benefits), and the imputed rent on owner-occupied housing.

Total income
> Personal income *plus* the value of social income in kind provided by the state.

McAuley describes the successive definitions as approximating more and more closely to the Haig-Simons, or comprehensive, definition of income as 'the sum of (1) the market value of rights exercised in consumption and (2) the change in the value of the store of property rights between the beginning and end of the period' (Simons, 1938, p. 50). Even so, the final concept of Total income still stops short of being comprehensive according to this definition, notably excluding capital gains and losses (the change in the value of assets). The exclusion of capital gains is likely to be more important in an economy with substantial private ownership of financial assets, but also applies to owner-occupied houses and to stocks of durables and consumer goods.

In none of the countries we consider did the definitions used in the survey data correspond exactly with the three concepts outlined above. In none of them do the data on the distribution of income include imputed rent for owner-occupiers. In this respect, and others, the definitions of income used depart from those laid down in UN guidelines (United Nations, 1977). There are other departures which affect individual countries. In Czechoslovakia income from bank interest is excluded from Money income; in the USSR Money income is gross of deductions. In the case of the UK, the Blue Book estimates (Tables BI1 and BI2) may be seen as aiming to measure Personal income, although they fall short in a number of respects (see Ramprakash, 1975). The FES data used in the other tables have a less complete coverage and omit much of fringe benefits and income in kind.

The definition of Personal income includes the estimated value of agricultural production consumed within the household. This requires an appropriate price to be set on the produce concerned, something which is far from being a trivial issue. In Chapter 6 we discuss the problem of interpreting income data in a situation of disequilibrium of markets when goods in short supply sell at two sets of prices, official prices and those prices established through private trading. In the USSR, consumption of agricultural production within the home is valued at *state* prices. In the case of many products, especially meat and fresh fruit, this may be expected to underestimate substantially their true value to the households concerned (see Chapter 6). The differences between state and private market prices and the practices of the central statistical offices in valuing agricultural produce cannot be expected to be the same throughout the region. In Hungary and Poland the valuation of consumed agricultural production was the statistical office's estimate of actual market prices (state prices in the case of meat in Poland).

Conclusions

A great deal of myth surrounds the subject of income distribution in Eastern Europe, not least about the availability and quality of data. Common impressions are dominated by the position with regard to the Soviet Union, but we have tried to demonstrate that the position in other Eastern European countries has been quite different. In the case of the earnings distribution, not only is information available for Czechoslovakia, Hungary and Poland, but the similarities in the sources we use with the corresponding survey in Britain (the New Earnings Survey) are more striking than the differences. Insofar as the earnings data are different, there are certain respects in which they are superior to those in Britain: for example, there appears to be less of a problem of non-response, and the series goes back to the 1950s rather than just to 1968.

The USSR *is* different and the information which has become available with *glasnost'* is less detailed than that available for many years in the other Eastern European countries. As far as the distribution of income is concerned, the USSR Family Budget Survey is a much less satisfactory source, given the unrepresentative nature of its sample, than the income and budget surveys in the other three countries studied here. The latter do indeed compare favourably with the information available for Britain. In Britain there has been no purpose-designed income survey, in contrast to Hungary. The surveys in Eastern Europe typically have had larger samples, have had higher response rates (except for Poland), have been able to substantiate earnings data from employers, have considered the deviations of survey results from macro aggregates, and have set out to collect information on annual income. The Eastern European sources have significant deficiencies, and there are undoubtedly aspects which are not adequately covered, such as the reporting of private incomes, legal or illegal, which may well have been a growing problem in the 1980s. It is important to bear these in mind when interpreting the data, but it must be remembered that data from *all* countries are deficient in some respect whether they come from market or Communist economies.

4 · The distribution of earnings

Different views are held about the distribution of earnings under Communism and about its evolution over time. As we have seen in Chapter 2, there are those who hold that there is no reason to expect earnings inequality to be less under Communism than capitalism, nor for it to rise with the transition to a market economy. The economies of the Soviet Union and Eastern Europe have been guided by a principle of distribution according to contribution, not need; and wage differentials and bonuses have been set with regard to incentives to invest in human capital, to enter occupations with unpleasant conditions, to bear responsibility, to work hard on the job, and to move to industries or areas selected for an expansion of employment. On this view, wage differentials under Communism were governed by economic imperatives rather than by concern with equality.

This contrasts with the view that controls over the labour force allowed Communist regimes to compress earnings differences in pursuit of social justice. The resulting distribution of earnings was, on this view, significantly less unequal in the Communist countries of Eastern Europe than in comparable Western countries, and we should expect the transformation to a market economy to lead to greater earnings dispersion. Or, on a dynamic view, there was a trend over time to less inequality, a trend which would cease, or be reversed, if there were a move to a market economy.

In this chapter, we examine the evidence about the overall distribution of earnings in Eastern Europe, including the differences between the earnings of men and women and the dispersion within countries. As explained in Chapter 1, we take for purposes of comparison the distribution of earnings in the United Kingdom.

4.1 Comparing earnings: East and West

The overall earnings distribution has been examined in detail by Lydall (1968), in which he painstakingly assembled evidence for a wide range of countries. To facilitate comparisons across countries, he defined (p. 60) a

'Standard Distribution', which related to the earnings before tax of adult males, in all occupations, in all industries except farming, in all areas, working full-time and for the full period. (In many cases data were not available on precisely this basis and Lydall made approximate adjustments.)

Lydall's results show that the most equally distributed earnings distributions around 1960 were those in Czechoslovakia and Hungary, which appear distinctly different from the Western European countries. The level of inequality in Poland was comparable to that in the group of Western countries with least inequality, such as Denmark and Sweden and, at that time, the UK. Lydall also refers to the 'few straws' of evidence about the USSR post-1934 and concludes that:

we may guess that the dispersion of all employee incomes in the Soviet Union is somewhat greater than in Hungary and less – on a pre-tax basis – than in the United States or most of Western Europe; but the dispersion of manual workers' earnings may well be greater than in Western Europe. (1968, p. 162)

The data of Lydall were analysed further by Pryor (1973), who made explicit allowance for other systematic reasons why earnings dispersion may be expected to vary across countries, in particular that earnings inequality declined with the level of development and increased with the size of population. Allowing for these, he concluded that there was on average a six percentage point difference in the Gini coefficient.

In her article 'Are Earnings More Equal under Socialism?', Chapman documents a sharp fall in earnings inequality in the Soviet Union since the Second World War and concludes that by the 1950s:

the degree of inequality among Soviet wage and salary earners had been reduced to roughly the level prevailing among American nonagricultural wage and salary earners in the early 1970s. In the 1970s, the Soviet earnings distribution has been considerably more equal than the American. (1979, p. 52)

As for other Communist countries, she states that:

The sharp reduction in inequality in the Soviet Union has reduced it to the degree of equality that had earlier been achieved in Poland and Yugoslavia, though differentiation of Soviet earnings is still somewhat more unequal than in Bulgaria, Czechoslovakia, and Hungary. (1979, p. 51)

Redor (1988), with more recent evidence, reaches the conclusion that, comparing Western and Soviet-type economies:

there appears to be no systematic difference in the overall dispersion of earnings. If the United States, at the beginning of the 1980s, was the country with the greatest earnings inequality, in the rest of the ranking one finds mixed together both Western and Soviet-type economies. (1988, p. 67, our translation)

The evidence regarding the Soviet Union in particular is rather mixed. Pryor's figures for 1959 show the fifth percentile (from the top) in the Soviet Union as earning more relative to the median than the corresponding group in the United States, the United Kingdom and other Western European countries (except France). On the other hand, the frequency distribution for Soviet earnings in 1966 drawn by Wiles and Markowski (1971, p. 505) including also the United Kingdom and Poland (1967), suggests that 'one might perhaps say that Poland and the UK have more poor earners ... As to the rich, the [evidence] leaves no doubt: Poland is more unequal than the USSR, less than the UK' (1971, p. 507). Such differences in findings may of course be due to the changes over time in the Soviet earnings distribution. More recent evidence is summarised by Bergson as showing:

a rather striking similarity in inequality, as measured, between the USSR and Western countries. Inequality in the USSR fluctuates in the course of time, but only rarely does any particular percentile ratio fall outside the range delineated by corresponding measures for Western countries. (1984, p. 1065)

At the same time, he develops further the normalisation for differences in the stage of development and population size, and this leads him to conclude that, allowing for such conditioning factors, 'inequality in the USSR in the early seventies may have been somewhat low by western standards' (1984, p. 1092).

In our study, we have sought to cast further light on the comparison of earnings by assembling in the Statistical Appendix data on the overall distribution for Czechoslovakia, Hungary, Poland, the USSR and the United Kingdom. We have attached considerable importance to the provision of evidence covering the shape of the distribution as a whole, rather than simply a few summary statistics, and covering as full a run of years as possible. The sources are those described in the previous chapter, and the qualifications made there should be borne in mind when reading the present analysis. It is also the case that we shall be leaving certain important questions of interpretation until Chapter 6. The extent of payment in kind, the role of second-economy earnings, the existence of price subsidies, all affect the comparison of Eastern and Western Europe.

In Section 4.2, we compare the degree of earnings dispersion in the five countries in the middle of the 1980s and examine whether any general conclusion can be reached about the relative degree of inequality under Communism. As will already have been clear from our summary of earlier evidence, there are differences *between* Communist countries, and these receive particular attention. The trends over time are the second important topic and this is treated in Section 4.3. As explained in Chapter 2, the dynamics of distributional change affect our evaluation of the Communist record and of the post-transformation developments.

The focus of our analysis is on the overall distribution, and we do not in this book investigate the differences in earnings by industry, by occupation, by age or other important dimensions. There are however two aspects which must be considered. The first dimension is that of gender. The impact of economic transformation on the position of women has not, in our view, received the attention which it deserves. Section 4.4 is devoted to the relative earnings position of men and women under Communism. Was equal pay more nearly approached?

The second dimension is that of distribution within geographical regions, a matter which is essential in considering the post-Union USSR. In Section 4.4 we consider the distribution of earnings within countries: England, Wales and Scotland in Britain, the Czech Lands and Slovakia, and by republic of the former Soviet Union. It is of evident interest to explore the distribution of earnings in, for example, Ukraine, Belarus and Moldavia, as well as of course in Russia. In addition, it casts light on the role of population size evoked in discussions of the USSR as a whole.

4.2 The distribution of earnings in the mid 1980s

In this section we consider the evidence about the distribution of earnings in the five countries in 1986 (1987 in Czechoslovakia). As will be further explored in Section 4.3, the degree of dispersion has changed over time, and our conclusions should be read as relating to a particular epoch in the post-war history of the countries. The year 1986 (and 1987) has been chosen as the most recent year for which data are available for all countries and which are relatively untouched by reforms which preceded the end of Communism. In the Soviet Union, the Gorbachev wage reform was introduced by a decree of 17 September 1986, whereas our data relate to March 1986. The Hungarian data for 1986 pre-date the introduction of the personal income tax, which was accompanied by the grossing-up of earnings. In the case of Poland, the choice of 1986 avoids the earlier years of the decade when the rise of Solidarity may have affected both the real distribution and the statistical reliability of the figures.

The coverage of the earnings distribution corresponds to that of Lydall's 'Standard Distribution', in that it covers:

all workers, in all occupations, in all areas, working full-time and for the full period.

But there are three significant differences. We cover in principle:

both males and females (not just males),

workers of all ages (not just adult workers),

all employment (not just non-agricultural employment).

Earnings are defined to be money income from employment before tax or other deductions and include all overtime, bonus and payments by results.

The description just given is the principle we sought to apply in selecting data; in practice, as has been made clear in Chapter 3, the data are not always available on precisely this basis. The implications of the differences between the sources are discussed below, but we should reiterate the conclusion of Chapter 3 that the earnings data used here enjoy, by the standards of international comparisons, a high degree of comparability.

In Table 4.1, we summarise some of the main features of the overall earnings distribution. For this purpose, we consider the earnings in each country at specified percentiles expressed as a percentage of the median: P_i denotes the earnings of the i-th percentile from the bottom relative to the median expressed as a percentage. These percentiles are interpolated from the original data, which are grouped in ranges. A value of 55.7 for P_{10} in Great Britain means that the person 10 percent up from the bottom earned 55.7 percent of the person in the middle. Since the .7 may give a false impression of accuracy (not least on account of the interpolation), we often round in the text to the nearest percentage, taking 56 percent in this case. This value may be compared with 62 percent in Hungary. This does not of course mean that the person 10 percent up from the bottom earns *more* in Hungary than in Great Britain. We are not comparing the absolute levels of earnings, rather the *relative* earnings, taking the median as the basis for comparison.

As we have already seen, it is misleading to treat the Communist countries of Eastern Europe as a bloc, and it is evident from Table 4.1 that there are considerable differences, first between the USSR and the three countries of Central Europe, and second between the countries of Central Europe. If we take the ratio of earnings at the top decile to earnings at the bottom decile (P_{90}/P_{10}), then this *decile ratio* has a value of 2.45 in Czechoslovakia, rising to 2.64 in Hungary, 2.77 in Poland and then jumping to 3.28 in the USSR. Even rounding to one decimal place (which in the case of Czechoslovakia, for example, allows there to be an error of two percentage points in the bottom decile or five points in the top decile, without affecting the calculation), we have a clear ranking:

$$P_{90}/P_{10}$$

	P_{90}/P_{10}
Czechoslovakia	2.5
Hungary	2.6
Poland	2.8
USSR	3.3

Earnings dispersion is distinctly greater in the USSR. It is lowest in Czechoslovakia, followed by Hungary, with Poland having an intermediate position, nearer to Hungary than to the USSR. Moreover, the differences in the decile ratio are due to differences in the earnings of the bottom decile as well as differences at the top.

Table 4.1 *Summary of earnings distribution in 1986–1987*

All full-time workers (male and female)

	Gini	P_{10}	P_{25}	P_{75}	P_{90}	P_{95}	P_{90}/P_{10}
Czecho-slovakia 1987	19.7	63.2	78.3	125.8	154.6	173.4	2.45
Hungary 1986	22.1	62.0	77.9	128.7	163.9	192.5	2.64
Poland 1986	24.2	60.9	77.6	129.3	169.1	206.5	2.77
USSR 1986	27.6	55.7	72.1	136.4	182.8	—	3.28
Great Britain 1986	26.7	55.7	72.9	135.3	179.7	217.3	3.23

Note:
P_{10} denotes the earnings of the bottom decile relative to the median, expressed as a percentage. P_{90}/P_{10} is the decile ratio.
Sources: Statistical Appendix Tables CSE1 (continued), HE1, PE1 (continued), UE1, and BE1 (continued).

It should be emphasised that the use of P_{90}/P_{10} as an indicator of dispersion is not affected by the shortcomings of the data at the top and bottom of the distribution. The omission of benefits in kind accruing to those in the top 10 percent does not affect the value of this indicator, so that, if the advantages of the nomenklatura are largely confined to those above this point in the earnings scale, then our conclusions would not be changed by their inclusion. Errors of interpolation which particularly concern the top and bottom intervals do not affect the P_{90}/P_{10} ratio, providing that the top and bottom intervals include less than 10 percent of the population, as is the case with the data used in constructing Table 4.1. (It is for this reason that we do not show a figure for P_{95} for the USSR in Table 4.1, since the open top interval covers more than 5 percent.)

The Gini coefficient, in contrast, is a measure summarising evidence for the whole distribution. (As explained in Chapter 2, the Gini coefficient measures the area between the Lorenz curve and the line of equal incomes.) It should be noted that it may be sensitive to the method of interpolation at the top and bottom. For example, we have assumed in constructing Table 4.1 that the open interval at the top of the earnings distribution in each country follows the Pareto Law, a statistical regularity observed by Pareto in the last century and which can at best provide an approximation. There is however a gap of some two percentage points between each of the Central European countries, and more between them and the USSR. Rounding to the nearest percentage point, we have:

	Gini coefficient (percent)
Czechoslovakia	20
Hungary	22
Poland	24
USSR	28

The ranking is the same as with the decile ratio, which is of interest since the Gini, unlike the decile ratio, is influenced by the shape of the distribution at all percentiles. Looking at Table 4.1, we can see that there is a clear pattern to the percentiles. Those below the median (P_{10} and P_{25}) get progressively smaller as a proportion of the median as we move down the table, and the percentiles above the median tend to get progressively larger.

Comparison with Great Britain

In this book we are concentrating on the comparison with Great Britain and we show figures for this country in Table 4.1. This comparison does not allow us to make any general statement about the differences between Communist and Western economies, since there is no reason to expect Britain to be representative of Western Europe, still less of the OECD in general. We have not attempted to include any other Western countries since this would, in our view, require a systematic comparison of the data sources of the kind given in Chapter 3 for the five countries under consideration. Differences in findings may arise between sources based on employer surveys (as here) and those based on household surveys (as in the US). Data from tax returns may tell yet another story. Differences may arise on account of the population coverage, of differences in the definition of earnings, and of the degree of detail in which data are available. For instance, the French earnings data, from the Déclarations Annuelles, which have some similarity with the New Earnings Survey for Britain, show a value for the decile ratio of 3.16 in 1986 (CERC, 1989, Table 14, p. 34). This is slightly below the figure for Britain in Table 4.1, but it should be noted that the French data exclude a number of important categories of employees (as described in Chapter 3) and we are not therefore comparing like with like.

It is possible that a comparison with Sweden or West Germany or Spain may lead to different conclusions, but as far as Britain is concerned the findings in Table 4.1 are that the distribution of earnings was substantially more unequal than in the Central European countries. In fact the distribution is close to that in the Soviet Union. The summary statistics suggest there was slightly less inequality in Britain: the Gini coefficient is 27 percent compared with 28 percent in the Soviet Union. This may be contrasted with the earlier finding of Wiles and Markowski (1971) that there were fewer low paid and fewer high paid in the USSR than in Britain. A detailed comparison of the percentiles shows that in 1986 they are in fact close except for the top of the distribution:

	Great Britain	USSR
P_{10}	55.7	55.7
P_{20}	67.4	66.2
P_{30}	78.0	78.4
P_{40}	89.0	88.8
P_{60}	112.3	112.9
P_{70}	126.6	127.5
P_{80}	145.7	147.3
P_{90}	179.8	182.8

The difference in the decile ratio is due entirely to the difference in P_{90}. That our findings are at variance from those of Wiles and Markowski is probably due to the changes in the distribution over time, as discussed in the next section.

The degree to which earnings are less dispersed in Central Europe than in Britain is quite striking. To find the person earning twice the median you have to go up to the top 2.5 percent in Czechoslovakia, whereas in Britain there are more than 6 percent earning more than twice the median. The difference in the bottom decile is equivalent to an earnings gain of some 12.5 percent. If the transition to a market economy causes earnings dispersion in Czechoslovakia to rise to the British level, with the low paid getting less in relative terms, then it will require a rise in average earnings of an eighth to compensate them.

Limitations of the comparison

How far are the findings regarding relative earnings inequality affected by the differences in data sources and methods described in Chapter 3? It is indeed possible that some part of the differences are explicable in this way. The Czechoslovak data for example only take account of bonuses paid in the month in question; if bonuses paid in other months of the year go disproportionately to the well paid, then this would cause the degree of dispersion to be understated. The New Earnings Survey (NES) data for Britain relate in part to weekly earnings, and this may cause the observed dispersion to be greater than it would be if we could measure earnings over the same time period in both countries. On the other hand, there are factors working in the opposite direction, such as non-response to the NES which may cause the low-paid to be under-represented.

Perhaps the most important differences concern the coverage of agriculture and of private employment. Earlier studies, such as that of Lydall, concentrated on non-farm employment; here we in principle cover all employment, but there are important exclusions. To the extent that those engaged in farming are self-employed, as in Poland, the exclusion does not affect the distribution of earnings among *employees*, although it may affect the way in which we interpret the results. However, in Czechoslovakia, workers in agricultural co-operatives are not covered, and they account for about one tenth of the total labour force (see Sources and Methods). In Hungary, workers in agricultural co-operatives are included, but not those employed on private farms. In the USSR those working on collective farms are excluded.

The treatment of employees in the *private sector* varies across Eastern European countries. In Hungary the earnings data are described as covering those employed in private ventures with a legal identity (not including private farms). In Poland, private sector employment is not included, and this is quite significant: about 10 percent of the labour force was engaged in 1989 in private sector non-agricultural work. Of the Soviet Union, Chapman says that:

No earnings, legal or illegal, from the private sector are included. The opportunities for private income are probably quite unevenly distributed among individuals and occupations, but this distribution may well not parallel the distribution by level of earnings from the job in state enterprises and institutions. Thus the distribution of total actual earnings may differ significantly from the distribution of earnings as reported. (1979, pp. 49–50)

The comparison may also be affected by the differences in hours. In Britain there is considerable variation in weekly hours of work. In April 1990, average weekly hours for full-time workers were 40.5, but 13 percent worked thirty-five hours or less and 8 percent worked more than fifty hours a week. The distribution of hourly earnings in 1986 for all workers paid on adult rates exhibited a decile ratio of 3.06 (New Earnings Survey 1986, Table 41, p. B50). This cannot however be directly compared with the figure in Table 4.1, since it excludes those juveniles (and others) not paid on adult rates (3.5 percent of the sample) and those for whom hours could not be calculated (7.4 percent of the sample). The variation in hours in Eastern Europe appears to be less marked, but it is an aspect which warrants further investigation. (See, for example, the evidence about overtime working in the USSR summarised by McAuley, 1981, pp. 28–30.)

Conclusion

The position regarding the overall distribution of earnings in the middle of the 1980s is that, with the qualifications just expressed, the degree of dispersion appears to be least in Czechoslovakia, followed by Hungary, and then by Poland. The difference from Great Britain is quite marked, as is that from the Soviet Union. The information for the USSR, more solidly based than that available when earlier comparisons were made, suggests a degree of dispersion not dissimilar to that in Great Britain.

4.3 Changes over time in the distribution of earnings

Changes in the distribution of earnings over time mean that comparisons such as those just presented may not apply at other dates. The changes over time are of interest too in their own right. We begin by illustrating these points by reference to the comparison of Czechoslovakia and Britain.

Czechoslovakia and Britain

Czechoslovakia stands out in its low level of earnings dispersion. This may be attributable to its history. We have already quoted Teichova to the effect that 'the desire for greater equality had deep historical roots in the social consciousness of broad segments of society' (1988, p. 101). According to Brada, commenting on the current economic transition, 'one intellectual legacy . . . is a strong . . . concern for economic equity to be achieved largely through state intervention' (1991, p. 172). In the 1950s:

Through a policy of faster wage increases for the lowest paid unskilled workers and slower increases for skilled workers, the government actually succeeded in significantly accelerating a process which had its roots in the 1930s, that is, the trend towards reduced differentials between skilled and white-collar workers. (Teichova, 1988, p. 109)

Our data, which start in 1959, are shown in the form of the decile ratio in Figure 4.1. The overall impression is one of considerable stability in the earnings distribution. Over the period as a whole, the decile ratio varied between 2.30 and 2.53, and the earnings of the bottom decile varied between 62 and 66 percent of the median. The Gini coefficient varied between 18.5 and 20 percent. As it has been put by Večerník, 'all the basic features of the structure of earnings inequality were established in the initial post-war period and firmly fixed for the future' (1991a, p. 238). The distribution appears to have been remarkably stable over the thirty years.

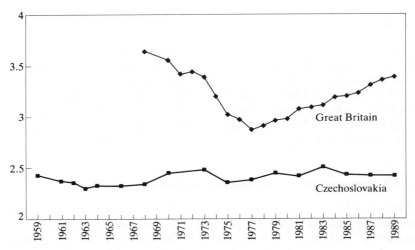

Figure 4.1 Decile earnings ratio: Czechoslovakia and Great Britain
Sources: Tables CSE1 and BE1.

At the end of the 1960s there was some rise in dispersion, with the decile ratio reaching 2.5 at the end of the decade. The slightness of the change may however be considered surprising in view of the campaign for 'de-levelling' in the 1960s (Phelps Brown, 1977, p. 48 and Myant, 1983 and 1989) and the declaration by the 1968 Party Action Programme that wage levelling was an obstacle to growth. According to Adam (1984, p. 164), the restructuring of the wage scales in 1972 led to an increased spread between top and bottom grades for manual workers (it may be seen from Table CSE1 that P_{90} reaches its maximum in 1973), but at the same time there was a reduction in intersectoral differentials. As Adam notes, 'apart from production and working conditions, social factors, including historical relationships, play an important role' (1984, p. 165).

The distribution of earnings in Czechoslovakia certainly appears stable when compared with that for Great Britain, also shown in Figure 4.1. (As we have brought out in Chapter 3, the data series in Britain is less extensive, starting only in 1968.) The decile ratio in Britain started at 3.65 in 1968 and then fell during the 1970s, reaching a value of 2.9 in 1977, the year which brought the distribution closest to that in Czechoslovakia. The Gini coefficient fell from 28 percent in 1968 to 23 percent in 1977. The earnings of the bottom decile rose from 48 percent to 58 percent of the median. This fall over the 1970s was associated in part with the improvement of the relative earnings position of women (it was over this period that the Equal Pay legislation was implemented), but there was also a reduction in dispersion for male workers: the decile ratio for men aged twenty-one and over fell from 2.46 in 1970 to 2.32 in 1977 (Royal Commission on the Distribution of Income and Wealth, 1979, Table 2.16, p. 46). A role is likely to have been played by the post-1970 incomes policies which incorporated flat-rate, rather than percentage, elements (see Mayhew, 1981), such as the 1975 policy of increases of £6 a week for all workers, except those earning more than £8,500 a year (within the top percentile).

This change in Britain over the 1970s is of interest because it shows that the kind of difference that may be found *across time* is not very much smaller than that found *across countries*. The decline of five percentage points in the Gini coefficient in Britain in the decade following 1968 (with a Conservative government in office for nearly four of the ten years) may be compared with the seven point difference between Britain and Czechoslovakia in the mid 1980s, and a difference of three percentage points with Poland. It is similar in magnitude to the six percentage points found to be the difference between Eastern Europe and Western countries by Pryor (1973). Moreover, there are reasons to link the change over time with explicit government policy measures.

Since the late 1970s, the picture has changed. There has been a distinct upward trend in earnings inequality in Britain. The Gini coefficient by the late 1980s was back to 28 percent. The decile ratio rose from 2.9 in 1977 to 3.2 in 1986. Between 1986, the year used in our comparisons in Table 4.1, and 1990 the decile ratio had risen further to 3.4, an amount equal to the difference between the ratios for Hungary and Czechoslovakia. This rise was attributable largely to a rise in the relative position of the top decile, which increased from 167 percent of the median in 1977 to 187 percent in 1990, while the bottom decile slipped from 58 percent to 55 percent of the median.

This fall then rise in inequality in Britain must be borne in mind when making comparisons with the other Eastern European countries, to which we now turn.

Soviet Union

Earnings differentials in the Soviet Union have attracted much interest. In Figure 4.2, we have combined the estimates for the decile ratio made for 1956–1976 by Rabkina and Rimashevskaia (1978), reproduced in Table UE2, which have been widely used by other authors (for example, Ellman, 1980), with our own interpolations from the published earnings surveys (Table UE1) for 1981–1989. (The available survey data do not allow us to interpolate the decile ratio for years before 1981, since the bottom earnings group contains more than 10 percent of workers.) The degree of compara-

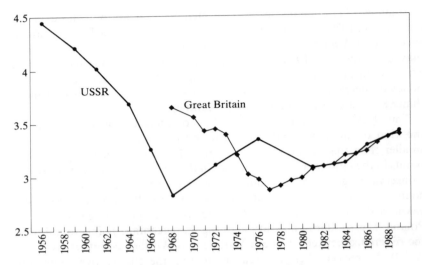

Figure 4.2 Decile earnings ratio: USSR and Great Britain
Sources: Tables UE1, UE2 and BE1.

bility is hard to assess. The series given by Chapman (1989, p. 16) has a value for 1981 of 3.3, which is distinctly higher than our calculation of 3.08. On the other hand, she cites Aleksandrova and Fedorovskaia (1984) as reporting a value of 3.0 for 1981. It should be noted that, unlike earlier authors, we have not made use of a lognormal distribution fitted to the data points; in our view this gives too much weight to a particular functional form, and we prefer a method of interpolation that passes exactly through the observed data points. It should also be pointed out that the 1984 and 1989 estimates in Table UE1 are taken from a different source, being based on the March survey of households rather than the census of enterprises.

Without making any assumption about the comparability of the sets of estimates, we may draw the conclusion that between 1956 and 1968 there has been a 'marked reduction in earnings inequality in the Soviet Union' (McAuley, 1979, p. 213), but since that date the overall trend has been in the opposite direction. According to the Russian authors, the ratio rose from 2.8 in 1968 to 3.35 in 1976; and our estimates show it as rising from 3.1 in 1981 to 3.4 in 1989. If our 1981 figure is comparable with that for 1976, then there was a fall between these years.

These changes over time are important in interpreting earlier findings. The evidence cited by Lydall related to the late 1950s, when earnings inequality was high by standards of later years, and this may explain the differences from later findings. The distribution in 1966, the year studied by

Wiles and Markowski (1971), was much closer to the low point of inequality in 1968. Bergson (1984, p. 1066) refers to 'the early seventies'. In these years, the distribution did indeed appear to be substantially less unequal than in Britain. After that, earnings inequality fell in Britain below the Soviet level, only to return to a comparable level in the 1980s. The way in which the Soviet distribution tracks the British one from 1981 to 1989 is indeed quite remarkable. Altogether, it is clear that it would be possible, by choosing different dates, to arrive at the conclusion that earnings dispersion was greater, less, or the same in the Soviet Union as in Britain.

The factors lying behind the changes in earnings dispersion over time in the USSR have been examined by many authors. McAuley notes that 'significant changes in the dispersion of earnings seem to coincide with the major innovations of state wage policy' (1979, p. 223). He refers to the re-organisation of the wage structure over the period 1956-1965 and the role of the minimum wage. According to Chapman, 'an effective minimum wage was introduced in 1957 (the first since 1937) and this was raised from 27–35 roubles a month to 40 roubles' (1991, p. 179). A major increase to 60 rubles was announced in 1968 (on the eve of the fiftieth anniversary of the Revolution), leading to a sharp contraction in wage scales (Chapman, 1983). The 1970s saw a further round of wage reform, with the minimum wage being set at 70 rubles by the end of 1977. This reform was protracted and, as has been emphasised by Chapman (1983), in interpreting the figures it is important to bear in mind the timing of wage changes: the rise in the decile ratio in 1976 reflected the fact that the wage reform was incomplete. The completion of the reform brought the decile ratio in 1981 back to a level comparable with that in the early 1970s (although not the 1968 level). Between 1981 and 1986 the decile ratio increased, and this reflected the fact that more recent wage reform has aimed at widening differentials (Oxen-stierna, 1990, p. 242). As described by Chapman, 'Gorbachev's wage reform in the material sectors, initiated in September 1986 and virtually completed by the end of 1989 ... has clearly reversed the earlier trend toward equality, as shown by the decile ratios for 1986 and 1989' (1991, p. 178). The minimum wage has fallen as a percentage of average wages (Sziraczki, 1990, Table 1).

Poland

The decile ratio for Poland is shown in Figure 4.3, where it should be noted that there is a break in the comparability of the series in 1970, for which two figures are shown. After a fall in the late 1950s, there is little trend in the decile ratio from 1961 to 1970. The Gini coefficient remained at 25 percent throughout the 1960s (Table PE4). The earnings of the bottom decile varied

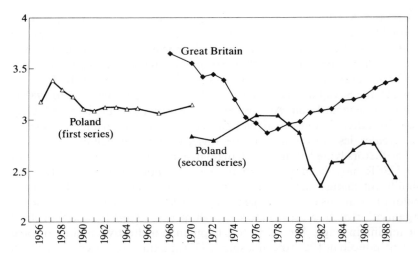

Figure 4.3 Decile earnings ratio: Poland and Great Britain
Sources: Tables PE1, PE4 and BE1.

in the 1960s between 55.6 and 57.0 percent of the median; and those of the top decile from 173 to 178 percent of the median (rounding to the nearest percentage point).

Over the 1970s, there was a detectable increase in dispersion. Earnings at the bottom decile fell by a modest amount, but the top decile increased from 166 percent of the median in 1970 to 176 percent in 1978, and the Gini coefficient rose by one percentage point. As may be seen from Figure 4.3, this took the measured dispersion above that in Britain. This was followed in 1980–1982 by a significant improvement in the position of the lowest decile (from 59 percent of the median to 66 percent) and a reduction in differentials at the top. The Gini coefficient fell by three percentage points. It has been argued that this in part reflects problems with the data:

the spectacular drop in relative dispersion of earnings between 1980 and 1982 claimed by the official statistics is probably exaggerated, because the official statistical data in this period of turmoil are particularly unreliable. (Flakierski, 1986, p. 72

But he also says that:

there is no doubt that even the partial implementation of Solidarity's wage and incomes policy has reduced inequalities. (1986, p. 72)

In response to demands for an equal absolute increase (2,000 zlotys per month) for all employees to compensate for price increases, and the Gdansk

Accord of 31 August 1980, relatively equalising wage adjustments were made, although in the judgment of Flakierski 'the increases in wages were too small to affect the overall relative dispersion of wages substantially' (1991, p. 97).

After 1982, dispersion tended to increase again, with a deliberate policy of larger increases for non-manual workers (Flakierski, 1991, p. 99); and the Gini coefficient in 1986, at 24 percent, was four percentage points higher than in 1982. The relative position of the bottom decile fell back to 61 percent of the median in 1986 and 1987. But, as Figure 4.3 brings out, this in turn was reversed, with a decline in dispersion between 1987 and 1989. In 1989 the bottom decile had increased its earnings relative to the median from 61 percent to 65 percent; the earnings at the top decile had fallen from 169 percent to 159 percent; and the Gini coefficient had fallen to 21 percent.

The history of the earnings distribution in Poland is therefore one of considerable change since 1970, particularly in the period since 1978 which has seen a fall in dispersion in 1980–1982, followed by a rise up to 1987, and then a decline, so that 1989 saw the lowest degree of inequality in any year apart from 1982. Whatever the implications for the subsequent transformation, this pattern of change means that care must be exercised in making cross-country comparisons. Taking 1989 as the year of comparison rather than 1986 yields the following results for Poland and Czechoslovakia:

	Poland	Czechoslovakia
P_{10}	65	62
P_{25}	81	76
P_{75}	126	124
P_{90}	159	150
P_{95}	188	172
Gini	20.7	19.8

The Czech figures are relatively similar to those in Table 4.1 for 1987, but the Polish figures are now quite different and suggest that the difference between the distributions was very much less marked. The Polish distribution appears to have less inequality at the bottom, with the bottom decile having a better relative position, but more inequality at the top. By the same token, it may make quite a difference which base year is chosen when comparing the post-transition distribution with that under Communism.

Hungary

The Hungarian earnings distribution shown in Figure 4.4 consists of four separate segments, each linked by overlapping years. The first distinction is between the data up to 1970, which relate only to the *state* sector, thus excluding co-operatives (agricultural and non-agricultural) and the later

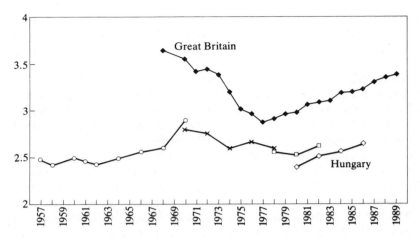

Figure 4.4 Decile earnings ratio: Hungary and Great Britain
Sources: Tables HE1, HE4 and BE1.

data which cover the whole *socialised* sector. The subsequent breaks in the series concern the inclusion of part-time workers up to 1978, and the exclusion of wage supplements up to 1980.

Earnings data exist back to 1951, but for years prior to 1957 there is insufficient detail to allow the decile ratio to be calculated. The late 1950s/ early 1960s show broad stability, with the Gini coefficient for the state sector close to 20 percent and the bottom decile earning around 65 percent of the median. This was followed, as observed by Flakierski (1986), by a period from the mid 1960s to the early 1970s when the dispersion of earnings increased. Between 1962 and 1970 the Gini coefficient rose to 23 percent and the earnings of the bottom decile fell from 65 to 57 percent of the median. Part, but not all, of this rise was reversed in the 1970s. The trend towards equalisation came to an end around 1980, since when there has been a distinct upward trend in inequality.

The decile ratio for 1988 is not shown in the diagram, since it has to be interpreted in the light of the introduction of the personal income tax in January 1988. This income tax is levied on personal income on an annual basis and is individual-based (i.e. the incomes of husbands and wives are not combined). As introduced in 1988, there was a fixed 1,000 forint per month deduction for working costs, followed by a 4,000 forint zero rate band. (In 1988 the median gross monthly earnings were around 7,800 forints.) The scale was progressive, rising from 20 percent to 60 percent.

One of the aims of the tax was to treat on a par income from principal employment and from additional occupations and business activity:

the uniform taxation of personal incomes makes also possible to discontinue the unjustified differences existing to-day in the regulation of enterprises, co-operatives and other forms of entrepreneurial activities ... This is an indispensable requirement of constituting a market. (Ministry of Finance, 1987, pp. 6–7)

Here our concern is with the impact on earned incomes. When the tax was introduced, earnings resulting from the main job or co-operative membership were increased to compensate for the effects of the personal tax deducted, whereas this did not apply to other sources of income. It is this grossing-up that is in part responsible for the observed rise in inequality in earnings before income tax in our tables in the Statistical Appendix.

Conclusion

The five countries studied here exhibit a variety of patterns of change over time in the distribution of earnings. These appear to reflect at least in part deliberate acts of government policy, such as Equal Pay legislation in Britain, the minimum wage in the USSR, the response to Solidarity in Poland. Whatever the realities that lie behind these statistics, the variation over time means that any cross-country comparison must be made with caution. In Figure 4.5 we have shown the relative earnings movements in the five countries over the 1980s, and it is evident that the relative positions have changed to a considerable extent. For the comparison pre- and post-transition, with the exception of Czechoslovakia, it may make quite a difference which base year is chosen for the comparison.

4.4 The earnings of men and women

Do women earn less under capitalism? According to Moroney (1979), who took issue with the radical economists who had associated gender inequality with the institutions of capitalist economies:

tests cast serious doubt on the proposition that relative earnings of women have differed systematically according to the broadly defined systems capitalism and socialism. (1979, p. 607)

Moroney reached this conclusion on the basis of data for male/female earnings in a range of countries. At that time, no data were available for the USSR, and he considered on the socialist side Czechoslovakia (1949–1970), Poland (1972) and Hungary (1962 and 1972). These data came from Michal (1973); who had earlier noted that the gender differential appeared to be similar to that in France or Scandinavia. On the other hand, as observed by Moroney, there were significant differences among 'capitalist' countries. Women *did* do significantly better in relative terms under Communism than in countries such as Australia, Canada, the UK and the US.

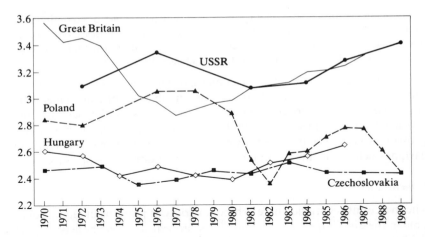

Figure 4.5 Decile earnings ratio for five countries 1970–1989
Sources: Tables CSE1, HE1, PE1, UE1, UE2 and BE1.

One route by which Communist countries may have achieved greater gender equality is the early adoption of equal pay criteria. According to Michal:

The principle of 'equal pay for equal work' is officially applied in Eastern Europe; differences between earnings of men and women apparently originate in the high proportion of women in economic sectors with below average earnings, and in the different occupational pattern of women's employment. (1978, p. 217)

He notes that in Czechoslovakia in 1975 women accounted for 76 percent of employment in the 'trade and catering' sector, which had below-average earnings, and conversely only 17 percent of employment in construction.

Writing about the Soviet Union, McAuley (1981, p. 14) draws attention to the fact that sexual equality is embodied in the 1936 Constitution and repeated in the Brezhnev Consitution, but notes that lower average earnings for women may result from occupational segregation or from their supplying fewer hours (for example, working less overtime). He assembles a range of evidence on the differential in male/female earnings which is interesting but in some cases rather special: for example one of the estimates relates to a sample of newly weds in Kiev (1981, p. 21). Female earnings range from 58 to 72 percent of those of men, and he concludes that the differential is 'on a par with those to be found in Western Europe in the 1960s' (1981, p. 26).

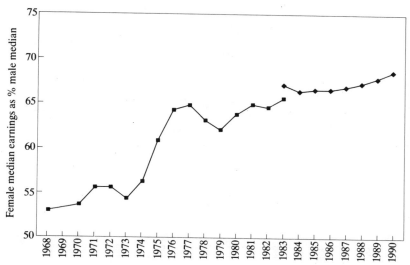

Figure 4.6 Female median earnings relative to male: Great Britain 1968–1990
Source: Table BE3.

Trends in the male/female differential

The 1970s and 1980s in Britain saw a marked upward trend in female earnings relative to male. Figure 4.6 shows the ratio of median female earnings to median male earnings (for adult workers). This period has seen the Equal Pay Act, passed in 1970 and fully implemented by 1975, as well as egalitarian incomes policies that may have particularly benefited women. In 1970 women earned 54 percent of the median for men; by 1975 this had risen to 61 percent, with the increase continuing to 64 percent in 1980 and (with a break in the series) 67 percent in 1986 (and 70 percent in 1991, New Earnings Survey 1991, Table 15). The conclusion drawn from any comparison with other countries will clearly depend sensitively on the year chosen. In terms of the ranking given by Gunderson (1989, Table 1, p. 47), in 1960 Britain had – apart from Japan – the largest differential, along with Canada and Australia, but by 1980 the differential was considerably less than in the United States, France and West Germany.

Turning to Eastern Europe, we may summarise the position in the mid 1980s in terms of the median earnings of women relative to men (in percent):

Czechoslovakia 1987	66
Hungary 1986	74
Poland 1985	74

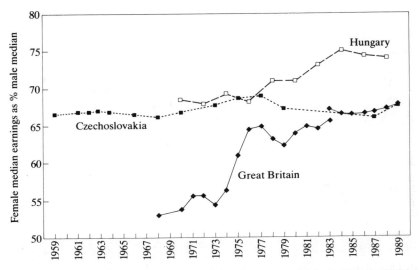

Figure 4.7 Changes over time in female/male median earnings in three countries
Sources: Tables CSE2, CSE3, HE2, HE3 and BE3.

There appears to be a difference between Hungary and Poland, on the one hand, and Czechoslovakia, on the other. It is interesting that the country with the lowest overall inequality should be marked by a greater gender differential. As is pointed out by Večerník, 'its weight within a generally egalitarian structure is particularly predominant' (1991a, p. 244). He goes on to refer to the division by type of job: 'the hierarchy of earnings in Czechoslovakia falls into two parts, the bottom for women and the top for men. Only university-educated women have a chance of invading "men's space"'.

The difference between Czechoslovakia and Hungary is one that has developed since the mid 1970s. As may be seen from Figure 4.7, the female/ male earnings ratio rose appreciably in Hungary after 1976, whereas it did not rise, or actually fell, in Czechoslovakia. (It should be noted that we have treated the Hungarian figures as a continuous series.) The same diagram shows that Britain has in this respect succeeded well in catching up with these two Eastern European countries. (Data are only available for a few years in Poland.)

To these figures we may now add information for 1989 for the USSR, albeit based on a somewhat different source (the March 1989 household survey). Median earnings for women were 71 percent of those for men in the USSR. This suggests that the gender differential was broadly the same as that achieved by the same date in Britain.

Table 4.2 *Summary of earnings distribution for men and women in 1980s*
All full-time workers.

	Gini	P_{10}	P_{90}	P_{95}	P_{90}/P_{10}	Female median/ male median (%)
Czechoslovakia 1987						
males	16.2	69	140	161	2.03	
females	17.2	73	149	170	2.05	66.1
Hungary 1986						
males	21.0	64	159	187	2.47	
females	20.0	66	158	183	2.39	74.3
Poland 1985						
males	23.9	63	167	—	2.65	
females	17.5	66	147	—	2.24	73.7
USSR 1989						
males	26.5	54	178	217	3.28	
females	24.4	57	176	209	3.09	70.9
Great Britain 1990						
males	27.4	56	172	225	3.25	
females	24.5	62	181	208	2.91	68.7

Sources: Statistical Appendix Tables CSE2 (continued), CSE3 (continued), HE2, HE3, PE3, UE3 and BE2.

Distribution by gender

The *distribution* of earnings among men and women is summarised in Table 4.2. This casts light on the view that earnings dispersion is less for women relative to that for men (as found by Michal, 1978, p. 217 and Vielrose, 1978, p. 230). The evidence of the latter author refers to Poland, and here the picture is clear. The decile ratio and the Gini coefficient are a lot lower for women than for men. The distribution of earnings among women in Poland is indeed noticeably less unequal than the overall Czech distribution. Put another way, the differential between each woman in the Polish earnings distribution and her male counterpart widens substantially as we move up the earnings distribution – see Figure 4.8. The female top decile earns 65 percent of the male top decile, but a woman at the bottom decile earns 77 percent of the male bottom decile.

Earnings dispersion is also less among women than among men in Great Britain, with the decile ratio for women being 2.9 in 1990 compared with 3.25 for men. But the pattern is different from that in Poland, as may be seen from Figure 4.8. While the position is similar for the bottom decile, the differential widens more sharply up to the median. But the relative position

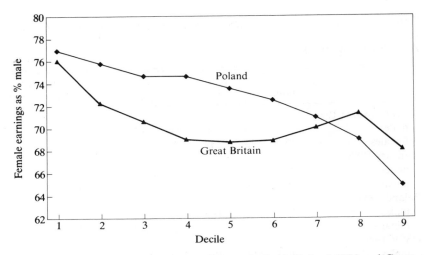

Figure 4.8 Female/male earnings at different deciles in Poland 1985 and Great Britain 1990

Source: Table PE3 and interpolated from Table BE2.

of women tends to rise again in the upper half of the distribution, until the top decile, in contrast to the continuing fall in Poland.

Is the Polish pattern of less dispersion for women typical of Eastern Europe? The evidence in Table 4.2 does not indicate any common pattern. There is somewhat less inequality among women in Hungary and the USSR, but it is much less pronounced. In Czechoslovakia the pattern appears quite different, with the summary measures being slightly higher for women than for men. Although the bottom decile is relatively higher for women than for men, the upper deciles are quite noticeably higher.

Conclusions

Examination of the differences between men and women has thrown light on the overall degree of dispersion in Eastern European. We have seen that the low overall inequality of earnings in Czechoslovakia was achieved *despite* a wider female/male differential than in Hungary and Poland. The dispersion among men and women considered separately is a lot lower than for the two sexes combined: the decile ratio is little over 2. Viewed another way, the low degree of inequality for men has been accompanied by a wider gender gap. In contrast, in Poland, not only is the gender gap smaller, but the distribution among women is close to that in Czechoslovakia. In Poland it is the high degree of inequality among men that is responsible for its overall dispersion.

These differences in dispersion patterns affect the comparisons across countries. If we consider the distribution just for men, then the earlier ranking is confirmed, but the gap between Czechoslovakia and Hungary/Poland becomes much larger: the decile ratio is 2.03 against 2.47 and 2.65. The distribution for women, on the other hand, shows a much smaller gap between Czechoslovakia and Poland, with Hungary now in third place, and inequality definitely less in Great Britain than in the USSR.

4.5 Differences within countries and the Soviet republics

The differences within countries are particularly relevant to the USSR, for reasons that are now more obvious than when we began writing this book, but also because the greater earnings dispersion observed in the USSR than in the countries of Central Europe may be attributed at least in part to its greater size. According to Wiles, 'the U.S.S.R. is a very big country, so surely it is bound to show more inequality on that ground alone?' (1974, p. 53). He goes on to suggest that 'big countries have regions with deep historical differences ... is it [the USSR] not a group of egalitarian regions, the averages of which history has separated, while the U.K. is a group of inegalitarian regions whose history has not been so divisive?' (1974, pp. 54–55). On the other hand, the imposition of central planning, with centralised wage determination, may have been expected to have had a more powerful equalising impact than in market economies.

The effect of population size is found to be significant by Pryor (1973) in his statistical analysis of differences in the earnings distribution across countries. More concretely, he finds no significant impact on P_{15}, which we take to apply also to the bottom decile, but the top decile, P_{90}, is predicted to increase with population size. According to his estimates (1973, p. 449), the top decile in the USSR, with population 290 million, may be expected to be higher than in Hungary, with population 10 million, by a factor of:

$$(290/10)^{0.042} = 1.15$$

(0.042 being the parameter which he estimated), so that instead of a value of 160 percent of the median, we might expect a value of 184. Put another way, the decile ratio might rise from 2.6 to 3.0. On this basis, the effect of size is potentially important.

Britain and Czechoslovakia

Before turning to the geography of the Soviet Union, we begin by considering two of the smaller countries for which we have earnings data by region: Czechoslovakia and Britain. The issue of regional distribution is particularly acute in the former case in view of the pressures for dissolution of the country into separate Czech and Slovak republics, but earnings in Scotland and Wales are not without interest for the same reason. The New Earnings Survey (Table BE4) shows that there are indeed quite sizeable differences in *average earnings* between countries within Great Britain. Average earnings for men in Scotland in April 1990 were 92 percent of those in England and in Wales the figure is 86 percent; for women the corresponding figures are 92 percent and 88 percent. (Here we are not covering Northern Ireland, which is part of the UK but not of Great Britain.)

Does the *distribution* of earnings differ across countries within Britain? As far as the low paid are concerned, this does not appear from Table BE4 to be the case. The bottom decile for women is slightly higher in Wales and Scotland (64 percent in both cases compared with 62 percent in England), and for men it is virtually identical. In the upper part of the distribution, however, the upper tail for men is less extended in Wales, with the top decile being only 165 percent of the median compared with 182 percent in England, with the result that the decile ratio is 2.85, compared with 3.1 in England, a sizeable difference. Coupled with the difference in average earnings, this implies that only 9.2 percent of men in Wales earned more than £400 a week compared with 17 percent in England. The distribution for women, on the other hand, appears to have much the same shape as in England. In Scotland, the top decile for men is the same percentage of the median as in England, but there is some suggestion that the top decile is higher for women, although when combined with the lower mean this still means that only 12 percent earned more than £300 a week, compared with 13.5 percent in England.

These differences within Great Britain provide a point of reference when examining republic differences in Eastern Europe, although it should be borne in mind that the extent of price variation may be different in the latter case. The ratio of average earnings in the Czech Lands to those in Slovakia is shown in Table CSE4. (It should be noted that the Czech Lands have a labour force which is slightly more than double that of Slovakia.) Throughout the period since 1959, the difference for women has been small – less than 5 percent. For men, the difference was initially around 10 percent, which was comparable to the figure for 1990 for men in Scotland, but this fell during the 1960s to reach 5 percent in the early 1970s. In 1989 the difference was much the same as for women – about 4 percent.

What about the distribution within the Czech and Slovak republics? For all workers, male and female, the evidence in Table CSE5 shows the decile ratio to be the same in both republics separately as in the country as a whole: the Gini coefficient is effectively 20 percent in each case. Looking in more detail, there is a tendency for the bottom decile to be higher in Slovakia, the difference for men between 69.6 percent in Slovakia and 67.5

percent in the Czech Lands being nearly sufficient to offset the difference in mean earnings. But the differences are small, and overall the impression is that there are no marked differences between the republics. In short, there seems to be no story to tell.

Differences in average earnings by USSR republics

The differences between republics in the former Soviet Union are much more striking, although perhaps less than would be suggested by Wiles' reference to 'deep historical differences'. We show in Table UE4 the ratio of average earnings in rubles in each republic to that in the Russian Federation. Russia represented a major part of the USSR (in 1988 it accounted for 55 percent of employment – Le Cacheux, 1990, Table 3, p. 24). In 1989, average earnings varied as a percentage of those in Russia from 69 percent in Azerbaidzhan and 73 percent in Moldavia to 104 percent in Estonia. Taking as a yardstick 86 percent – the ratio of earnings in Wales compared with England (for males) – then eight of the fifteen republics were below this level, including the Ukraine with 19 percent of employment.

Has there been a levelling over time within the unified state? Figure 4.9 shows the movement of earnings differentials over time since 1940 for a selection of republics (those with more than 1.5 percent of employment in 1988). The pattern is not uniform. In Belarus and Uzbekistan there was a distinct rise in average earnings, relative to Russia, in the 1960s. In the case of Belarus there was a further rise in the 1980s, but in Uzbekistan the average fell quite sharply, particularly in the second half of the decade. In fact, for five of the six republics shown in Figure 4.9 there was a marked divergence from the Russian average during the late 1980s. For a number of republics this was a continuation of a longer-run trend. From Table UE4, it may be seen that in 1950 average earnings in Ukraine were within 5 percent of those in Russia, but by 1989 they had fallen to 84 percent. Azerbaidzhan is recorded as having had the same average earnings as Russia in 1950, but by 1989 these had fallen to 69 percent.

Distribution of earnings by republics

Is the distribution of earnings less dispersed within republics? If we consider a republic such as Belarus, which is comparable in population size to Hungary, do we find much less inequality than in the USSR as a whole? The distribution by republic in 1981 and 1986 is shown in Table UE5. Taking the example of Belarus, we can see that the decile ratio is 2.9, which is higher than the 2.6 found in Hungary in that year, and a little higher than in Poland (2.8), but much closer to these numbers than to the 3.3 recorded in the

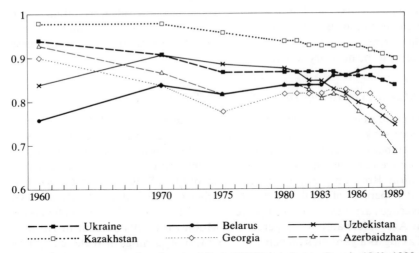

Figure 4.9 Average earnings by republic in USSR relative to Russia 1960–1989
Source: Table UE4.

USSR as a whole. The top decile in Belarus is 164 percent of the median, compared with 183 percent in the USSR. Part way between is Ukraine, with a population of 52 million, where the top decile is 175 percent of the median, and the decile ratio is 3.0 (see Table UE7, which is based on slightly more detail, being taken from the Republic's statistical abstract).

Size is not however the only explanation of differences in earnings dispersion, and we do not find that all of the republics have an decile ratio of less than 3.3. In Table 4.3 we show the republics ranked in order, together with the five countries considered in our study. Kazakhstan, with a population of 17 million, had in 1986 a decile ratio which was the same as for the USSR as a whole, as did Turkmenia and Estonia. Georgia and the Russian Federation had ratios of 3.4 and the greatest inequality was to be found in Armenia, where the top decile earned 204 percent of the median. Notwithstanding the earlier comment about Belarus and Hungary, it is striking that *all* the Soviet republics have a higher decile ratio than Czechoslovakia, Hungary and Poland.

Looking at absolute, rather than relative, earnings, we can see that the proportions earning 120 rubles or less varied from under 20 percent in Estonia and 22 percent in Russia, through 30 percent in the Ukraine and 37 percent in Moldavia, to 41 percent in Georgia and 45 percent in Azerbaidzhan. At the top end of the scale, only 3.3 percent earned more than 300 rubles in Moldavia, 4.4 percent in the Ukraine, 5.9 percent in Belarus and Azerbaidzhan, compared with 10.1 percent in Armenia and 12 percent in

Table 4.3 *Decile earnings ratios for countries
and Soviet republics in ascending order 1986*
All full-time workers

Czechoslovakia (1987)	2.45
Hungary	2.64
Poland	2.77
Moldavia	2.86
Belarus	2.88
Ukraine	2.97
Uzbekistan	2.98
Kirgizia	3.02
Lithuania	3.05
Tadzhikistan	3.13*
Azerbaidzhan	3.20*
Latvia	3.20
Great Britain	3.23
USSR	3.28
Kazakhstan	3.28
Turkmenia	3.30
Estonia	3.33*
Georgia	3.35
Russian Federation	3.36*
Armenia	3.46*

Note:
* these entries involved interpolation in an open
interval.
Sources: Statistical Appendix Tables CSE1
(continued), HE1, PE1 (continued), UE1, UE5 and
BE1 (continued).

Russia. The earnings distribution for the whole Union appeared to be the
result of differences both in average earnings by republic and in the
distribution within republics.

The earnings data in Table UE6 are taken from the March 1989
Household Survey and are not therefore fully comparable with those
discussed so far (the broad picture is similar in terms of republic rankings,
except that Armenia now appears to have less inequality). This source
provides information about the earnings distribution for men and women.
According to the household survey, for the USSR as a whole, women
earned on average in 1989 some 29 percent less than men. The figures for

many republics lie within five percentage points, but in certain republics the gender differential is quite significantly less. This applies particularly to those with the lowest average earnings: Moldavia (where women earned 22 percent less on average), Kirgizia (21 percent) and Armenia (23 percent). It seems likely that the minimum wage played an important role here, in that the earnings distribution is not simply scaled-down.

How has the distribution changed over time within republics? The information in Table UE5 covers the two years 1981 and 1986, a period when dispersion widened in the USSR as a whole. Such a widening is found for all republics, with the exception of Turkmenia, and the same republics were to be found with decile ratios above that for the USSR, except that Georgia moved from below to above the USSR. A longer run of years is given for two republics in Tables UE7 and UE8, taken from the individual republic yearbooks.

Conclusions

The most evident conclusion from the mass of earnings distribution data assembled here is that there is considerable diversity across countries and across time. There is a marked difference between the Soviet Union, on the one hand, and the Central European countries. Earnings dispersion changed quite substantially over time in the Soviet Union and in Poland. This means that it is not easy to draw clearcut conclusions about the comparison of earnings inequality under capitalism and Communism.

Among the Eastern European countries, Czechoslovakia stands out. The low recorded degree of earnings dispersion in Czechoslovakia is indeed remarkable, as is the relative stability of the distribution over a period of three decades. This may be explicable by the historical development of the country, but it would be interesting to know more. Within Czechoslovakia, the inter-republic difference in average earnings is small; and the ratio of median female to male earnings is lower than in other Eastern European countries.

Next in the ranking comes Hungary, where the difference from Britain is clear in all years studied. The changes over time exhibit somewhat the same pattern as in Britain, with a decline in dispersion up to 1980 and then a rise over the 1980s. The ratio of median male to female earnings is rather lower than in Britain.

The position in Poland is an intermediate one. In the mid 1980s the degree of dispersion was undoubtedly less than in Britain, but there has been considerable change over time. The 1980s saw an apparent fall, then a rise, and finally a fall, in earnings differentials. In the 1970s inequality had risen, taking the inequality indicators above those in Britain. Of particular interest are the relative earnings of men and women. Not only is the male advantage on average smaller than in other countries, except for Hungary, but there is distinctly less earnings dispersion among women – the reverse of the situation in Czechoslovakia. As a consequence, the distribution of earnings *among women* in Poland is much closer to that in Czechoslovakia.

Finally, we turn to the Soviet Union. We have seen that, by choosing different dates, it is possible to arrive at the conclusion that earnings dispersion was greater, less, or the same as in Britain. The degree of dispersion, after apparently falling sharply from 1956 to a low point in 1968, varied over the 1970s with the protracted wage reform of that decade. The coincidence of the rise in inequality over the 1980s with that in Britain is striking. There is considerable difference in money earnings between the constituent republics, and this appears to have widened over the years rather than narrowed. What happens within the individual republics is now of great interest. There are considerable differences in the degree of dispersion, but the least unequal still exhibits greater inequality than the countries of Central Europe.

5 The distribution of household incomes

We turn now to the distribution of household net incomes. How much inequality is there between people in respect of the total income coming into their household? The previous chapter looked at the differences in individual earnings by full-time workers; here we take account of the possibility that:

an individual may have work income from sources other than his or her main employment, such as a second job or self-employment income or income in cash or kind from farming private plots,

an individual may have capital income, such as the interest on money held in a savings bank,

there are people in addition to those in full-time work, such as pensioners, children, and the sick and disabled,

a family or household often comprises more than one person, so that we are considering the income of the unit, as compared with individual earnings.

there are income and social security taxes to be subtracted from income, and state transfers such as pensions or child benefit to be added.

These factors are likely to affect the measured degree of dispersion. The second and third may lead to dispersion being greater, insofar as there is more inequality in income from capital, at least in Western countries, and pensioners and others not in work tend to have lower incomes. If second economy jobs are done by those with higher wages, this reinforces inequality. To the extent that transfer incomes are less unequal, this operates in the opposite direction, and inequality may be reduced by progressive income taxation. The fourth difference – the household unit – may tend to reduce the observed degree of dispersion, in that we are in effect averaging the incomes of different household members. Lower paid women may be living with better-paid men.

Overall, in Western countries we would expect the distribution of income to be more unequal than that of earnings among full-time workers. This

106

may not however apply in Communist economies, where, for example, investment income is much less significant. Evidence from the former state of East Germany, for instance, shows the income from capital of private households to have been less than 4 percent of gross wages and salaries in 1983 compared with 13 percent in West Germany (Deutscher Bundestag, 1987, Tables 4.1.1 and 4.1.2). Pryor (1973) concludes that the existence of property income raises the Gini coefficient in developed capitalist countries by between three and six percentage points, although he goes on to argue that:

the greater inequality of labor income in the West is probably a somewhat more important source of income inequality between systems than the existence of property income. This tentative conclusion ... runs quite contrary to the conventional (both Marxist and non-Marxist) wisdom ... that focuses almost exclusive attention on property as the chief causal factor underlying differences in income inequality between East and West. (1973, p. 89)

(We have discussed these different causes of inequality in Chapter 2.)

In the distribution of personal income in Western countries, at least as important as capital income is that arising from state transfers. Eastern European countries have also had well-developed social security systems and provision of social benefits (such as housing and medical care). As a proportion of net material product, their total expenditure on transfers in cash and kind (excluding education but including health) in 1980 was not dissimilar from that (as a percentage of GDP) in Italy, Spain and the UK (ILO, 1985, Table 2). At the same time, the structure of transfers may well have been different. As far as cash transfers are concerned, unemployment protection was a conspicuous absence, and social security has tended to be related to the workplace rather than providing universal coverage. We consider this issue further in Chapter 8.

In Western societies many households contain no earner: for example, in Britain in the late 1980s, a third of all households contained no worker (FES Report 1987, Table 1, p. 1). In part the absence of earners from many households in the West is the result of the high rates of unemployment in Western countries during the 1980s, and this has evident implications for Eastern Europe in transition, as unemployment rises in countries where previously very low rates had been recorded. It also arises because more elderly people live on their own, whereas in Eastern Europe and the USSR, there are more multi-generation households (reflecting both housing conditions and the level of income). There may also be a higher labour force participation rate by pensioners in the East. Wiles and Markowski commented at the beginning of the 1970s that 'the pure pensioner, definitely not working and living in a small household of his own, is not a common feature in Poland, whereas he – or he and his wife, or just his widow – are 11% of all British households' (1971, p. 368). A major difference between East and West is in the level of participation of married women in the labour force, which will affect the outcome of combining the earnings of husbands and wives to form total household income. Eastern Europe has had a high rate of female labour force participation, much of it in full-time work.

These are some of the elements which enter the determination of the overall distribution of household or family income. In Section 5.1, we review the earlier writing on the comparison of income distributions across Communist and market countries. The remainder of the chapter examines the evidence assembled in our Statistical Appendix about the distribution of household income in Czechoslovakia, Hungary, Poland and the USSR. As we have described in Chapter 3, much of the evidence for Central Europe has in principle been available for many years, but in the case of the former Soviet Union we are able to draw on material which has only become available in the very recent past. Commenting on the idea that suppression by the Soviet authorities of information about income distribution may have been due to the relatively great inequality, Ofer and Vinokur said that 'the test of this hypothesis will come if and when the Soviet Union ever achieves a higher level of equality' (1980, p. 2). Neither they, nor we, envisaged that the test might come about because of a change in policy towards publication of distributional statistics.

The material presented here allows analysis of relative income inequality East and West (Section 5.2), of the trends in inequality over time (Section 5.3), and of the distribution between and within the republics of the former USSR (Section 5.4). The rich set of data now available about the USSR and Central Europe suggests many hypotheses about the differences in the distribution of income in East and West. In this chapter we can only scratch the surface, examining in Section 5.5 the role of differences according to household size, the effect of using an equivalence scale, and the individual life-cycle.

In discussing the distribution of income, we tend to use the terms 'inequality' and 'dispersion', or 'differences', as having the same meaning. In this, we are following well-established practice. Kuznets, in his pioneering study of incomes in the US, set out by stating that:

When we say 'income inequality', we mean simply differences in income, without regard to their desirability as a system of reward or undesirability as a scheme running counter to some ideal of equality. (1953, p. xxvii)

It is important to emphasise that the mere existence of income differences does not necessarily imply economic injustice. Not only is economic welfare many-dimensioned, so that we have to take account of other differences such as those in age, family circumstances, labour market activity, etc., but also any normative conclusion about inequality depends on the underlying moral judgments. We are not seeking to make normative conclusions.

5.1 Comparing incomes: East and West

According to Lydall, 'the most difficult international comparisons of inequality are those between socialist and nonsocialist countries' (1979, p. 32). We believe that he may well be right in this view, but not for the reason he gives, which is 'the fact that socialist countries publish so little relevant information'. Rather, the major difficulties seem to us to be those of the comparability of data from different countries and of the interpretation of income distribution data in the context of very different economic and social systems – a subject taken up in Chapter 6. As far as the publication of information is concerned, we have already argued that, the former Soviet Union apart, a considerable volume of material is (and was) available.

The available information for Eastern Europe has indeed been used by a number of writers. Lydall himself drew on the work of Michal (1978) to compare the distribution of income in the United Kingdom with that in Czechoslovakia, Hungary and Poland. Comparing the percentiles of the distribution, and the Gini coefficient, in the early 1970s, he reached the conclusion that 'there is little difference between the United Kingdom and this group of countries' (1979, p. 33). (The data used for the UK were those of Lansley (1977).) A similar conclusion has been reached by Morrisson (1984) in a comparison which encompasses a wider range of socialist countries: the four countries considered here, as well as Bulgaria and Yugoslavia. Morrisson pays particular attention to the non-monetary advantages accruing to the privileged elite in Eastern Europe and included in his estimates are approximate adjustments. It is these adjustments in part which lead him to the finding that the income share of the top deciles are relatively similar in, for example, Czechoslovakia and the UK. Even though the relative incomes of the lowest deciles (the bottom 4 deciles) are higher in Eastern Europe, Morrisson reached the overall conclusion that:

Czechoslovakia excepted, East European countries have *not* a more egalitarian income distribution ... all the other East European countries belong in the same range of income distribution as the most advanced of the Western countries. (Morrisson, 1984, pp. 126–127)

The Gini coefficients for the individual distribution of household per capita incomes (that is, taking individuals ranked according to the per capita income of their household) are 22 percent for Czechoslovakia and 24 percent for Hungary, compared with 25 percent in Sweden and the UK. The Gini is 31 percent for Poland and the USSR, compared with 30 percent in Canada and 34 percent in the US. (The data used by Morrisson relate mainly to the early or mid 1970s.)

This ranking accords with the findings of Bergson in his survey of the evidence about income inequality under Soviet socialism:

Soviet income inequality probably has been found to be greater than often supposed. It is very possibly as great or greater than that in Sweden, and not much less than that in some other Western countries such as Norway and the United Kingdom. Income inequality in the USSR is commonly assumed to be less than that in the U.S. That is doubtless so, though not by so wide a margin as sometimes imagined. (1984, p. 1073)

Bergson reaches this conclusion by arguing that the estimates of McAuley (1979), on which he draws, tend to understate income inequality in the Soviet Union. McAuley himself reaches the rather different conclusion:

These estimates ... yield a value of 3.14–3.21 for the decile coefficient, which implies that there is a moderately unequal distribution of incomes in the USSR. Estimates of this statistic for other Eastern European countries, quoted by Wiles, tend to be lower, but by the same criterion, inequality in the USSR was less than in the United Kingdom and substantially less than in either the USA or Italy. (1979, p. 66)

The view that there is less inequality in Eastern Europe is indeed supported by the results of Wiles (1978). His estimates of the decile ratio for the per capita income distribution in Czechoslovakia, Hungary, Poland, the USSR (and Bulgaria), along with those for the UK, Italy, Sweden, Canada, the US and West Germany are shown below (Wiles, 1978, Table 7.17, p. 191):

Bulgaria 1965	2.62
Poland 1971	2.88
Hungary 1972	3.04
USSR 1967	3.11
Czechoslovakia 1965	3.15
Sweden 1971	3.58
West Germany 1969	3.83
United Kingdom 1969	3.93
Italy 1969	5.86
Canada 1971	5.90
USA 1974	6.25

These figures led the commentator on his paper to conclude that:

during the period considered, the USA and Canada had the most unequal distribution, followed by Italy (an example of 'Catholic Europe'), Sweden and the UK (examples of 'Protestant Europe'), with the socialist countries displaying the lowest inequality of this kind. (Michal, Discussion of Wiles, 1978, p. 193)

This conclusion is in line with that of Pryor:

we can estimate that the Gini coefficient of total income inequality is at least .10 less in the East than in the West, other things remaining equal (e.g., level of economic development). (1973, p. 88)

The degree to which the estimates quoted above are comparable one with another is an issue which may be debated. Wiles' article is entitled 'Our Shaky Data Base'. He draws attention to the problem that Western data are typically expressed in terms of the *household* distribution of *total household* income, whereas Eastern European countries produce estimates of the *individual* distribution of *household per capita* income (as we have discussed in Chapter 3). The latter he feels to be the more relevant, 'since it is human beings not [households] that have stomachs and feel the cold' (1978, p. 178) and he emphasises the problems of interpolating the published Western data to put them on a per capita basis. The interpolation is not necessary where there is access to the original micro-data, and the progress that can be made in improving the degree of comparability is illustrated by the comparison of micro-data for Hungary and the Netherlands made by government statisticians from the two countries (Bruinooge *et al.*, 1990). Their findings show that the Lorenz curves for the two countries cross when the distribution is based on total household income, but that there is clearly less inequality in Hungary in the distribution of *per capita income*. They, like Wiles, stress the differences in practice between East and West in this respect, noting that in the Netherlands 'per capita distributions are hardly ever used' (1990, p. 43).

To summarise, we again have two different schools of thought: those who have found income inequality to be no less in the communist countries of Eastern Europe than in the West and those who find these countries to have less inequality. We have however seen in the case of earnings that the results of such a comparison may vary with the date at which it is made; moreover there are major problems in ensuring that the estimated distributions are constructed on the same basis. In the next section we consider the evidence regarding the mid 1980s paying particular attention to the degree of comparability.

5.2 The distribution of income in the mid 1980s

In this section we consider the evidence about the distribution of net household income in the five countries in the mid 1980s. As explained in the previous chapter, we take this period as one which is relatively recent but also not affected by the changes which were becoming apparent in some of the countries by the latter part of the 1980s. In Table 5.1, we show data for 1985 in Czechoslovakia, Poland and the USSR. In Hungary the income

Table 5.1 *Summary of income distribution in 1982–1985*

	Individual distribution of household per capita income								
	P_{10}	P_{25}	P_{75}	P_{90}	P_{95}	P_{90}/P_{10}	Gini	RHI	HIM
Czechoslovakia 1985	66.4	81.4	127.1	160.3	182.9	2.41	19.9	13.9	1.76
Hungary 1982	62.0	79.5	128.6	162.1	187.8	2.61	20.9	15.0	1.82
Poland 1985	57.6	75.0	134.2	175.1	209.2	3.04	25.3	17.8	2.06
USSR 1985	53.7	74.3	135.3	177.3	206.9	3.30	25.6	18.2	2.08
United Kingdom 1985	52.0	71.8	144.5	200.9	248.7	3.86	29.7	21.2	2.74

	Cumulative decile shares									
	S_{10}	S_{20}	S_{30}	S_{40}	S_{50}	S_{60}	S_{70}	S_{80}	S_{90}	S_{95}
Czechoslovakia 1985	4.9	11.6	19.2	27.4	36.3	46.0	56.6	68.4	82.1	90.0
Hungary 1982	4.9	11.3	18.6	26.7	35.6	45.3	56.0	67.9	81.4	89.4
Poland 1985	4.2	9.9	16.6	24.2	32.7	42.1	52.7	64.7	78.8	87.4
USSR 1985	3.9	9.4	16.1	23.7	32.2	41.8	52.6	64.9	79.4	88.0
United Kingdom 1985	3.5	8.6	14.7	21.7	29.7	38.8	49.2	61.5	76.5	85.9

Notes:
RHI is the 'Robin Hood Index' and measures the amount of income (expressed as a percentage of total income) which has to be redistributed from those above the mean to bring about equal income.
HIM is the 'Hungarian Inequality Measure' and is the ratio of the average incomes of those above the mean to the average income of those below the mean.
Sources: Statistical Appendix Tables CSI1 (continued), CSI2, HI1, HI2, PI1, PI2, UI1, UI2, BI3 and interpolation from Table BI3.

data are only available for 1982 and 1987 and we take the former year on the basis that trends to increased inequality were already evident by 1987 (see below). The sources for the data from each country were described in Chapter 3. The Czechoslovak data refer to *money* income: they exclude the value of income in kind, including that from agriculture. The data from the other sources approximate the wider concept of *personal* income (see Chapter 3) but depart from this definition by excluding the imputed rent from owner-occupation and the value of certain fringe benefits. We return at the end of this section to the limitations of the data.

The estimates of the distribution of income in Eastern Europe in Table 5.1 all relate to the *individual distribution of household per capita income*. This involves:

the choice of the household as the unit over which income is added, so that we are considering income as being shared within the household;

adjusting for differences in household size by simply dividing by the number of people, so that 10,000 forints income for a household of four people is recorded as 2,500 per person;

counting each person as one, so that the household just described is recorded in the income tables as entering four times in the range 2,401–2,600 forints (range taken from Table HI1 in the Statistical Appendix).

In Britain, the official 'Blue Book' series departs from this practice in all three respects: incomes are added only over the tax unit (which is broadly man, wife and dependent children), no adjustment is made for family size, and each tax unit is treated as contributing 1 to the distribution (it enters a single time rather than in respect of each person). The difference may be seen in the example of:

Mr and Mrs Puskas and daughter aged twelve, with income of 6,900 forints, living in the same household as their grown-up son and his friend, who have incomes of 4,300 forints and 3,900 respectively.

In Hungary the total income is added to give 15,100 forints, or 3,020 forints per person, and the household is treated as five people in the range 3,001–3,200 forints. In the British tax unit data, we have three separate units, with incomes of 6,900, 4,300 and 3,900 respectively which each enter a single time in the ranges 6,601–7,400, 4,201–4,400 and 3,801–4,000.

The official statistics do not present data in Britain in per capita terms; for this reason we have in Table BI3 given our own calculations for the per capita distribution in the UK based on the original micro-data. The results for the UK in Table 5.1 draw on this. As is discussed further in the next section, they show a rather different picture from the official Blue Book series.

E

What do the figures in Table 5.1 tell us? If we look first at the percentiles, we find that Czechoslovakia has the least inequality, as in the case of earnings. The bottom decile has an income which is 66 percent of the median, compared with 62 percent in Hungary, 58 percent in Poland, 54 percent in USSR and 52 percent in the UK. The lower quartile follows the same ranking, with Czechoslovakia and Hungary relatively close: 81 and 80 percent, respectively, compared with 72 percent in the UK. Above the median, the percentiles suggest a rather different picture from the findings in the case of earnings dispersion. Czechoslovakia and Hungary appear to be grouped together as exhibiting the least inequality. Poland and the USSR appear to form a second group, with a marked difference in the upper part of the distribution between these countries and the UK. The top decile in Poland is 175 percent of the median, in USSR it is 177 percent, but in the UK it is 201 percent.

Overall, the position is summarised clearly by the decile ratio (rounded to one decimal place):

Czechoslovakia   2.4
Hungary   2.6
Poland   3.0
USSR   3.3
UK   3.9

The decile ratio for incomes in the USSR is the same as that we found for earnings in the previous chapter, as is that for Hungary and, effectively, Czechoslovakia. The differences are in Poland, where the decile ratio for incomes is somewhat higher (3.0 against 2.8), and the UK where there is much higher value (3.9 against 3.2). The move from the earnings distribution to an income distribution has a much larger impact on recorded inequality in the UK.

The distribution of income is more commonly presented in terms of *shares of total income*, which are the ingredients for drawing the Lorenz curve introduced in Chapter 2. The shares are clearly influenced by the methods of interpolation used in the open-ended top and bottom intervals. In the lower part of Table 5.1, we show the cumulative income shares, with S_{10} denoting the share in total income of the people who make up the bottom 10 percent, S_{20} denoting the share of the bottom 20 percent (which includes the bottom 10 percent), and so on. The shares of the bottom 10 percent are estimated to be 4.9 percent in Czechoslovakia and Hungary, 4.2 percent in Poland, 3.9 percent in the USSR and 3.5 percent in the UK. Looked at from the point of view of the bottom 10 percent in the UK, this means that a switch to a 'Czech/Hungarian' *distribution* of income would yield the same cash advantage as a 40 percent increase in *average* income with the distribution remaining unchanged. Put another way, if the price of economic progress in Czechoslovakia and Hungary is a fall in the share of the bottom 10 percent to that in the UK, then an increase of 40 percent in real average income is necessary for the lowest 10 percent simply to maintain their absolute level of income.

Moving up the cumulative distribution, the share of the bottom fifth is 11–12 percent in Czechoslovakia and Hungary, compared with 8.6 percent in the UK. The 'advantage' of the more equal Czech distribution is in this case equivalent to a difference of about 35 percent in average income. Poland and the USSR continue to hold an intermediate position. This continues up to the bottom half of the distribution, who have 36 percent of total income in Czechoslovakia and Hungary, 32–33 percent in Poland and the USSR and 30 percent in the UK. The extent of differences in the distribution for the Central European countries is shown graphically in Figure 5.1. On the vertical is shown the increase in average income which would be necessary to compensate the bottom x percent for a move to a UK distribution of income, for different values of x from 10 to 50. In terms of the trade-off between average incomes and distribution, this may be seen as the 'demand curve' of a person concerned with the absolute income of the bottom x percent. In the case of the bottom 30 percent in Poland, for example, a rise of 13 percent on average would be necessary to compensate for a move to the UK distribution.

The fact that the shares S_x are in each case higher, or no lower, for Czechoslovakia than for Hungary means that the Lorenz curve lies nearer to the line of equal incomes. (We do not actually draw the Lorenz curves, since the differences can be seen clearly from Table 5.1.) This applies right up the income scale: the share S_{90} is 82.1 percent in Czechoslovakia, compared with 81.4 percent in Hungary, which means that the top 10 percent in Czechoslovakia have a share of 17.9 percent, compared with a share of 18.6 percent in Hungary. (Whether or not this difference is statistically significant is a question that requires more information about the standard errors surrounding these figures.) The Lorenz curve for Czechoslovakia clearly lies a lot further inside that of the UK.

The Lorenz curves may be used to compare other countries. The curve for Hungary lies inside that for Poland, the USSR, as well as that for the UK. The curves for Poland and the USSR in turn lie inside that for the UK. With a sole exception, we have a situation of 'Lorenz dominance', where when comparing two countries we can say for one of the two countries that the bottom x percent have a larger (or no smaller) share whatever value of x we choose. The exception – where the Lorenz curves cross – concerns Poland and the USSR. For shares up to S_{70}, Poland does better, but S_{80} and above are higher in the USSR.

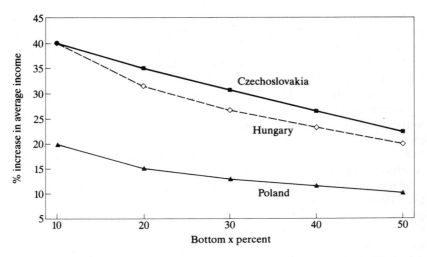

Figure 5.1 Distributional 'advantage' in Czechoslovakia, Hungary and Poland relative to UK

Note: The diagram shows the percent increase in average income necessary to compensate for increased inequality: for example, a 40 percent increase in average income would be needed to compensate the bottom 10 percent in Czechoslovakia were the distrbution of income to become like that in the UK.
Source: Table 5.1.

Measures of inequality

A quantitative indication of the extent of differences in the income distribution can be provided by a measure of income inequality. The use of such measures does however involve, explicitly or implicitly, judgments about the weight to be placed on different parts of the distribution. It is interesting therefore to note the differences in the measures used in different countries.

A favourite in many countries is the 'miraculous Gini', as it was described by *Fortune Magazine*. From Table 5.1, we can see that the Gini coefficient is 20 percent in Czechoslovakia and 30 percent in the UK. Between these two countries there is indeed the ten percentage point difference found by Pryor (1973, p. 88). Nor is Czechoslovakia exceptional, as some writers have suggested. The Gini coefficient for Hungary is nine percentage points less than that in the UK. It is only for Poland and the USSR that the difference is reduced to four percentage points.

Statisticians in Eastern Europe have tended to emphasise other measures of inequality, ones which are described by Éltető and Frigyes as having 'plausible economic interpretation' (1968, p. 384). Before describing their measures, we first refer to the 'maximum equalisation percentage' made popular by the UN Economic Commission for Europe (1967, Chapter 6) and used extensively in Poland. It involves taking those decile groups whose share exceeds 10 percent and adding the excess of these shares over that level. For 1985, we have (see Table PI2) the following:

	share	contribution to maximum equalisation percentage
7 decile	10.6	0.6
8 decile	12.0	2.0
9 decile	14.1	4.1
10 decile	21.1	11.1

so that the total value of the index is 17.8. The index approximates the share of total income which has to be taken from those above the mean, and transferred to those below the mean in order to achieve equality. (It is an approximation since it is based on data grouped by deciles.) In graphical terms, it is the maximum vertical distance between the Lorenz curve and the line of equal incomes – see Figure 5.2. Algebraically, it is half the mean deviation divided by the mean. It is also known as the Pietra ratio (see Kondor, 1971). Here, in view of its simple interpretation, we refer to it as the *Robin Hood Index* (RHI) (a suggestion due to Joanna Gomulka). From Table 5.1 it is clear that Robin Hood would have less work to do in Hungary and Czechoslovakia and quite a lot more work in the UK, where he would have to transfer 21 percent of total income.

The Hungarian statistical office has used as a measure of inequality a variation on the relative mean difference. This is the ratio of average income above the mean to average income below the mean (see Éltető and Frigyes, 1968). In terms of the Lorenz curve, it is the ratio of the slope marked m_A to the slope marked m_B in Figure 5.2. The relationship between this measure and the Robin Hood Index changes as the proportion of the population above the mean changes. The values of the *Hungarian Inequality Measure* (HIM) are shown in Table 5.1. In the UK the average income of those above the mean is 2.74 times that of those below the mean, which is quite a lot higher than in Poland and the USSR where the ratio is double. In Hungary, the value is 1.82, and Czechoslovakia has again the least inequality, with a value of 1.76. In considering these values, it should be borne in mind that the figures for Hungary and the UK are calculated from the micro-data (as are those for the decile ratio) and therefore do not need interpolation, whereas the other figures are interpolated.

Limitations of the data

The conclusions drawn from these statistics may change when we take account of the deficiencies of the data. In Chapter 3, and the Sources and

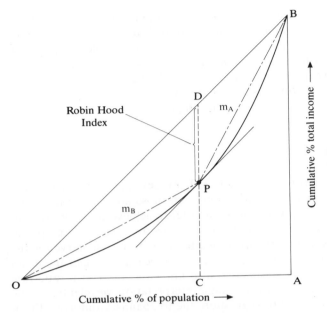

Figure 5.2 Definition of inequality measures

Notes: The point P is where the Lorenz curve has slope equal to that of the line of equality OB (i.e. 45°) and indicates the mean: OC of the population are below the mean, and CA are above.

The distance CD is the share of total income that those below the mean would receive if incomes were equal, and the distance CP is their actual share. The Robin Hood Index is the difference between CD and CP. It is the maximum vertical distance between the Lorenz curve and the line of equality OB.

The Hungarian Inequality Measure is the ratio of the slope m_A to the slope m_B, where m_A is the average income of those above the mean, and m_B is the average income of those below the mean.

Methods section, we have described at some length the sources of data on household incomes and their limitations. Here we concentrate on those which may have caused inequality to be *under*stated in Eastern Europe, and then those which may cause inequality to be *over*stated in the UK.

The first reason for understatement of inequality in the USSR is the problem of the sample design. In Chapter 3, we have described the limitations of the way that the sample is drawn for the Soviet Family Budget Survey (FBS), which is the source for the data in Table 5.1. There can be no doubt that the survey is unrepresentative, and this has led some writers to discount entirely results based on this source. The under-representation of pensioner households may be expected to cause inequality to be understated. As explained in the Sources and Methods section, this under-representation may be less serious in the 1980s than in the past. A second major problem is that the panel nature of the FBS leads it to be unrepresentative of the working population, in that it is biased towards those with longer service records and that it suffers from attrition. Both of these may cause inequality to be understated.

In the three Central European countries, the sample design is comparable with that in the UK, with the exception of the exclusion in Poland of households whose principal source of income is the private non-agricultural sector. The latter may cause inequality to be understated, as may differential non-response in all three countries: for example, there are signs that response is lower in large cities, where there may be more of both high- and low-income households. It should be noted that the level of response is different across countries and that in the case of Poland non-respondents were substituted with other households with similar characteristics (see Sources and Methods).

Among respondents there is a problem of incomplete reporting or coverage of income. The coverage of agricultural production is one problem that affects Eastern Europe to a greater degree than the UK. As explained in Chapter 3, in the case of Czechoslovakia, the distribution examined here does not include the value of farm production for own consumption. This may cause the degree of inequality to be overstated insofar as this source of income is proportionately more important at the bottom of the scale. In the case of the other Eastern European countries, an estimate of this income is included but there are issues concerning the valuation of output. The use of state prices for farm produce may cause incomes such as those of collective farm workers in the USSR to be understated.

One of the most important problems is the omission or under-recording of income from private business activity, illegal activities and from overseas remittances. Assessing the possible effect of unrecorded incomes on the *distribution* of income is a daunting task. An impressive attempt to do so for an Eastern European country is the study for Hungary by Éltető and Vita (1989), whose basic set of results we report in Table 5.2, together with our derived statistics. The authors took as their starting point the micro-data in the 1982 Hungarian Income Survey. The survey sample for this year was divided into seventy-one sub-groups on the basis of sex, occupation and type of residence, and the individuals in each were subjected to a separate micro-simulation treatment in respect of 'hidden' income, defined by the authors as 'unauthorized and/or tax-evading productive and service activities, tips, gratitude payments' (1989, p. 4). This simulation increased the

Table 5.2 *Estimated effect of unrecorded income on the individual distribution of household per capita income in Hungary 1982*

Lower value of range in forints	Reported income	Including estimates of unrecorded income		
		Low	Medium	High
1	6.4	5.7	5.4	5.1
1,801	9.7	8.4	8.0	7.6
2,201	13.9	12.1	11.2	10.8
2,601	15.0	13.7	13.0	12.5
3,001	14.0	13.2	12.6	11.8
3,401	10.8	10.8	11.0	10.6
3,801	12.1	12.6	12.6	12.4
4,401	9.0	10.6	11.4	12.1
5,201	4.6	5.9	6.4	7.0
6,001	4.5	7.0	8.4	10.1
TOTAL	100.0	100.0	100.0	100.0
Mean	3,385	3,618	3,718	3,847
Median	3,140	3,297	3,395	3,475
Percentages of the median				
P_{10}	63.0	62.0	60.2	59.4
P_{25}	79.0	77.7	77.0	76.1
P_{75}	129.0	130.9	131.6	133.4
P_{90}	162.0	167.8	169.3	173.2
Decile ratio	2.6	2.7	2.8	2.9

Notes:
Income is annual income divided by 12.
The data in the first column differ from those for 1982 in Table HI1 in that there are fewer ranges; the summary statistics here have been interpolated using the smaller number of ranges to ensure comparability with the other columns in Table 5.2. The means are as in original source.
Source: Éltető and Vita (1989), Table 3.

incidence and/or recorded amounts of hidden income in each sub-group, with for example high values of these parameters for doctors, dentists, hairdressers and beauticians living in Budapest. Within each group simulated amounts of hidden income for each individual were drawn from a lognormal distribution. The recorded data in the 1982 survey indicated that these forms of income accounted for only 2 percent of personal income.

Éltető and Vita experimented with three different assumptions increasing the proportion of hidden income in 'low', 'medium' or 'high' variants to 6, 8 or 11 percent respectively. The effect of the simulations were to increase inequality of incomes; we estimate from Éltető and Vita's results that the decile ratio of the individual distribution of per capita personal income would rise after adjustment from 2.6 to 2.9 under the 'high' variant. Referring back to Table 5.1, we can see that, even taking the 'high' variant, and even supposing no upward adjustment to be necessary to the UK figures, there remains noticeably less inequality in Hungary. The UK decile ratio is 3.9.

The quantitative results from this exercise cannot of course be seen as necessarily representative of the impact of under-recording of income in other countries in Eastern Europe. However, certain aspects of the Hungarian situation may be applicable. Tips and gratuities in the health system have been important in other countries. In Czechoslovakia, we were told that payments were made to all types of employees and that, according to one of the more authoritative estimates, tipping in the health system accounted for a quarter of all hidden income.

In the case of the USSR, there has been debate as to the distributional impact of illegal incomes. It has been suggested that illegal earnings in different jobs were inversely related to the official rates of pay. Alexeev and Gaddy make use of data for a sample of some 1,000 families which emigrated from the USSR to the United States in the late 1970s and early 1980s. The results show that the Gini coefficient for total income from all sources, legal and illegal, was only one percentage point higher than that for legal incomes for those coming from Russia, Belarus, Ukraine, Moldavia and the Baltic republics, but that it was seven percentage points higher for those from the Transcaucasus and Central Asian republics (Alexeev and Gaddy, 1991, Table 5.1). It should be noted that the results are based on a small and largely urban sample.

Finally, in writing about Eastern Europe, a great deal has been made of social income in kind and of the non-monetary advantages of the elite – the Party officials, top managers, academics, etc. The omission of this latter element without doubt causes inequality in these countries to be understated. These aspects are discussed in Chapter 6.

There are also factors which may cause the degree of inequality in the UK to be overstated. The measurement of income over a week or month may, as explained in Chapter 3, lead to a higher recorded degree of inequality than annual income. Estimates of the possible effect have been made by Nolan using the same data source as in Table 5.1, but for the earlier year of 1977. The effect on the inequality of pre-tax income is to reduce the Robin Hood Index from 24.9 percent to 24.2 percent (1987, Table 5.1, p. 71). On this basis we could account for only a modest part of the difference. Moreover, against this must be set a number of factors which may cause inequality to be understated in the UK. These include the higher non-response of the self-employed, the tendency for self-employment and investment income to be understated, and the omission of fringe benefits.

Conclusions

One way of summarising our findings in this section is to ask whether the overall distribution of income is more or less unequal than the distribution of earnings among full-time workers examined in the previous chapter. For the reasons indicated at the start of the chapter, the expectation in Western countries is that incomes would be more unequal, and for the UK this appears to be the case. The decile ratio for per capita income is 3.9 compared with 3.2; the Gini coefficient is 30 percent compared with 27 percent for earnings. In the Eastern European countries there is not the same difference between the distributions of income and earnings. With the exception of Poland, the decile ratio is essentially the same, and the Gini coefficient is actually *lower* for incomes in Hungary and the USSR. In Poland the decile ratio for income is 3.0 compared with 2.8, which is a much smaller difference than recorded for the UK. Put another way, a difference between Czechoslovakia and the UK in decile ratios for earnings of 0.8 has become a difference of 1.45 for incomes.

5.3 Changes over time in the distribution of income

In comparing our findings with those of earlier writers, we have to remember that most of their evidence relates to the 1970s or 1960s. In this section we consider the changes in the distribution of income over time, taking each Eastern European country in turn. Was the distribution in the 1980s typical of the post-war period or was it the result of a progressive move over time towards greater equality? Was there a period of equalisation followed by a reaction as new economic mechanisms were explored in the 1960s? As described by one group of Hungarian authors:

At the beginning of the fifties we consciously attempted to reduce exaggerated income differences that had developed in the atmosphere of capitalist economic conditions. However, in the last fifteen years the opinion has been repeatedly voiced that income differences which had been so brought about did not sufficiently stimulate the raising of productivity. (Hoch *et al.*, 1978, p. 95)

This chapter differs from the previous one in that we have no direct UK benchmark to apply in each case. This is because the main historical series in the UK – the Blue Book series – is not directly comparable with the

Table 5.3 *Comparison of Blue Book tax-unit distribution with individual distribution of household per capita income in the FES in the UK*

	P_{10}	P_{25}	P_{75}	P_{90}	P_{95}	$P_{90}/_{10}$	Gini	RHI
Tax unit 1984/5	47.6	62.0	167.0	247.2	302.9	5.19	36.0	26.5
Household per capita 1985	52.0	71.8	144.5	200.9	248.7	3.86	29.7	21.2

Cumulative decile shares:

	S_{10}	S_{20}	S_{30}	S_{40}	S_{50}	S_{60}	S_{70}	S_{80}	S_{90}	S_{95}
Tax unit 1984/5	2.7	6.9	11.8	17.8	24.9	33.5	43.9	56.9	73.5	84.0
Household per capita 1985	3.5	8.6	14.7	21.7	29.7	38.8	49.2	61.5	76.5	85.9

Sources: Statistical Appendix Tables BI1 (new), BI2, BI3 and interpolation from Table BI3.

Eastern European data. (It is for this reason that we have taken in the previous section a distribution based solely on the Family Expenditure Survey (FES).) The Blue Book estimates not only draw on other sources but also show the tax unit distribution of *tax unit* income, rather than the individual distribution of per capita income. As may be seen from Table 5.3, where the Blue Book estimates for 1984/5 are compared with the per capita household distribution for 1985 used in the previous section, the Blue Book estimates show a picture of much greater inequality in the UK. If the Blue Book series is taken, the Gini coefficient rises to 36 percent in place of 30 percent, and the decile ratio becomes 5.2 compared with 3.9. The differences in the top percentiles are especially marked.

The Blue Book series goes back to 1949. From Table BI2 it may be seen that the share of the top 10 percent fell from 27 percent in 1949 to 22 percent in 1976/7. It is this fall in inequality at the top that is the main cause of the decline in the Gini coefficient shown in Figure 5.3 (the 'old series'). There was a fall of four percentage points. At the same time, the increase of the share of the bottom half of the population was only one percentage point, so much of the redistribution was in fact towards those in the upper-middle of the income range. As a result, the Robin Hood Index declines much less: only from 24 percent in 1949 to 23 percent in 1976/7. This illustrates how the indices capture different aspects of the distribution.

The break in the series in Figure 5.3 is a purely statistical matter, but it also coincides with a change in direction in the trend. Inequality clearly increased from the late 1970s (Atkinson, 1991b). The share of the top 10 percent rose from 23 percent in 1975/6 to 26.5 percent in 1984/5. In contrast

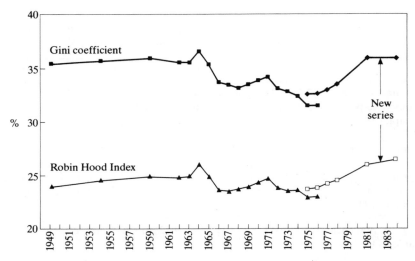

Figure 5.3 Blue Book tax-unit income distribution in UK 1949–1984/5
Sources: Tables BI1 and BI2.

to the earlier period, the Gini coefficient and the Robin Hood Index both moved together, increasing by three percentage points, so this was a different kind of distributional change, with the top income groups gaining at the expense of the bottom. This makes it very interesting to know what happened after 1984/5, but this is the last published figure in the Blue Book series. We have to rely instead on other sources based, like our earlier calculations, solely on the FES. The official figures in Table BI5 are the closest to those we presented for 1985, although they still differ in being based on equivalent income rather than per capita income (see below). They confirm the rise in inequality after 1979, with the rise being particularly marked from 1983 to 1987. The Robin Hood Index rose from 18.5 in 1983 to 21.3 in 1987. (It should be stressed that these figures are not comparable in level with that of 21.2 given earlier for 1985.)

These changes over time have – as in the case of earnings – to be borne in mind when considering the comparison with Eastern Europe, as do the differences in the different types of estimate for the UK. The earlier authors cited did not use the Blue Book series; they used the FES data and, with the exception of Lansley's figures cited by Lydall (1979), their findings were expressed on a per capita basis. This applies to the work of Wiles (1974 and 1978), Morrisson (1984) and Bergson (1984), although it should be noted that the per capita estimates of Sawyer (1976) used by Bergson related to

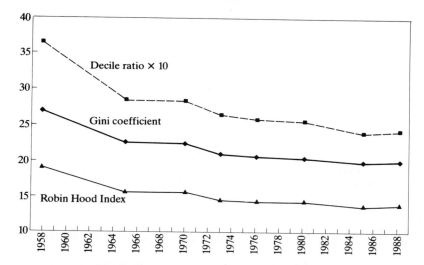

Figure 5.4 Individual distribution of per capita household income in Czechoslovakia 1958–1988

Sources: Tables CSI1 and CSI2.

pre-tax income. The adjustment to a per capita basis was made, not from the micro-data as in our estimates for 1985, but from interpolation of the published tables (the FES reports or the CSO *Economic Trends* analysis). Comparing our 1985 findings with those of Wiles for 1969 the correspondence in terms of percentiles is very close: in both cases the decile ratio is 3.9. The UK distribution estimated by Morrisson for 1975 on the other hand exhibits quite a lot less inequality and this contributes to his conclusion that – apart from Czechoslovakia – there is a similar degree of inequality to that in Eastern Europe.

Czechoslovakia

What have been the trends over time in Eastern Europe? Have they followed the same pattern as in the UK, with inequality first falling (up to the mid 1970s) and then rising? In the case of Czechoslovakia, the answer appears to be 'no'. Over the period since 1958 the degree of inequality fell, at first sharply and then gradually – see Figure 5.4, where we summarise the position in terms of the decile ratio (multiplied by 10 to put it on the same scale), the Gini coefficient and Robin Hood Index.

Particularly interesting is the movement of the income distribution

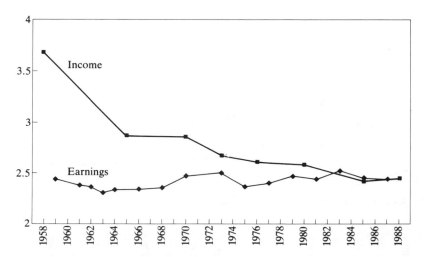

Figure 5.5 Decile ratios for income and earnings in Czechoslovakia 1958–1988
Sources: Tables CSE1 and CSI1.

relative to the – much more stable – distribution of earnings. Figure 5.5
gives the decile ratio for the two distributions, and shows how the difference
between them has narrowed to the extent of disappearing in the 1980s. The
evolution of income distribution in Czechoslovakia has to be considered as
depending not just on the policy regarding wage differentials but also on
other sources of income, particularly the role of social benefits. For the
period up until 1976 Hiršl has commented that 'a changed level of social
benefits considerably contributed to the levelling out of the growth rate of
general income in households with a different number of wage earners and
dependent children. This applied to the entire period 1960–1976' (1980,
English summary, p. 4).

This may also be related to the marked narrowing of the difference in
average incomes between the Czech Lands and Slovakia. Whereas the
earnings data were characterised by an initial differential of 11 percent in
favour of the Czechs (Table CSE4), later falling to around 4 percent, the
difference in average *incomes* is recorded as 72 percent in 1958 (Table CSI4).
The relative advantage of the Czechs fell to 37 percent in 1965, to 21 percent
in 1970, and then to about 10 percent in the 1980s. From Table CSI5 it may
also be seen that this was accompanied by a much sharper reduction in
inequality in Slovakia. In 1958 there was considerably greater inequality in
Slovakia than in the Czech Lands: the Robin Hood Index being 21.4
percent, compared with 16.9 percent in the Czech Republic. By 1988 the
difference had been eliminated.

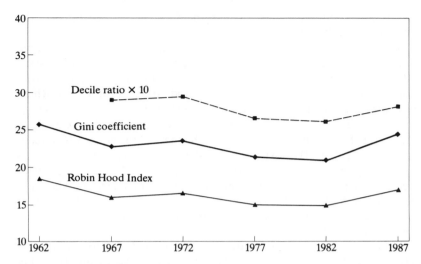

Figure 5.6 Individual distribution of per capita household income in Hungary 1962–1987

Sources: Tables HI1 and HI2.

Hungary

In Figure 5.6 we show for Hungary the movement over time in the three summary indicators of inequality in the individual distribution of per capita income. In contrast to the position in Czechoslovakia, these do suggest a U-shaped pattern over time, but with the increase coming between 1982 and 1987, and with there having been an earlier increase between 1967 and 1972. (With income surveys only being carried out every five years, the trends cannot be tracked very precisely.) The rise in inequality between 1982 and 1987 was quite marked. The Gini coefficient rose by three and a half percentage points, and the Robin Hood Index by two percentage points. The reversal of the earlier trend towards equalisation broadly took the situation back to that at the beginning of the 1970s.

The (modest) rise in inequality between 1967 and 1972 may be associated with the New Economic Mechanism established in 1968. We have seen that earnings differentials widened at this time and according to Flakierski 'the reform was consciously aimed at increasing earning differentials in the socialist sector' (1986, p. 18). He goes to say that 'at no time, however, has the leadership pursued a deliberate policy of increasing the dispersion of per capita household incomes' (1986, p. 18). The rise in inequality does indeed appear quite modest (a rise in the decile ratio for example from 2.89 to 2.94), certainly when compared with a rise in the decile ratio of earnings in the state sector from 2.6 to 2.9.

Turning to the more recent period, it is of particular interest that income inequality in Hungary did not rise until after 1982. Many people regard 1978 as a turning point in the recent economic history, this being the year in which the 'new economic policy' was declared, and it is the year in which real wages were at their highest (Andorka, 1989, p. 138). Moreover, the rise in inequality has taken place more at the top than at the bottom. A comparison of 1987 with 1977 shows that the share of the bottom 10 percent is the same (Table HI2), whereas the share of the top 10 percent has increased by more than two percentage points. Despite large price increases, those at the bottom appear to have managed to keep up. According to Andorka (1989), this has been achieved through a further increase in female employment and a more than proportionate rise in social income, particularly pensions.

An important factor in accounting for increasing dispersion of incomes in Hungary in the 1980s is likely to be the growth of the second economy during this period. Kupa and Fajth (1990) illustrate the changes in second economy work between 1977 and 1986 with data from time budget surveys. The proportion of non-agricultural skilled male workers cultivating a private agricultural plot on an average day rose from 26 percent to 40 percent (Table 3.1/b, p. 10). Kupa and Fajth comment that overall 'in 1987 2.1 million of the 3.8 million households earned at least 10 thousand forints with supplementary work. Since the time of declination in real wages the increase in their number can be estimated as 0.3–0.5 million' (1990, p. 10).

Poland

In Figure 5.7 we show two series for Poland. The first is a series covering all households and we have been able to construct this from 1983 to 1989. As explained in Sources and Methods, the data are published separately for different types of households. While it would in principle have been possible to combine the figures for different groups for the earlier period, we felt that the more readily available estimates for worker households would be sufficient to indicate the trend in the years prior to 1983. It has also to be remembered that there was a major change in the budget survey design in 1982, with a rotating design being introduced, and that there are reasons to believe that the results for subsequent years are rather different.

To a considerable extent, the changes over time mirror those in the earnings distribution: a modest rise in inequality over the 1970s, a sharp fall in the Solidarity period of 1980–1982, and a return to rising inequality in the 1980s although the break in the series in 1983 must be borne in mind. There is however a fall in inequality in 1988 followed by a sharp rise in 1989. The

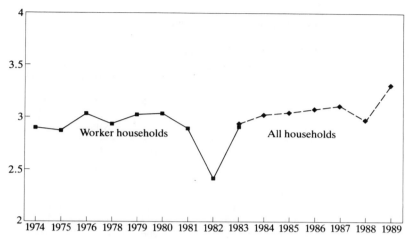

Figure 5.7 Decile ratio for individual distribution of per capita household income in Poland 1974–1989

Sources: Tables PI1 and PI4

fall in 1988 may have been the result of the increased latitude allowed in wage settlements, combined with the union pressure for equalising adjustments.

The most striking feature of Figure 5.7 is the fall in inequality in 1982. This may be at least in part a statistical artefact, reflecting the change in sampling design; and it has been alleged that the statistics at this time were less reliable. According to Flakierski, 'the official statistical data for this period of turmoil are particularly unreliable' (1991, p. 99). But, as he explains, there are substantial reasons for expecting a fall in inequality as a result of the measures introduced in response to Solidarity. The incomes policy package of Solidarity is described by Flakierski as 'one of the most egalitarian programmes ever defined in a socialist country' (1991, p. 96). In Chapter 4 we referred to the demand for an undifferentiated wage increase in compensation for inflation, but the Gdansk Accord also called for the establishment of a social minimum and for increases in social benefits. These measures were however only partially implemented, and there was only partial indexation of pensions and other social transfers.

Soviet Union

Earlier comparisons of income inequality in the Soviet Union and the West such as those of Bergson (1984) and Morrisson (1984) have relied largely on the work of McAuley (1979) and Ofer and Vinokur (1980).

Table 5.4 *Comparison of income distribution estimates for USSR*

Individual distribution of household per capita income

	McAuley 1967	Ofer-Vinokur 1973	Family Budget Survey		
			1980	1989 All	1989 Workers/ employees
Median (rubles)	56	83	101	140	143
P_5	—	51	—	—	—
P_{10}	57.7	56	53	52	53
P_{25}	76.6	73	73	72	72
P_{75}	133.6	131	136	136	136
P_{90}	176.9	178	174	182	181
P_{95}	—	216	200	—	—
P_{90}/P_{10}	3.1	3.15	3.25	3.53	3.40
S_{10}	—	3.5	4.0	3.4	3.5
S_{20}	—	9.1	9.6	8.6	8.9
S_{30}	—	15.7	16.3	14.9	15.2
S_{40}	—	23.2	24.2	22.2	22.5
S_{50}	—	31.8	32.9	30.5	30.9
S_{60}	—	41.3	42.6	39.8	40.2
S_{70}	—	51.8	53.5	50.4	50.6
S_{80}	—	63.7	66.0	62.4	62.6
S_{90}	—	78.0	80.5	76.7	76.8
Gini coefficient	—	26.8	24.5	28.9	28.4
Robin Hood Index	—	18.7	17.4	20.2	19.8

Note:
The data of McAuley relate to the non-agricultural population; the data of Ofer and Vinokur relate to the European urban population; those from the FBS relate to households of worker-employees and collective farm workers.
Sources: McAuley (1979), Table 3.1 p 57; Ofer and Vinokur (1980), Table A1; Statistical Appendix, Table UI3.

McAuley discusses both the Family Budget Survey, the source of the estimates for 1985 above, and the periodic March Household Survey, of which we have also made use. He describes the Family Budget Survey as being, at that time, 'of questionable value in the analysis of income distribution' (1979, p. 53), and he therefore uses the periodic survey. In Table 5.4 we give McAuley's results for the individual distribution of household per capita income in the non-agricultural population which he reconstructed from the graphs in Rabkina and Rimashevskaia (1972). These figures refer to income gross of tax and relate to 1967.

The source used by Ofer and Vinokur is quite different from the Family Budget Survey which is the basis for the estimates quoted for the 1980s, being a survey of some 1,200 emigrants from urban areas of the former Soviet Union to Israel, who reported in retrospect on their economic conditions in the USSR during their last year of normal residence (around 1973). The sample was evidently unrepresentative and was re-weighted with the aim of bringing it into line with the European urban population of the USSR. The re-weighting took account of the type of household, the labour force activity of the household head, the sex, education and occupational status of the household head, but could not of course get away from the fact that the entire sample consists of Jewish emigrés. The sample is also a small one: 1,222 households containing 3,984 individuals. Against these limitations must be set the advantages of access to micro-data. The findings for the individual distribution of household net per capita income from this survey are shown in the second column of Table 5.4. (We focus on the individual, rather than the household, distribution for reasons of comparability with the estimates in the previous section.)

Given the very different sources, and the differences in coverage, the two distributions of McAuley and Ofer-Vinokur appear to be close. The McAuley figures differ in covering the rural non-agricultural population, in including the Asian republics, and in relating to income before tax. These differences may lead us to expect inequality to be higher. Bergson suggests that inequality may be understated in the McAuley data on account of the omission of households with no gainfully employed members and the incomplete coverage of private income. The same criticisms apply to the Family Budget data also shown in Table 5.4 although the under-representation of pensioners may now be less serious. In the case of 1989, we show two sets of estimates: one for all households, the other covering the households of worker/employees, thus excluding those on collective farms. This provides some indication of the effect of limiting coverage to the non-agricultural population. There is relatively little difference, with the decile ratio excluding collective farms being 3.4 in place of 3.5.

Given the differences in the sources, and the uncertainty surrounding the interpolation (which affects particularly the estimated shares, Gini and Robin Hood indices), no strong conclusions can be drawn about the trends in the USSR up to 1980. All that one can say is that the FBS distribution in 1980 appears to be fairly similar to those found by McAuley and Ofer-Vinokur, and used in the earlier comparisons.

Since 1980 there has been an apparent widening of income inequality.

The decile ratio has risen from 3.25 to 3.5, especially on account of a rise in the top decile relative to the median. The Gini coefficient increased from 24.5 percent to 29 percent; and the Robin Hood Index increased from 17 to 20 percent. We have seen that earnings differentials widened over this period in what Matthews has called Gorbachev's 'drive against equal incomes' (1989, p. 8). The encouragement of co-operatives may be expected to have had the same effect but these are not covered in our data. Working in the opposite direction are improvements in social security introduced in accordance with the Twelfth Five Year Plan (approved in June 1986). These included the introduction of a degree of indexation for pensions in payment, increases for registered invalids, and extension of child benefit. On the other hand, the fact that the minimum pension is tied to the minimum wage means that it has been left behind along with the official minimum wage. The importance of the minimum wage in this connection is stressed by Rimashevskaia (1990). According to Matthews, 'Gorbachev has not shown any special interest in social security' (1989, p. 27), and his assessment is critical:

Apart from the relatively modest levels of improvement so far registered, the proposed timing is disappointing. Implementation was promised 'during 1986–1990 and over the period up to 2000.' . . . the policies did not include any advance toward what is termed 'national assistance' in the United Kingdom, that is automatic state aid for people whose income is below a recognized level. This has remained a serious gap in an otherwise reasonably comprehensive system. (1989, pp. 29–30)

Social policy is discussed further in Chapter 8.

Conclusion

The earlier finding that the extent of dispersion of incomes in Eastern Europe is similar to that of earnings does not imply that the latter is the sole determinant of income inequality. As is brought out by the discussion in this section of the trends in different countries, the two distributions do not always move together and the income distribution, while heavily influenced by that of earnings, also reflects other determinants, notably the contribution of social incomes.

The different countries exhibit rather different changes over time, but it is noticeable that Hungary, Poland and the USSR all shared with the UK a pattern of rising inequality over the 1980s. Again Czechoslovakia stood out – see Figure 5.8, which summarises the changes in the four Eastern European countries since 1970 in terms of the Robin Hood Index.

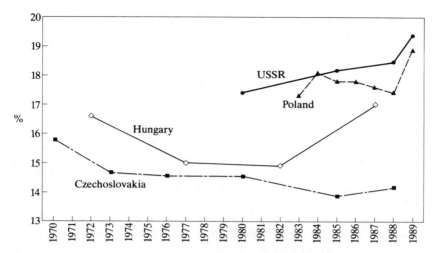

Figure 5.8 Income distribution in four countries: Robin Hood Index
Sources: Tables CSI2, HI2, PI2 and UI2.

5.4 Differences between and within Soviet republics

The reduction of regional disparities was one of the goals of Communist governments. We have seen that in Czechoslovakia there was a marked reduction in the difference between average incomes in the two republics. In Hungary, Éltető and Láng report that 'although regional differences in Hungary are not as large as in many other countries ... in past years a certain amount of levelling has occurred' (1971, p. 312). In contrast, in the Soviet case doubt has been cast on the success of government policy in reducing regional disparities. According to McAuley:

although all republics in the USSR enjoyed substantial increases in per capita incomes, there was little if any reduction in interrepublican variation. If the Soviet government did become more concerned about the extent of regional disparities in the standard of living in the late fifties, and if it actively sought to reduce them, its policies must be adjudged to have failed during the 1960s. (1979, p. 99)

More recently, Zaslavskaya has stated that regional differences remain important: 'the territorial criterion is the strongest determinant of differences in a person's socio-economic status' (1991, p. 138). In this section we examine the evidence about average per capita incomes and about the distribution of income within republics.

To put the discussion in context, we may note that the differences in average income between England, Scotland and Wales are small. According to Table BI6, the Scottish mean income per capita is 97 percent of that in England and the Welsh is 99 percent. These differences are much smaller than the differences in average earnings recorded in Chapter 4.

Average incomes

In the previous chapter we considered the regional disparities in average earnings per worker. These are only one factor entering the determination of disparities in average income. As noted in one study of Uzbekistan, wages 'in some cases comprise only a small proportion of total personal income. Perhaps particularly in Soviet Central Asia, 'non-wage' income and income from the private sector – legal and illegal – play an important role in household budgets' (Lubin, 1984, p. 179). Nor need regional disparities in income be as large as those in earnings; as in the UK other sources of income, notably government transfers, may play an equalising role across republics.

In Table UI6 in the Statistical Appendix, we have assembled evidence on average per capita income by republic from two sources. The first set, covering 1960–1970, are the estimates of McAuley (1979); the second set are from the Family Budget Survey. These are not necessarily comparable, and the shortcomings of the Budget Survey have already been rehearsed: for instance, that it is unlikely to capture adequately the illegal private income just referred to. The average republic incomes are expressed relative to that in the Russian Federation (RSFSR). In 1988, the republics could be grouped in terms of their percentages of the RSFSR average:

Baltic republics: around 110 percent,

Belarus, Ukraine: around 100 percent,

Kazakhstan, Georgia and Moldavia: 80–90 percent,

Armenia and Azerbaidzhan: around 70 percent,

Uzbekistan, Kirgizia, and Turkmenia: around 60–65 percent,

Tadzhikistan: around 50 percent.

In some republics, the relative income position is closer to that of Russia than is the position for earnings. This is true of the Baltic republics, Belarus, Ukraine, Georgia and Moldavia. But in the others, particularly some of the poorest, the disparities in terms of income are larger than for earnings. It is also interesting to compare the average incomes of worker households, excluding those employed on collective farms. The relative mean incomes, derived from Table UI3 for 1989, are consistent with the classification above except that Ukraine falls to 85 percent of the RSFSR, Azerbaidzhan to 60 percent and Uzbekistan to 55 percent.

Over time, there have been examples of convergence of the republic

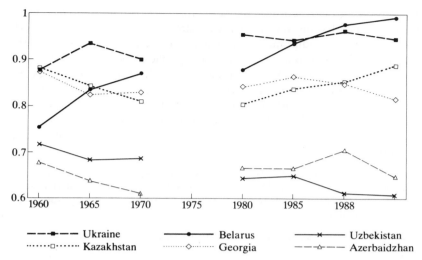

Figure 5.9 Average per capita income by republic in USSR relative to Russia 1960–1988

Sources: 1960–1970: McAuley (1979, Table 5.1, p. 109), personal income series; 1975–1988: Goskomstat (1989, p. 47), worker/employee households.

average incomes towards that for the RSFSR. Belarus is an example, as may be seen from Figure 5.9 where we show the changes over time in the six largest republics (in terms of population). The average income in Kazakhstan rose from 80 percent of that in Russia in 1975 to 90 percent in 1988. Moldavia rose from 81 percent to 87.5 percent. But seven out of the eleven non-Baltic republics failed to make significant progress towards achieving a higher relative income, and a number fell behind, particularly some of the poorest Asian republics. Even allowing for the possibility that missing income may be more important in these cases, one can understand the reasons for inter-republic tensions.

One of the differences in our presentation of the findings from the earnings distributions is that we are now adjusting for household size by dividing by the number of household members. As noted by McAuley, it has been claimed 'that difference in demographic structure, the higher birth rate in Central Asia resulting in more children and larger families, means that per capita income fails to measure living standards adequately' (1979, p. 112). He examines the effect of allowing for the demographic composition with an equivalence scale (see the next section) and suggests that it has very little effect on inter-republic variation. Using aggregate data, it is not possible to allow for economies of scale within households (since this depends on the distribution of the population between households), and it can be argued that his allowance for children is rather high: 0.75 for girls and 0.83 for boys (adult males = 1). Cazes and Le Cacheux (1991) use the example of Estonia, one of the richest republics, and Tadzhikistan, the poorest, to illustrate the possible impact of an adjustment which gives less weight (0.5) to children than a per capita calculation. As they show, the average per capita income in Estonia is 2.4 times that in Tadzhikistan but total income divided by the total number of equivalent adults in the republic differs only by a factor of 2 (1991, p. 173). The same point is made in a different way by a Russian author:

While the family load indicator (number of dependents per working person) is 0.45 in Estonian workers' and employees' families and 0.59 in Estonian collective-farm families, the corresponding figures in Tadzhikistan are 1.31 and 1.56, respectively. (Pern, 1989, p. 81)

The issue of family size, and of the number of earners, is taken up below.

Income inequality

According to the Family Budget Survey, in 1989 the Gini coefficient for the USSR as a whole was 29 percent, and the decile ratio was 3.5. Is income inequality significantly lower in individual republics? Our capacity to answer this question is limited by the form in which the data are published, since the top and bottom ranges contain for individual republics a large proportion of observations. Over half the population of Tadzhikistan are in the range below 75 rubles per month; more than a fifth of Estonians are in the top range. In Table 5.5 we have included only those republics for which the proportion in the top and bottom ranges were less than 20 percent. This still involves extrapolation in open intervals and the results should be treated with considerable caution. The only republic with less than 10 percent in both top and bottom intervals is Ukraine.

With this qualification in mind, we may see from Table 5.5 that the degree of income inequality within individual republics does appear to be substantially less than for the USSR as a whole. In the case of the Ukraine and Belarus, the Gini coefficient is 24 percent, meaning that these countries are less unequal than Hungary. Close behind, and ahead of Poland, are Armenia and Moldavia. On the other hand, Kazakhstan, and Georgia are more unequal than Scotland.

5.5 Household composition, equivalence scales and the life-cycle

We have seen that differences in household size are important in the comparison of the different Soviet republics. More generally, households in

Table 5.5 *Gini coefficients and decile income ratios for countries and republics*

Individual distribution of household per capita income (1989 unless indicated)

	Gini	Decile ratio
Czechoslovakia (1988)	20.1	2.44
Ukraine	23.5	2.76
Belarus	23.8	2.73
Hungary (1987)	24.4	2.81
Moldavia	25.8	3.08
Armenia	25.9	3.14
Poland	26.8	3.31
Latvia	27.4	3.08
Lithuania	27.8	3.11
RSFSR	27.8	3.16
Scotland (1985)	28.6	3.68
USSR	28.9	3.53
Kazakhstan	28.9	3.46
Georgia	29.2	3.53
Wales (1985)	29.5	3.69
United Kingdom (1985)	29.7	3.79
England (1985)	30.3	3.83

Sources: Statistical Appendix Tables CSI1 (continued), HI1, PI1 (continued), UI3 (continued), BI3, and BI6.

Eastern Europe tend on average to be larger than in the West. This reflects the housing shortage and the lower standard of living, independent living for the elderly being in part a 'luxury' which can only be afforded in rich countries. The fact that there are more large households lends particular significance to the per capita adjustment; it is likely to affect the comparison of income inequality between East and West and the composition of the low-income groups (relevant to Chapters 7 and 8).

Certainly one finds more large households in the lowest ranges. The report on the USSR 1989 Budget survey comments that:

Of the families with incomes below 75 rubles, families with 5 or more members dominate (52–66%), and the families with an average per capita income of more than 200 rubles per month tend to have 2–3 members. (Goskomstat, 1990a, p. 6, translation by S Marnie)

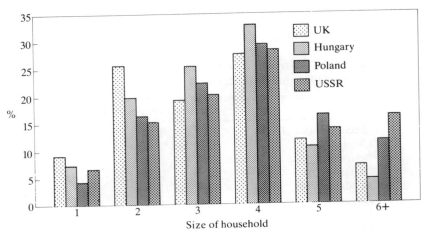

Figure 5.10 Distribution of individuals by household size in four countries

Note: The data refer to active households only in the case of Hungary and worker/employee households only in the case of the USSR. For the UK and Poland the data refer to 1985. The data from Hungary refer to 1987 and those from the USSR to 1989.

Sources: UK FES (1985, Table 1, p. 1), taking 6+ as 6.5 persons; Hungary: Statistical Yearbook (1988, Table 35.4, p. 432); Poland: see Table PI1, size 3 includes pensioners 3+; USSR: Goskomstat (1990b, p. 6), taking 6+ as 6.5 persons.

In the case of Czechoslovakia in 1988, Table CSI6 in the Statistical Appendix shows that households with two or more children are concentrated towards the bottom. If we take a per capita income of 1,200 crowns per month, then about 15 percent of the total population has an income below this level, and about the same percentage has an income of 2,400 crowns per month or more. Among households with two children, the proportion below 1,200 crowns is about the overall average, but only 1.5 percent are to be found above 2,400 crowns. Among households with three children, nearly a third are below 1,200 crowns and virtually none are above 2,400.

In Figure 5.10 we show the proportion of individuals in households of different sizes in 1985 in the UK, Hungary, Poland and the USSR. There are more single-person, and many more two-person, households in the UK. In Hungary there are more three- and four-person households, whereas in Poland and the USSR the difference from the UK appears to be more among those with five or more members. An indication of the difference is that more than one in three of the UK population live on their

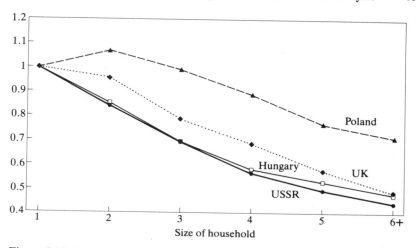

Figure 5.11 Average per capita income by household size relative to one-person household in four countries

Note: The data refer to active households only in the case of Hungary and worker/employee households only in the case of the USSR. For the UK and Poland the data refer to 1985. The data from Hungary refer to 1982 and those from the USSR to 1989.

Sources: Hungary: Statistical Yearbook (1982, Table 19.22, p. 302); UK: Table B17; Poland: Table P15; Goskomstat (1990b, p. 242).

own or with only one other person, whereas in Poland the corresponding proportion is one in five.

In general, income does not rise proportionately with household size, and there tends to be an inverse correlation between household size and per capita income. Comparing six different countries, including both developed and developing, Kuznets drew attention to 'an impressive *negative* association between size of household and household income per person' (1989, p. 287). That this holds for the Eastern European countries considered here is shown by Figure 5.11, which gives the average income per capita in households of different sizes, expressed as a proportion of the average for single-person households. The decline with household size is similar in the UK to that in Hungary and the USSR, although in Poland the gradient is less pronounced (and two-person households fare better). The same pattern is shown in a different way in Table CSI3 for Czechoslovakia. The average household size in the lowest income range is 3.9; it declines to around 3 in the middle ranges; and then falls progressively to around 2 at the top of the income scale. Of course, there are large households with a correspondingly large total income, but they are not the rule.

While average per capita income falls with household size, it does so less than proportionately, as may be deduced from Figure 5.11. In other words, total income rises with household size. This means that a calculation which gives less weight to differences in household size than the per capita adjustment we have been using might show a rather different picture. This brings us to the possibility of an adjustment via the use of an equivalence scale.

Equivalence scales

The use of equivalence scales to adjust for differences in household composition may affect the conclusions drawn. The sensitivity of measured inequality to the choice of scale has been explored in the UK by Coulter *et al.* (1991) using the parameterisation in terms of γ described in Chapter 3. This means dividing total income by H^γ to give equivalent *income*, where H is the number of persons and γ is a parameter varying from 0 (make no adjustment for size) to 1 (per capita adjustment). The scale used in official CSO/DSS estimates, such as those in Tables BI4 and BI5, is taken by Coulter *et al.* as corresponding approximately to a value of $\gamma = 0.6$. The simpler OECD scale of 1 for the first adult, 0.7 for other adults and 0.5 for each child (aged less than fourteen) corresponds broadly to a value of 0.72.

Does the choice of γ affect the conclusions drawn? Using data for the UK for annual household disposable income for 1986, Coulter *et al.* show that the shares S_{10} and S_{20} tend to first rise as γ is increased and then fall; and the share of the top 10 percent first falls and then rises. As a result, the Gini coefficient has a U-shape, with a minimum around γ equal 0.55 – or close to the value which corresponds to the CSO/DSS choice. The extent of variation is two and a half percentage points. The Robin Hood Index falls from 23 percent at 0 to 21 percent at 0.5 and then rises to 22 percent with a per capita adjustment. For the indices used here (although not for all indices) moving to a calculation of equivalent income, with a value of γ around 0.6, can be expected to reduce the measured degree of inequality.

The results for the UK in the Statistical Appendix, Table BI3, confirm that the move to a CSO/DSS equivalence scale from a per capita distribution reduces the measured inequality. The Gini coefficient in 1985 falls by three percentage points, the decile ratio from 3.8 to 3.1, and the Robin Hood Index from 21 to 19 percent. These differences are not dramatic, but of some importance in terms of the issue of East–West comparisons. The comparison by Lydall (1979, p. 33) of the distribution of equivalent income in the UK with that of *per capita income* in Eastern Europe may have partially contributed to his conclusion that there was little difference.

The analysis by the Hungarian statistical office of income distribution has also compared per capita and equivalent distributions. The equivalence scale used is summarised in the note to Table HI3. For a family of two earners with two children, the allowance is 2.67 times that for a single-person household, which may be taken as corresponding to a value of γ of about 0.7. In all three years, the decile ratio is reduced on moving to an equivalent income basis: for example from 2.8 to 2.5 in 1987. (It should be noted that the equivalence scale is not the same in each year.) This change is less than that just described for the UK and the fall in the Robin Hood Index is also much smaller: by only half a percentage point.

Weighting

To this point, with one exception, each person has had equal weight in the calculations, but income distributions are sometimes presented which give each *household* an equal weight. (The exception is the Blue Book series for the UK, which gives each tax unit an equal weight.) In a household distribution, each individual has a weight equal to $1/H$ where H is the size of the household. That this change in weighting alone can affect the findings is shown by Table CSI3, which gives the household distribution of household per capita income in Czechoslovakia. The Gini coefficient rises by two percentage points, and the decile ratio goes from 2.43 to 2.65.

The effect of changing both the weighting *and* the equivalence scale is shown for Hungary in Tables HI3 and HI4 and for the UK in Table BI3, where the household distribution of household income is equivalent to taking $\gamma = 0$. The combination of these two changes can produce a large increase in recorded inequality, compared with that in the individual distribution of per capita income, as has been stressed by Morrisson (1984). In the UK, the Gini coefficient rises by four percentage points, the Robin Hood Index by three and a half percentage points, and the decile ratio from 3.9 to 5.1. In Hungary the changes are even larger: the Robin Hood Index rises by six percentage points and the decile ratio from 2.8 to 5.4. Using the decile ratio as the measure of inequality would reverse the previous ranking of Hungary and the UK.

In our view there is little to recommend a household weighting, and we use the individual weights, but the magnitude of the changes which can be caused by a change in definition should serve to remind readers that these issues of definition are not matters to be relegated to footnotes.

The life-cycle

The observed differences in household size are associated with the differences in the individual life-cycle, as has been emphasised in Western analyses of income distribution. Paglin (1975) and others have claimed that systematic variation of income with the life-cycle is responsible for a significant part of the observed inequality, this being an example of the importance of distinguishing between income *differences* and income *inequality*.

Life-cycle differences may affect the comparison of income distribution in East and West in two different ways. First, there may be differences in the number of households at different stages of the life-cycle. The fact that there are more elderly in the West may, depending on their relative incomes, lead to a larger proportion of low-income units. Secondly, the life-cycle itself may be different between East and West. If there are more three-generation families, then this may reduce the tendency for per capita or equivalent income to rise and then fall with the life-cycle. A couple who have not yet had children may not be living independently from their parents; the middle-aged couple whose children have grown-up may be supporting elderly relatives. The economic implications of different stages of the life-cycle depend on the extent of social support of families with children and of the elderly.

The life-cycle in Czechoslovakia is illustrated by Figure 5.12. The average income per head rises with the age of the household head up to the age group 55–59 and then falls, so that above 70 the average income is below that for the youngest households. The average household size reaches a peak in the age range 35–39, when there are 1.8 dependent children.

Associated with life-cycle differences is variation in labour force participation. In Czechoslovakia, the average number of economically active persons per household is over 2 between the ages of 45 and 54, and then falls sharply with age – see Figure 5.12. This may also exercise an independent influence on the distribution of income. The distribution of income will, other things equal, be different in a society where all married women are in full-time employment from that in a society where a significant proportion are not in paid work or are only employed part-time. The role of the number of earners in determining the position of the individual household in the income distribution has been shown empirically by Élteto and Láng (1971) with reference to the Hungarian survey data for 1967. While the average per capita income of the household tends to rise with the earnings of the household head, the relation between earnings and income is fairly weak: 'all earnings categories include households with low, medium and high per capita incomes ... the income position of the individual families is not a simple mechanical repetition of their earning position' (1971, pp. 318-319). Important factors are the number of earners and the number of dependants: 'the differences in incomes are far more due to the varying compo-

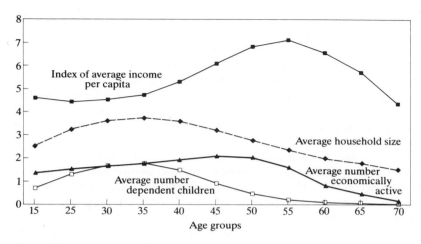

Figure 5.12 Life-cycle in Czechoslovakia 1988
Source: Microcensus (1988), table on households by age.

sitions of the households and to the different ratios of earners to dependants' (Élteto and Láng, 1971, p. 319).

The untangling of these strands requires a more extensive analysis than we can provide here. The identification of the life-cycle effect is not easy. With cross-section data – a snapshot at a point in time – we may seek to separate out that part of the observed dispersion associated with life-cycle differences in family size and labour force participation. However it is not clear how to interpret such a decomposition and it is difficult to identify households at different stages of the life-cycle. The diversity, and fluidity, of household circumstances is such that they cannot easily be pigeon-holed into categories. Longitudinal data may allow individual life histories to be constructed. A number of the Eastern European household surveys contain panel elements, which could be used for this purpose, but this is for the future.

Conclusions

The aim of this chapter has been to summarise *what the statistics show* about the distribution of household income in three countries of Central Europe, the former Soviet Union and its constituent republics, compared with the United Kingdom. The italicised phrase is important, since we have stressed the problems of interpretation which surround the concept of income in Eastern Europe, and we shall be taking up some of the most important of these problems in the next chapter. We have also emphasised the shortcomings of the statistical data – in both Eastern Europe and the United Kingdom – and the results should be read bearing in mind our earlier discussion of the sources and their limitations.

Taken at face value, the figures show that the difference in income inequality between the UK and Eastern Europe in the mid 1980s was greater than for the distribution of earnings examined in Chapter 4. The expectation in Western countries is that *incomes* would be more unequal than *earnings*, and for the UK this appears to be the case: the Gini coefficient is 30 percent compared with 27 percent for earnings. In the Eastern European countries there is not the same difference between the distributions of income and earnings, so that the contrast between East and West is heightened. For earnings, the difference in the Gini coefficient between Czechoslovakia and the UK was seven percentage points; for incomes, it becomes ten points. Unlike the earnings distribution, there is a clear difference in income inequality between the UK and the USSR. The USSR is now closer to Poland and four of the republics (Ukraine, Belarus, Moldavia and Armenia) record a lower degree of inequality than Poland (the first two also have less inequality than Hungary).

The finding that the extent of dispersion of incomes in Eastern Europe is similar to that of earnings does not imply that the latter is the sole determinant of income inequality. Examining the trends over time in different countries, we find that the two distributions do not always move together and the income distribution, while heavily influenced by that of earnings, also reflects other determinants, notably the contribution of social incomes. The different countries exhibit rather different changes over time, but it is noticeable that Hungary, Poland and the USSR all shared with the UK a pattern of rising inequality over the 1980s. Again Czechoslovakia stands out as having had a relatively stable distribution since the 1970s.

The comparisons summarised above are based on the *per capita* distribution of income, which is the basis adopted in many Eastern European analyses. If we have to choose between a per capita basis and treating all households as identical, as in the official Blue Book series in Britain, we would certainly opt for the former. There is however a case for moving to the intermediate case of an equivalence scale which rises less than proportionately with the number of household members. We have shown how this may affect the conclusions drawn (and this issue is further discussed in Chapter 7 in connection with the measurement of poverty).

6 Interpreting income data

The reader used to reports of queues and shortages in Eastern Europe may well be wondering about the significance of the evidence on incomes presented in the previous chapter. How can we *interpret* data on money incomes from Eastern Europe? If many goods were not readily available in the market and were rationed in some way, did differences in recorded incomes correspond to differences in living standards? If goods were supplied by enterprises, or were reserved for the privileged elite, how does this change our view of relative inequality? The reader who has heard accounts of the subsidies provided by Communist governments may ask about the balance between the payment of wages and the provision of social benefits. If there was widespread provision of basic goods either free or at subsidised prices, how does this affect our comparison of the distribution of income in the pre-1990 East and West?

These issues are evidently important, and it is for this reason that we have devoted the present chapter to this subject. At the same time, it must be remembered that they are not unknown in Western countries. Governments in Western Europe provide social benefits in kind and subsidise the purchase of certain essential goods such as housing and public transport. Fringe benefits are a significant part of the remuneration of managers and others in the private sector. The main difference in kind, as opposed to degree, concerns the *availability* of goods in the market, although even here there have been periods in Western economies where queues have developed, especially in the housing market.

The issues in the context of the USSR have been described by Bergson (1984), on whom we draw at several points in this chapter. The central problem facing the researcher wishing to draw conclusions from information on distribution of income is that the 'incomes that are compared, while expressed in monetary terms, are supposed to represent commensurate differences in real income. Income, that is, should ideally be received in a monetary form, and be freely exchangeable for goods and services at

F

established prices that are uniform for all households in any market area' (Bergson, 1984, p. 1057). Where this condition is not satisfied, the distribution of personal income may fail to give an adequate measure of the distribution of the standard of living, and there may be problems in interpreting changes over time in real incomes.

We begin in Section 6.1 with an issue familiar from the public finances of Western economies: the impact on the distribution of personal income of the government budget via social benefits. This refers to benefits in kind, cash transfers already having been included in the personal incomes discussed in Chapter 5. We make use of the findings from official studies that have been made in Hungary, Poland and Czechoslovakia, which may be compared with those made by the Central Statistical Office in the UK. In Section 6.2, we consider the distributional impact of price subsidies and indirect taxes, looking at evidence from Hungary, Poland and the UK. We then consider in Section 6.3 the non-wage benefits paid by virtue of employment, notably those to the privileged elite. These are particularly significant where goods are not available on the market, and in Section 6.4 we take up the issue of shortages and differential prices.

Two points should be borne in mind throughout the chapter. First, the different issues, despite being discussed in different sections, are closely interrelated. For example, price subsidies may cause shortages which may both increase the significance of non-wage benefits and bias official calculations of consumer price movements. Second, we are able to give only limited evidence on the quantitative importance of the different problems of interpretation of income data. We present a number of different examples but what we provide is far from being a comprehensive guide to interpretation of data from all five countries for all periods.

6.1 Social benefits

It is widely believed that the socialist distribution system gave greater weight to social benefits at the expense of the general level of wages. Income was channelled from enterprises to the state, which in turn paid benefits to households in the form of cash transfers and in-kind benefits. To the extent that these social benefits were more or less uniformly distributed, the effect would be equalising, compared with a proportionate increase in wages. Benefits may be equalising too in other dimensions. Benefits may reduce differences between the households of workers and those of farmers (see, in the case of Poland, the analysis by Okrasa, 1988). They may narrow the gap in living standards between those in work and the retired population. They may reduce geographical differences. In the case of the Soviet Union, McAuley draws attention to the fact that:

although there are differences between the republics and between urban and rural areas in the scale of educational and medical service, essentially the same system is provided in all parts of the country. An attempt is made to impose common standards, and these standards are those of an industrialized European state. ... Differences between the Soviet Central Asian republics and the countries immediately south ... are particularly striking. (1979, p. 287)

On the other hand, there are questions which have to be investigated before we can reach any firm conclusion concerning the role of social benefits. Are these social benefits in reality equally distributed in quantity and quality? Who in fact receives them? How are the benefits to be valued?

In this section, we consider some of the evidence about social benefits, particularly the state provision of education and health care. By social benefits, we mean benefits in kind provided free. This excludes state spending on goods which are traded at subsidised but non-zero prices, this being the subject of the next section. It excludes cash transfers, which have already been included in the distributional figures; the point of departure is indeed household income including cash transfers, referred to as household *disposable income*.

The question with which we are particularly concerned is the extent to which in-kind benefits are distributed independently of income. If there is a systematic relation with disposable income, are they positively or negatively related? If we rank individuals (or households in the case of the UK data) by disposable income, do we observe a larger or smaller share going to those at the bottom? The presentational device that we use is the *concentration curve* due to Mahalanobis (1960) and developed for this purpose by Kakwani (1977). This curve is formed by calculating the cumulative shares of benefit going to different income groups (see the upper part of Figure 6.1). If everyone were to receive the same amount, then we would have have a straight line of *uniformity*: the bottom 10 percent get 10 percent, etc.

The concentration curve is like a Lorenz curve, but differs in that people are ranked not by the amount of benefit, as would be the case in the Lorenz curve for benefit, but by their disposable income. This allows the Lorenz curve for disposable income and the concentration curve for benefit to be plotted on the same diagram. The ranking by income means that it is quite possible that the concentration curve lies above the line of uniformity. If social benefits are concentrated on the lower-income groups, then they receive absolutely more than those higher up the distribution. This is illustrated by case A in Figure 6.1, where in the lower part we show the amount of benefit per head received at different income levels. In case B, the amount of the benefit rises with income, and the concentration curve lies below the line of uniformity. Of particular interest in this situation is whether the benefit rises less steeply, or more steeply, than disposable

income. If the concentration curve lies inside the Lorenz curve for disposable income (i.e. the benefit rises less steeply), then the benefit still
contributes to reducing overall inequality. It is of course quite possible that
the concentration curve *crosses* the line of uniformity.

The graphical device of the concentration curve leads in turn to the
concentration coefficient (Kakwani, 1980), which is a widely used summary
measure. The concentration coefficient corresponds to the Gini coefficient,
in that it depends on the area between the concentration curve and the
line of uniformity, but again differs in that the ranking is according to
disposable income not the amount of the social benefit. As a result, the
coefficient can be negative. This happens when the concentration curve lies
above the line of uniformity (or, in the case of a crossing, when the area
above the line of uniformity more than outweighs the area below). The case
where the social benefit is uniform (the same absolute amount for everyone)
provides a benchmark, since in this case the concentration coefficient is
zero. If the benefit is β percent of average disposable income, then the Gini
coefficient for income plus benefits is reduced in relation to that for income
alone by a factor $\beta/(1 + \beta)$ when we take the benefit into account. With a
uniform benefit equal for everyone to 10 percent of average disposable
income, a Gini coefficient of 22 percent would be reduced by two percentage
points. More generally, where the social benefits vary across the population, the Gini coefficient for income plus benefits is reduced relative to the
Gini coefficient for disposable income alone by an amount equal to $\Delta \equiv \beta/
(1 + \beta)$ times [Gini for disposable income – Concentration coefficient of
benefits] plus an adjustment for the re-ranking which takes place between
the two distributions. (The addition of non-uniform social benefits may
change people's position in the income distribution.) A concentration
coefficient of *minus* 11 percent would therefore, with β equal to 10 percent,
contribute a further one percentage point reduction to the Gini coefficient
compared to a uniform benefit. (This ignores the re-ranking adjustment.)

This suggests that social benefits which are uniform, or which have a
systematic negative relation with income, may have a powerful equalising
impact. At the same time, there may be variation in the amounts of social
benefit received by those who are otherwise identically placed in income
(and other relevant characteristics, such as household composition).
Differences may exist, for example, in the social benefits received by urban
and by rural households, or simply between one district and the next. Some
people may live within reach of a public facility and others may live too far
away to take advantage of the benefits. By introducing such 'noise' into the
distribution, the equalising impact of social benefits in kind may be
reduced. This is potentially of some importance in East–West comparisons,

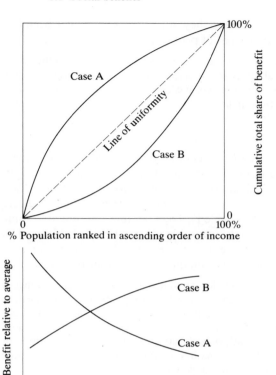

Figure 6.1 Hypothetical illustration of concentration curves

Notes: People are ranked along the horizontal axis in terms of their disposable income. The bottom diagram shows the amount of benefit, expressed relative to the average, received by people at different income levels (all differences other than in income are ignored). The top diagram shows the concentration curve, which gives the cumulative share of total benefit going to different cumulative groups. The top two diagrams are linked by the fact that at any point the slope of the concentration curve is equal to the level of the benefit (relative to the average) shown at the corresponding point of the bottom diagram.

In case A, the benefit falls steadily with income, starting from a value greater than the average. This means that in this example the slope of the concentration curve is initially greater than 1 and that the curve is everywhere above the line of uniformity.

since it has been argued that social policy in Eastern Europe has been less concerned with the equal treatment of people in the same position:

The redistribution of income through social transfers in Poland – and in the East – pays more attention to vertical equity across particular socio-economic groups than in the West, but at the same time it is less successful in meeting the objective of horizontal equity. (Okrasa, 1988, p. 637)

United Kingdom

In the United Kingdom, social benefits in kind are covered in the official Central Statistical Office analysis of the impact of the government budget. In 1988, health services and education (including school meals and welfare milk) each accounted for 12 percent of general government expenditure (Central Statistical Office, 1991, Table 1). Together they amounted to some 15 percent of average household disposable income (1991, Table 3). The official study allocates the total amount spent by the government as a benefit to individual households. The method used is described as follows:

Education benefit to individual households is imputed by reference to the number of pupils and students in the state sector ... and to the type of education they are receiving ... No benefit is allocated for pupils at private schools ... Data are available on the average cost ... of providing the various types of health care ... and it is possible to estimate the use made of each service on average by individuals of different ages and sex. Using this information, an imputed benefit from the state health service can be allocated to each individual. (1991, p. 113)

The Central Statistical Office study is based on the same data from the Family Expenditure Survey that we used in Chapter 5, but with the difference that the household, rather than the individual, is taken as the unit of analysis. Moreover, households are ranked according to equivalent income, using the official equivalence scale, rather than according to per capita income.

The results of imputing social benefits in kind to households in the United Kingdom in 1988 are shown in Figure 6.2 in terms of the concentration curves for education and health spending where households are ranked in terms of equivalent net income. Decile group 1 is the bottom 10 percent of households. For purposes of comparison with the in-kind benefits, the cumulative shares of *total* disposable income are also plotted in Figure 6.2. The benefits in kind are, on this basis, allocated more progressively than disposable income, in that they are close to the line of uniformity. In other words, they have an equalising effect. The concentration curve for health benefits lies clearly above the line of uniformity, and the concentration coefficient is some *minus* 9 percent. (Here, and in all later calculations, we assume in calculating the coefficient that income within each decile

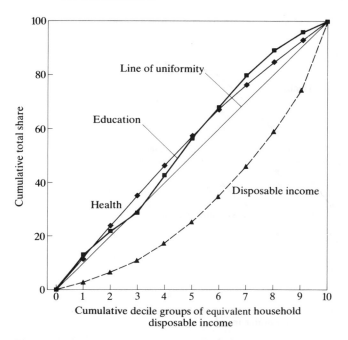

Figure 6.2 Distributional incidence of education and health spending in UK 1988

Source: Central Statistical Office (1991, Table 4).

is equally distributed: i.e. we take the linearisation of the concentration curve. This gives a lower bound on the absolute value (where the curve does not cross the line of uniformity).) Given that the Gini coefficient for disposable income is around 34 percent, this makes the difference between the Gini and the concentration coefficient $(34 - (-9)) = 43$ percent. It is this equalising factor that enters the earlier expression Δ for the impact of benefits on the overall distribution and which may be regarded as a measure of the leverage the benefit has.

The picture for education is less clear, with the concentration curve dipping at one point below the line of uniformity. This reflects the life-cycle dimension of redistribution. In Figure 6.3 we show the position excluding retired households (where the income of retired members accounts for over half of total household gross income). (In this case, the data are shown for *quintile*, rather than decile, groups.) The bottom 20 percent of non-retired households received more than 30 percent of allocated education benefits, and the spending is more progressive than health. It is also true that there is

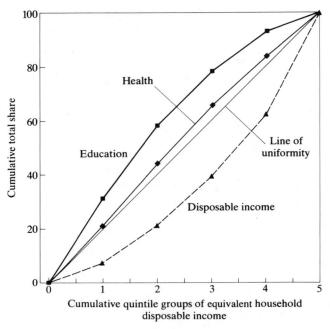

Figure 6.3 Distributional incidence of education and health spending in UK
1988: non-retired households
Source: Central Statistical Office (1991, Tables D and H).

a life-cycle element in health spending, with the elderly being allocated a
disproportionate share, but the picture is different in that within this group
the allocated benefit is relatively uniform. Overall, the coefficient of
concentration for education is similar to that for health – around *minus* 9
percent.

Hungary

This kind of calculation suggests that in the UK social benefits in kind from
education and the National Health Service are relatively equalising. The
same kind of finding has been reported in Eastern Europe. In Hungary,
estimates are made of *social income in kind*, including public health,
education, social welfare, culture, sports and recreation. In 1987 the total
amounted to some 16 percent of total personal income (see Table HI5 in the
Statistical Appendix). The Hungarian definition is more extensive than that
in the UK study just cited in including items such as social welfare, whereas

the personal social services are not allocated in the UK exercise. If we take just health and education, then the Hungarian figure is 12 percent – or less than the 15 percent in the UK.

As explained in Sources and Methods, the benefits in kind are allocated to individual households in the Hungarian Income Survey on the basis of their demographic characteristics and reported usage. The latter represents an important difference from the UK studies which make no reference to actual usage (no data being available in the Family Expenditure Survey). Table HI7 in the Statistical Appendix shows that the amount allocated falls steadily as a percentage of total disposable income, indicating a progressive impact. In Figure 6.4 we show the results from a more recent study by Kupa and Fajth (1990), based on updated data from the 1987 Income Survey combined with the Household Budget Survey (in order to allocate subsidies – see the next section). These authors explain that about 60 percent of health spending was allocated on the basis of days spent in hospital; the expenses of out-patient care were distributed on the basis of indicators of health status, such as health care expenses, consumption of medicines, number of hospital days and number of days of sick leave; the remaining general health care expenses were allocated uniformly per person. In the case of education and nurseries, the allocation was based on participation, as in the UK. The value of social support services (family care, welfare nurses, daytime homes for the elderly, etc.) was allocated to individuals aged under fourteen and over sixty-five in the lower-income categories, differentiated between Budapest, rural towns and villages.

The resulting estimates of the incidence of social income in kind in Hungary in 1989 are shown in Figure 6.4. This takes the same form as the earlier Figure 6.2 for the UK, but with the difference that we are here considering the *individual* distribution and that they are ranked by *per capita* rather than equivalised income. The total for all benefits is slightly above the line of uniformity, indicating a fairly even distribution and one certainly more progressive than disposable income. Looking at the individual spending categories, education appears to be the most progressive, and the concentration coefficient is *minus* 12 percent. The effect on the distribution is however less, since the Gini coefficient for disposable income is lower than in the UK and hence Δ is smaller. Interestingly, the share of health benefits tends to rise somewhat with income, and the concentration curve lies below the line of uniformity, although not far removed. This may reflect the different method of allocation. Overall, the concentration coefficient for all benefits is a relatively modest *minus* 3 percent.

The concentration curves for all benefits in kind and for health benefits lie close to the line of uniformity, but this does not imply that everyone receives the same amount. It only implies that each decile group receives the same

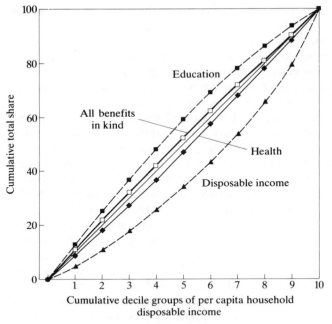

Figure 6.4 Distributional incidence of social benefits in kind in Hungary 1989
Source: Kupa and Fajth (1990, Tables 1.2.2/b and 39).

share. *Within* an income group there may be considerable dispersion, and this adds to inequality. The extent of dispersion is illustrated in the case of health benefits in Figure 6.5, which groups households according to whether the allocated health benefit is less than 5 percent of disposable income, between 5 and 10, between 10 and 20, or more than 20 percent. (The average over all households is 5.5 percent.) This is an aspect which warrants further investigation.

Poland

In Poland, official studies were made of the effect of social benefits on the income distribution in the 1970s (GUS, 1981, Dmoch, 1979 and 1983 – see Topińska, 1991 for references). The combined impact of both cash and in-kind benefits has been studied by Okrasa, who has compared the Polish experience with that of Western countries such as the UK (Okrasa, 1987 and 1988). Here we make use of the study by Topińska (1991) for 1989. In this year, state budget expenditure on social benefits in the form of

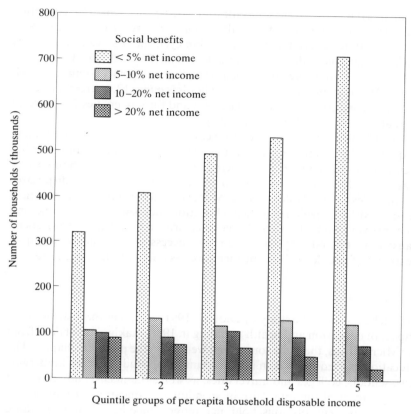

Figure 6.5 Dispersion of social benefits in kind as percent of net income in Hungary 1989

Note: The unit shown in the diagram is the *household*, classified by per capita income (i.e. the quintile groups are of *individuals*).

Source: Kupa and Fajth (1990, Table 148).

education represented 6 percent of household money incomes, and health and social welfare represented 5.5 percent (Topińska, 1991, Table 2). As in Hungary, these were rather smaller percentages than in the UK.

The distributional impact in Poland was assessed using data from the household budget survey, which was our source of income distribution information in the previous chapter. The procedure of allocation to individual households is similar to that in Hungary in that health care is based on actual usage in terms of hospital days and outpatient consultations. Education is allocated according to participation. The results are summarised in terms of the concentration coefficients, which for education are *minus* 4.3 percent and for health *minus* 4.8 percent (Topińska, 1991, Table 21). If, to reduce the influence of life-cycle factors, we consider only worker households, then the values are *minus* 5.9 and *plus* 3.9 percent, respectively. Within the educational spending category (Topińska, 1991, Table 22), the coefficient for primary schools is *minus* 12.6 percent, whereas that for secondary schools is 17.0 percent and for universities 21.6 percent (virtually the same as for final income).

Social benefits in kind do therefore contribute to a sizeable reduction in inequality, the difference between the concentration indices and the Gini coefficient for disposable income being some 30 percent for all households. This is less than the 43 percent in the UK, mainly because disposable income is less uneqally distributed. Moreover, the progressive impact may be reduced by dispersion in their allocation independent of income and other relevant characteristics. As has been argued by Okrasa (1988), social transfers in Poland may have been less successful in ensuring the equal treatment of people in the same income class and with the same needs.

Czechoslovakia

In Czechoslovakia, the study by Dlouhý (1991) examines the distributional impact of education and health spending in 1988, making use of data from the Microcensus, the same source that we used in the previous chapter. The education expenditure taken into account in the study covered kindergartens, schools, colleges and universities, as well as canteens, and accounted for 65 percent of the total current spending on education. It represented some 6.5 percent of household net money income. Health spending amounted to some 10 percent of household net money income recorded in the Microcensus. The total is therefore similar to that in the UK. Educational spending was allocated simply using three age categories, but four different methods were employed in the case of health spending.

The results for the distributional impact of social benefits are summarised in terms of the concentration coefficient, which for education was *minus* 15.7 percent (Dlouhý, 1991, Table 10). This represents a substantially more progressive effect than in Poland, and is a little larger in its impact than is educational spending in Hungary. Moreover, if to reduce the life-cycle effect we take only worker households (in that pensioner households derive less benefit from education), then the index becomes *minus* 19.6 percent. It is also interesting to note that the coefficient is virtually zero for the category 'secondary, vocational and university', but substantially negative for elementary schools and, even more, kindergartens. In the case of health care, an allocation based on age and its relation to the reported incidence of infectious diseases led to a coefficient close to that for education (Dlouhý, 1991, p. 14), but the other methods of allocation (by number of persons hospitalised, or number of hospital days, or reported sickness) all led to values close to zero, the value which would be found with a uniform provision.

Criticism

In the UK, the official estimates have been challenged from a number of directions. In particular, it has been argued that 'almost all public expenditure on the social services in Britain benefits the better off to a greater extent than the poor... [This is] true for services whose aims are at least in part egalitarian, such as the National Health Service, higher education, public transport and the aggregate complex of housing policies' (Le Grand, 1982, pp. 3–4). (Transport and housing are covered in the next section.)

Why are different conclusions reached? First, it is questioned whether the Central Statistical Office method correctly identifies the beneficiaries from state spending, and it is suggested that it is the middle and higher income groups who in fact benefit most. In the case of education, there is evidently a tendency for the children of middle class, and higher income, parents to be over-represented amongst those who stay on at school after the minimum leaving age and among students in higher education. However, insofar as the official estimates are based on actual participation, this is captured in the estimates cited above. We have indeed noted that these sectors of education made virtually no contribution to progression in the case of Poland, and that they were substantially less progressive than other forms of education in the case of Czechoslovakia.

In the case of medical care, it is argued (Le Grand, 1982, Chapter 3) that the better-off in Britain make greater use of the health service, when judged according to their need in terms of sickness, although this claim is controversial (see for example O'Donnell and Propper, 1991). The official study not only fails to take account of actual use but also does not relate use to sickness. The Central European estimates quoted above *do* attempt to employ indicators of use, but are still open to the objection that use needs to be related to sickness. If the poor have greater need for health care, then spending on health services cannot necessarily be taken as equalising. At the same time, this raises fundamental questions about the nature of social objectives.

A second criticism of the statistical studies is that they take no account of the variation in the *quality* of service. It has been argued that in the USSR that:

the 'quality' of services provided from social funds varies greatly. While free benefits are available to everyone, where is the guarantee that a worker will receive the same medical care in his raion polyclinic that a minister receives in his departmental polyclinic? (Dmitriev, 1989, p. 60)

In the case of Poland, Topińska notes that:

Given that schools and medical centers in the countryside are more poorly equipped than those in the cities, 'true' relative per capita transfers for education and health care for farmers and mixed [households] could be even lower than estimated. (1991, p. 23, n. 22)

It is difficult to make any correction, but it is quite possible that, when this is taken into account, the equalising effect of social benefits may be less.

Finally, there is the problem of *valuation*, which has been much discussed. The procedures described above allocate the total budgetary expenditure, assuming that the total value to households is equal to the total cost in terms of current public spending. There is however no reason to suppose that the value placed on the benefits by individual households will, in aggregate, necessarily coincide with government cost. Nor should any failure for these two values to coincide be taken as evidence of inefficient decision-making. State spending on education or health care may have characteristics of a *merit good* (Musgrave, 1959), where the social valuation differs systematically from the private valuation. Even where the total value coincides, the allocation by individuals may not coincide with receipt of the benefit. If for example there are external benefits from education or medical care, then other members of society should be credited with part of the gain. Pensioners may benefit from education even though no one in their household is in school or college. Even if the goods are purely private in their benefits, a collective decision process will not ensure that the amounts supplied are those that would be chosen by each individual household. An additional forint spent on education may be valued more by a particular household than an additional forint on health care, or the reverse.

It should be clear that the problem of valuation is a difficult one and that there are a number of approaches which could be adopted – see for example Smolensky *et al.* (1977) and Smeeding (1982). Suppose that there were to be agreement that the benefit should be valued in terms of the well-being of the recipient, or more precisely the amount of money which would need to be given to the household to keep it at exactly the same level of utility if the benefit were to be taken to away, known as the *equivalent variation*. It is not at all clear how this could be implemented in a situation where there is no significant market provision. In the case of medical care, we might interpret the procedures followed as ones in which the actual medical resources are valued; in contrast the UK procedure may be seen as attempting to measure the insurance premium that would have been payable in a system of private provision (if premia are related to the characteristics that are used to impute benefit in the statistical study). The treatment of education has to be dynamic, in that a major part of the benefit accrues in the future to the children, and a valuation of the future stream of benefits is not easily made.

Conclusions

In his comparative study of income distribution East and West, Morrisson (1984) cited evidence from Hungary which suggested that the inclusion of in-kind social benefits reduced inequality by the same amount (a two percentage point reduction in the Gini coefficient) as in the UK, the US and France. Our examination of more recent evidence for three Central European countries shows that there are indeed similarities in the general impact of social benefits in kind, but there are noticeable differences when we examine individual spending categories. Moreover, the difficulties in evaluating these benefits mean that any conclusion must be highly qualified.

6.2 Subsidies and indirect taxation

The extent of consumer subsidies in Communist countries have been at the forefront of discussion. According to the World Bank, 'subsidies are an issue of immense importance in Poland ... consumer subsidies represent some 10 percent of GDP ... This is an extremely high ratio by international standards' (1989, p. iv). According to the IMF *et al.*, in the USSR 'the containment of subsidies is recognized as a key component of any reform effort' (1991, Vol. 1, p. 268). In this section we consider the role of consumer subsidies.

It is of course rather artificial to focus, as we do, on the explicit direct subsidies to *consumption* and not to consider the impact of *producer* subsidies. The subsidy given to tinned fruit is considered but not the subsidy to the manufacture of the tin. Flour in Poland in 1987 received a substantial subsidy but there was no direct subsidy for bread (World Bank, 1989, p. 23). The dividing line between a production and a consumption subsidy may at times be difficult to draw. Moreover, the relative weight of producer and consumer subsidies varies across time and countries. In both Hungary and Poland in 1988 total consumer and producer subsidies represented about 15 percent of GDP, but in the former consumer subsidies accounted for about one-third whereas in Poland the figure was two-thirds (Abel, 1990, and World Bank, 1989, Tables 1.1 and 1.4). Producer subsidies were dramatically reduced in the early 1980s in Poland from around 18–20 percent of GDP in 1980/1 to 8 percent or less from 1982 onwards. As with other aspects of our analysis it is important to bear in mind that results that hold for one point in time do not necessarily apply to others.

Consumer subsidies are not unknown in Western economies. In the

1970s in the UK, in addition to the long-standing subsidies for housing, there were consumer subsidies on milk, butter, cheese, household flour, bread and tea. Total consumer subsidies allocated in the Central Statistical Office estimates were 3.6 percent of household disposable income in 1975 (1976, p. 108). Today there are no food subsidies and housing subsidies have been reduced, and, although subsidies on travel (concessionary bus and rail fares) are more important, the total is only 1 percent of disposable income (Central Statistical Office, 1991, Table 4 (Appendix 1)).

Subsidies may take the form of tax concessions rather than explicit subsidies, and these have been widely employed in Western countries. Prest and Barr refer to the 'shadowy distinction' between explicit and implicit subsidies, observing that 'in recent years it has been widely recognized that governments often prefer to give tax concessions rather than make outright expenditures' (1985, p. 15). A good example in the UK is the relief provided against income tax for the interest paid on mortgages taken out to purchase owner-occupied property. This nearly doubled in real terms between 1976/7 and 1989/90, while direct public spending on housing was halved (Hills, 1991, Table 3.1). This 'tax expenditure' does however appear in the distributional statistics as a tax reduction, so that it has already been taken into account in the figures considered in Chapter 5.

It is therefore on the impact of consumer subsidies in Eastern Europe that we concentrate here, particularly drawing on the systematic studies of their impact for Hungary and Poland in the late 1980s which have been undertaken by the World Bank or with World Bank finance (World Bank, 1989, and Kupa and Fajth, 1990). The calculations for Poland relate to 1987 and cover subsidies which came to 11 percent of GDP, including:

food	3.4%
housing	2.9%
transport	1.6%
energy	1.3%
health and medicines	0.9%

(World Bank, 1989, Table 2.1). The calculations for Hungary relate to 1989. The most important forms of subsidy, expressed as a percentage of the total, are:

housing investment	46.7%
heating	14.9%
medicine	11.0%
transportation	10.2%
rent	6.2%
dwellings	4.2%
food	3.1%

(Kupa and Fajth, 1990, Table 1.2.2./d).

In the case of Poland, the calculation starts by taking the total cash amount of the consumption subsidy for each good recorded in the state budget and dividing this by the total retail value (at the post-subsidy price) of sales of the subsidised good in state outlets (World Bank, 1989, annex 3, p. 1). This figure, which may be called the subsidy rate, is then multiplied by the recorded expenditure on the good in question for groups of households shown in detailed tabulations from the budget survey data (the Polish study did not use the micro-data). Call this figure 'imputed subsidy income' from the good in question. Summing the calculations across all subsidised goods gives the estimates of each household group's total subsidy income. A similar procedure appears to have been followed in the Hungarian study, but this was conducted at the level of the individual household (Kupa and Fajth, 1990, appendix, p. 5). (A slightly different procedure is suggested by KSH, 1989, p. 30.)

The results of the Hungarian study are shown in Figure 6.6 in terms of the concentration curve for subsidies. In contrast to the case with social benefits in kind, the subsidy concentration curves lie below the line of uniformity and therefore contribute less to reducing inequality. The concentration coefficient for all subsidies is 15 percent (World Bank, 1991c, Table 3.5). This *positive* value for the concentration coefficient is still less than the Gini coefficient for disposable income (23 percent), so that subsidies contribute, at least in total, to reducing overall inequality. The tendency for the value of the subsidy to rise with income is particularly marked for the housing investment subsidies. If these, and the medicine subsidy, are excluded, then the curve for consumption subsidies is closer to the line of uniformity (see Figure 6.6). The concentration coefficient for consumption subsidies, excluding housing investment subsidies, is 10 percent, which means that there is quite a large leverage compared with the overall coefficient for disposable income.

The Hungarian study shows that there is considerable variation in the estimated amount of subsidy as a proportion of disposable income. In part this is associated with life-cycle differences. In Figure 6.7, we show the concentration curves for four of the most important household types. That for inactive households is close to the line of uniformity. Within active households, there is a great deal of variation. The curve for households with no children exhibits considerable inequality, but where there are children, the subsidies are much more progressive, and the curve for active households with two children lies above the line of uniformity.

The results of the Polish study are presented in terms of concentration coefficients, and these are shown for the main subsidies and different household types in Table 6.1. Overall, the coefficient for all consumer subsidies is 12 percent. This implies a difference of some ten percentage points from the Gini coefficient for disposable income (also shown in the table), so that subsidies altogether make a sizeable contribution to progres-

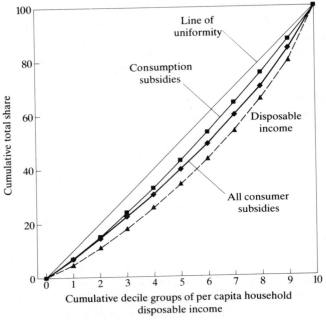

Figure 6.6 Distributional incidence of consumer subsidies in Hungary 1989
Source: Kupa and Fajth (1990, Tables 1.2.2/b and 39).

sion. This does however conceal a wide variation in individual subsidies, a point stressed by the World Bank (1989). Subsidies to families with have a negative coefficient, indicating that the lower-income groups receive more absolutely. These subsidies are evidently very redistributive. For food and medicines, the coefficient is positive, but less than the overall average. Food subsidies of 7 percent of disposable income contribute to Δ about one percentage point reduction in the Gini coefficient. For energy and housing the difference is smaller. For transportation, the overall coefficient is virtually the same as for disposable income, and we can see that there are big differences between farm and non-farm households. Finally, for culture (theatres, cinemas, etc.) the coefficient is higher than the Gini.

Valuation of Subsidies

These results are of considerable interest, but the calculation of the value of subsidies and their distributional incidence raises a number of problems which must be borne in mind, not least because these calculations may

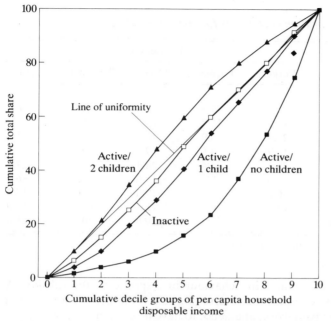

Figure 6.7 Distributional incidence of consumption subsidies by household types in Hungary 1989

Source: Kupa and Fajth (1990, Table 87).

influence the direction of policy in Eastern Europe.

How can the procedure of estimation be interpreted in the light of the theory of household behaviour? Figure 6.8 shows an individual household's choice between good X, which is subsidised and good Y, which is not. The good Y is taken to have a price of 1 (i.e. is a *numeraire*). In the upper diagram (Figure 6.8a), the line AB indicates the budget constraint faced by the household in the absence of any subsidy, the downward slope being p the price of X. The budget constraint in the presence of a subsidy for X is given by AC, where the downward slope is $p-s$, where s is the subsidy. The household chooses to consume at the point P. In effect the empirical procedure treats the value to the household as equal to the difference between its expenditure on X at subsidised prices and the cost at the price p. The 'imputed subsidy income' of the household estimated from budget survey data is given by AD in Figure 6.8a (using good Y as a numeraire). The amount depends on the household's choice along the post-subsidy budget constraint.

Calculations of this type are open to the criticism that no account is taken

Table 6.1 *Concentration coefficients for consumer subsidies in Poland 1987*

	Households				
	Workers	Farmers	Mixed	Pensioners	ALL
Subsidy:					
Foodstuffs	7.2	7.5	7.6	5.8	6.6
Energy	13.9	15.7	17.7	12.5	13.2
Transportation	23.0	3.9	14.4	21.9	21.1
Medicines	10.9	4.8	9.3	6.9	9.5
Culture	28.1	23.4	28.3	29.6	27.9
Family	− 5.6	− 12.4	− 15.0	− 27.4	− 6.0
Housing	16.5	19.8	19.6	12.4	14.9
All	13.2	10.2	11.7	10.6	12.0
Disposable income	22.2	22.4	20.6	21.0	21.8

Source: World Bank, 1989, Table 2.17.

of the household's change in behaviour in response to the subsidy. A subsidy is in this sense just the reverse of a tax. If an income tax causes a person to give up paid work, and hence to have no cash income, we do not conclude from the fact that the revenue is zero that the taxpayer is bearing no cost from the tax. In the case of a tax, we can measure the burden in terms of the compensating cash transfer required to keep the household at exactly the same level of utility as in the absence of the tax. In the same way, the value of a subsidy can be measured by the distance AE in Figure 6.8a, which is the amount (measured in terms of the numeraire Y) which would keep the household on the same indifference curve if the subsidy were abolished (see, for example, Rosen, 1985). (This is again the *equivalent variation* of the price subsidy.) This means that what we may call the 'true value', AE, of the subsidy to the household is overstated by the imputed subsidy income, AD. The extent to which the imputed subsidy is an overstatement is determined by the household's preferences, as indicated by the curvature of the indifference curve in the diagram.

For many subsidies, there is a limit X^* to the quantity which can be purchased at the subsidised price. This limit may be a formal one, incorporated into the regulations, although the effectiveness of such regulations depends on the extent to which individual consumption can be monitored. In this situation, the household may or may not be able to buy more of the good at the non-subsidised price. In the lower part of Figure 6.8 (Figure 6.8b), we show the case where further purchases may be made at price p, and where the household chooses to do so. It may be seen that in this

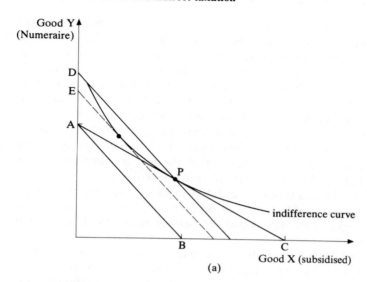

(a)

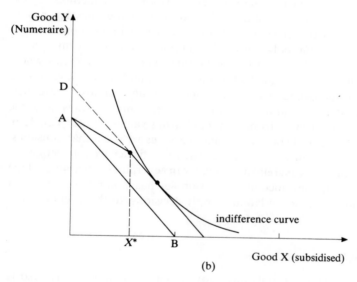

(b)

Figure 6.8 Valuation of subsidies.

case the value of the subsidy is indeed equal to AD. The subsidy on the X^* intra- marginal units of the good is just like a cash transfer of sX^*.

The limit on purchases at the subsidised price may arise not officially but on account of shortages, in which case a secondary, private market for X may develop in which the price is higher than the subsidised, or state, price. Where the situation is that shown in Figure 6.8b, with households purchasing the maximum X^* at the subsidised price and then making additional purchases at the higher secondary market price, the value of the subsidy is sX^*. This means that the correct imputation of subsidy income depends on an accurate identification of the mix of purchases at the subsidised and unsubsidised prices. It would be wrong to treat the entire consumption as having taken place at the subsidised price. If, for instance, richer households make a greater proportion of transactions in the secondary market, this implies that the egalitarian effects of subsidies is understated.

From this analysis, it is clearly necessary to examine the consequences of shortages and of access to goods at subsidised prices. These will be taken up again in Sections 6.3 and 6.4. Here, we end with two general methodological points. First, the evaluation of the welfare benefits of subsidies depends on the extent of departure from market prices elsewhere in the economy, and on the degree of monopoly power. The importance of the former in the Soviet Union is clearly recognised by the IMF *et al.*: 'in an economy where practically all commodity and factor prices are administered, the economic concepts of subsidies and taxes can become so broad as almost to lose their meaning, insofar as administered prices, wages, interest rates, and the exchange rate all deviate from market-clearing values' (1991, Vol. 1, p. 267). Secondly, it should be stressed that the issues are wider than subsidies, or social benefits, and that what is needed is a firmer welfare economic justification for the measurement of income in general. The treatment of the distribution of money income, for example, has not related observed earnings, which depend on labour supply decisions, to the level of utility generated.

Subsidies, indirect taxes and controls

Price subsidies are not the only way a government may influence prices so as to further distributional goals and a focus on subsidies to the exclusion of other methods may be misleading. Indirect taxes are an obvious example. In Eastern Europe consumer prices have been influenced by positive turnover taxes and a full study of the distributional impact of government price policy in pre-reform Eastern Europe would take into account the effect of these taxes in addition to that of the price subsidies (see for instance

Juhász (1979) on turnover taxes in Hungary in the 1970s). In the case of the USSR, it has been argued that:

the better-off win on the subsidies and lose to the poor on the turnover tax (calculated per capita) with regard to clothes (excluding knitwear) by 5 times, on knitwear 9–11 times, on shoes 12–15 times, on household goods 10–12 times, on furniture 8–9 times. However, the balance of distribution of subsidies and turnover tax to low and high income groups of the population shows that the major part (by 1.5 times) goes to the latter. (Rutgaizer, Shmarov and Kirichenko, 1989, p. 61 [translated by S. Marnie])

The distributional impact of indirect taxes can be estimated using budget survey data although the procedure gives rise to a number of conceptual difficulties similar to those we have discussed for price subsidies.

In addition, we need to consider the impact of price *controls*, as distinct from either subsidies or taxes. In an economy in which the state owns all sales outlets and stands to bail-out any in financial trouble, the distinction between a control and a subsidy may be considered rather academic. However, in an economy with a substantial private sector, this is no longer the case. Price controls may be general, as part of an anti-inflationary policy, or they may be specific and have distributional aims. Whereas, price subsidies by the state represent redistribution of income from tax-payers to consumers, price controls on private firms represent a redistribution of income from the firm's shareholders to consumers. An important instance in recent years in the UK are the controls put through the regulatory process on price increases of privatised public utilities such as water, electricity and gas. In effect, the state insists that a part of the monopoly profit is handed back to consumers.

A complete abolition of consumer price subsidies in pre-reform Eastern European countries would still have left their governments with instruments for manipulating prices to further distributional aims. One implication is that discussion of income distribution in the post-reform period needs to take account of the impact of these instruments. Moreover, it seems almost inevitable that some forms of control will be retained. Even in arguing for '*total liberalization of prices*' (p. 146) in the state sector (author's own italics), Kornai (1990) notes that there will be 'a few permanent exceptions' whose prices are regulated in most market economies and he cites public services and the output of natural monopolies.

6.3 Privileges for the elite and non-wage benefits from work

One of the features of the former USSR that has attracted considerable Western attention is the provision of substantial benefits in kind to a small elite group of top Party and government officials, army officers, managers, scientists, academics, etc. (see, for example, the study by Matthews, 1978). These included the provision of superior housing, provision of cars and chauffeurs, holiday homes (dachas), access to foreign currency for travel, access to foreign currency shops where imported goods could be purchased, etc. At the same time, non-cash benefits are not limited to the elite, and the more evident privilege at the top should be seen as part of structured pattern of differential remuneration. Bergson (1984, p. 1059) cites the example of the research complex near Novosibirsk where service workers were allocated apartments with 77 square feet per person, junior scientists received 97 square feet per person, senior researchers got an additional 216 square feet, and academicians were allocated a whole cottage. Particularly in the USSR, the 'quality' of the enterprise one worked for was a most important determinant of living standards independent of the level of earnings.

Non-wage benefits of this kind may appear unrelated to the rest of this chapter. However, there is a close connection. In a situation where enterprises were all state controlled, there was little difference in principle between enterprise and state provision of benefits in kind (even if there were considerable difference in the distribution). Benefits in kind for the elite may have been the 'incentive' side of state transfers in kind, which offset at least in part the 'equalising' elements examined in Section 6.1. Secondly, enterprise provision played a particularly important role in a shortage economy. Where enterprises could obtain supplies of scarce consumer goods, through barter with other producers, they were able to give their workers access to goods that would otherwise have been unavailable. Being able to purchase at state prices, via one's enterprise, a good in short supply could be a valuable benefit in kind. At the very least, it eliminated the need to queue. There is therefore a link with the next section on shortages and differential prices.

In the West, these benefits in kind are referred to as 'fringe benefits', but this should not be taken as meaning that they are necessarily small in scale or extent. Indeed, in a country such as Britain, minor 'perks' or better working conditions associated with better-paid jobs are so widespread as to scarcely warrant mention. Substantial benefits are available to top managers in the private sector. Eric Newby describes accepting a senior position in the early 1960s in the John Lewis Partnership, a large UK retail and wholesale supplier:

I soon discovered that I had become a member of a hierarchy within the Partnership which comprised the upper crust, and one which was able to indulge itself with a minimum of expenditure in pastimes that I had previously thought of as only being available either to the very rich or to members of the upper class. As a member of this hierarchy I could spend my weekends in a splendid country house in Hampshire, one that was equipped with good cellars and with excellent pheasant shooting and with some of the finest fishing in the world immediately outside its door. In summer I could go yacht racing in the Channel with other members of the upper hierarchy – none of the lower ones were ever present when I was a member of the crew. (1982, p. 192)

This does not seem very different from some of the descriptions of the privileges open to members of the nomenklatura in the former USSR.

Obtaining quantitative, rather than anecdotal, evidence about the scale and distribution of payments in kind is not easy. In Britain, the Royal Commission on the Distribution of Income and Wealth (1979) distinguished between 'welfare' benefits, generally available to all employees in a firm, including free or subsidised meals, sports facilities, and goods at discount prices, and benefits intended to attract and retain staff, particularly executives, which were concentrated at the top end of the earnings scale. The survey evidence quoted by the Commission showed 67 percent of executives with full use of a company car, 62 percent with free life assurance, 44 percent with free medical insurance, and 10 percent with low interest loans (1979, Table 9.9). The overall conclusion of the Royal Commission was that:

there is little doubt that if account were taken of employee benefits, working conditions and other aspects of employment, the dispersion of the earnings distribution would be increased. The effect within the top one per cent of employees must be particularly marked. (1979, p. 233)

In the mid 1980s over 80 percent of a sample of firms providing company cars reported using seniority as one of the criteria for receipt of this benefit (sometimes the only criterion) and at that time the purchase of company cars accounted for about a half of all new car sales (Ashworth and Dilnot, 1987, p. 24). The imputed value of this benefit has in part been subject to income taxation, although the government admitted that the position in 1988 was that 'a typical company car might be taxed on only about a quarter of its true value' (reported in Dilnot et al., 1991, p. 23), and it was only in 1991 that most of the tax advantages of this benefit were removed.

What is the likely impact of such benefits in kind on the degree of income inequality in Eastern Europe? One brave attempt to estimate the effect of benefits for the nomenklatura is that of Morrisson (1984 and 1985). He starts from estimates for the size of the 'privileged' population varying from 0.2 to 1.5 percent in the USSR and of 0.7 percent in Poland (1984, p. 125). As has been noted by several writers, adjustment for the missing income in kind of a group of this size would not affect the estimated decile ratio (P_{90}/P_{10}) or other percentiles below the elite group. (These measures *would* of course be affected by more generally distributed non-wage benefits received by those lower down the distribution.)

The shares in total income and the Gini coefficient would however be affected. In order to show what he believed to be the *maximum* impact of the special advantages of the 'privileged', Morrisson made an adjustment to the data on household income distribution for a number of Eastern European countries, including the four we consider in this book, by assuming that these advantages in every country represented at most half the recorded income of the top 5 percent of the distribution. Summary inequality measures of the income distribution were then estimated for each country with and without the adjustment for top incomes. In between these, Morrisson argues, 'the true distribution certainly lies' (1984, p. 126).

To treat the elite population as being as extensive as the top 5 percent seems to be casting the net wide. In contrast, Bergson (1984, p. 1070) takes the elite population as 0.3 percent of the urban population, and Morrisson himself refers to 1.5 percent (1984, p. 126n.). Here we present an alternative calculation, taking the latter figure to represent the elite population, and asking how large the payments to the top 1.5 percent would have to be for the Gini coefficient in Eastern Europe to be equal to that in the UK in 1985 (29.7 percent). It should be borne in mind that this can only be an approximate calculation since we are interpolating in an open upper interval to arrive at the share of the top 1.5 percent. (Also, since this is only an illustrative calculation, we use the linearised Lorenz curve drawn in terms of deciles to calculate the Gini coefficient.) The calculation shows that the increase in their income necessary to raise the Gini coefficient to the UK level would be around 125 percent in the USSR and Poland. We would have to more than double the income of the top 1.5 percent. In the case of Hungary, the income of the top 1.5 percent would have to be multiplied by a factor of some 4.5; for Czechoslovakia it would require a five-fold multiplication.

This calculation is clearly arbitrary, and attributes no value to what may admittedly be the lesser but nonetheless widespread non-wage benefits received by those at lower points of the income distribution.

6.4 Shortages and prices

At the start of the chapter we noted that the interpretation of information on money incomes depends on the ability to convert those incomes into goods and services at established prices. On the other hand, 'with prices below clearing levels, money income ceases to be the sole determinant of capacity to acquire goods; to a degree, fortitude in searching out supplies and standing in queues, and plain luck, become consequential' (Bergson, 1984, p. 1058). In this section we first present some of the evidence about the extent of shortages and differential prices across the Eastern European countries before examining the consequences for the interpretation of distributional issues.

Evidence of shortages

In the case of the USSR, the existence of shortages have been noted by many Western observers. Matthews (1986) reports his observations on the availability of food in Moscow in the summer of 1978:

some foodstuffs, including bread, certain milk products, cheese and butter, appeared to raise no problems. Eggs, sugar, biscuits and teas were reasonably plentiful, while tinned fish and vegetables, though expensive, were not hard to find. The purchase of anything over and above such staples, however, presented great difficulty. (1986, p. 60)

Shortages are attested not just by Western visitors, but also by official comments. Bergson quotes the report in the newspaper *Pravda* in 1979 of complaints regarding interruptions in the supplies of 'medicine, soap, detergents, toothbrushes and toothpaste, needles, thread, diapers and other goods produced in light industry' (1984, p. 1058). He goes on to say that, while shortages have persisted for some goods, they have only been intermittent for others. In more recent years it appears that shortages have become a major feature of economic life in the USSR.

Popular impressions regarding shortages in Eastern Europe are often dominated by the Soviet Union, but Poland is another country where there have been marked shortages. The extent of formal rationing has been described by the World Bank:

the range of rationed goods was especially wide at the beginning of the 1980s. The list of rationed goods in 1981–2 contained besides meat and sugar (rationed since 1976), butter and other greases, flour, candies and chocolates, cigarettes, vodka, soap, shoes and gasoline. Milk, bread, eggs, fruits and vegetables had never centrally fixed rations during the last period. The number of rationed goods was step by step reduced, going down to only two of them, i.e., meat and gasoline, in 1987. (World Bank, 1989, p. 5)

Shortages in Hungary at the beginning of the 1980s have been described by Farkas and Pataki who concluded on the basis of opinion poll evidence that 'it may be stated unambiguously that simple successful purchases requiring little energy and time are not typical in Hungary' (1984, p. 291). The respondents in the poll, interviewed in Spring 1981, reported that at that time milk and dairy produce were in best supply and then in order of decreasing availability:

detergents, washing ingredients and perfumery, household machines, durable cultural consumer goods, deep-frozen and semi-finished products, meat, fruit and vegetables, fuel, clothing articles for adults, small items needed every day, children's clothing articles, furniture, shoes and finally building materials. (Farkas and Pataki, 1984, p. 300)

The situation was nonetheless less serious than in the USSR or Poland, and there was an improvement in supply over time. Rationing did not occur as in Poland. Temporary acute shortages of particular goods continued through the 1980s such as soft tissue lavatory paper according to one report we were given and razor blades according to another. Some services were very difficult to secure, such as the installation of a telephone line. The serious shortages of building materials facing individuals wishing to build or extend their own homes appear to have persisted, but these types of goods cannot be considered as part of a normal consumption basket. In general, most consumption goods seem to have been in good supply in Hungary in the 1980s.

Differential prices

Shortages in official retail outlets are often associated with the emergence of higher free market prices in other outlets, which may be legal or illegal. According to the World Bank study for Poland referred to above, rationing of meat was accompanied by prices in the free market which were in 1988/9 some three to four times higher than the official price in state shops. In the USSR, on which we concentrate here, the differences between state trade prices and those in collective farm markets have been widely noted. Lubin gives a graphic description for the Central Asian republic of Uzbekistan:

In 1980, in the markets of Tashkent alone, there were more than 13,000 stalls selling fruit and vegetable products at prices often two to five times official retail prices. During the year I spent in Tashkent, the official price of meat was between two and three roubles per kilo; on the market, it was often sold for between eight and twelve roubles per kilo. Eggs, when available in government stores (an extremely rare occurrence), cost 15 kopeks each; on the market they sold for twice as much. (1984, p. 186)

Differences between the two sets of prices may be hard to assess in some cases. The account given of the situation in Tashkent by Lubin continues 'I never discovered the official prices of oranges or cottage cheese (*tvorog*), since they were never available in government stores during that entire year'.

Taking the former Union as a whole, official data show that the difference between collective farm market prices and those in state trade outlets rose very substantially between the early 1960s and 1990, with a sharp rise at the end of the period (IMF *et al.*, 1991, Vol. 1, p. 414).

However, the picture at any one time varied between and within republics and from product to product. For example, looking at official data for prices in May 1989, we see that the ratio of the collective farm market price for potatoes to that in state trade outlets was 7.8 in Moscow, 6.3 in Tashkent, 5.3 in Rostov (in the Russian Federation), but only 2.3 in Kiev (the capital of Ukraine) (*Statistickii Press Biulleten'*, 1990, no. 15, pp. 21–24). The ratios for onions in the same four cities were 3.88, 2.90, 6.55 and 3.55 respectively. The variation is caused principally by differences in the collective farm market prices, but not exclusively. McAuley notes that the Union was divided up into a number of price zones and the official state trade price in general increased 'as one moves north and east of Moscow' (1979, p. 115). In interpeting the differences between state trade prices and those in collective farm markets, it should be noted that there may be differences in the quality of goods between the two sorts of outlet.

An alternative to looking at official data on prices is to consider those recorded in survey data as being actually paid. Detailed information is indeed available on this in the former USSR. Household survey data show prices paid at different points in the income distribution in each republic (IMF *et al.*, 1991, Vol. 2, Table IV.6.16, pp. 207–209). At the same time, these data need to be treated with some caution, not least since they are drawn from the Soviet Family Budget Survey which we have described as being a rather low quality source. (The data may be found in more detail and given separately for worker/employee and collective farm households in Goskomstat, 1990a, Vol. 1, pp.106–117, and Vol. 2, pp. 124–135.)

It is tempting to interpret these data in the light of the discussion below of the distributional implications of shortages. There are factors which would lead us to expect prices to rise with income level and others that suggest that they should fall (and again there is the issue of variation in quality). However, as noted by the IMF *et al.* study, 'it is difficult to generalise' (1991, Vol. 2, p. 156). Even if we look only at the prices averaged across the whole distribution clear patterns do not immediately emerge. The average price paid for meat in 1989 is notably high in Uzbekistan, the republic with the second lowest average per capita income (see Table UI6), but the average price paid for vegetables is low in relation to those in Russia, Ukraine or Belarus for example. There is clearly substantial variation in prices across republics but it is not easy to summarise or interpret.

Distributional implications of shortages

If governments control prices and set these so low that supplies of goods are exhausted, then the implications of the resulting shortages depend on how goods are allocated. Effective rationing could be highly egalitarian. If ration points are distributed equally, and these replace money income in determining access to goods, then the resulting distribution of consumption should be less unequal than that resulting from market-clearing. The statistics in Chapter 5 would overstate the degree of inequality in consumption (although inequalities in money wealthholdings would be increasing).

Where the allocation process is based on queuing, this may again be equalising. It has been suggested that the opportunity cost of spending time in queues is less for the poor (for example, pensioners). While there are economies of scale in queuing, which reduce the average waiting cost per unit for the rich, this is countered by the fact that shops typically limit the amount that can be purchased per transaction (Stahl and Alexeev, 1985). Moreover, queuing is often regarded as a 'fair' process. In his review of principles for allocating scarce resources by institutions, Elster (1991) classifies queuing and waiting-lists as ranking high in terms of fairness.

There are, however, qualifications to this argument. First, there are discriminatory sales practices. Not all buyers are treated equally in the face of shortages. One of the significant non-wage benefits discussed in the previous section is that of access to goods in short supply. The most obvious case is the ability of the privileged to buy goods in closed shops unavailable to others.

Second, when goods are in short supply this is likely to lead to a secondary market in which much higher prices are established, as we have seen. This may occur either through resale of goods bought at official prices or through direct sales of production outside the official sector. In this case money regains its value and with detailed knowledge of the price structure and volumes of trade at different prices an interpretation may be put on the distribution of income although the ability to re-sell goods bought at the lower prices would need to be considered. However, shortages would continue to be seen as relatively egalitarian; people can still stand in line to buy at the lower price (although in this case the value of time spent queuing may become an issue which cannot be ignored). Or as put by Bergson, 'the tendency towards dampening of real relatively to money income differentials [brought about by shortages] should be mitigated but not eliminated' (1984, p. 1058).

Third, even the queuing in the primary allocation mechanism may cease to be seen as 'fair'. Places in a queue may be bought and sold. Morrisson (1985, p. 205) cites reports of old age pensioners and adolescents undertaking paid queuing on the behalf of others and we may also include in the category of sale of queue places the apparently widespread activity of tipping in order to secure a good in shortage. Employers may vary in their attitudes to absenteeism in order to queue. Queuing favours extended families which can practice division of labour.

Implications of shortages for price indices

Official calculations of price indices are of considerable interest in any study of distributional issues in pre- and post-reform Eastern Europe. Evidence of changes in real incomes may be used to indicate a decline or improvement of living standards. In general the official poverty lines in Eastern Europe described in Chapter 7 are updated for price increases; the quality of the index used has a considerable bearing on the extent of measured poverty. Social security benefits may be up-rated in line with movements in the price indices as has been the case with a number of benefits in the UK. In this case the quality of the index has an effect on actual as well as measured living standards. Social security benefits over much of the Communist period were not subject to regular up-ratings in line with consumer price inflation but indexing of key benefits may become an important feature of government attempts to secure acceptance of reform packages in the transition period. Finally, if different income groups experience different consumer price inflation rates then relative measures of inequality, such as those we used in Chapters 4 and 5, are not measures which are 'price-free'. Similarly, if different regions have different price structures, then identical summary statistics of the income distribution across regions imparts different information about the distribution of consumption opportunities. This is particularly important in the USSR in view of its size.

The shortages of consumer goods which we have considered above have important implications for the calculation of price and real income indices. As put by Kordos:

the real incomes index has a different meaning in the environment of a strong economic imbalance which dominated in Poland in the eighties than in the balanced economy. In the environment of a strong economic imbalance it provides information on the potential not actual purchasing power of the population. (1990, p. 5)

In the situation of shortages and secondary markets, it may still be possible to calculate real income, but the appropriate price index is one based on a mix of official and secondary market prices rather than the official price alone. This is particularly significant during a transition to a market economy, where the movement in an index based on official prices may overstate the effective rise in prices. In this situation a sharp deterioration of an index of money incomes deflated by an index of this latter sort would overstate the decline in real living standards. If poverty thresholds are indexed by changes in official prices then the rise in poverty will be overstated.

The failure to include secondary market prices in the price index can be expected to cause price inflation to be overstated in the transition period.

The reverse will have been true in the pre-reform period in times of worsening shortages if secondary market prices were not included, although when supply was improving inflation would have been overstated.

The quality of the price indices in practice in Eastern Europe have been the subject of review by Heston and Summers (1990) and Gardner (1991). The former (who exclude the USSR from their analysis) consider pre-reform Hungary to be 'at the more comfortable end of the spectrum ... with a price collection system involving a large sample of items [over 2,000] and outlets visited by enumerators' (Heston and Summers, 1990, p. 2). The collection of price quotations by visits to actual retail outlets is clearly an important feature of accurate collection of representative price data. The indices in Poland and Czechoslovakia are considered by Heston and Summers as intermediate cases, also with large samples of items and with that in Poland being less dependent on official prices than the Czechoslovak index. On the other hand, the official USSR index of state retail prices which was used for many years comes in for considerable criticism. This covered only state retail outlets and was based on official list prices rather than those actually charged during transactions with consumers. A new index introduced in 1989 appears to be a significant improvement since it does not rely on list prices, and prices in collective farm markets or secondary markets are now included.

Conclusions

Do differences in money income imply differences in standards of living? As we have seen in this chapter, this question arises even more acutely in Eastern Europe than in Western economies. The problems of interpreting evidence on the distribution of incomes are heightened by the system of pricing, distribution and reward. We have seen how the meaning of money income is affected where there are marked shortages of some goods, where rationing mechanisms operate in a way that has significant distributional consequences, where there is substantial subsidisation of consumer prices, where the state provides free of charge certain goods and services, and where some individuals receive notable non-wage benefits.

In considering the implications, it must be remembered that Eastern Europe cannot be treated as a bloc. The shortages or subsidies in one country, for example, have not necessarily been found in another. The quality of official calculations of price indices differs across the region. The interpretation we put on income data within Eastern Europe may well vary from country to country. Equally, there has been considerable variation in the picture when considering the distribution within a single country over time. Income in 1968 may not have meant the same as income in 1988 and this is important to bear in mind when considering trends in inequality.

At the same time, a number of these issues are similar in principle if not extent to those in Western countries. OECD countries provide substantial social benefits in kind and subsidise consumption of particular goods, such as housing and transport. Fringe benefits represent a significant part of executive remuneration. As a result, 'in the appraisal of equity . . . the ideal is hardly realised anywhere' (Bergson, 1984, p. 1057). This may lead some readers to reject the whole project of attempting to measure the extent of inequality. However, for those who attach importance to the question of distribution, the only satisfactory response is to allocate more statistical and analytical resources to the resolution of these difficulties, or the evaluation of their consequences. The development of methods for comparing distributional outcomes is important not just for the historical question of comparing Communism and capitalism. The comparison of the post-1990 distribution with that prevailing under the Communist regime is going to raise many of the same problems as the comparison of East and West pre-1990.

7   Measuring poverty

Poverty was for many years a subject of great sensitivity for the Communist governments of pre-reform Eastern Europe. This is true even in countries where there was substantial published information on the inequality of earnings and household incomes. Poverty was treated in a different light from inequality. It was regarded as one of the distinguishing features of capitalism, and 'it was an official conviction that one of the great achievements of socialism was to combat [poverty] effectively and for ever' (Szalai, 1989, p. 1). Of the USSR, Matthews wrote in 1986 that 'public discussion of poverty as such is virtually banned in the USSR itself, and even specialist Soviet writers cannot easily broach it' (1986, p. xi).

This does not mean that the subject was not investigated. There is indeed a long tradition of work on subsistence minima in the USSR. A notable study is the book by Sarkisyan and Kuznetsova (1967), of which 10,000 copies were apparently published (Matthews, 1986, p. 208). This refers to calculations having been made in 1956/7 of normative consumer budgets, showing the minimum required for material security, established as part of the planning process. Their book contained further calculations of subsistence minimum levels made in 1965.

Alongside the discouragement of public discussion of poverty, there was therefore research in the USSR on social minima. This meant that the opening up of the subject with *glasnost'* could draw on existing work. When Gorbachev issued in May 1991 a Presidential Decree (reproduced in Table 7.1) ordering the calculation of minimum consumer budgets which were to be used for policy purposes, he was not breaking new ground in terms of research. What was new was the publicness of the discussion. The *USSR Yearbook '90*, for example, published in English, French, German, Spanish and Swedish, reported that 'nearly 40 million people live below the poverty line' (p. 279), a figure given publicity by Prime Minister Ryzhkov at the first Congress of People's Deputies, held in June 1989.

In Hungary, the Central Council of Hungarian Trade Unions made

Table 7.1 *Presidential decree on the subsistence minimum, USSR, May 1991*

Article 1
Minimum consumer budgets are to be worked out for the country as a whole, for republics and regions; they are to be used for forecasting changes in the standard of living of the population, defining the minimum wage, pensions, benefits, grants and other social payments and also state expenditure on food in hospitals, hostels, schools, nurseries, etc.

Article 2
The selection of goods and services in the minimum consumer budgets will be defined for various social-demographic groups. In establishing minimum consumer budgets, average purchasing prices will be used.

Article 3
The consumer basket will include:
food products, clothing, medicine and chemist items, furniture and household goods, housing and local services, cultural and holiday services, everyday services, transport and communications, nursery school places for children.

Article 4
The minimum budget will be reviewed at least once a year, taking into account growth in the index of consumer prices; at least once every 5 years, the composition of the consumer basket will be reviewed.

Source: Izvesitiia, 22 May 1991, translation by S Marnie.

poverty estimates in 1955/6, but 'many people debated the necessity of such calculations under socialist conditions, and the series was dropped' (Salamin, 1991, p. 2). Other poverty calculations were carried out in the central statistical office in 1968, and a survey on poverty was conducted by Kemeny in 1969, following up the households in the lowest income decile of the 1967 Income Survey (Salamin, 1991). But publication of both the results of his survey and of his calculations in the early 1970s of subsistence minima were forbidden. Similarly, analyses were made by Benda and Vita of the composition of the bottom decile in the 1977 Income Survey, but the circulation of their manuscript even among social scientists was prohibited (Szalai, 1989, p. 1). Calculations of social and subsistence minima, however, were made again by the Central Statistical Office from 1984.

In Czechoslovakia, calculations have been made of social minima since the middle of the 1960s. Hiršl and others during the 1970s worked on low income households (for example, Hiršl, 1971b, 1971c), and some of the findings were made available in English (Hiršl and Kučerák, 1978).

In Poland, Kordos notes that the notion of a social minimum had been an issue since 1956, observing that it 'usually caught public attention after each social crisis' (1991, p. 8). He reports the first publication of calculations of the social minimum as being in 1957, but in the years 1970–1976, the Polish Central Statistical Office calculations 'were confidential results meant only for the state authorities' (Kordos, 1991, p. 8). The Gdansk Accord of 1980 between Solidarity and the Polish government led to the official establishment of a 'social minimum' income level (Flakierski, 1991, p. 97). These calculations were made and published in 1981 by the Institute of Labour and Social Affairs, and the subject was widely debated in the press (Kordos, 1991, pp. 8–9). Publication of the level of the minimum ceased following the introduction of martial law in 1981 and was not re-started until 1988, but calculations continued to be made throughout this period.

The opening up of public discussion about poverty in Eastern Europe has received prominence in the West. The *World Development Report 1990*, devoted to the subject of poverty, gives figures for Poland based on the Institute for Labour and Social Affairs social minimum (World Bank, 1990, p. 108–109). A background paper for the report contains in addition estimates for Hungary and Yugoslavia (Milanovic, 1990a). The study of the Soviet economy by the IMF, World Bank, OECD and EBRD reports the estimates for the USSR, including the variation across republics (IMF *et al.*, 1991, Vol. 2, p. 154).

The evidence from Eastern Europe does indeed invite comparison with the West. The figure of 40 million poor in the USSR is strikingly similar to the widely publicised one of 44 million in the European Community (O'Higgins and Jenkins, 1989) – an area with broadly similar population. The IMF *et al.* study compared the ruble poverty line applied in the USSR with the $370 a year cut-off used in the *World Development Report 1990*, according to which 33 percent of the population in developing countries was regarded as in absolute poverty (World Bank, 1990, p. 28). Using data from the Israeli and American surveys of emigrés from the USSR, Ofer and Vinokur have examined the results of applying the relative poverty standards used in studies by the OECD, the European Community and others, concluding that their comparison:

does not show that the first 'socialist' society has any advantage. On the contrary, the number of Soviet households that lived in relative poverty in the 1970s was higher than in Sweden, Norway, the Netherlands, the United Kingdom, Belgium and the Federal Republic of Germany, and lower than in the United States, Canada, Italy and Ireland. (Ofer and Vinokur, 1992, p. 250)

Such conclusions about poverty in Eastern Europe – whether seen in absolute terms, or comparatively – raise many questions. What do we mean by 'poverty'? How can a poverty line be established? How can we choose between absolute and relative poverty lines? Is there any sense in which the figure for 40 million poor in the USSR is comparable with that of 44 million for the European Community? It is evident that the answers to these questions involve matters of judgment. The choice of a poverty line is a matter about which people can legitimately disagree. It is equally evident that the answers given will vary from country to country, reflecting their past history, their culture, their dominant social values, and the economic context. Such differences arise within the European Community, where the Rowntree tradition in Britain differs from the French notion of 'precariousness' which differs in turn from the emphasis in Dutch research on subjective evaluation. Such differences arise between West and East. To the extent that this happens, differences in reported poverty rates may be as much a reflection of differences in the measuring rod as of real differences in circumstances.

This chapter is concerned with issues of methodology, rather than with substantive findings. We seek to bring out the distinctive features of the definition and measurement of poverty in Eastern Europe. We begin however with the measurement of poverty in Western countries. Let us suppose that there had been no analysis of low incomes and subsistence and social minima in pre-reform Eastern Europe. What choices might be suggested by the voluminous literature on the analysis of poverty in the West? This is the subject of Section 7.1. The choices that *were* made in Czechoslovakia, Hungary, Poland and the USSR in the pre-reform period are the subject of Section 7.2. The special issue of the treatment of household composition is addressed in Section 7.3. In all three of these sections we try to make clear where the different circumstances of East and West call for different approaches. Movements in poverty lines over time are analysed in Section 7.4. How should our criterion of poverty change with time? This methodological discussion provides the underpinning to our use in the next chapter of the estimates of poverty incidence, and composition, in Eastern Europe based on the official, or semi-official, poverty lines.

We restrict ourselves in this chapter to analysis of income, expenditure and the consumption of private goods. Our lack of treatment of other factors must be recognised as an important omission. The *World Development Report 1990* noted the importance to 'welfare' widely defined of 'health, life expectancy, literacy, and access to public goods or common property resources. Being able to get clean drinking water, for example, matters to one's standard of living, but it is not reflected in consumption or income as usually measured' (World Bank, 1990, p. 26). On these grounds, the Report supplemented conventional poverty measures with measures of other social indicators. Sipos (1991) draws attention to similar indicators in

Eastern Europe and in addition underlines the impact on living standards of environmental pollution. For reasons of space we do not discuss these aspects of living standards, but this should not be taken as implying that we believe them to be unimportant.

7.1 The study of poverty in Western economies

What can be learned from the Western analyses of poverty that is relevant to its measurement in the Communist countries of pre-reform Eastern Europe? To make the question concrete, suppose we were to start with the dollar values of the official US poverty line. In this calculation, based on the work of Orshansky (1965), the cost of a minimum needs food basket is multiplied by the reciprocal of the share of food in net household income. The calculation is made for different family types. Converting these dollar values to domestic Eastern European currencies at purchasing power parity exchange rates, and using data on the distribution of household incomes in the Eastern countries of the kind examined in Chapter 5, we could then calculate the number of poor people in Eastern Europe according to the US official poverty line.

Such an exercise would certainly be of interest. It would provide an estimate of the number of persons in the pre-reform Eastern European countries who would be considered poor by one well-known Western standard. But it would raise a number of issues which need careful evaluation. There are technical questions concerning the method. What is the appropriate exchange rate at which to convert? What is the appropriate concept of income and time period for its measurement? There are questions concerned with the differences between the economic and social context. Do shortages of consumer goods mean that a poverty line based on income has little meaning? Is the American treatment of the needs of families of different size appropriate in societies where there is more widespread provision of social benefits in kind? There are fundamental questions about the meaning of poverty that arise in any society. Is poverty concerned with standards of living or with command over resources? Is the standard an absolute one, or one that is relative to the circumstances of a particular society at a particular date?

Income, expenditure and goods

The first point to be made about the measures of poverty considered here is that the identification of poverty is assumed to be based on the objective circumstances of the household and not on the household's own assessment of its level of well-being. The measurement of poverty is concerned, in this approach, with the resources and not with the welfare of the family in question. For those approaching the subject from a welfare–economic perspective, it may be described in the terminology of Sen (1977) as a 'non-welfarist' approach. It is neither necessary nor sufficient that a household feels itself to be deprived. This is not of course to deny that the feelings of deprivation, exclusion or frustration associated with low levels of resources may be a powerful reason for our concern in the first place.

This approach based on observed indicators of resources can be criticised as essentially 'paternalist'; that it represents society imposing its own valuation – a further indignity for the poor. Since such paternalism might be associated in the minds of readers with a Communist but not with a democratic state, we should emphasise that such an approach has been the traditional basis for the investigation of poverty in Western countries. The main exception is the work of van Praag and colleagues on perceptions of poverty (for example, van Praag *et al.*, 1982 and Hagenaars, 1986).

Observed indicators of poverty may take a variety of forms, and three broad approaches may be distinguished:
(a) consumption of specific goods,
(b) total expenditure,
(c) total income.
Under the first of these, we specify required amounts of a bundle of goods, $X^* = X^*_1 \ldots X^*_n$, and label as poor all those whose consumption fails to reach any of the individual required amounts in the bundle. This gives a multi-dimensional indicator of poverty. People are poor unless they consume at least the minimum amount of each item in the bundle. They are poor if they have too little to eat, have inadequate housing, or are ill-clothed. In the context of developing countries, such considerations have been discussed under the heading of 'basic needs'.

The alternative to such a multi-dimensioned approach is to seek to reduce the analysis to a single indicator, as has been common in studies of poverty in OECD countries. (Recent reviews may be found in Atkinson, 1989, and Callan and Nolan, 1991.) From the list of minimum requirements, X^*, we could calculate the cost of purchasing them at prices P, to arrive at a minimum level of spending:

$$E^* = P \cdot X^*$$

One can interpret in these terms the poverty standard developed by Orshansky (1965) for the United States, where the $P.X^*$ was based on the value of food requirements and the total requirements were reached by dividing by the estimated share of food in total spending:

$$E^* = P \cdot X^* / \text{share of spending on food}$$

The problems in implementing such an approach are considered below.

The approach just described identifies people as poor on the basis of their *expenditure*. There is however a choice between expenditure, and *income* as the indicator of poverty. Views differ as to whether we are concerned with low income or low spending, yet this fundamental distinction is rarely made explicitly and people often change from one to the other. The European Community calculations began by using income (see O'Higgins and Jenkins, 1989), but later, with little comment, switched to expenditure (Eurostat, 1990). The distinction is an important one, since people may have low-income but be able to maintain expenditure by borrowing or drawing on savings. Budget studies commonly report significant dissaving by low-income groups, and the poverty count on the basis of expenditure may be lower than that using income. It is possible that low expenditure in part reflects choice and in this case income may exceed expenditure: 'to *choose* not to go on holiday or eat meat is ... of no interest to those concerned with poverty. To have little or no *opportunity* to take a holiday or buy meat is entirely different' (Piachaud, 1981, p. 421).

The choice between income and expenditure may be seen as depending on whether we are concerned about a household's *standard of living* or about its *right to a minimum level of resources*. Are we concerned with how far they actually enjoy a specified level of consumption or with their entitlement, as citizens, to a minimum income, the disposal of which is a matter for them? That these can lead to different results is illustrated by the fact that, until recently, the official poverty line in the US was higher for men than for women. On a standard of living approach, it may be defensible to set differing minima, reflecting differing nutritional requirements, but on a rights approach such differentiation would be hard to justify.

The Western choice between these different approaches – consumption of specific goods, total expenditure, or income – may or may not be relevant in Eastern Europe. The choice is above all a matter of social judgment, and this involves wider considerations. Thus, the right to a minimum level of income may be seen as a pre-requisite for participation in a democratic society, with this having priority over other distributive principles. Or, considerations of equality between the sexes may preclude setting different minima for men and women, even though food needs may be different. But the choice also depends on the economic environment. Most importantly, when moving to an Eastern European context we have to take account of the implications of multiple markets and shortages of goods. With state price controls, and private markets, the price of a basket of goods may vary greatly depending on access to the different markets. In an economy with shortages, income may exceed expenditure because of forced saving due to the absence of goods to purchase. The shortages may be sufficiently severe to warrant a definition of the poverty line based on the consumption of specific goods.

The level of the poverty line

The application in Eastern Europe of the US official poverty line, or the World Bank \$370 line, might be interpreted as an *absolute* measure of subsistence needs, independent of the time and place to which it is applied. The search for an objective basis for such an absolute standard has however proved elusive. The following quotation from Marx is familiar but here perhaps particularly appropriate: 'the number and extent of [a worker's] so-called necessary wants...are themselves the product of historical develop-ment and depend, therefore, to a greater extent on the degree of civilisation of a country' (quoted by Coates and Silburn, 1970, p. 24). As numerous other authors have held, there can be no such thing as a single absolute poverty standard. Subsistence needs must reflect in part the standard of living of the country in which those needs are being assessed.

In the case of the American poverty line, its originator noted that 'there is no generally acceptable standard of adequacy for essentials of living except food' (Orshansky, 1965, p. 5). This explains the rationale for the use of food requirements, multiplied up by the inverse of the food share, but it also brings out how the poverty standard can be affected by the level of development. The average food share in net income can be expected to be higher in Eastern European countries due to their lower level of develop-ment. This would imply a lower poverty standard than one based on average food shares in the US.

In principle, a minimum cost diet can be derived from specified require-ments of nutrients and information about the nutritional content of different foodstuffs and their prices. This is often seen as a merely technical matter. The *World Development Report 1990* describes how 'a consump-tion-based poverty line can be thought of as comprising two elements: the expenditure necessary to buy a minimum standard of nutrition and other basic necessities and a further amount that varies from country to country' (World Bank, 1990, p. 26). The calculation of the first part is seen as 'relatively straight-forward', but in practice this is far from the case. There is room for genuine difference of opinion between experts on matters of nutrition. Moreover, it has long been known that the minimum number of calories can be purchased at a total cost much below people's actual food spending (Stigler, 1945).

Account has to be taken of actual eating habits: 'even with food social, conscience and custom dictate that there be not only sufficient quantity but sufficient variety to meet recommended nutritional goals and to conform to customary eating patterns. Calories alone will not be enough' (Orshansky, 1965, p. 5). The US poverty line indeed starts from an 'American-style' diet. Rowntree included tea in his original subsistence diet for British households, despite its absence of nutritional value (Atkinson, 1983, p. 226). Equally, if expert opinion about the health consequences of different foodstuffs differs from conventional eating habits, it is not evident that the former should prevail in the construction of minimum diets. If people persist in eating meat rather than cheaper lentils, their actual nutritional intake may be below the desired standard even though they could in principle afford the expert diet.

It is apparent that the idea of a purely scientific, indisputable, basis for a subsistence income is illusory. It is a matter of judgment and, as Rein explains in the American context, of political realities:

The first working definition of poverty used by the Council of Economic Advisors [CEA] established the extent of American poverty at about 34 million persons, or roughly one-fifth of the population. More refined estimates, if they were to be politically acceptable, had to be consistent with CEA's estimate ... As a consequence, technical decisions ... have come to reflect not only our understanding of the meaning of subsistence but also the political views and realities which provide the framework for professional judgements. (Rein, 1970, p. 56)

On this basis, the application to Eastern Europe of the US official poverty line, or any other Western line, would be a political judgment, made consciously in the light of its likely implications for the size of the poverty population. There is circularity in that the poverty standard is set with an eye to the likely outcome.

At the opposite extreme from an absolute approach is one that is expressly *relative*. In the official calculations for the European Community, a household is considered poor if its income (or expenditure) is less than 50 percent of the national average. This is the basis for the figure given earlier of 44 million poor persons in the Community in 1985 (O'Higgins and Jenkins, 1989). A household in Spain is classified as poor if its expenditure is less than half of the average for all Spanish households. The difference in the level of economic development between Spain and Germany, for example, is not reflected in the calculation of the number of poor Spaniards.

The relative approach has the virtue of making explicit the choice that has to be made, but the cut-off of 50 percent remains again purely a matter of judgment. A basis for such a judgment may be sought in the determination of the scales for social transfers that perform the function of a social safety net. There is indeed an important difference between countries such as the US, where the poverty line has no direct connection with the social security system, and countries such as the UK, where the social assistance level has commonly been taken as a poverty standard. Until 1988 this was indeed the basis for the official estimates of the number of 'Low Income Families' (Department of Health and Social Security, 1988). The role in the

UK of Income Support (previously Supplementary Benefit, and before that National Assistance) is to provide a minimum level of resources, and the choice of this level indicates the effectiveness of the safety net. (The choice also has practical implications where there is a bunching of people at the Income Support level, since the inclusion or exclusion of those at the safety net level can make a considerable difference to the estimated proportion in poverty.) Table BP1 in the Statistical Appendix shows the social assistance rates for different family types.

The adoption of a benefit level as the poverty cut-off may be treated as the 'revealed preference' of the government for a poverty criterion. On the other hand, it fails to distinguish between the targets and achievements of policy (Atkinson, 1991c). The determination of transfers will reflect a trade-off with other objectives and benefit levels may be constrained by consider-ations of costs or incentives. A government may set one target as an aspiration, while recognising that it cannot immediately be achieved, and it is the aspiration that it is relevant to the measurement of poverty.

Geographical scope

Looking to the future may also suggest going beyond the *national* average income in selecting a point of reference. The European Community is developing into a political confederation, with some common social goals including redistribution of income between the Member States. It might be argued that this should be reflected in the use of a *Community* average in the calculation of the incidence of poverty in the Community, and this has been done in the calculations of Eurostat (1990). A household is poor if its expenditure is less than half of the Community average. This would result in higher incidence of poverty in the poorer Member States and a lower incidence in richer ones. The poverty line in Spain, for example, would represent two-thirds of the national average rather than one half as before (Atkinson, 1991a). Another possibility would be to take a weighted average of the national and the Community average as the basis for the calculation. This would reflect both the differences in the levels of development across the Community as well as the notion of social cohesion between the constituent countries.

The European Community is obviously very relevant to Central Europe. If Hungary, Poland and Czechoslovakia are to join the European Community at a future date, the official Community poverty line in those countries could be set with respect only to their own national averages. On the other hand, the calculations could reflect the goal of raising living standards in these countries towards the average level in the existing members of the Community. The former USSR raises the same problems in reverse. If we were to measure poverty pre-reform in the USSR on the same basis as in the European Community calculations, should we take 50 percent of the all-Union average household expenditure as our poverty line or should the line be expressed relative to the average in each constituent republic? As we have seen in Chapter 5, there are substantial diferences in average incomes between republics. Put another way, should the break-up of the Union mean that we switch overnight from the all-Union average to a national figure?

The household, the family and the individual

Statements about poverty typically refer to individuals: there are 40 million poor *people* in the USSR. What this means however is that there are 40 million people living in *households* whose average income (or expenditure) per capita is below a poverty line. Adoption of the household as the unit of analysis appears to be standard practice in Eastern Europe, and this applies to the estimates discussed below, but it should be recognised that there has been considerable debate in the Western literature as to the appropriate choice of unit. A narrower unit could be defined in terms of blood relationship or marital relationship, or of dependence.

The social assistance scale in Britain refers to the inner family, i.e. excluding any grown-up children or other relatives in the household. The same applied to the official calculations of 'low-income families' made in Britain up until 1988, but since that date the official figures have referred to 'households'. The effects of the adoption of this wider definition have been investigated by Johnson and Webb (1989), who estimate that the proportion of the British population with income below 50 percent of the mean in 1983 was 11.1 percent on the inner-family definition and 8.1 percent on a household basis. In other words, the adoption of a wider unit could lead to a significant decrease in measured poverty.

The choice of unit depends both on social judgments and on the empirical question as to the degree of sharing within the household. If our concern is with standard of living, then some items of spending, like housing, have the attributes of public goods for individual members of the household and the benefits may be fairly equally shared. Other items may be essentially individualistic and there may be considerable inequality *within* the household. The same applies on a minimum rights interpretation of poverty, which is essentially individualistic. Questions then have to be asked not just about the income transfers within the household but also about the conditions on which they are made. Transfers from children to elderly parents, for example, may only take place if the old person lives with the children and may induce dependence. The difficulties in obtaining information about relations within the household, or about the distribution of consumption benefits, is however such that we typically have to treat the household, or the family, as a unit. At the same time, we should recognise that, in ignoring intra-household inequality, we may be misrepresenting the extent and nature of poverty, as is shown by Haddad and Kanbur (1990) in the context of a developing country.

The structure of the poverty line

A calculation of poverty in Eastern Europe based on the US official poverty line would impose not just a particular *level* of the poverty line but also a particular *structure*. This applies most obviously to the treatment of household size. As we have discussed in earlier chapters, a variety of equivalence scales have been employed to adjust for differences in household size and composition. These differences stem in part from the differences in conception that we have already identified. A standard of living measure, based on a food budget and food shares, will depend on how nutritional needs vary with composition. How do the minimum food needs of a child of ten compare with those of an adult man? A minimum rights measure could, in the limit, lead to a per capita scale.

Not only are the scales different, but so too are the results. Buhmann *et al.* (1988) examined the sensitivity of the proportion below 50 percent of the median income in the nine OECD countries then included in the Luxembourg Income Study. Depending on the scale applied, the UK ranked third or sixth (out of nine) in terms of the poverty count. With one scale, the elderly account for some two-thirds of the poor in West Germany and the UK, whereas with a scale similar to that applied by the OECD the proportion is a little over one third. The choice of equivalence scale appears to affect both the extent and the composition of the low income population.

This means that if different countries use different equivalence scales in their official poverty lines then another dimension is added to the comparison of poverty between countries. If a country gives generous benefits in respect of children then it may record low child poverty if the equivalence scale used in its poverty line treats children as being close in their needs to adults. This may not be true if the equivalence scale from another country is used which gives a lower weight to children. Alternatively, if the country's equivalence scale gives less weight to the elderly then the proportion of the poor who are old may appear much less than that in another country using a different equivalence scale. Differences in demographic composition between counties could exacerbate the comparison. The relation between the equivalence scales East and West is discussed in Section 7.3 below.

One of the factors influencing equivalence scales is the role of housing costs, and this item as a whole has been the subject of much debate. In Britain, in his analysis of the problems of calculating subsistence needs, Beveridge considered housing costs (which he equated with rent) as being one of 'Three Special Problems':

Rent has three characteristics differentiating it from other forms of expenditure: (i) rent varies markedly from one part of the country to another; (ii) rent varies markedly as between different families of the same size in the same part of the country; (iii) expenditure on rent cannot be reduced during a temporary interruption of earning as that on clothing, fuel or light can. (Beveridge, 1942, p. 77)

As a result, the Sub-Committee helping Beveridge, which included the pioneers in poverty measurement Sir Arthur Bowley and Seebohm Rowntree, concluded that in the calculation of a subsistence minimum 'in regard to rent ... no single figure can be justified on scientific grounds as fitting the needs' (Beveridge, 1942, p. 77). The implication is that the measurement of poverty should be on the basis of income (or expenditure) *net of housing costs*:

In the social surveys which have been made shortly before the present war of living conditions in various British towns, Mr Rowntree and others, in judging subsistence needs and estimating what proportions of the population are in poverty or in varying degrees above it, have invariably and unavoidably allowed for the actual rent paid by each family. (Beveridge, 1942, p. 79)

The British social assistance scheme in general makes separate provision for the costs of housing, and studies of poverty, such as that of Abel-Smith and Townsend (1965), have repeated the pre-war practice of looking at income net of housing costs.

The measurement of poverty net of housing costs is not typical of Western practice and the relevance of the British example to pre-reform Eastern Europe may be limited by the differences in housing markets. The large variations in housing costs noted by Beveridge for Britain in the 1940s may not be representative of those in Communist countries, where the state may have been able to achieve a greater equality in housing costs through its ownership of large segments of the housing stock and where the levels of rent were low. On the other hand, the shortages of housing meant that the free market price for housing could be very high for those at the margin. And the issue may become of increasing relevance as a result of the liberalisation of housing prices during the reform process.

Conclusions

Two main conclusions may be drawn from this section. The first is that there are several different dimensions to the measurement of poverty, with choices to be made concerning the indicator of poverty, the determination of the poverty line, the scope of geographical coverage, the choice of unit of analysis, the equivalence scale, and the treatment of housing. The second is that there is a wide variety of practice in Western countries and that within these countries there have been significant changes over time.

7.2 Poverty lines in pre-reform Eastern Europe

There have been, as we saw earlier, calculations of social minima in all four countries studied here. In this section we consider these in turn. The comparison of *method* is our main focus. The comparison of the *results* is more difficult, and we limit ourselves to expressing the minima as a proportion of median earnings for all workers. (In the next chapter we consider how many persons had income beneath these minima.) As a point of reference, we may note that on 6 April 1988 the Supplementary Benefit scale in Britain represented 22 percent of median earnings for a single active person and 28 percent for a single pensioner. (Earnings are calculated net of National Insurance contributions and income tax liability for a single person.)

USSR

There is a long tradition of minimum budget studies in the USSR. The 1918 RSFSR Labour Code made explicit reference to the establishment of a subsistence wage and, according to Matthews (on whose work we draw extensively here), this:

gave the investigation of family budgets an almost constitutional justification. In 1918 standard minimum budgets were worked out ... primarily for industrial workers. The main problems of compilation were practical, rather than conceptual. The cost of many items, particularly foodstuffs, varied greatly ... chronic shortages and the inexorable march of inflation soon made nonsense of most statistical data. (1986, p. 15)

Three-quarters of a century later, these problems have a contemporary ring. Matthews goes on to say that:

as the economic crisis deepened, economists found it expedient to replace the assessment of a subsistence minimum with that of a selection of food items only ... Only in the mid-twenties did rising living standards enable budget calculations to be expanded again to include non-comestibles. (1986, p. 15)

According to Matthews, the calculation of subsistence minima was suspended towards the end of the 1920s.

The calculation of standard minimum budgets in the USSR was revived by Khrushchev in the mid fifties, when a number of research institutes were requested to prepare subsistence minima as part of the framework for the 1959–1965 Seven Year Plan (see McAuley, 1979, p. 18, and Matthews, 1986, p. 19). This research was summarised in the budgets published by Sarkisyan and Kuznetsova (1967), referred to by Matthews as the 'Khrushchev' Minimum Budgets and which are reproduced in Table UP1. In addition to the 'current minimum', there was also a 'prospective minimum' and a 'rational budget'. The prospective budget looked to the future possibilities which 'expanding production would bring for broadening the circle of minimal essential needs, whose satisfaction requires a higher family income' (quoted in Matthews, 1986, p. 21). The rational budget looked even further into the future, being set at a level some three times the current minimum.

In the 1980s new work was undertaken. In 1987 Goskomtrud and Goskomstat were required to define and publish annually a minimum subsistence level (Rimashevskaia, 1990). The food elements in the budget were based on norms worked out by the Institute of Nutrition for twelve sex–age groups of the population (Gur'ev and Zaitseva, 1990). According to these authors, the calculation of the cost is based on the average actual prices paid in state and cooperative trade, as well as taking account of prices on collective farm markets. The selection of non-food goods and services is based on expert evaluations and on actual expenditure of families with a low per capita income. The resulting figure calculated by Goskomstat in 1988 was 78 rubles per month, or 84 rubles taking account of collective farm prices. For 1989 the figure was adjusted to 81 rubles, or 87 at collective farm prices. These represented 45 percent and 48 percent, respectively, of median gross earnings for all workers, a proportion which is about double that for the single active person in Britain. Separate figures were calculated for different family sizes and structures (age, sex and type of employment) and different geographical regions. The latter are important and it should be emphasised that the figure of 78 rubles represented a national average.

Czechoslovakia

Calculations of subsistence and social minima for different household types in Czechoslovakia have been made since the middle of the 1960s. (The history and method of the calculations is given in Hiršl and Kučerák (1978) and Hiršl (1990b).) At that time, a minimum standard was determined for a single pensioner at 1967 prices (Bútora, 1969). This was based on estimates of necessary food consumption determined by nutritional experts plus requirements for clothing and footwear based on actual expenditure by pensioner households plus other items ascertained directly or taken from observed budgets (Hiršl and Kučerák, 1978, p. 57). The 1967 estimate was in turn the basis for the estimates of Hiršl (1971a), who made use of an equivalence scale estimated in 1966/7 by Moravová (1966) to arrive at minima for other household types. Minima for 1970 were reached by multiplying by average per capita income growth in 1967–1970. Subsequently, a second concept – the subsistence minimum – was set as 75 percent of the social minimum.

It was observed that in 1970 the social and subsistence minima equalled 56 percent and 42 percent respectively of average expenditure per adult equivalent. As a result, since 1970 the minima in each year were set as 56 and 42 percent of the adult equivalent net income. Total per capita income was calculated as the sum of per capita net income indicated by macro statistics and of per capita income in kind recorded in the Microcensus. It was then divided by the average adult equivalent per person, based on the demographic structure of the population. The resulting calculations are given in Table CSP1. The subsistence minimum figure for a single active person for 1988 was some 40 percent of median earnings (taking a broad average of the figures for 1987 and 1989), and the social minimum was over 50 percent. For a single pensioner the figures were lower, the subsistence minimum being virtually the same percentage as Supplementary Benefit in Britain (28 percent) and the social minimum being 36 percent.

An alternative approach described by Hiršl and Kučerák (1978) made use of a minimum food basket and a regression analysis of the relation between actual food spending and household cash income. The social minimum is the amount of cash income which is consistent with actual food spending equal to the minimum food basket. According to the authors, this 'underlines the social character of the minimum levels of living' (Hiršl and Kučerák, 1978, p. 60). We understand that this led to very similar levels of the social minimum (Pekník and Kučerák, 1974).

Hungary

As part of its work on poverty in 1968, calculations of social minima had been made by the central statistical office (KSH). This social minimum or 'minimum of socially justified needs':

was considered as an income which is an income adequate to meet not only the conventionally accepted basic needs, but (assuming rational economic behaviour) it also incorporates the acceptable, though modest satisfaction of needs . . . that are widely justified by the society at the given general economic, social and cultural level. (Salamin, 1991, p. 2)

It was based on a basket of goods and services. Later in 1972 the KSH investigated the use of regression analysis of household budgets (Salamin, 1991).

In 1984 the KSH began making regular calculations of a social minimum level of income, with retrospective results being derived for 1982. (The results were published for the first time in the 1987 statistical yearbook.) Two calculations are made. The higher is the 'minimum of socially justified necessities' or *social minimum*. The second, the *minimum subsistence level*, is:

an income lower in amount than that of the social minimum, rendering possible merely to satisfy the very modest necessities conventionally qualified as essential to ensure continuous living. (*Statistical Yearbook* 1987, English–Russian edition, p. 328)

Most attention in Hungary has focused on the lower line, the minimum subsistence level. Our description here is of the method used up to 1989 in which year there was a marked change in methodology.

The calculation began by establishing a minimum cost food basket for a number of different household types. (The description here draws on a note by Éltető (1990).) The Hungarian Research Institute for Food and Alimentation determined the energy and nutritional needs (protein, carbohydrate, fat and various vitamins and minerals) of different types of persons (e.g. child of a certain age, active adult, inactive adult) and the content of about 150 different food-stuffs. The total minimum cost of attaining the given nutritional needs was then determined subject to constraints on the food-stuff contents and to upper and lower bounds of quantities of these foods in 'typical' Hungarian diets as indicated by consumption levels in the Budget Survey.

The second stage of the calculation was a regression of food expenditure on income net of housing costs using micro-data on households with below average per capita income in the Budget Survey. (This regression was run separately for households with and without an active earner.) The resulting relationship was used to work back from necessary food expenditure to the subsistence minimum income net of housing costs for each household type. This is similar to the alternative method described for Czechoslovakia.

The final stage was to add observed actual average housing costs (both rent and mortgage interest) of households of the relevant size and type with below average per capita income in the Budget Survey. The resulting figures for 1982–1989 are set out in Table HP1. In 1986 the minimum subsistence for a single pensioner represented 46 percent of median earnings, and the social minimum was 53 percent.

Poland

The Institute of Labour and Social Affairs (ILSA), part of the Ministry of Labour, first calculated the social minimum level of income in 1980 and has done so every year from 1983 onwards. A calculation was made each quarter and a summary annual figure was also produced. Figures are produced for four different types of household composition (see Tables PP1 and PP2).

The social minimum was composed by pricing a basket of goods under seven headings (see Table PP2), the basket having been fixed in 1983 (with the exception of the meat standard for adults which was reduced in the period 1984–1988 when shortages of this good were widespread). The food standards for the different household types were specified by nutritional experts; the housing standard was taken as the rent on a state-owned apartment. The basket was priced using official price indices supplied by GUS with the exception of the most important item, food, which we were informed was priced using actual prices recorded in the Budget Survey. The standard is adjusted over time for price changes on a quarterly basis. In September 1988 the social minimum for a single active person was 51 percent of median earnings, and that for a single pensioner was 46 percent.

Comparison

The poverty lines in the four Eastern European countries have a number of similarities. Like the US official poverty line, they are quite independent of social security benefits and they are based on a basket of goods. Despite the standard of living orientation of the derivation of such a basket, the scales are applied to total incomes rather than total expenditure. The unit of analysis is the household. In all countries the scale for a single-person household appears to be nearer a half of median earnings than the figure of a quarter found in the UK. As is brought out by Milanovic (1990a), this difference may be due to the fact that there is no direct link with benefit payments or it may be associated with the lower level of development. Alternatively, it may reflect different social preferences.

But there are also differences. The food minima vary, which is not surprising in view of our earlier discussion of the difficulties in choosing even this most basic item in a subsistence basket. For example, Salamin (1991 p. 9) notes that the current minimum in Hungary is based on a daily intake of 2,700–2,800 calories for a person of working age (with separate figures for other nutrients), whereas calorie intake for the worker in the Khrushchev budgets varied from 3,361 in Central Asia to 4,033 in the Far North (Sarkisyan and Kutznetsova, 1967, p. 86, and Matthews, 1986, p. 55) reports variation also by family member. In the USSR, Poland and Czechoslovakia, the basket covers all goods, rather than being a multiple of food spending; in Hungary and Czechoslovakia (alternative calculation) the minimum is arrived at by a more sophisticated version of the food share method used in the US based on regressions of food spending on income.

The Hungarian calculation gives a special place to housing costs. There are differences in the equivalence scales implied by the different minima, and these are the subject of Section 7.3. There are differences, discussed in Section 7.4, in the procedures for up-rating the minima over time, the explicit indexation to per capita net income for example being a distinctive feature of Czechoslovakia. Despite similarities, the pre-reform measures from Eastern Europe illustrate some of the variations in approaches to measurement of poverty which always occur.

Comparison of the minimum budgets

We now turn to a more detailed comparison of the scales in different countries, beginning with the composition of the minimum budgets. In the case of the Polish social minimum and the Khrushchev minimum budgets from the USSR of the 1960s, we know the share of food and of the other main expenditure headings in the calculations. Table 7.2 shows the breakdown of these two minima for comparable family types: urban worker families with two adults and two children. (Details for other family types and also for 1989 are given for Poland in Table PP2 in the Statistical Appendix and the composition of other Khrushchev budgets in Table UP2.) Matthews has argued that the Khrushchev budget was 'strongly characteristic of an advanced industrial society' (1986, p. 19). But as he himself went on to point out, there are distinctive features of its composition which 'reflected many specific constraints of Soviet reality'. The high share of food expenditure – over 50 percent – was noted as one of these. The share of food is vitually the same in the Polish social minimum budget of 1989, and would be higher still if the calculation excluded the item 'other expenditures' which is a 10 percent addition to the total of the items higher in the table.

Matthews argued that the share of food in the budget would have been lower if other items had been priced 'at capitalist rates'. We may note the low share of housing in both budgets. This reflects the low housing costs for many persons in pre-reform Eastern Europe due to substantial subsidies. (We return to the issue of housing costs below.) But 'capitalist' pricing would also have led to a rise in food costs, since where these were incurred at official prices there was a substantial subsidy. The net impact is unclear. The food shares in both budgets in part reflect the level of development of the pre-reform Communist economies of Eastern Europe. This was substantially lower than that in many Western countries and, as has been widely observed, food shares fall with the level of development. (This is reflected in the lower food shares in the other Khrushchev budgets in Table UP2 in the Statistical Appendix which were prepared for projected higher average standards of living.)

Table 7.2 *Composition of Polish social minimum in 1983 and 'Khrushchev' minimum family budget, circa 1965*

Urban worker family with two adults and two children: percent of budget allocated to various headings

	Poland, 1983		USSR, c.1965
Food	57.6	Food, bought meals	55.9
Clothing, shoes	14.5	Clothing, footwear	20.9
Housing	10.2	Housing, communal services	5.4
Hygiene, health	2.7	Toiletries, medicines	2.2
Culture, education	2.4	Culture goods, sportswear	1.3
		Cinema, theatre, etc.	1.7
Transport, communications	3.4	Transport, post, telegraph	2.3
Other expenditures	9.2	Furniture, household goods	2.6
		Holidays, various services	1.4
		Hairdressing, baths, laundry	2.3
		Membership fees, other expenses	1.2
		Tobacco, alcoholic drinks	2.7
TOTAL	100.0	TOTAL	100.0

Source: Tables PP2 and UP1

Account has also to be taken of the inability of households to reproduce the linear-programming required to arrive at the calculations of the least cost nutritional diet. Their budgets may not exhibit the 'rational management' assumed in the Hungarian calculations. This may be a particular consideration in economies marked by shortages. As asked by Boldyreva, 'how can our budget be rational when everything is scarce?' (1989, p. 94). As in the West, the insistence on purchasing certain items due to dietary custom must be allowed for. The food minimum at the base of the Hungarian subsistence and social minima take account of 'typical' Hungarian diets. The Khrushchev budget allowed for 'the actual eating habits of the population' (Sarkisyan and Kutznetsova, 1967, p. 88 [translation by S. Marnie]). It also contains an explicit allowance for tobacco and alcohol. Matthews argues that this allowance is 'unrealistically low' (1986, p. 20) but it could be argued that there should be no place for these items in a subsistence minimum.

We have noted the low share of housing costs in the Polish social minimum and the Khrushchev budgets and the existence of substantial subsidies to housing in pre-reform Eastern Europe. Such subsidies applied evidently to rented accommodation, but costs for owner-occupiers may have been no higher, since in a number of Eastern European countries there were subsidies through low interest loans. At the same time, the problem of the diversity of housing circumstances discussed in Section 7.1 is a real one in Eastern Europe. The assumption made in constructing the Polish minimum that housing costs can be represented by the rent of a state-owned flat household is described as 'far from reality' (Kordos, 1991, p. 10). The allowance for housing in minimum budgets almost certainly underestimates the costs by a substantial amount for those with neither their own home nor secure tenancy of state housing. In other words, the costing does not reflect the general problem of housing shortages in Eastern Europe. For this reason the calculation of the minima in Hungary in the 1980s by the Central Statistical Office took average actual housing costs of those households with below average per capita income, as we have described.

Shortages, variation in prices and geographical differences

At the root of the problem of housing costs is the idea that the price varies in an unavoidable way across households, and that this defies the selection of a single price with which to cost the good. With this exception, little attention is paid in Western countries, such as Britain, to the choice of prices, P, used to determine the cost of the subsistence basket of goods, X^*. The shortages of goods in Eastern European countries makes this an important issue as we have already noted. Goods may be available on the free market but at a cost greatly in excess of those in state outlets. It might be argued that, given adequate data, the price vector, P, should be set as a weighted average of state and free market prices. The weights could be determined, for example, by the volume of trade at each set of prices of low-income households. But if a particular household has expenditure in excess of the critical level, E^*, solely because it has been forced to make a higher than average proportion of its purchases of scarce goods at free market prices, should it be considered as being above the poverty level? The analogy with housing costs would suggest not.

The types of prices used in practice in the construction of the Eastern European poverty lines have varied from country to country and with the type of expenditure heading concerned. In Hungary, the minimum food requirement was costed with a mix of official and 'free' prices, and the relationship between food expenditure and net income, together with the housing cost element, were both estimated with Budget Survey data recording purchases at actual prices. In Poland, the cost of the food basket was based on prices of actual purchases recorded in the Budget Survey, with other prices taken from the official retail price index. In the poverty line announced in 1989 in the USSR, a distinction was made between the value of the basket calculated at state prices and the higher value at a mix of state and collective farm market prices. The difference was some 7 percent.

Variation in prices geographically means that minimum standards may need to vary by city or by region, and this may be accompanied by differences in requirements associated with differences in climate. This is likely to be particularly important in the USSR, where the application of a single Union-wide poverty line would make little sense if concern is with the standard of living achieved. The same applies within the vast area of the Russian Federation.

This was well recognised by the authors of the Khrushchev budgets. The budgets for 1965 reported by Sarkisyan and Kutznetsova were constructed for nine different regions of the Union for the single worker and for four regions for the family of four (1967, p. 9). For each region, the calculations were made for one or two republics or for a selection of provinces (oblasts) considered typical. The relative cost of the minimum budget for the single worker in the nine regions is shown in Table 7.3. There are clearly substantial variations. Commenting on reasons for the differences, Sarki-syan and Kutznetsova noted that:

the difference in the various levels of price differentiation is significantly greater than the difference in the basket of the food products. Non-food products show the opposite tendency. There is an insignificant difference in prices, but a significant difference in the composition of the basket, especially in the regions with specific natural-climatic tendencies. (1967, p. 86, translated by S. Marnie)

Table 7.3 *Cost of 'Khrushchev' minimum family budget in different regions relative to Ukraine*

	Ukraine = 100
Central oblast (territory)	114.8
Ukraine	100.0
Central Asia	95.6
Kazakhstan	116.2
Urals	118.8
East Siberia	123.6
Far East	133.8
Iakutsk ASSR and Magadanskaia oblast:	
(a) regions with equal status to Far North	152.5
(b) regions of the Far North	181.8

Source: Sarkisyan and Kutznetsova, 1967, Table 18, p. 85, figures without taking tax payments into account.

The calculations in the late 1980s by Goskomstat of minimum budgets also varied by region but we do not know the details.

7.3 The treatment of household composition in poverty lines

We have discussed at length the treatment of household size and composition in the measurement of household incomes. We have demonstrated, for example, how through the selection of different equivalence scales one can gain different impressions about the extent of inequality of household incomes or of differences in inequality between countries. The issue is no less important when we come to the measurement of poverty. The choice of an equivalence scale has a direct impact on the size and the composition of the group labelled as poor. In this section, we examine the treatment of this issue in Eastern Europe, compared with that in Britain. As will become clear, there are some interesting differences.

Poverty lines from Eastern Europe are sometimes presented in terms of per capita income amounts for different family types, but this does not imply that the equivalence scale used to produce the line for each type is on a per capita basis. The poverty lines in pre-reform Eastern Europe show considerable departures from a per capita scale, as is clear from Table 7.4, which assembles the equivalence scales implied by the poverty lines from

Table 7.4 *Equivalence scales in Czechoslovakia, Hungary, Poland and the UK*

	Czecho-slovakia	Hungary	Poland	UK SB	UK HBAI
Scale with single pensioner = 1.00					
Elderly Households					
Single person	1.00	1.00	1.00	1.00	1.00
Couple	1.93	1.71	1.77	1.60	1.64
Active age households					
Single person	1.45	—	1.12	0.79	1.00
Couple	2.67	2.36	—	1.28	1.64
Couple with 2 children	4.05	3.77	3.72	1.82	2.40
Scale with couple + 2 children = 1.00					
Active age households					
Single person	0.36	—	0.30	0.43	0.42
Couple	0.66	0.63	—	0.70	0.68
Couple with 1 child	0.83	0.85	—	0.85	0.84
with 2 children	1.00	1.00	1.00	1.00	1.00
with 3 children	1.16	—	—	1.15	1.16
with 5 children	1.48	—	—	1.45	1.48

Note:
Czechoslovak figures refer to the subsistence minima in 1988. Hungarian figures refer to the subsistence minima for urban households in 1988. Polish figures refer to December 1987. UK SB figures refer to Supplementary Benefit in 1988 and in the case of active age households refers to the situation where the household head is unemployed. The HBAI figures are those before deduction of housing costs. Children in the UK calculations are taken to be on average aged 8–10.
Sources: Statistical Appendix Tables CSP1, HP1, PP1 and BP1, and Hiršl and Kučerák (1976), pp. 63–64, and Central Statistical Office (1990, p. 111).

Poland, Hungary and Czechoslovakia. The information we have for each country differs in detail. We show in the table the equivalence scales for the two households types for which we have information for all countries: a single elderly person and a household with a head of working age containing two adults and two children. For comparison we show the equivalence scale implicit in the British Supplementary Benefit scheme in 1988 and that used in the official study *Households Below Average Income*.

In all three Central European countries the poverty line for households with the head of active age is higher than for elderly households of the same size. However there are notable differences between the countries. The social minimum for a single person of active age in Poland is only 12 percent higher than for a single pensioner, whereas in Czechoslovakia the difference between subsistence minima for these two household types is 45 percent. Hungary would appear to be an intermediate case, but nearer to the Czechoslovak position: the active couple with no children have a subsistence minimum which is 38 percent greater than that of an inactive couple (the minimum for a single active person is not given in this source). There are also differences between the treatment of household size within the two types of household, active and elderly. Czechoslovakia makes less allowance for economies of scale among the elderly than the other two Central European countries, with the scale for a couple being nearly double that for a single pensioner. This does not apply in the case of the active population, where in Poland the scale for an active family of four is 3.33 times that of a single person compared with 2.78 times in Czechoslovakia.

Comparison with Britain

How do the Central European equivalence scales compare with those applied in Britain? In Table 7.4, we show in the first column for the UK the Supplementary Benefit (SB) scale for families of different types. The second column shows the scale applied in the official study of *Households Below Average Income* (HBAI). The latter differs in that it is the scale applied to income before deduction of housing costs. It is therefore more directly comparable with the Eastern European scales, in that the SB scale is exclusive of housing costs (as discussed in Section 7.1). It should be noted that in both cases the scale varies with the age of the children, and we have taken children on average aged 8–10.

The most obvious difference in Britain is that the poverty line for the active household is *less* than that for an elderly household of the same size in the case of the SB scale, or the same in the case of the HBAI scale, whereas in Eastern Europe the active age households receive a higher allocation. The single active person has a poverty line 21 percent lower than a single pensioner which may be compared with the 45 percent addition in the case of Czechoslovakia. If the poverty line were the same in cash terms for a single pensioner, then the SB scale for a single unemployed man would be only some 54 percent of the scale for his counterpart in Czechoslovakia.

Why is there this difference? The SB scale in Britain refers to the amount of social assistance provided to a person who is unemployed (the same rate also applies to active age heads other than the unemployed, receiving social assistance for less than a year.) The assistance scale in turn reflects a variety of considerations. In the pre-war social security system in Britain, unemployment benefit and sickness benefit were set at a higher level than the retirement pension. The justification in terms of different subsistence needs was examined by Beveridge, who concluded that the subsistence require- ments of people of active working age were greater than those of the retired – by 6.5 percent, comparing single men (Beveridge, 1942, paras. 222 and 225). Nonetheless, Beveridge noted the 'strong public opinion in favour of securing for the aged something more than bare subsistence' (1942, p. 98), and the scales were, following his recommendation, set at the same rate in 1948. However, in 1966 a long-term addition was introduced with Supple- mentary Benefits, specifically excluding the unemployed, and from 1973 there was a higher long-term scale rate. This feature of the assistance system, attributable to concerns with cost and incentives to work, reflects the conflicting considerations which influence a scale derived from social security benefits, as opposed to one which represents purely a social objective.

The second feature of the comparison with Britain is that in general there are greater economies of scale with respect to household size built into the British social assistance figures. The scale for a pensioner couple is 60 percent more than for a single pensioner, compared with over 70 percent in Poland and Hungary, and 93 percent in Czechoslovakia. The scale for a couple with two children is 2.33 times that for a single active person, compared with 2.78 times and 3.33 times respectively in Czechoslovakia and Poland. (The variation with different numbers of children appears to be similar between the four countries, although the UK scale does vary with the age of the child.)

In the USSR, the Khrushchev budget for an urban family of four in the 1960s was 51.4 rubles per capita per month. According to McAuley, the equivalence scale was not given in the original (Sarkisyan and Kuznetsova, 1967) but he estimates from another source that the budget for a single worker was 58.20–59.40 rubles a month (1979, p. 18). This implies a scale of 3.46–3.53 for the family of four relative to the single worker. The estimates of Kapustin and Kuznetsova (1972) for the cost of subsistence in the central provinces in 1969, including direct taxes, give values of 247.72 rubles per month for a family of four and 81.94 rubles for a single worker (McAuley, 1979, Table 5.6). The ratio is close to 3. On this basis, in the USSR too there is substantially less allowance for economies of scale.

The reasons for these differences with household size between the scales of Britain and the Eastern European countries are not easy to explain. As already noted, the basic amounts of the British social assistance benefit are not intended to cover housing costs, so that we cannot look for an explanation in terms of larger housing costs relative to total expenditure in Britain leading to greater economies of scale. Moreover, the HBAI scale is similar and it refers to income before housing costs.

Differences in equivalence scales

The analysis by Buhmann *et al.* (1988) suggests that the differences may lie in the methods employed. They distinguish four types of approach:

(a) *expert statistical*, where standards of minimum adequacy are applied for statistical purposes,

(b) *expert programme*, where scales are used to calculate benefits for social protection programmes,

These two correspond to the distinction we have drawn between minimum targets and benefit scales; to these Buhmann *et al.* add

(c) *observed consumption*, where scales are derived from observed differences in consumption by households of different sizes,

(d) *subjective evaluations*, based on questionnaire evidence on the income necessary to achieve specified levels of well-being.

Buhmann *et al.* (1988) find that in general the resulting equivalence scales give more weight to economies of scale as we move from (a) to (d). As explained in Chapter 3, they summarise the differences by expressing the number of equivalent adults as H^γ where H is the number of persons in the income unit and γ is a parameter measuring the elasticity of household 'needs' with respect to household size. They characterise equivalence scales used in statistical work by the OECD and other bodies by an elasticity of 0.72, whereas those used in policy-making – embodied in social security benefit scales or in official poverty lines – are lower (around 0.55). Relating these to the present discussion, the scales for a four-person household in Czechoslovakia and Poland would give values of 0.74 and 0.87, respectively, which are in the expert statistical range and above, as are the values implied by the scales for the USSR. The SB scale in Britain corresponds to a value of 0.61.

The values based on observed consumption patterns tend to be lower, and Buhmann *et al.* (1988) take 0.36 as representative, and those based on subjective evaluations (of what is needed to 'get by') have relatively low values for the elasticity (around 0.25). This suggests that other methods may give rather different equivalence scales, and this is illustrated by an interesting series of studies in Poland. Szulc (1991) takes the value of the social minimum calculated by the Institute of Labour and Social Affairs (ILSA) for a single pensioner household as the starting point for the poverty line but estimates his own equivalence scale on the basis of econometric analysis of consumption patterns using micro-data from the Budget Survey for 1987 and 1988.

The estimate by Szulc of the difference in needs between active and inactive households is similar to that implied by the ILSA scale. Needs for single-person household with head aged 16–29 and 30–44 are higher by 15

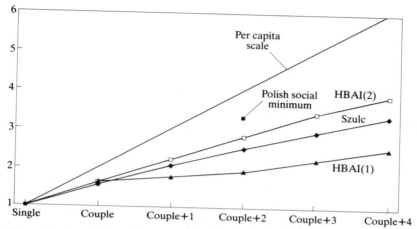

Figure 7.1 Comparison of equivalence scales in Poland and UK

Notes: The Szulc scale relates to urban households where the head is aged 30–44.

The two HBAI scales relate to different ages of children. HBAI(1) assumes that the children are spaced one year apart aged up from 0; HBAI(2) assumes that they are aged down from 18.

Sources: Table 7.4, Szulc (1991, p. 80) and Central Statistical Office (1990, p. 111).

percent and 16 percent respectively than that of a person living alone age sixty-five or over (1991, p. 80). The comparable figure in the ILSA scale shown in Table 7.4 is 12 percent. (Both sets of calculations refer to urban households.) However, there are considerable differences between the two scales when it comes to household size. Szulc estimates the additional needs for a two-person elderly household to be only 61 percent compared with 77 percent in the ILSA scale. A couple with two children with the head aged 30–44 is estimated to have needs 2.53 times those of a single person aged 30–44 living alone. The ILSA figure is 3.33 – see Figure 7.1. The estimates of Szulc may be compared with those in the British HBAI scale, as is brought out in Figure 7.1. The British scales depend on the age of the children and we have shown two cases: a lower line where the children are aged 0 and upwards at one year intervals and an upper line where they are aged 18 and downwards. It may be seen that the Szulc estimates are bracketed by the two British scales.

In Poland there has also been a recent study based on subjective evaluations (Podgórski, 1991). Compared with the ILSA social minimum, the subjective poverty lines derived in this study are higher for small households and typically lower for larger households. They do therefore conform to the picture of Buhmann *et al.* in that they embody greater economies of scale. For employees' households, the scale for a four person household is 2.05 times that for a single person (Podgórski, 1991, Table 4.3). This corresponds to a value of around 0.5 for the parameter γ, so that the degree of economies of scale is still less than that in Western studies summarised by Buhmann *et al.* (1988), a finding that Podgórski attributes to the difference in the level of development. It may also be noted that the differential between the subjective scales for employees' households and those for pensioners is wider (some 30 percent).

The subjective evaluation approach has also been used in Hungary, where the results of Baranyai and Salamin indicate again that there are less substantial economies of scale than in the Western poverty lines. The scale for a household of a couple with two children and an active earner is 2.78 times that for a single pensioner (Szalai, 1989, Table 3), compared with 2.66 in the estimates of Podgórski for Poland. Comparison of the results of applying an evaluation approach in Czechoslovakia with those found in the US leads Večerník to conclude that 'children are not cheap in Czechoslovakia' (1991b, p. 7).

Conclusion

The equivalence scales which have been applied in Eastern European differ in giving a higher allowance to active workers than to inactive, rather than lower as in the British social assistance scale, and in giving greater weight to the needs of larger households. There are also differences between countries, with for example Czechoslovakia having a larger differential than Poland for active households. This implies that care is needed in comparing analyses of the poor in the different counties based on the poverty lines concerned. For example, other things being equal, one would expect to see a higher share of active households among the 'poor' in Czechoslovakia.

The differences in the scales may in part, but only part, be related to differences in the methods used to arrive at the scales. The use of observed consumption behaviour or subjective evaluations tends to produce scales in Eastern Europe which rise less with size. But the choice of method is in itself a matter of judgment, and we regard the differences as an expression of the revealed preferences in these countries. There may be particular features of the pre-reform Eastern European countries that required the use of a scale quite different to that found in the West, such as the lesser importance of housing costs, which may be expected to change with the transition process. But there may also be a greater social weight attached to the needs of families with children, a feature which may continue to be present in the post-reform period.

7.4 Changes over time in the poverty line

The movement over time of poverty lines is a subject of considerable interest. If the rise or fall of poverty is taken as an indicator of the effectiveness of changes in government policy towards those on low incomes, then the answer will in part depend on the choice of adjustment of the poverty line over time. Whether or not poverty has been increasing in Eastern Europe may depend on how the goalposts have been moved from year to year. In particular, we may distinguish between indexation to *prices* and indexation to *average wages or incomes*. Does the poverty line preserve a constant real value over time, or is it a constant percentage of average incomes?

Practice in Western countries varies. The use of 50 percent of average income as a poverty cut-off in the European Community means that it is automatically indexed to average income. As the Community gets richer, so too the poverty line will rise in real terms. If there is no change in the distribution of income, then the proportion of the population which is poor will remain unchanged.

In contrast, in the US the official poverty line has been indexed in line with prices. Between 1960 and 1988, the poverty line for a family for four rose by exactly 300 percent (US Department of Health and Human Resources, 1990, Table 3.E1). Personal income per capita, on the other hand, grew during this period by 649 percent, more than twice as much (*Statistical Abstract of the United States*, 1978, Table 725 p. 449, and 1990, Table 706, p. 437). In 1965 the official poverty line was 46 percent of the median income for a family of four; by 1986 it had fallen to 32 percent (Sawhill, 1988, p. 1076). If the relative distribution had remained unchanged, then this growth in income relative to the poverty line would have led to a fall in the official poverty count. Conversely, if the poverty line had been indexed by average incomes the proportion of persons classified as poor would have been considerably higher. The 1990 *Statistical Abstract* shows that setting the poverty line higher in real terms by only 25 percent in 1987 would have led to an increase of one third in the number of persons classified as poor (Table 744, p. 459).

Views regarding the poverty line change over time. The social assistance level in Britain has been adjusted with changing economic conditions and political decisions. Between 1975 and 1980 the 'long-term' social assistance rate (applicable to pensioners amongst others) was indexed by law to whichever was the faster rising of prices or earnings. Since 1980 the link has been with prices, with consequences that may be seen from Figure 7.2, which shows the movements in the social assistance rate for a single person (taken at the point of up-rating) and average earnings (for all workers).

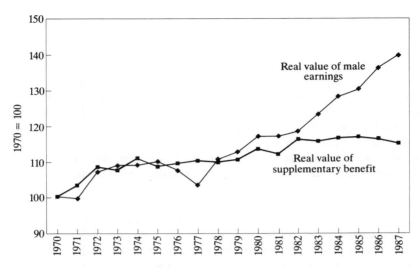

Figure 7.2 Real value of supplementary benefit scale and earnings in Britain 1970–1987

Note: The supplementary benefit scale relates to a single householder, ordinary (not long-term) rate.

Source: Social Security Statistics (1989, Table 46.11).

With the exception of 1981, average earnings rose in real terms in each year from 1978 to 1988. The cumulative rise between April 1977 and April 1988 was about one third. During the first half of the period, the social assistance scale rose at least in line with earnings, but in the early 1980s it levelled off in real terms. The real value of the social assistance scale in 1988 was only a few percent above that in 1977. The effect of the change in policy has been to convert the assistance scale from one rising in line with earnings to one that represented a declining fraction of average earnings over time. The change reflects a shift in political opinion as to whether those on low income should share in rises in average earnings.

How did the poverty lines in the pre-reform period from the Central European countries change over time? With the exception of a temporary change to the food basket in Poland which we noted earlier, all changes were the result of the method selected for indexation of the level of a poverty line calculated at one point in time. If the poverty line was price-indexed, what did this imply for its movement relative to average incomes or wages?

Poland and Hungary

The poverty lines for Poland and Hungary from the 1980s were both in principle indexed in line with prices. In the case of Poland, the combination

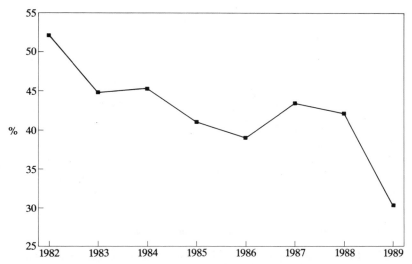

Figure 7.3 Social minimum in Poland as percent of average earnings 1982–1989

Note: The earnings data refer to September; the data for the social minimum are for a single pensioner and also relate to September, except in the case of 1986 when the figure is for August.

Sources: Social minimum supplied by I. Topińska, earnings data from Table PE1.

in the 1980s of high inflation rates and shortages (described in Chapter 6) makes the issue of the quality of the indexation particularly important. In this respect we may note that the food items in the social minimum basket, which as we have seen accounted for over half the total cost, were adjusted in line with average purchase prices recorded in the budget survey. Nonetheless, questions remain about the extent to which the real value was maintained. In this connection, the comparison between the social minimum and average earnings is of especial interest.

The movement in the social minimum as a percentage of average earnings is shown in Figure 7.3 for 1981–1989. The ratio is that of the Polish social minimum for a single pensioner to the level of average earnings, where the latter is taken from the earnings census presented in Chapter 4. The data for both the minimum and the average earnings refer to September of each year, with the exception of 1986 when the minimum refers to August. This correspondence in timing is important in view of the substantial inflation within each year, particularly in the latter part of the period. (The social minimum is calculated four times a year.) The especially high inflation rate in 1989 – the level of the social minimum doubled between September and December – may imply that the ratio for that year in the diagram should not receive too much attention.

H

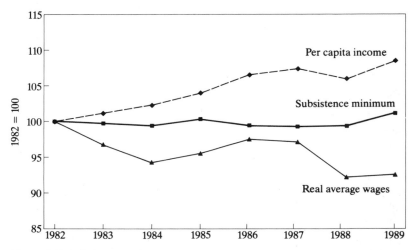

Figure 7.4 Subsistence minimum, per capita income and average wages in real terms in Hungary 1982–1989

Note: The subsistence minimum in each year is the summary figure for all households.

Sources: Table HP1 and Statistical Yearbook (1989, Table 1.14).

Even leaving on one side the 1989 figure, the pattern seems clear. There was a downward tendency over the 1980s in the ratio of the social minimum to average earnings, broken by a rise from 1986 to 1987. On this evidence, indexing the social minimum to average earnings would have resulted in larger nominal increases in its level during 1982–1989 than actually occurred.

For Hungary, we have noted that the price index in the pre-reform period has been considered among the best in Eastern Europe. Figure 7.4 shows the movements in the real value of the subsistence minimum level ('all households' figure) during 1982–1989, taking the value in 1982 as equal to 100. It confirms that there was very little change. The diagram also shows the changes in the real value of per capita income and of earnings during the period, again setting the series to 100 in 1982. (We took the indices for these latter series direct from published sources, rather than constructing them from our data in the Statistical Appendix.) Real income per capita grew through the period, by a total of 8.7 percent by 1989 compared with 1.3 percent for the subsistence minimum. Had the poverty line been indexed by income more people would have been considered poor by the end of the 1980s than was the case with indexation by prices. On the other hand, indexation by average *earnings* would have had the opposite effect. Real earnings fell between 1982 and 1984 by nearly 6 percent, and again in 1988 (by 5 percent) after a recovery in 1986 and 1987 to almost the 1982 level.

Czechoslovakia

In the calculations for Czechoslovakia which we present, indexation was in line with changes in average *income*. The social and subsistence minima originally calculated for 1970 were set in subsequent years as the same percentages of average income per equivalent adult. As noted by Hiršl and Kučerák:

> The selected concept has a strong dynamic character. It takes the concrete figures referring to the various minimum levels to be a function of the actually attained standard of living. This means, that under conditions of regular growth of income accompanied by, on the whole, stable prices typical for CMEA countries, the contents of the category of the minimum levels of living will substantially rise within a period of 5 to 10 years. (1978, pp. 66–67)

Between 1970 and 1988 the subsistence minimum for active age households rose by 79 percent (Table CSP1). This may be compared with a figure of only 24 percent for the change during this period in the official index for consumer prices for goods and services (World Bank, 1991a, p. 181). The implied movement in the real value of the subsistence minimum is illustrated in Figure 7.5. Had the minima been indexed in line with prices, as with the US poverty line, then the minima would have been much lower in 1988 and measured poverty could be expected to be significantly lower as a result.

The Czechoslovak approach may be seen as a hybrid between the absolute and relative concepts of poverty. The initial level of the minimum was justified by reference to a bundle of goods, but the minimum was adjusted over time to maintain a specified relation with average incomes.

USSR

An alternative approach is to carry out periodic revisions to the bundle of goods, with the poverty line being indexed by prices in between revisions. Such a procedure is set out explicitly in the Gorbachev Presidential Decree in May 1991 on the minimum consumer budget. This decree stated that the composition of the basket of goods should be reviewed at least once every five years and that it would be adjusted at least once a year in the light of inflation (see Table 7.1). Such periodic revisions could in principle take into account changes in availability of goods and in preferences, as well as changes in average living standards.

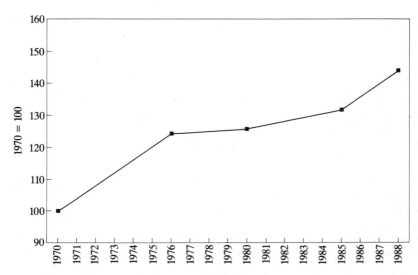

Figure 7.5 Subsistence minimum in real terms in Czechoslovakia 1970–1988

Note: The subsistence minimum in each year is for a productive age single adult household.

Sources: Table CSP1 and Vienna Institute for Comparative Economic Studies (1984, Table II/2.3, p. 159) and World Bank (1991a, Table 7.1, p. 181).

There have indeed been revisions to the basket of goods in the USSR, as is evidenced by the changes in the quantities of items between the Khrushchev 'current minimum' diet of the 1960s and the food basket used in the calculations for the 1988–1989 USSR poverty line. These are shown in Table 7.5. There are large increases in the norm for milk and dairy products, fruit, eggs, a moderate rise for meat, and decreases for all other items. For seven of the ten headings the direction of the change (but not necessarily the amounts) is in line with that foreseen in the 'prospective minimum' diet by those responsible for drawing up the Khrushchev budgets. The exceptions are sugar, vegetables and bread products. The changes may reflect a variety of factors. One may be changes in availability of goods. (It should be noted that the 1965 diet refers to an urban family of four, wheras the reference family for the 1988–1989 diet is not specified in the original source.)

Conclusions

The method of adjustment to the poverty standard has particular relevance at a time of economic transition, since it will affect the conclusions drawn with regard to the performance of the new economic system. The choice

Table 7.5 *Differences in food products in subsistence minima in USSR 1965 and 1988–1989 (Per capita kilos per year)*

	1965	1988–1989	% change
Meat and meat products	44.0	54.0	+ 23
Fish and fish products	23.0	18.0	− 22
Milk and dairy products	146.0	331.0	+ 127
Eggs (number not kilos)	124	234	+ 89
Sugar	30.0	25.0	− 17
Vegetable fat	16.0	10.0	− 38
Potatoes	137.0	89.0	− 35
Vegetables	121.0	110.0	− 9
Fruit	28.6	65.0	+ 127
Bread products	145.0	97.0	− 33

Sources: Matthews (1986, Table 3.1) for 1965 and Gur'ev and Zaitseva (1990) for 1988–1989.

obviously depends on the social objectives. Those adopting a dynamic criterion of equity (see Chapter 2) may be concerned with the absolute living standards of the poor compared with the past. The aim of policy is to prevent deterioration of their position relative to that at the end of Communism. For this purpose a price adjustment is appropriate. Others may attach importance to relative deprivation, for example to ensure participation in the new society, and this would point to adjustment in line with average incomes.

The choice will also be influenced by the economic circumstances of the transition, particularly the difficulties in measuring price changes, to which we have made reference. If the official price index failed to adequately capture higher free market prices in the pre-reform period, then 'liberalisation' of prices through removal of subsidies may lead to the index overstating the change in actual prices between pre- and post-reform periods, as we argued in Chapter 6. A poverty line indexed by official prices may overstate the growth in poverty between the pre- and post-reform periods. This may be an argument for indexing by incomes rather than prices, if we believe that changes in incomes are better measured. On the other hand, such a procedure would mean that any reduction in real incomes during the transition process would be transmitted to the poorest section of the population. As has been indicated in the frequent references to the social safety net, a government may well want to protect the poorest from a general decline in average real incomes. This may point to the need for fresh calculations of the social minima – following in the long-established tradition in Eastern Europe.

8   Poverty and the safety net

It is commonly held that the state in pre-reform Eastern Europe provided an all-embracing comprehensive system of cash benefits. 'Under the planned economy the state assumed responsibility for the provision of social benefits in the same way that it controlled the entire economy. The right to state-provided social welfare from cradle to grave was a fundamental tenet of the socialist system' (Beddoes and Lindemann, 1991, p. 7). Writing of Czechoslovakia, Cornell relates that 'a citizen received income from the state at all stages: at birth, through childhood and education, at marriage, at the birth of children, during employment (in that the state as employer guaranteed every citizen a job), after retirement, and even at death (for survival and funeral costs)' (1991, p. 34). On this view, the social security systems in Eastern Europe under Communism are seen as similar to those of developed Western countries. (We use the phrase 'social security' to cover all cash transfers.)

The Eastern European safety net may even appear to have been more generous and wide-ranging than that in the West: 'the concern in Czechoslovakia is not the provision of adequate but rather of excessive social safety nets' (Cornell, 1991, p. 31). This leads some people to argue that, in the process of economic transition, the pre-existing schemes should be scaled-down with the object of balancing the state's budget and improving incentives to work.

Support is leant to the idea of comprehensive social security in pre-reform Eastern Europe by international comparisons of the extent and cost of social security schemes. As has been observed by Ferge:

on the face of it, the social security system of the state socialist countries in Europe did not differ fundamentally from that of the developed market economy in general. If one studies international handbooks [of social security] . . . the great dividing line has never been between 'socialism' and 'capitalism', but rather between both of them, and the Third World, or Europe together with North America, Japan, New Zealand and Australia, one the one hand, and the remaining continents on the other. (1991a, p. 69)

214

She points out that by 1980 the cost of social security in terms of percent of GDP was typically in excess of 10 percent and often 20 percent in the first group but rarely reached 10 percent in the second group. To take a specific example, expenditure in Hungary in 1988 on social insurance alone amounted to 15.5 percent of GDP (National Administration of Social Insurance, 1989, Table 2.4). Looking at the details of schemes listed in international reference works on social security, one finds a considerable amount that seems familiar to the Western eye: for example, family allowances, earnings-related pension schemes, sickness benefits, etc.

With support from the state from 'cradle to grave', we might be surprised, on this view, to find a significant element of poverty under Communism. Surely poverty had indeed been 'abolished' and the poverty lines with which we were concerned in Chapter 7 of little practical importance? As, however, the experience of Western countries has demonstrated, it is quite possible for the problems of poverty to persist despite the existence of an elaborate social security system. Transfers of 15 percent or more of GNP in the West have not totally eradicated concern about poverty. Safety nets that are generous on paper may be flawed in reality if there are categorical conditions restricting eligibility or incomplete take-up by those eligible (Atkinson, 1991d). Nor are Western safety nets necessarily generous. In the US, for example, the income cut-offs for Aid to Families with Dependent Children are such that families may be ineligible for help but still below the official poverty line (Williams *et al.*, 1982, p. 495).

The experience of Western countries does not indicate that the existence of social security ensures the eradication of poverty, and the same appears to be true in Eastern Europe. According to Matthews, in the USSR 'for the great majority of people ... recourse to social security meant an inevitable lapse into poverty. Successive Soviet leaderships have obviously not been able, or willing, to save them from a fate all too familiar to recipients of state benefits under capitalism' (1986, p. 125). According to Ahmad, in Eastern Europe as a whole, 'prior to the transition the social security system was inadequate in preventing poverty and need' (1991, p. 2). (See also Kopits, 1991.) This has happened not just on account of the limitations known from Western schemes but also because, despite the superficial similarity, there are important differences between social security East and West. Ferge, after pointing to the apparent parallels, goes on to say that:

In most western countries it has been recognized that classical ... social insurance is just one element of the welfare system and that genuine protection of existential security can be attained only by a social security system ... In socialist countries, only social insurance, namely, employment-related benefits, have become accepted. Social security, as a more fundamental concern, has been ignored. (1991a, pp. 70–71)

In the first section of this chapter, we provide a brief description of some of the features of social cash transfers in Eastern Europe before 1990. It should be emphasised that the section is not intended as a comprehensive guide to social security pre-reform. Rather, the intention is to show how, as in the West, there may be gaps in the safety net, giving rise to concern about poverty which is the subject of the rest of the chapter. Section 8.2 considers the evidence from studies of poverty in Czechoslovakia about the extent and composition of the poverty population, where these studies are based on the social minimum analysed in Chapter 7. Section 8.3 deals with poverty in Hungary and Poland. The final Section 8.4 discusses poverty in the former USSR, with especial reference to the differences in poverty across republics, a subject which has become of even greater interest with the break-up of the Union. Our concern is throughout with the situation before 1990 and with understanding the background against which the post-Communist safety net must operate.

8.1 The pre-reform safety net

In simple terms, the Communist societies of Eastern Europe can be seen as providing a safety net through a combination of full employment, generous family benefits, and social insurance linked to employment. Employment was guaranteed and even though wages were low, many basic requirements were provided free or at subsidised prices. There was no need for unemployment benefit or social assistance to those without resources.

This is of course a stylisation, and in this section we examine some of the reasons why the situation was different in practice. In considering the reality, it is important to bear in mind that, just as in the West there are widely differing systems of social security, so too in Eastern Europe there is variation between the different Eastern European countries: 'although the social security systems had been constructed along some assumptions common to all communist societies, the institutional settings and the performance of the systems ... vary considerably' (Buettner, 1991, p. 1). In particular, we would expect to find differences between the USSR and the countries of Central Europe on account of the differences in the historical route by which they arrived at their systems of social security.

Family benefits

Eastern Europe is widely perceived by Western observers as having provided a generous set of family and maternity benefits. This perception is illustrated by Figure 8.1, taken from a study by the International Labour Office (1989). Expressed as a proportion of average earnings, family benefits in the three Central European countries were the highest among the

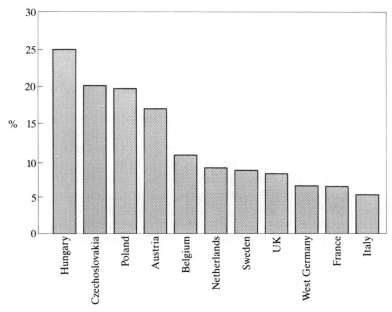

Figure 8.1 Family allowances for two children as percent of average earnings in early 1980s in eleven European countries
Source: ILO (1989, Table 8).

countries shown (they were also similar in Bulgaria and Rumania). With family allowances approaching a quarter of average gross earnings as in Hungary, they represented a major addition to income. The motives for such provision were not solely those of anti-poverty policy, but these programmes gave a significant level of income support.

At the same time, the form and effectiveness of these programmes varied considerably, both across countries and over time, as is well brought out in the case of Poland by Wiktorow and Mierzewski:

The history of child allowance in Poland is very complicated. Since 1948 the allowance differed for each successive child in the family. Between 1950-52 and 1970-84 the allowance varied also in relation to the income of the head of the family ... between 1984 and 1988 the child allowance varied only in relation to the income of the head of the family ... In 1989 a flat rate, equal for all children, was introduced. Since 1990, the allowance for each child has been equal to 8 per cent of the average remuneration in the previous quarter. (1991, p. 210)

This means that the 1990 allowance of 16 percent of average earnings is similar to that shown for Poland in 1984 in Figure 8.1, but that there is an important difference in that the allowance in 1984 was subject to an income test. Western experience suggests that there may be problems of incomplete take-up with means-tested benefits. There are a number of reasons for this. Some of these, such as the perceived stigma attached to the receipt of the benefit, may depend on the particular culture and be influenced by history, and may not have applied in Eastern Europe. Others, such as imperfect information amongst potential claimants about the benefit and the eligibility conditions, or the time costs of claiming, may apply more generally and be a source of concern in Eastern Europe.

Income-testing also applied to the family income supplement introduced in the USSR in 1974, according to which families with a per capita income of less than 50 rubles a month were entitled to a supplement of 12 rubles a month per child up to the age of eight (McAuley, 1979, p. 282). Eligibility was defined in terms of total income, including income in kind, and evidence of income had to be submitted once a year. It is claimed that the rate of take- up is high (IMF *et al.*, 1991, Vol. 2, p. 158), although McAuley expresses a cautionary view: 'since the procedures for establishing entitlement seem to me to be fairly bureaucratic, I would be surprised if all those who qualify for a particular allowance in fact receive it' (1991, p. 202). To the extent that any eligible families do not claim, the supplement has reduced effectiveness and there may be a basis for concern about poverty among families with children. A family allowance free of a means-test was paid to two-parent families only for the fourth and subsequent child (McAuley, 1979, p. 281, and 1991, p. 201) and in 1979 its level had been unchanged since 1948.

Entitlement to family benefit may also be subject to other conditions, particularly association with employment. The family allowance in Hungary was paid only to parents who had twenty-one days employment during a given month (Ferge, 1991b, p. 20). In Czechoslovakia, family allowance was likewise paid only to those with regular employment (Hiršl, 1973, p. 143). He reports that in 1973 between 50,000 and 80,000 children were not covered by the allowance for this reason. These figures may be compared with that of 116,000 for the total number of children beneath the subsistence minimum in 1970 (Table 8.1 below), and it is exactly those families excluded from receipt that one might expect to be on the margins of poverty. In Poland, the large private farming sector only became eligible for family allowances in 1983 (Wiktorow and Mierzewski, 1991, p. 209).

The picture of universal and generous child benefit in Eastern Europe has therefore to be qualified; its effectiveness in preventing child poverty may have been reduced by means-testing and other restrictions.

Social insurance

Social insurance was the predominant form of cash transfer in Eastern Europe, but differed from Western systems in several respects. First, there was an almost complete absence of unemployment benefit. Ferge notes that the 1985 edition of the well-known reference work *Social Security Programs Throughout the World*, published by the US Department of Health and Human Services, lists Hungary as having an unemployment assistance scheme dating from 1957, but she explains that this never functioned in practice (1991a, p. 89). This reflected the ideological emphasis placed on work in Communist society, together with the official view that unemployment was, like poverty, a distinguishing feature of capitalism. Throughout much of the post-war period the excess demand in Eastern European labour markets disguised the absence of income support for the unemployed. But with the slow-down in Eastern European economies in the 1980s this became a more obvious hole in the safety net. (In Hungary, it was in fact the last Communist administration which introduced a proper unemployment benefit scheme, in 1989.)

A second major difference concerned the indexation of benefits to the retired. In the macro-economic circumstances of Eastern Europe, with low or zero official rates of inflation, benefits in payment were subject to only periodic increases. In the USSR, pensions were determined in relation to past earnings at retirement and once determined were not adjusted unless they fell below the level of the minimum pension (McAuley, 1979, pp. 270–271). In 1985 a modest degree of augmentation was introduced for those who had been retired for at least ten years (Matthews, 1989, pp. 27–28.)

The indexing of pensions which did take place was particularly directed at minimum pensions, and this could have a substantial redistributive impact. In Czechoslovakia, the minimum pension doubled between 1970 and 1988, which may be compared with an increase in the average pension of only 70 percent (Dlouhý, 1991, p. 10) and about 80 percent in the social minimum. In Hungary, calculations by the Central Statistical Office show that a pension awarded in 1980 of 1,500 Forints a month actually rose by 7 percent in real terms by 1986, having taken into account increases during the period (Statistical Yearbook, 1989, Table 19.17). The real values of 1980 pensions of 2,000 forints and 4,000 forints fell in this period by 3.2 percent and 22.2 percent respectively. (Average earnings in 1980 were around 4,500 forints.) Notwithstanding this protection of the real value of the lowest pensions, it is clear that a significant number of pensioners remained in danger of being below the poverty line. For example, the per capita subsistence minimum in Hungary in 1987 for a married inactive person was 2,530 forints per month, but 13.9 percent of pensioners had a monthly pension beneath 2,500 forints in January of that year (Statistical Yearbook, 1987, Table 20.3).

To the extent that pensions in payment were not protected against inflation, this would have weakened the effectiveness of the safety net. We have too to take account of the fact that the social insurance system was not universal in coverage. In the USSR, collective farm workers were covered for the first time in legislation in 1964 which introduced a separate pension scheme. As described by George, 'at the bottom of the pile were the collective farm workers whose contribution to the economy was deemed low – both their wages and their benefits were pitifully inadequate' (1991, p. 2). One of the features of the 1990 pension legislation was that it brought all the population, except the military, into a single unified scheme (Telyukov, 1991). In Poland, private farmers were only brought into the pension system in 1977 (Wiktorow and Mierzewski, 1991, p. 209). The dependence of social insurance benefits on employment history meant that there was no provision, or limited provision, for those who did not satisfy the contribution conditions. This led to problems in the USSR for 'a minority of housewives, mothers and persons with unusual career patterns' (Matthews, 1986, p. 114), and 'able-bodied people who earned a living by private practice, contractual work, or other marginal activity were generally left outside the provisions of the state system' (pp. 114–115).

Social assistance

Social assistance may be considered as the floor of the safety net, and in Western societies it is typically seen as providing for those not covered by social insurance or whose entitlement is restricted. In Eastern Europe, however, many years of official denial of the existence of poverty was reflected in only very rudimentary social assistance schemes providing means-tested benefit of last resort. In Poland, a social assistance law had formally been in force since 1923 but Kazmierczak (1990) argues that it had 'no practical significance in the post-war period' (p. 1). Ksiezopolski notes the 'very low status' (1991, p. 177) attributed to anyone who did receive social assistance. In the case of the USSR, McAuley has argued that such schemes as there were offered little scope for discretion and were relatively small in scale (1991, p. 202). In Czechoslovakia, the Commission of Experts set up in 1990 to study subsistence benefits for those on low incomes commented that 'the present system of supplementary social welfare [dating from 1985] in fact only cares for a small part of needy families' (Hiršl, 1990a, p. 2). In Hungary, social assistance was completely abolished in 1949 and was revived only partially in the 1960s and 1970s (Ferge, 1991b).

Where means-tested assistance existed, it appears, at least in the case of the Central European countries, to have been very discretionary and entirely under local council finance and control. According to Ferge, the revival of social assistance in Hungary in the 1960s and 1970s was along the lines of its nineteenth-century form, with the result that it was stigmatising and 'handed only to "the deserving poor"' (Ferge, 1991a, p. 75). This may be expected to have reduced take-up of the benefit by those eligible. While there was in both Czechoslovakia and Hungary a centrally determined official cut-off level of income above which there was no eligibility for benefit, there does not appear to have been an obligation on the local councils to make payments to persons qualifying which would bring their incomes up to that line (Thompson, 1991, and World Bank, 1991b). Of Hungary, the World Bank has noted:

there appears to be no *right* to social assistance, in the sense that any individual demonstrating financial need (and meeting any other specified criteria) is guaranteed payment, with an appeals procedure providing for redress in the case of an assessment with which the claimant disagrees. (1991b, p. 88)

The view that there was a 'right' to social security 'from cradle to grave' is clearly incorrect in this case. Nor did a household have the right to be assessed independently of wider family ties; in assessing need, account was taken in both Czechoslovakia and Hungary of relatives outside the claimant's household who could provide support.

Evidence from Hungary on numbers of social assistance payments to adults suggests a sharp distinction between regular payments and 'exceptional' payments. The former provided ongoing support while the latter could be paid up to six times a year (Zam, 1991, p. 188, World Bank, 1991b, Annex VIII). Access to regular support was clearly restrictive and the number of payments per year showed little change during the 1970s and 1980s. However, there was an enormous expansion in the number of exceptional payments:

	number of:	
	regular payments	exceptional payments
1970	51,361	55,594
1975	51,579	96,449
1980	51,212	186,271
1985	48,671	446,235
1989	47,406	781,122

(*Statistical Yearbook* 1989 [English–Russian edition], Table 20.10, and *Statistical Pocket Book of Hungary*, 1989, p. 56).

The 781,122 payments in 1989 were paid to a total of about 420,000 persons, a figure representing 5.4 percent of the adult population (Zam, 1991, p. 188). Whether these figures show a growing need or a progressive relaxation of the regulations is a matter for interpretation, but either way the number of payments by the mid 1980s is notable. There was a separate social assistance scheme for children in Hungary, again with exceptional and regular payments. In 1989, exceptional payments were made in respect of 348,781 children, and regular payments in respect of almost 80,000, or 12.5 percent and 2.9 percent respectively of all children.

Summary

The sketch we have given of social security in pre-reform Eastern Europe has of necessity been a brief one. A number of features which we have identified are indicative of 'holes' in the safety net, although the picture varies across countries and across time. The existence of such holes explains the concern about possible poverty, and in the following sections we consider evidence from Eastern Europe on how many people were poor and who they were. From the discussion in this section, it appears that potentially vulnerable groups are families with children, the elderly, and those outside the state sector.

8.2 Poverty in Central Europe

What have been the findings of studies of poverty in Eastern Europe? How many people were poor in Eastern European countries, taking the social minima described in Chapter 7 as a guide-line? Are the holes in the pre-reform safety net which we have described in the previous section associated with a higher incidence of poverty for particular groups? In this, and the next two sections, we review a selection of the findings reached in different countries, beginning here with Czechoslovakia, where we have seen the distribution of income to be less unequal than in the other three countries. In section 8.3 we consider the situation in Hungary and Poland, two countries where – in contrast to Czechoslovakia – the social minimum was, in principle, indexed in line with prices rather than income. Finally, we turn to the USSR and its constituent republics, where there is a difference in the amount and quality of data which may be used to assess the numbers of poor people.

Our concern is with *studies* of poverty, not with the production of original results. The data on income distribution assembled in the Statistical Appendix, and examined in Chapter 5, may appear to lend themselves directly to poverty calculations, but considerable caution needs to be exercised. There is for instance the conversion from a per capita distribution to one based on an equivalence scale, as typically applied in poverty lines. Or there is the distinction between active and non-active households. The accuracy of poverty calculations depends on how far the data correspond in richness to the characteristics embodied in the poverty criteria. In this connection, there is an important distinction between analyses based on micro-data (we do not at this stage have access to the micro-data) and those based on interpolation from published tables.

We are particularly interested in seeing how the situation changed over time. Was there a steady downward trend in the extent of poverty? Or were the economic problems of the Eastern European economies in the 1980s associated with a rise in poverty and a change in the composition of the poor? We should not expect the situation to be the same in the three Central European countries nor in the former USSR. There have been marked differences in the recent economic and political experience, with implications for the incidence of poverty and the composition of the poor.

At the same time, there are common features which may expected to result in the composition of the poor having similarities across the four countries, and common differences in relation to Western countries. There is the absence of open unemployment in the pre-reform period in Eastern Europe, to which we have already referred. This is in obvious contrast to the situation in Western countries, where the unemployed have been prominent among the poor. There are demographic differences. For example, the share in the total population of children aged under 15 rose slightly in Czechoslovakia, Hungary and Poland between 1975 and 1985, compared with a fall in every European Community country during the same period (ILO, 1989, Table A.1). (The USSR also recorded a fall.)

Czechoslovakia

We have seen in Chapter 5 that income inequality in Czechoslovakia fell over the post-war period, first steeply, and then more gradually. Between 1970, the first year considered here, and 1988 the share of the bottom 10 percent rose from 4.3 percent to 5.3 percent. Does this correspond to a fall in poverty? In seeking to answer this question, we draw on the work of Hiršl, using the Microcensus data. (We are grateful to him for having made available to us in English the results of his research which have appeared in a number of papers.)

The estimates by Hiršl of the incidence of poverty in Czechoslovakia in the years 1970–1988 are shown in Table 8.1, where poverty is measured in terms of the social and subsistence minima described in Chapter 7. (The subsistence minimum is set at 75 percent of the social minimum.) These estimates of incomes below the minima are based on interpolation by Hiršl from detailed tabulations rather than the survey micro–data. The table gives both absolute numbers (in thousands, the figures being grossed-up to the population level) and percentages of the total population.

The percentage of the population living in households with incomes below the social minimum fell quite noticeably from 1970 to 1988 (see Figure 8.2). In 1970, over 10 percent of persons had incomes beneath the social minimum. This was still true in 1976 but by 1985 the figure had fallen to just under 7 percent, only to rise again slightly in 1988. The number of

Table 8.1 *Number of households and persons living in households with income beneath the social and subsistence minima, Czechoslovakia 1960–1988*

The numbers are given in thousands and are also given in brackets as a percentage of all households or persons of that type

	Social minimum			Subsistence minimum		
	Households	All persons	Children	Households	All persons	Children
1970	568	1,502	487	109	315	116
	(12.3)	(10.6)	(12.0)	(2.4)	(2.2)	(2.8)
1976	583	1,493	500	115	289	96
	(11.7)	(10.1)	(11.4)	(2.3)	(2.0)	(2.2)
1980	506	1,233	423	60	141	49
	(9.5)	(8.2)	(9.3)	(1.1)	(0.9)	(1.1)
1985	406	1,039	386	50	142	59
	(7.7)	(6.8)	(8.3)	(1.0)	(0.9)	(1.3)
1988	404	1,141	456	49	120	46
	(7.3)	(7.4)	(10.0)	(0.9)	(0.8)	(1.0)
	Czech Lands: social minimum			Slovakia: social minimum		
	Households	All persons	Children	Households	All persons	Children
1970	355	805	216	213	697	271
	(10.6)	(8.3)	(8.5)	(17.0)	(15.6)	(18.0)
1976	355	848	269	228	645	231
	(10.0)	(8.5)	(9.5)	(15.8)	(13.6)	(14.8)
1980	303	686	220	204	547	203
	(8.0)	(6.7)	(7.5)	(13.1)	(11.1)	(12.6)
1985	235	552	195	171	487	191
	(6.4)	(5.4)	(6.5)	(10.5)	(9.6)	(11.4)
1988	236	641	251	168	500	205
	(6.2)	(6.3)	(8.7)	(9.9)	(9.7)	(12.5)

Source: Information provided by M. Hiršl based on his estimates interpolated from Microcensus data.

persons beneath the lower subsistence minimum was always small and has fallen from just over 2 percent in 1970 to under 1 percent ten years later. Unlike the case with the social minimum, there was no rise in poverty as measured by the subsistence minimum in 1988.

When considering these movements, it is important to note how the social and subsistence minima have been adjusted over time. This, as we

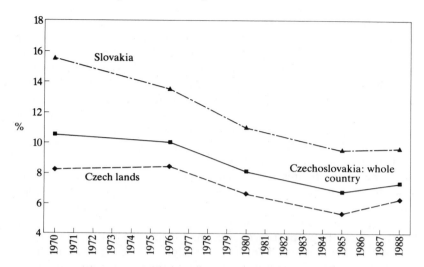

Figure 8.2 Proportion of persons below social minimum in Czechoslovakia 1970–1988

Source: See Table 8.1.

explained in Chapter 7, has been in line with average income and not prices. Between 1970 and 1988, the minimum grew by 45 percent more than the official price index (see Figure 7.5). In other words, the measurement of a substantial reduction of poverty in Czechoslovakia between 1970 and the end of the 1980s – by nearly one third as measured by the social minimum – has been *after allowance* for real income growth. This represents a significant achievement.

How has the picture changed between different groups in the population? Table 8.1 suggests that there has been a rise in the relative importance of child poverty, a rise that might in part be expected due to their rising share in the population as a whole. As we have noted earlier, the share of the Czechoslovak population aged under fifteen grew between 1975 and 1985. The proportion of children living in households beneath the social minimum was exactly 10 percent in 1988, 2.6 percent more than the figure for the population as a whole (households below the poverty line having above-average numbers of children). The incidence of child poverty, on this measure, has always been above that in the population as a whole, but there was a sharp increase between 1985 and 1988. In 1988, children accounted for 40 percent of those below the social minimum, compared with 37 percent in 1985, and 32 percent in 1970. Put another way, the total number of children below the social minimum has not fallen greatly, whereas the total number of adults has fallen by a third. Further evidence of a rise in child poverty in the second half of the 1980s may be the increase in expenditure on means-tested benefits for child nutrition, by some 29 percent between 1985 and 1988 (Kroupová and Huslar, 1991, p. 158) although this could reflect a change in the supply of social assistance rather than the demand. The situation of single-parent families seems to have been particularly poor, at least in the one year for which we have a figure. The proportion of children in such families with incomes beneath the social minimum in 1976 was 28 percent (Hiršl, 1979, p. 6) compared with figures for all children in that year of 11 percent.

Looking at the figures for the subsistence minimum we see that the proportion of children which are poor on this basis has again always exceeded the figures for all persons. However, the changes in the series at the end of the period differ compared with those for the social minimum. There is a rise in the proportion of poor children in 1985 but a fall in 1988, to a level below that in 1980. Children form a slightly lower share of the group beneath the subsistence minium than beneath the social minimum.

In the case of numbers beneath the social minimum, Table 8.1 also distinguishes between the two republics, the Czech Lands and Slovakia. In Chapter 5 we saw that there had been a convergence in average incomes between these two republics. Much of this took place in the 1960s, but it continued in the 1970s. It is therefore interesting to see that, while poverty in Slovakia is notably higher in every year, there has been a convergence between the two republics, as is shown by Figure 8.2. The proportion of persons beneath the social minimum in Slovakia in 1970 was nearly double that in the Czech Lands but this differential has fallen continuously. The Slovak figure was only 50 percent higher in 1988. And, whereas, the Slovak figure barely rose in 1988 compared with 1985, the proportion of people beneath the social minimum in the – richer – Czech Republic rose by nearly 1 percent and it is clearly this (larger) republic which is behind the rise in that year for the whole country. The same sort of picture emerges if we focus on just children. The proportion of children beneath the social minimum rose by 2.2 percentage points between 1985 and 1988 in Czech Lands but only by 0.9 points in Slovakia. The 1988 figure for children in the Czech Republic was actually *higher* than in 1970, whereas that in Slovakia had fallen by nearly a third from its 1970 level.

Poverty and activity status
Table 8.2 gives proportions of persons with incomes below the social and subsistence minima distinguished according to the activity status of the head of household, the information being shown separately for each republic. The proportions beneath the social minimum for three types of

Table 8.2 *Percent of persons beneath the social and subsistence minima by household type, Czechoslovakia 1970–1988*

	Farm	Manual	Non-manual	Pension/ work	Pure pension	Other
Czech Lands: social minimum						
1970	2.2	7.8	3.7	4.3	26.7	25.3
1976	1.0	8.9	3.7	1.5	23.5	50.3
1980	0.8	6.6	4.1	1.8	18.0	39.7
1985	0.4	5.8	3.8	1.6	11.9	41.9
1988	1.1	7.8	5.7	1.5	8.5	33.6
Slovakia: social minimum						
1970	6.3	16.6	6.0	8.2	45.6	42.3
1976	4.5	14.4	5.3	6.0	44.4	58.7
1980	3.5	12.2	5.1	4.2	37.1	51.3
1985	2.6	11.5	5.9	4.5	22.1	59.5
1988	3.2	12.8	6.7	4.0	17.6	47.3
Czech Lands: subsistence minimum						
1970	0.7	1.6	0.8	1.3	3.7	19.5
1976	0.2	1.3	0.6	0.5	3.1	37.3
1980	0.1	0.4	0.6	0.1	1.5	23.5
1985	0.0	0.6	0.5	0.1	0.7	19.6
Slovakia: subsistence minimum						
1970	1.7	3.6	1.0	2.6	6.8	24.7
1976	1.1	2.8	1.1	2.0	11.9	37.1
1980	0.3	1.3	0.7	0.7	4.2	29.4
1985	0.1	2.3	0.7	0.7	2.7	33.9

Note:

Farm – head of household is a member of an agricultural co-operative.

Pension/work – head is non-working pensioner and other member is working.

Pure pensioner – head is pensioner and no-one in household works.

Other – head is not economically active in either state or co-operative sector, nor a pensioner.

Source: Information provided by M. Hiršl based on his estimates interpolated from Microcensus data.

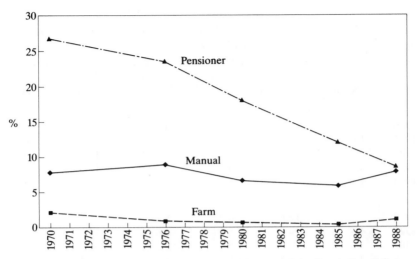

Figure 8.3 Proportion of persons below social minimum in Czech Republic by activity status 1970–1988

Source: See Table 8.2.

household head in the Czech Lands are shown in Figure 8.3: farm (meaning employed in an agricultural co-operative), manual worker and 'pure' pensioner (meaning the head is a pensioner and no person in the household works). The differences in poverty by household type, as measured by income beneath the social minimum, are striking, as are the differences in the movements in the series over time. It may be noted that the 'other' category in the table covers households where the head is not economically active in the state or co-operative sector, and nor is he or she a pensioner. The high incidence of poverty in this – small – group may reflect their not being eligible for social insurance.

The position of 'pure' pensioner households is interesting. In 1970 this group had a poverty rate slightly above 25 percent in the Czech Republic and 45 percent in Slovakia. Since 1970 there has been a rapid decline, reaching 8.5 percent and 17.6 percent respectively in 1988. By 1988, there was in the Czech Republic little difference in the position of pensioners and persons in households of manual workers. Poverty (on this measure) in the manual households has fluctuated during the period and in 1988 was the same figure as in 1970. This is consistent with the view that there has been an increase in child poverty.

It is striking that the lowest poverty rate of all is among persons in the farm households, and this is true throughout the period. The apparently favourable position of this group in Czechoslovakia contrasts markedly with pictures of rural poverty found in other countries.

Finally, it is notable that poverty rises in 1988 compared with 1985 in all household types headed by an active person and falls in all those headed by an inactive person (this is true of those types not illustrated in Figure 8.3 and it is also true in Slovakia.)

Conclusions

The evidence presented above shows that, judged by a relative standard (56 percent of average income per equivalent adult), poverty has declined over the past two decades in Czechoslovakia. The decline has been especially marked for pensioners, reflecting the policy of increasing minimum pensions, and in Slovakia, reflecting the reduction in income disparities between the republics. Of more concern is the increase in the relative importance of poverty among children and it is the active households which have shown a rise in poverty between 1985 and 1988.

8.3 Poverty in Poland and Hungary

The social minima in Poland and Hungary differ from that in Czechoslovakia in being indexed to prices rather than average incomes. We would therefore expect to see a rather different pattern of change over time. It is also the case that the 1980s were a turbulent decade in Poland, when the poor may have been especially vulnerable. Various writers have considered the changes in poverty during the period, and we draw heavily on the analysis of Milanovic (1990b), Kordos (1990, 1991) and Szulc (1990 and 1991). These studies are all based on data from the annual household budget survey and take a similar starting point for the poverty line in the calculations. However, their calculations differ in the definition of the poverty line for different household types, equivalence scales and method of calculation. These differences have implications for the results obtained.

Milanovic, in his work for the *World Development Report 1990*, used the published data which formed the basis for our Table PI1 (his period of analysis was slightly different). He took as his starting point the one-person social minimum in each year for worker and pensioner households described in Chapter 7. (The level of the minima in each year are given in Table PP1. Milanovic estimated values for 1978 and 1979 by adjusting the 1982 value for movements in prices). The minima calculated by the Institute for Labour and Social Affairs (ILSA) apply to an urban household. For mixed and farmer households, Milanovic took a value of 80 percent of the minimum for the worker's household. To adjust the levels of the poverty line for household size, he took the equivalence scale published in the budget survey reports. With the aid of the detailed tables published in the survey report on per capita income distribution by household type and household size, he then estimated the number of poor persons by interpolation. The results (see Figure 8.4) show poverty rising from under 10 percent in 1978 to nearly 24 percent in 1983. There is then a slight fall to 1986 before an increase in 1987 followed by a sharp fall to 15 percent in 1988.

The calculations of Kordos (1990, 1991) are based on the Polish central statistical office definition of a 'low-income' household as one with per capita income below 2,500 zlotys in 1981 prices, a figure close to the per capita value of the ILSA social minimum for a four-person worker household in that year (Kordos, 1991, p. 12). (A figure of 2,000 zlotys was taken for 1980.) In other words, the calculation is made on a per capita basis with no allowance for economies of scale in respect of household size and no adjustment for the activity status of the household. The calculations again provide estimates of the numbers of persons living in poor households. From Figure 8.4, it may be seen that the series virtually coincides with that of Milanovic for 1981 and 1982. Thereafter it is between two and five percentage points higher. The Kordos series shows a continued fall in 1989.

Szulc (1991) takes the ILSA minimum for a one-person pensioner household and then, as we described in Chapter 7, calculates an equivalence scale on the basis of econometric results from a demand system of consumer expenditure. Unlike Milanovic and Kordos, Szulc estimates the number of poor *households*, rather than persons. He also differs from these authors in that a household is considered poor if its *expenditure* falls below the critical level, rather than its income. Besides Szulc's estimates of the number of poor households (the 'head-count' measure) which we report here, he also calculates other aggregate poverty indices. He does not have results for 1983. The series is also shown in Figure 8.4. The initial fall from 1980 to 1981 is in the reverse direction from the other series, but the broad impression is similar.

The fact that three different estimates produce broadly the same pattern is quite striking. There is no reason to expect the figures to coincide, or for the movements over time to be the same. The Milanovic calculations are based on interpolation from published tabulations; the others are based on micro-data. The Kordos series is on a per capita basis; the others use equivalence scales which allow for economies of scale. The Szulc estimates are based on expenditure and count the number of households; the others relate to income and count the number of people.

Given the major disturbances to the Polish economy, we may expect different groups in the population to be affected differently. Figure 8.5 shows the Kordos and Milanovic series for worker and pensioner house-

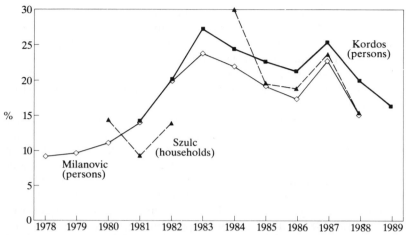

Figure 8.4 Proportion below social minimum in Poland 1978–1989

Sources: Kordos (1991, Table 2), Milanovic (1990b, Table 1) and Szulc (1991, Table 5).

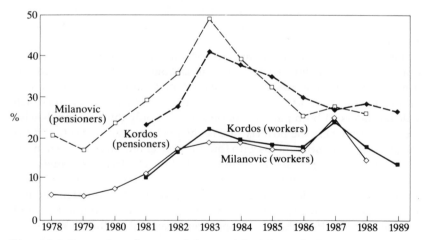

Figure 8.5 Proportion of persons below social minimum in Poland: Worker and pensioner households 1978–1989

Sources: Kordos (1991, Table 2) and Milanovic (1990b, Table 1).

holds separately. In all years pensioners have the highest poverty rate in both sets of calculations and the broad movements over time are similar. But there was a distinct widening of the differential in 1983, when pensioner households suffered an especially large rise in poverty; this in turn narrowed up to 1986. In 1987 poverty rose sharply for worker households, and the two groups had virtually the same incidence of poverty in that year. After 1987 the gap began to widen once more.

The relative position of all four types of household is shown in Figure 8.6, based on the Kordos series. In contrast to the situation in Czechoslovakia, the poverty rate is higher among farmer households than among worker households. The gap widens in 1983 to some ten percentage points, and any significant decline in farm poverty from the 1983 peak does not occur in the series of Kordos until 1988. (It should be noted that the series for farm households given by Milanovic shows the difference in poverty rates narrowing after 1983 and essentially disappearing from the mid 1980s. The reasons for this discrepancy are not clear, although differences in the level are in part explained by the fact that Kordos treats farm households as having needs that are equal to those of worker and pensioner households, whereas Milanovic assumes that they are 20 percent less.) It is interesting to note from Figure 8.6 that mixed farmer/worker households show a less marked rise in poverty in 1983 and that their poverty rate is the lowest of all groups at the end of the period.

The results of Szulc allow one to look at child poverty. Figure 8.7 compares the overall poverty rate in all households with that in households with children. This shows that two-parent households with one or two children have a poverty rate below the overall rate in each of the years which Szulc considers. If both parents are present, it is only the households with three children where the poverty rate is above the overall rate (the same is true of two-parent households with four or more children, not shown in the diagram). The poverty rate for couples with three children is 2.2 times that for couples with one child in 1988 (Szulc, 1991, Table 7). However, their poverty rate is exceeded by the poverty rate among single-parent households. A third of households headed by a single parent are poor in 1988 and it is only in 1980–1982 that the proportion is lower than this.

Hungary

Our analysis for Hungary draws on Szalai's background paper for the *World Development Report 1990*. Her estimates of poverty incidence are based on the official subsistence minimum and are calculated using both the biannual Budget Survey and the five-yearly Income Survey. We understand from the author that her estimates from the Income Survey are based on the

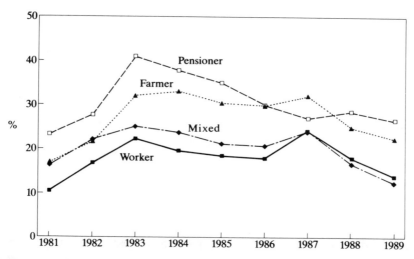

Figure 8.6 Proportion of persons below social minimum in Poland by household type 1981–1989

Source: Kordos (1991, Table 2).

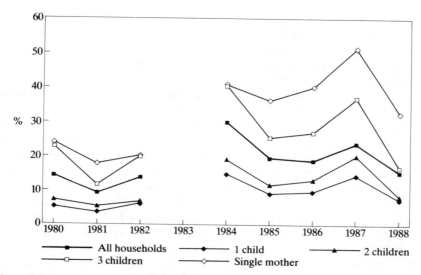

Figure 8.7 Proportion of households below poverty line in Poland by family size 1980–1988

Source: Szulc (1991, Tables 5 and 7).

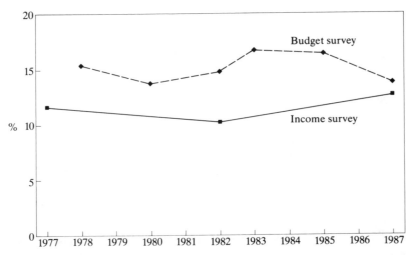

Figure 8.8 Proportion of persons below minimum subsistence in Hungary 1977–1987

Source: Szalai (1989, Table 4).

micro-data but those from the Budget Survey are interpolated from published results. The use of two sources providing independent estimates is of considerable interest and there are a number of differences between the two surveys which may lead to different results. (The surveys are described in Sources and Methods.)

The results of Szalai (1989) for the proportion of the population below the minimum subsistence level in 1977–1987 are summarised in Figure 8.8. Figures for the period 1977–1980 are based on her estimates of the subsistence minimum in these years since the official calculations began only in 1982. The estimates were made by adjusting the 1982 minimum by movements in average nominal per capita incomes recorded in the two surveys (Szalai, 1989, note to Table 1). This contrasts with the statistical office's calculations for the years after 1982 which index the 1982 minimum by *prices* (see Chapter 7). Since real incomes grew in Hungary during 1977–1982, the effect is to make Szalai's estimates of the subsistence minima for 1977–1980 somewhat *lower* than they would have been if indexing by consumer prices had been applied. For example, average per capita income grew in total by 3.8 percent more than the consumer price index between 1977 and 1982 (Table HI1 and *Statistical Yearbook*, 1989, Table 1.14) and adjusting the 1982 subsistence minimum figure to 1977 by the price index would have resulted in a 1977 estimate higher by this amount. This implies that poverty in 1977–1980 is slightly underestimated by Szalai on the basis of the 1980s indexing practice.

There are only two years in which there are data from both surveys, 1982 and 1987. The Income Survey shows less poverty in both these years, although the difference is only around one percentage point in the latter year. The figures from the Income Survey should be considered more authoritative, since the income data in this source are of a higher quality than those in the Budget Survey, the Income Survey's coverage and response rates are higher, and the sample of households is larger (see Sources and Methods). (We need also to take into account that the Income Survey results of Szalai are based on the micro-data.)

Of particular interest are the changes over the 1980s, in view of the fact that real wages peaked in 1978 and fell until the mid 1980s, whereas real incomes rose (see Figure 7.4). According to Andorka (1989), poverty increased between 1987 and 1989, but did not rise before 1987. Taking account of the recent increase, he concluded in 1989 that 'the number of poor people today is not larger than in 1982, possibly in 1977' (1989, p. 138). This conclusion is based on the per capita distribution from the Income Surveys. According to the application of the subsistence minima to the Income Survey micro-data by Szalai (1989), the proportion of the population under the subsistence minimum fell between 1977 and 1982 (the fall would have been larger if the 1977 subsistence level had been based on price indexing, rather than income indexing) and then rose by over a fifth between 1982 and 1987: from 10.3 percent to 12.7 percent. On this basis, there was a rise over the 1980s. The evidence of growing numbers of 'exceptional' social assistance payments in Hungary during the 1980s, to which we referred earlier, seems consistent with this although it is also the case that the number of such payments had been growing prior to this period. In contrast to the Income Survey data, the Budget Survey results of Szalai show poverty to be lower in 1987 than in 1982, and compared with 1978 there is similarly a decline.

The lack of a clearcut answer to the question whether poverty increased in Hungary in the 1980s may be attributable to the diversity of experience of different groups. We have already noted that real per capita incomes rose while real wages fell. It is helpful, as suggested by Szalai (1989), to look at the figures separately for persons in active and inactive households (Figure 8.9). Both Income Survey and Budget Survey record a halving of the proportion of persons in inactive households beneath the poverty line between 1977–1978 and 1987. We have a clear indication from the two different sources that the position of low-income inactive households improved substantially. The situation regarding active households is less clear. The Budget Survey suggests no overall change; the Income Survey shows poverty rising for these households by a third between 1982 and 1987.

As a consequence of these divergent trends, the incidence of poverty in

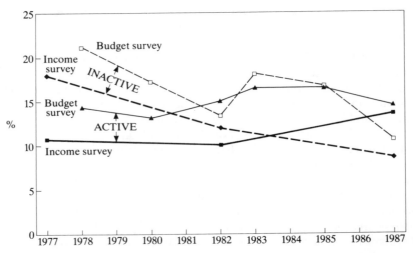

Figure 8.9 Proportion of persons below minimum subsistence in Hungary by activity status 1977–1987
Source: Szalai (1989, Table 4).

1987 was significantly higher among the active population than among the inactive. According to Szalai, 'while the typical poor of the sixties came from a rural setting, was relatively old, lived alone or with spouse on pensions or on welfare, the typical poor of the eighties lives in urban families, is relatively young, and brings up (several) children' (1989, p. 20). Among the active households, the risk of falling below the social minimum rises with the presence of children and with their number. In 1987 the risk of being below the subsistence minimum was 2.2 times higher for a family with three dependent children than for a family with one dependent child (Szalai, 1989, Table 11). This ratio is the same as that found for Poland. At the same time, a quarter of poor active households have only one child and over a third have two children, so that it is not purely a matter of large families.

Comparing the figures

The results presented in this and the previous section indicate that, measured according to official minimum levels of living, in the 1980s around 7.5 percent of the population in Czechoslovakia, 10–15 percent of the population in Hungary, and 10–25 percent of the population of Poland, were in poverty. Such figures cannot of course be taken as indicating anything about the *relative* severity of poverty in the three countries. The recorded level of poverty in each country depends on the criteria adopted in determining the official minimum. The recorded poverty rates reflect, in addition to substantive differences, differences in the level of the poverty line, in the equivalence scales, in the data employed, etc. All that can be concluded is that *measured by national standards* the problem of poverty in the 1980s was of significance in all three countries, particularly at certain periods in Poland when more than a fifth of the population were judged to be below the official minimum.

Over time, poverty appears to have fallen in Czechoslovakia in the 1970s and the first half of the 1980s, before rising slightly between 1985 and 1988. This decline in poverty is particulary notable given that the poverty line was indexed to incomes rather than prices, so that Czechoslovakia achieved a reduction in relative poverty. The poverty standard in Hungary and Poland, on the other hand, was indexed to prices. Moreover, it has to be viewed against a background of falling real wages. Seen this way, it is perhaps surprising that there is no clear evidence of a rise in poverty in Hungary. In Poland, the sharp rise up to 1983 is evident. After that date there has been a decline, punctuated by a rise in 1987.

In both Czechoslovakia and Hungary the position of low-income pensioners seems to have improved. In Hungary, the poverty rate among persons in inactive households, of whom the majority are presumably pensioners, fell sharply between 1977 and 1987, in which year it became significantly lower than that of active households, having previously exceeded it by a large margin in 1977. Poverty fell among pensioners in Czechoslovakia from 1970 right up until the last year we observe, 1988. In that year the poverty rate for pensioners almost equalled that of manual workers, having been far above it in 1970. The experience of pensioners in Poland is that the poverty rate for pensioners remained above that for worker households (although in making comparisons with other countries we have to bear in mind the differences in the relative social minima, with that for active households being higher in Czechoslovakia – see Chapter 7).

With the fall in the relative importance of poverty among pensioners, poverty among families with children has become relatively more important. In Hungary and Poland the risk of poverty was higher for families with three or more children. In Czechoslovakia there was concern about rising child poverty.

8.4 Poverty in the USSR

In some respects the analysis of the poor in the former USSR can follow similar lines to that in the Central European countries. The official figure of 40 million poor in 1989 – about 14 percent of the population – refers to the

Table 8.3 *Distribution of pensions in USSR July 1987*

	Worker/Employees		Collective farm workers	
Monthly pension	All pensions	Old age	All pensions	Old age
Up to 60 rubles	31.4	20.2	84.7	85.6
60–80 rubles	19.0	21.3	8.2	7.2
80–100 rubles	14.9	17.0	3.6	3.6
100–120 rubles	11.3	13.1	1.8	1.8
120+ rubles	23.4	28.4	1.7	1.8
total	100.0	100.0	100.0	100.0

Source: Statisticheskii Press Biulleten, 1989, No. 1, p. 142.

number of persons with per capita income beneath the subsistence minimum first calculated by Goskomstat in 1988. As in the Central European countries we can consider the position of different groups in the population in relation to the official poverty line.

For example, there were clearly considerable numbers of persons on low pensions in the 1980s. The average old-age pension at the end of 1989 was 88.7 rubles per month, compared with the subsistence minimum in that year of 81 rubles per capita at state trade prices and 88 rubles at state trade and collective farm prices (*Sotsial'noe razvitie SSSR 1989*, p. 108). The distribution of pensions for July 1987, based on survey data, is shown in Table 8.3, distinguishing between those persons previously worker/employees and former workers on collective farms. The Goskomstat subsistence minimum in 1988 was 78 rubles per capita. It may be seen that four out of ten old-age pensions for worker/employees were below 80 rubles. The low level of many of the collective farm pensions is particularly notable: virtually all pensions were below 80 rubles. We have earlier noted that pensions for this group were not introduced until the legislation of 1964.

In other respects, we are in a different situation when discussing the extent of poverty in the former Soviet Union. We do not know whether the figure of 40 million in poverty was based on a detailed set of minimum budgets varying with household size, composition, activity status, and other dimensions, or whether it was reached by applying a single per capita figure to the overall distribution. We do not have access to detailed breakdowns of the 40 million figure. With the exception of the Khrushchev minimum budgets from the 1960s, official estimates of a poverty line are only available from 1988. We do not have figures each year back to the early 1980s or before, and there are no estimates of the numbers of persons beneath the line at regular intervals.

At the same time, much more information now exists on low incomes in the USSR than was available to earlier Western writers on poverty in the former Union, such as McAuley (1979) and Matthews (1986). These studies refer to the period prior to the release by Goskomstat of detailed information on the distribution of income, as recorded in the Family Budget Survey. This restricted the conclusions which could be reached about the extent of poverty, even at the national level. Referring to the late 1970s, Matthews concluded that 'given the scarcity of information [on the distribution of income], anything more than a general assessment is out of the question' (1986, p. 23). He reported on the incidence of low incomes in a number of local studies in the second half of the 1970s (1986, Table 1.2, p. 24) together with evidence of other indicators of living standards, such as housing. For the late 1950s and early 1960s, McAuley was more bold and concluded that 'in spite of substantial increases in living standards since the late fifties, some 35-40% of the Soviet population had per capita incomes below the official poverty level in 1967–68' (1979, p. 70). However, his figures were based on estimates of all-Union income distributions reconstructed from diagrams with no published scales published by Soviet writers, and he counselled that these estimates 'should be treated with caution' (p. 62).

Poverty at the end of the 1980s: variation by republics

In 1989 the national subsistence minimum calculated by Goskosmstat (81 rubles or 88 rubles per month, depending on the prices used in the calculation) fell within the interval from 75 to 100 rubles in the per capita income distribution data (Statistical Appendix, Table UI3). Rather than interpolate within this interval, in which a substantial part of the distribution may be found in a number of republics, we have chosen to take the lower bound of 75 rubles as the national 'poverty' threshold. This choice is of course arbitrary. We might just as well have taken the upper bound of 100 rubles, a figure which Goskomtrud (the USSR Ministry of Labour) apparently estimated as a minimum subsistence threshold for 1988 (IMF *et al.*, 1991, Vol. 2, p. 154). This would have led to different conclusions about not only the numbers of persons with low incomes but also the variation across republics. At the same time, the 75 ruble figure is one that has also been taken by other authors. Commenting on the 1989 budget survey results, Goskomstat noted 'it is customary to count families with an average per capita income of below 75 rubles a month as poor' (1990a, p. 4, translation by S. Marnie).

Taking the Union as a whole, 31 million people, or 11 percent of the population, were estimated by Goskomstat on the basis of the Family

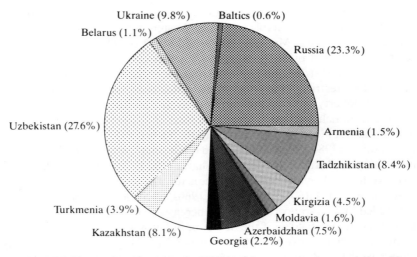

Figure 8.10 Share of total persons in USSR with per capita income below 75 rubles per month by republic 1989
Source: Table UI3.

Budget Survey data to have incomes beneath 75 rubles per capita of monthly income in 1989 (Table UI1). For what it is worth, this percentage is some third of the 35–40 percent estimate of the incidence of poverty in 1967–1968 referred to by McAuley (1979). If the poverty line were taken as 100 rubles per capita, then the 1989 figure would rise to 25 percent – or still well below the earlier estimate.

Of particular interest is the variation in the incidence in low incomes across republics of the former Union. The share of this total in each republic is shown in Figure 8.10. (We have amalgamated the Baltic republics for this figure.) Russia, with half the population of the Union, has slightly less than a quarter of the poor, classified on this basis. Uzbekistan, with only 7 percent of the Union's population, has more people beneath the 75 ruble level than any other republic, contributing over a quarter of the Union total in this category. Together, the five Central Asian republics (Uzbekistan, Kirgizia, Tadzhikistan, Turkmenia and Kazakhstan) contain just over half of the poor, whereas these republics make up only 17 percent of the USSR population.

The shares of low-income population in Figure 8.10 reflect both the size of population in each republic and the incidence of low income. The proportion of the population within each republic shown by the Family Budget Survey data with income below 75 rubles per capita is shown in

Table 8.4 *Percent of population in USSR republics with per capita monthly income beneath 75 rubles, 1989*

Baltic Republics	
Estonia	1.9
Lithuania	2.3
Latvia	2.4
European Republics	
Belarus	3.3
Russia	5.0
Ukraine	6.0
Moldavia	11.8
Transcaucasia	
Georgia	13.0
Armenia	14.3
Azerbaidzhan	33.6
Central Asia	
Kazakhstan	15.5
Kirgizia	32.9
Turkmenia	35.0
Uzbekistan	43.6
Tadzhikistan	51.2

Source: Statistical Appendix Table UI3.

Table 8.4, where we have grouped the republics under conventional geographic headings.

The enormous variation in the incidence of low incomes across republics is striking, from 2 percent in Estonia and the other Baltic republics to 50 percent in Tadzhikistan. With the exceptions of Azerbaidzhan and Kazakhstan, the incidence of low income gets progressively higher as we move down through the groups of republics. For example, in the 'European' republics of Russia and the Ukraine (we are clearly stretching geographical imagination to include the far east of Russia in Europe), only 5 and 6 percent respectively of the population are recorded as having income beneath 75 rubles per capita. In four out of five of the Central Asian republics the figure is a third or more.

The figures above refer to all households types in the Family Budget Survey. We now separate the totals between the two groups distinguished in the data: worker/employee households and the households of collective

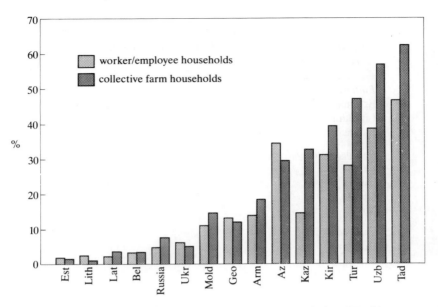

Figure 8.11 Proportion of persons with per capita income below 75 rubles per month in USSR by republic and worker/collective farm 1989
Source: Table UI3.

farm workers. At the national level, there were 10 percent of persons in worker/employee households with monthly per capita income beneath 75 rubles in 1989 compared with 20 percent in collective farm households (Table UI3). In Figure 8.11 we show how the incidence of low incomes in the two types of household varies between republics. In five republics – Ukraine, Georgia, Azerbaidzhan, Lithuania and Estonia – the figure for collective farm households is lower, although in all of these the difference from the figure for worker/employee households is small (and may be insignificant). In contrast, the Central Asian republics all display large differences between the two types of household. Low income appears particularly common among collective farm households in these republics and is higher here than among collective farm households in any other republic. In Kazakhstan, for example, which appeared the odd man out in the Central Asian group in terms of the overall incidence of low incomes, the incidence among collective farm households is more than double that in worker/employee households and is higher than that in Azerbaidzhan (which was shown in Table 8.4 as having a lower incidence of low incomes than Kazakhstan taking worker/employee households and collective farm households together). The small sample sizes of the collective farm house-holds in some republics (see Sources and Methods) may lead us to be cautious about the figures for some individual republics but the overall picture of widespread low incomes among the collective farmers in Central Asia is clear.

Explaining the numbers

How may we explain these differences in the incidence of low incomes across republics and between worker/employee and collective farm house-holds? Do they correspond to differences in living standards? Undoubtedly part of what we see in the data represents genuine differences in incomes and in living standards. But there are a number of issues which need to be clarified – not least in view of the attention that these figures have received.

First, there are large differences in household size between republics and a focus on per capita income may exaggerate differences in living standards. We have already commented on the differences in average household size in Chapter 5 and the remarks we made there apply again here. These differences are very important at the bottom of the income distribution. For example, in 1989, average household size in the interval of 50–75 monthly rubles per capita was 6.21 and 7.08 in worker/employee and collective farm households respectively in Uzbekistan but 3.89 and 4.74 in the Ukraine (Goskomstat, 1990a, Vol. I, pp. 31–32, and Vol. II, pp. 23). If the low income cut-off of 75 rubles per month were to be adjusted for household size on other than a per capita basis, it is probable that there would be a greater proportion of persons re-classified as above the cut-off in Uzbekistan than in the Ukraine.

Second, there is the question of the representativeness of the Family Budget Survey sample. We have discussed the problems with this source at some length in Chapter 3 and in the section on Sources and Methods. It needs to be emphasised that the survey is primarily one of the households of *working people*. (This is not clear from the published tables since the results are presented by Goskomstat grossed-up to the population of households of all types.) This implies, for example, that low-income pensioners are likely to be under-represented in the survey. This means that the overall incidence of low incomes in the population as a whole may well be understated by the budget survey data. It may also result in differences between republics being over-stated. In 1989, the ratio of persons above retirement age to those of working age was 0.325 in Russia and 0.379 in the Ukraine, compared with only 0.163 in Uzbekistan (IMF *et al.*, 1991, Vol. 2, p. 212). The proportion of pensioners who live in the households of working people may also vary between republics.

Thirdly, a single low-income cut-off of 75 rubles has been applied across the USSR as a whole, a calculation which ignores the differences in prices across republics which we described in Chapter 6. If prices are on average higher in the Central Asian republics then the low-income cut-off should be higher if we wish it to correspond to the same living standard in each republic. This would imply that the figures we have presented understate the incidence of low living standards in Central Asia. In Chapter 7 we noted how the authors of the Khrushchev budgets calculated minima for different regions. We need also to ask whether collective farm households face higher prices and have different needs to worker/employer households. Put another way, the subsistence minimum may be different for collective farm households. Earlier writers on poverty in the USSR have noted the problem: 'it would appear that no minimum budget has been published for them [collective farm households]; their income is subject to wide and uncharted variations, by geographical locations, farm and year; and there is the additional mystery of the private plot' (Matthews, 1986, p. 42). The problems with interpreting the data may suggest that we focus on consumption rather than income. The IMF *et al.* draw attention in their section on poverty to the information in the budget survey on average per capita consumption of different food stuffs by range of per capita income, the information being given separately for each republic (IMF *et al.*, 1991, Vol. 2, Table IV.6.15, pp. 204–206). This represents an important extra dimension to the comparison. As has been noted by Cazes and Le Cacheux (1991, p. 172), the differences are striking, with the average consumption of meat per head in Tadzhikistan and Uzbekistan being around a third of that in Lithuania, and with there being similar differences for other foods, vegetables being an exception. At the same time the differences between republics may be due to a number of factors, including dietary custom.

The reference by Matthews to the private plot in the quotation given above brings us to a final issue of interpretation. Income from private plots is in principle included in the Family Budget Survey. This is true whether the income is in the form of money derived from the sale of produce or whether in kind, when produce is retained for own-consumption. However, the income may not be fully reported. Moreover, the income in kind is valued at state prices which for certain goods undoubtedly under-estimates its free-market value given what we have described in Chapter 6 about the difference between state and collective farm market prices. Marnie (1992, p. 223) notes that a significantly higher proportion of total recorded income comes from private plots for collective farm households, about 20 percent for persons in collective farm households with less than 75 monthly rubles per capita in 1989 in the USSR as a whole compared with about 10 percent for the persons in worker/employee households in the same income class.

(She also notes the variation in the figure for the Central Asian republics.) If the income from plots is systematically under-reported or under-valued, then the incidence of low incomes among the collective farm households, relative to that in worker/employee households will be overstated. Lubin describes how:

> mountain shepherds are often envied as among Uzbekistan's wealthiest inhabitants. Because they, in practice, have a partial monopoly on Uzbekistan's meat production – a glaringly 'scarce' good – they are seen as earning tremendous sums from private sales of meat alone. (Lubin, 1984, p. 198)

The shepherd in the mountain ranges of Uzbekistan is not representative of agricultural employment in the republic, much of which is in cotton growing, but the example is clear.

In lieu of a conclusion

Much of this book has been concerned with the problems of collecting and evaluating statistical data on the distribution of income. We believe these to be important, and that the available information has – despite all the qualifications – a valuable story to tell. But we have also emphasised differences in perspective, and this is well illustrated by the example of Uzbekistan.

On the basis of the data we have presented, persons in collective farm households in Uzbekistan appear among the poorest groups in the former Soviet Union. Figure 8.11 shows 57 percent of persons in this group in 1989 with income per capita of 75 rubles per month or less. This figure is higher than those for worker/employee families in all republics. Among collective farm families, it is exceeded only in Tadzhikistan (62 percent). The picture obtained from these data is of large numbers of poor people. On the other hand:

> it is the rare Uzbek who dreams of trips to Paris, or even to Eastern Europe or to the Black Sea. Rarely would he or she wish to buy washing machines, or Soviet household amenities ... Russians, on the other hand ... tend to prefer to spend rubles on household goods, or summers in the Baltic away from Uzbekistan's desert heat. To the visiting Westerner's eyes, therefore, the Russian appears to be 'better off', but only when Western standards are applied. Within the framework of indigenous lifestyles, quite the opposite could well be the case. (Lubin, 1984, pp. 198–199)

As two Westerners writing on Central Europe and the former Soviet Union, we undoubtedly have used our 'Westerner's eyes'.

Sources and methods

This part of the book gives details of the data on which we have drawn and, in particular, describes the methodology of the earnings and income surveys used in each country. This provides fuller information on many of the issues considered in Chapter 3. We also refer to sources of social or subsistence minima ('poverty lines') within government ministries or agencies in each country. The main part of the material is organised by country in the following order:

Czechoslovakia (Section S.1)
Hungary (Section S.2)
Poland (Section S.3)
USSR (Section S.4)
Britain (Section S.5)

('Britain' may refer to either Great Britain or the United Kingdom, the latter including Northern Ireland; the precise coverage is made clear where relevant.)

The same order of countries is followed in the Statistical Appendix, to which the present section serves as a commentary. The Appendix tables for each country are indicated by the initial letters: 'CS' (Czechoslovakia), 'H' (Hungary), 'P' (Poland), 'U' (the USSR), and 'B' (Britain). These letters are followed by an 'E', indicating earnings distribution, 'I', for income distribution, or 'P' for 'poverty line'. Except where otherwise stated, the raw data in the tables are in the form in which they were published or made available to us: absolute frequency distributions where these were available and relative frequencies otherwise. We have not combined class intervals and have in a number of cases drawn on different sources so as to achieve a greater degree of detail.

The main purpose of the Statistical Appendix is to make accessible the raw data, but alongside we also give certain summary statistics: the mean, median, a selection of quantiles (expressed relative to the median), and measures of inequality such as the coefficient of variation and the Gini coefficient. Where, as is often the case, summary statistics have been based on interpolating the distribution from the information available, we have given the summary statistics *in italics*. (In several tables, some statistics are the result of interpolation, but others are known from the original source.) The methods of interpolation applied to grouped data to obtain summary statistics are described below in Section S.6.

We make no claims to providing an exhaustive account of earnings or income surveys for each country; we describe only those relevant to the data used here. Nor do we give a complete picture of each source which we cover; and there are undoubtedly aspects of which we are unaware or to which we have not been able to do justice in the space available. Our descriptions are based in the main on correspondence and interviews with officials in the relevant central statistical offices or government ministries (other sources are noted where appropriate). We refer to the statistical offices of each country by abbreviations as follows (these refer to the names as of Spring 1991):

Czechoslovakia – Federální Statistický Úřad (FSU),

Hungary – Központi Statisztikai Hivatal (KSH),

Poland – Główny Urzad Statystyczny (GUS),

USSR – Goskomstat (GKT),

UK – Central Statistical Office (CSO), Office of Population Censuses and Surveys (OPCS).

We refer to the statistical yearbooks of each country by the following abbreviations:

Czechoslovakia – *Statistická ročenka* (SR),

Hungary – *Statisztikai Évkönyv* (SE) and *Statistical Yearbook* (SY) (English-Russian edition),

Poland – *Rocznik Statystyczny* (RS),

USSR – *Narodnoe Khoziaistvo SSSR* (NK),

UK – *Annual Abstract of Statistics* (AAS).

The position with regard to statistical information in Eastern Europe is changing rapidly. We have chosen to use the past tense in order to avoid giving the impression that statistical practice in the pre-reform period has continued unaltered (in some cases we know that it has definitely changed), but this should not be taken as indicating that none of the methodology related here has survived.

We note here two points which apply to all, or most, of the Eastern European countries:

(a) a distinction is often drawn in published statistics between 'workers' and 'employees', the former being manual and the latter non-manual. We use the term 'workers' to cover both types, distinguishing between manual and non-manual if appropriate;

(b) where published tables refer to 'monthly' income this may in fact be annual income divided by twelve. We indicate on the relevant tables in the Statistical Appendix where this is the case.

S.1 CZECHOSLOVAKIA

(a) Earnings (CSE1–CSE5)

Source. Periodic enquiries on the distribution of gross earnings in Czechoslovakia were carried out through a 100 percent census of enterprises in the state sector and the non-agricultural co-operative sector. Enterprises were obliged to provide information on earnings for all their employees covered by the enquiry. The information requested took the form of the number of persons in discrete earnings bands. Up until 1979 the census was conducted by FSU and referred to earnings in May. From 1981 it was conducted by the Ministry of Finance and referred to earnings in November, but the data from the two sources, after editing by FSU, were said to be on a comparable basis and in Tables CSE1–CSE4 we treat them as a continuous series.

Coverage. Excluded from the census were members of the armed forces, employees of the Communist Party and affiliated activities (probably about 0.3 percent of the employed workforce in the late 1980s), those working in the private sector (another 0.3 percent of the workforce in 1989), and those working in agricultural co-operatives. The last of these groups represented about 650,000 persons in 1989 out of the total of about 950,000 persons employed in either state or co-operative agriculture. The total labour force at the end of the 1980s was about 6.5 million (the source of the employment figures in this paragraph is the FSU). Those employees not working a full month were also excluded: for example, those who joined or left the enterprise at some time during the month. Part-time workers were excluded.

Definition of earnings. Gross earnings for the month in question were defined to include overtime, allowances for being away from family and for unhealthy working conditions. No account was taken of any annual bonuses.

Presentation of results. Prior to the 1980s, a basic table on the size distribution of earnings was published in the statistical yearbook (SR). Information for a number of years up to 1981 was given in a historical abstract of Czechoslovak statistics (FSU, 1985). The information we have used is taken in part from the annual yearbook (SR) and in part from a 1990 FSU publication (of which only 100 copies were printed) providing a consistent time-series of data on the Czechoslovak labour market (FSU, 1990).

(b) Income (CSI1–CSI6)

Survey design. The income distribution data used here are derived from the Czechoslovak Microcensus, a household survey held periodically. Since 1970, 2 percent of all households were sampled, or about 100,000 in all. Surveying took place in March of each year collecting information about income in the previous calendar year (1973 is an exception in that information was collected in November for that year); the dates we refer to are the years to which the income information relates. The first Microcensus collected information relating to 1956 and sampled 0.75 percent of households; we have information neither from this survey nor from the third Microcensus relating to 1960. Our first data relate to 1958 (see Tables CSI1, CSI2, CSI4 and CSI5).

Random sampling on a territorial basis was used with a two-stage self-weighted selection process designed to ensure each permanently occupied dwelling had a equal selection probability. There was no panel element; a fresh sample was drawn for each Microcensus. The sampling frame for the 1988 Microcensus was an administrative register used to record addresses of all dwellings for the purpose of collecting a combined payment for gas, electricity and other utilities. The Microcensus results refer to 'common budget' households, defined as a set of persons in the same dwelling who share the main household expenditures (the self-declaration of persons in this respect being accepted by FSU). FSU defined three types of household: 'dwelling' (an address), 'common budget' (defined above and a sub-set of dwelling households), and 'census' (more restrictive than a common budget household and with a maximum of two generations). In the 1988 Microcensus there were (grossed-up to national level) 5,068,461 dwelling households, 5,288,803 common budget households and 5,436,725 census households. Information was collected through personal interview based on a short and simple questionnaire; details of income not provided at this time could be posted to the statistical office following interview.

Response. The total response rate to the Microcensus for 1988 (see Table S1) was at the low end of the range for response rates since 1970, the highest figure in this period being about 99 percent. Considerable efforts were made to achieve high response to the Microcensus (a regional office director being known to have made a personal visit to try and elicit response following an initial refusal by a household). We were told that there may occasionally have been some substitution carried out by interviewers in the event of non-response, despite instructions to the contrary, which would have had the effect of disguising non-response. One reason for the high level of response is that participation in the Microcensus was not onerous, the interview lasting about an hour and proxy responses being permitted for other household members. The refusal rate (a sub-set of non-respondents) in Prague was over 5 percent, compared with a national average of under 2 percent.

Income concept. The Microcensus collected information on annual net household income from different sources (the information was requested separately for each household member). Specifically excluded were income from bank account interest, travel allowances for business trips, and income from abroad in the form of remittances. (Macro-data for 1988 record foreign remittances in that year amounting to about 2 percent of net money income (Dlouhý, 1991, p. 2).) Remuneration for work in agricultural cooperatives was included; information was requested on all cash income coming from sales of produce either by those working on farms as a main occupation or by those with a private agricultural plot, distinguishing between sales to organisations and to individuals. Each member of responding households was asked to report all other forms of cash income (with the exception of the exclusions noted above) in a residual category of 'other income', distinguishing 'organised' (state) sources from other sources. 'Other income' could include tips, gratuities and any other form of legal or illegal income. (Examples are income from rent and transfers from persons outside the household.)

Information was sought on the amounts of each household's agricultural

Table S1 *Response to the Czechoslovak 1988 Microcensus*

	Sampled households	Total not responding	Refusals (sub-set of non-respondents)	Total response rate (%)
Czech republic	70,499	2,947	1,655	95.8
Slovak republic	31,081	510	267	98.4
Total	101,580	3,457	1,922	96.6

Source: Information supplied by FSU.

production consumed within the household (the 1988 questionnaire distinguished about a dozen categories of produce) and on other income in kind such as goods received free of charge or at a discount; the former was valued at average official retail prices for the year in question. However, the estimated cash value of all such income in kind was *not* included in the definition of income used for the published distributions of income which refer to 'money income' although tabulations do show the average value of income in kind (including agricultural production for own consumption) in each band of money income.

Substantiation and adjustment of data. Starting with the second Microcensus (1958), all information on earnings from employment was collected from employers, members of responding households being asked to supply the name and address of their employer in the previous calendar year. Where job changes had taken place during the year, this information was requested for each employer, together with the start and end dates of work in each case (the latter also being asked for in the case of retirement during the year). No information on earnings was requested from the respondents themselves. If an employer failed to give the requested data, something which happened in only about 0.1 percent of cases, earnings were imputed. Similarly, all information on social security benefits paid by employers were collected in the same manner, and (from 1965) information on pensions was taken from the relevant post-offices making the payments.

Presentation of results. Results relate to the distribution of household per capita annual income, this being given for both individuals and households. The sample figures were grossed up to the population level. A basic table of the size distribution of income was published in the statistical yearbook (SR), typically a year or two following the Microcensus. The majority of our tables are drawn from the reports on the Microcensus prepared by FSU. They provide considerable detail, including statistics on an individual and a household basis (Table CSI3) and a distribution by number of children (Table CSI6).

(c) Poverty lines (CSP1)

As described in Chapter 7, estimates have been made of social and subsistence minima. These were not published in the annual statistical yearbook, but estimates were contained in research papers written by Dr Hiršl during the period 1970–1988, of which in most cases 200 copies were made and distributed to university libraries and research institutes within Czechoslovakia as well as to government officials. In the early 1970s the calculations were also published in Czechoslovak scientific journals (e.g., Hiršl, 1971b, 1971c). See Hiršl (1990).

S.2 HUNGARY

(a) Earnings (HE1–HE4)

Source. Regular enquiries on the distribution of gross earnings in Hungary were carried out through 100 percent censuses of enterprises, which collected information on earnings in September (June in 1955 and 1956). Enterprises were obliged to supply for all their employees covered by the enquiry information on the number of persons in discrete earnings bands. The enquiry was carried out every second year since 1962, with earlier information dating back to at least 1951. (Earnings data were also collected by the quinquennial household Income Survey – see below – but we do not draw on these.)

Coverage. The data published for years prior to 1970 are limited to the 'state sector', defined as state-owned enterprises and state-owned farms. Information for the state sector, which continued to be available after 1970, is given in Table HE4. Data are available from 1970 covering the more extensive 'socialised sector', this being defined as the state sector plus co-operatives (agricultural or non-agricultural). This information is given in Table HE1 for all workers and in Tables HE2 and HE3 for males and females separately. From January 1982 private ventures were permitted (see Laky, 1984) and we understand that from this time those ventures which had a legal identity were included in the earnings enquiry under the heading of the 'socialised sector'. In January 1988, 86.8 percent of all employed persons were in state organisations, 11.6 percent in co-operatives and 1.6 percent in private ventures (SY 1988, Table 4.4). The armed forces were excluded, as were the self-employed and people working in specified areas close to Hungary's borders. Organisations employing fewer than fifty workers were excluded. These organisations (classified by KSH as those using the 'simplified order of statistics') employed 3.3 percent of the total employed workforce in 1988.

The enquiry covered workers of all ages, excluding apprentices. Those employees not working a full month were excluded (specifically those who missed more than three working days in the month): e.g. those who joined or left the enterprise at some time during the month. Also excluded are those persons who would receive the end of year bonus in the year in question from a previous employer rather than the current employer. In recent enquiries part-time workers were excluded, but the published data indicate that for years up to 1978 certain part-time workers were included. (The data for agricultural co-operatives refer to full-time workers only from 1986.) Results for 1978 were published on both bases (see Table HE1). The total number of part-time workers is relatively small: in 1987, for example, there were only 121,636 persons in part-time work compared with 3,190,786 working full-time (SE 1987, Table 4.11). Persons were only included in the enquiry in respect of their first job; as is discussed in the main text, second jobs have been very important in Hungary.

Definition of earnings. Gross earnings for the month in question included overtime, one-twelfth of any annual bonus, one-sixth of half-yearly bonuses and one-ninth of all additional earnings received between January and September (information based on the 1990 instructions to employers and notes to relevant tables in FKA 1980–1988). Allowances for meals and transport were excluded. The precise definition of earnings has changed over the years. For example, in certain years the statistics excluded the allowances paid to compensate for price increases for meat, etc., but in later years these were merged with wages in the statistics.

As discussed in Chapter 4, a progressive personal income tax was introduced in Hungary in January 1988, marginal rates (at that time) rising from zero to 60 percent. This was accompanied by a grossing-up of wages. This means that the distributions for 1988 should not be compared directly with those for earlier years.

Presentation of results. A selection of the results of the September earnings enquiry have been published in the annual statistical yearbook (SE and SY). For example, the results for 1988 are given in SY 1988, p. 70. The results have been published in detail every two years in the annual KSH publication, *Foglalkoztatottság és Kereseti Arányok*, referred to in our tables as FKA. This is the source of data used here from 1968. In this respect it is an improvement over the sources used in Atkinson and Micklewright (1991), (where it should be noted that an error wrongly attributed the 1972 data to Flakierski (1986)), in that the FKA tables provide more earnings bands than those published regularly in the statistical yearbook, which we have used for years prior to 1968.

(b) Income (HI1–HI6)

Survey design. The Hungarian Income Survey is the source for our income tables HI1–HI6. This household survey has in the past been held every five years. (See Vita, 1991, for a discussion of the survey's methodology and future). The survey covered either 0.5 or 1 percent of the target population. The 1988 survey, collecting information on 1987 incomes, interviewed some 20,000 households; the first survey carried out in 1963 collected information on 1962 incomes covering 47,871 individuals (SE 1964, Table 4.5, p. 299). Interviewing took place in March and sought information about income in the previous calendar year; the dates we refer to are the years to which the income information related (Table HI1 for example has data for 1962, 1967, 1972, 1977, 1982 and 1987).

The survey used a multi-stage random sampling process on a territorial basis and a fresh sample of addresses was drawn each time (there was no panel element). Random sampling took place from a master-sample of Census enumeration districts drawn every ten years (and modified regularly in the light of new residential construction); this master-sample has been used for all Hungarian household surveys carried out since 1976, including the Budget Survey (see below).

Information was collected through personal interview based on a detailed questionnaire with separate questions concerning different forms of income. Results refer to households, defined as a set of persons in the same dwelling who partly or entirely share living expenses. Calculations have been made by KSH of the effect of different adjustments for household size (see Tables HI3 and HI4).

A brief description of the Hungarian Budget Survey is relevant to the discussion in Chapter 6 of the distributional impact of price subsidies, which is based on Budget Survey data re-weighted using the Income Survey (Kupa and Fajth, 1990), and to Table HP1 which shows subsistence and social minima income levels, estimated by KSH in part using Budget Survey data. The Budget Survey used the same master-sample as the Income Survey and also had a multi-stage design. However, the design differed in several respects:

(1) The Budget Survey was held more often, every two years. (Prior to 1983 the survey was conducted annually but with a sample size of two-thirds that in the period since 1983.)

(2) In the event of non-response a substitute household was chosen from the same geographical area, having the same number of members and from the same social class (these two latter pieces of information being elicited by a preliminary 100 percent survey of the third-stage sampling units).

(3) There was a significant panel element (one third of the sample rotating out every two years).

(4) Prior to 1989, households containing a self-employed member were excluded from the budget survey. (Pudney (1991) reports examples referred to in KSH documentation as being private farmers, retail dealers, craftsmen, 'transporters', authors and freelance translators.)

(5) The achieved Budget Survey sample size in 1989 of just under 12,000 households was about half that of the Income Survey.

Response. The rates of response to the Income Surveys and to the Budget Surveys held in the 1980s are shown in Table S2. Response was substantially higher in the case of the Income Survey. Refusal to this survey was relatively low, accounting for less than a third of non-response in 1987. Refusals are more important for the Budget Survey, the proportion of refusals among non-response rising from about 50 percent in the early 1980s to 70 percent in 1989. According to Pudney (1991, p.5), KSH indicate that response to the Budget Survey was lower from high-income households, and households of the elderly; Kupa and Fajth (1990) report that the self-employed and households of young married couples had lower response rates. Response was lower in towns and, in the case of the Budget Survey in 1987, the rate was 62.2 percent in Budapest, compared with 76.2 percent overall. In producing the results, the Income Survey data were re-weighted by region in order to compensate for the regional pattern of response.

Income concept. The Income Survey collected information on net household income over the past year, distinguishing a large number of sources. Incomes from agricultural production (including that from small private plots) was estimated by KSH on the basis of the information given on production of a wide range

Table S2 *Response to the Hungarian Income Survey and Budget Survey*

	1982 Income Survey		1987 Income Survey	
	Total response rate (%)	Refusal rate (%) (sub-set of non-response)	Total response rate (%)	Refusal rate (%) (sub-set of non-response)
Budapest	86.3	5.8	77.9	8.7
Counties	91.3	1.6	84.0	4.6
Total	90.6	2.2	83.1	5.2
	Budget Survey			
	1983	1985	1987	1989
Towns	72.7	73.5	70.9	69.6
Villages	83.2	82.6	81.2	79.9
Total	78.4	78.4	76.2	74.5

Source: Information supplied by KSH.

of produce. Output which was sold was valued at producer prices; output which was consumed within the household was valued at consumer prices. In the survey for 1987 responding households were asked about the total production of several dozen different agricultural products and then asked to indicate the proportion of each product consumed themselves; this reply could be 'nothing', 'about a quarter', 'about a half', 'about three-quarters', or 'all'. Both production for sale and that for consumption were included in the definition of income used for the distribution of income which refers to 'personal income'. In the case of reported pensions and family benefits, appropriate annual values were calculated by KSH given knowledge of retirement and birth dates and any upratings during the year.

Efforts were made to collect information on tips, gratuities and income from unlicensed economic activity, and respondents were asked to report the average monthly or annual amounts of these items. In the 1987 survey, for example, KSH requested from respondents the average amounts of time per month spent in various different 'second job' activities such as skilled and unskilled construction work, repair work and non-manual work. KSH then imputed income in the light of locally typical hourly pay rates established by the survey interviewers. (The detailed questions about 'hidden incomes' were asked only of economically active earners; other groups were asked a simple question about the annual amount of all such income.)

The value of 'social income in kind', such as education, health and sport, was estimated by the KSH for each household on the basis of macro estimates of the value of such income, the socio-demographic characteristics of the household, and information given by respondents to the Income Survey about usage of state services (e.g. frequency of visits to hospital, local doctor, museums, concerts, etc.).

The imputed value of social income in kind was not included in the definition of 'personal income' in the published income distribution although tabulations show the average value of social income in kind in each band of personal income (see Table HI5).

Households in the Budget Survey were asked to keep diaries recording their expenditures and incomes for two consecutive months during the year (the requested diary periods of those households agreeing to respond was distributed uniformly across the year by the KSH). Households were then visited after the end of the year at which time information was sought about income for the entire year; annual income was therefore the basic income concept in both Income and Budget Surveys.

Substantiation of data. For the Income Survey, the KSH substantiated information on earnings (and income derived from membership of a co-operative) by asking members of responding households to supply the name and address of their employer in the previous calendar year (this was almost invariably given). KSH then requested earnings figures from the employers who were obliged to comply with the request. Where job changes had taken place during the year, this information was requested for each employer, together with the start and end dates of work in each case (the latter also being requested in the case of retirement during the year). If an employer failed to give the necessary data (or could not be contacted by KSH), which happened in about 5–7 percent of cases, the earnings figure reported by the respondents were taken.

The KSH compared aggregate reported agricultural production in the Income Survey with macro estimates and typically found that the former was lower. When this occurred, reported agricultural production was inflated by KSH so that the totals corresponded. (For some agricultural products macro estimates were lower than those recorded in the Income Survey and in this case the Income Survey amounts were reduced by KSH.) The same treatment was given in the 1987 survey to self-employment income which was also found to be under-recorded compared with macro estimates.

There was no substantiation of earnings data with employers for the Budget Survey and the income data in this survey were considered less reliable by KSH. Prior to 1989 recorded expenditure in the Budget Survey exceeded recorded income, but in 1989 this position was reversed. Reported income data in this year may have been more accurate as a result of respondents having had their personal income tax (PIT) returns to help their memories (the PIT was introduced in 1988).

Presentation of results. Results of the Income Survey were typically published by KSH in three volumes, the first giving preliminary results, the second giving the main results and the third exploring the relationship between per capita income and earnings. (The main report of the 1987 survey had the title *Jövedeleme-loszlás Magyarországon* but for earlier surveys was *A Családi Jövedelmek Színvonala és Szóródása*; the third volume, on earnings, was titled *A Keresetek Színvonala, Szóródása, és Kapcsolata a Családi Jövedelemmel*). These were all published in Hungarian only. A substantial selection of results from the survey for 1972 was published in English (Hungarian Central Statistical Office, 1975). A basic table giving the individual distribution of per capita income by class intervals was published in the statistical yearbook, typically in the year following the survey, and in later years the yearbook gave a more substantial selection of tables (e.g SY 1982, pp. 298–309, and SY 1988, pp. 427–443).

Tabulations produced by the KSH from the Income Survey are available on a number of bases (see Tables HI3 and HI4): (i) the household distribution of total household income, (ii) the individual distribution of household per capita income, and (iii) the individual distribution of 'consumption unit' income, defined as equivalised household income. The tables in the statistical yearbook refer to the second of these distributions, and contain a reduced number of class intervals of income compared with the main KSH Income Survey publications. It should be noted that we have been able to augment the Statistical Appendix tables (HI1 and HI3) using information on the precise values of the median and top and bottom deciles which were supplied to us by KSH and which are unpublished. (Those for 1987 are also used in Section S.6 to investigate the accuracy of interpolation.)

(c) Poverty lines (HP1)

As described in Chapter 7, calculations of subsistence minima have been made by KSH at a number of dates since 1968. Results for the subsistence minimum were published for the first time in the 1987 statistical yearbook and have been published in subsequent yearbooks. (The calculations for 1968 have not been published in this source.) The same source gives also the rather higher *social minimum* level, which receives less prominence in Hungary.

S.3 POLAND

(a) Earnings (PE1–PE4)

Source. An annual enquiry on the distribution of earnings of full-time workers in the socialised sector in Poland was held in September of each year up to and including 1989. Up until 1980 the enquiry was a census of employers. From 1981 sample surveys of enterprises were conducted. Sampling took place from the REGON list of business establishments (described in Olenski, 1991). The selection probability for an enterprise depended (positively) on its size (in terms of number of employees) and the number of other enterprises in its industry. If the number of enterprises fell below a certain level, all establishments were selected and this occurred in about a quarter of industries. The procedure resulted in about 20 percent of all enterprises being selected. All employees within the selected enterprises were included in the survey. The information requested from the enterprise was the total persons in a number of discrete earnings bands. Information distinguishing the distribution of earnings for men and women was requested in some years (separate distributions for men and women for 1972 and 1985 are shown in Table PE3).

Coverage. The survey referred to the socialised sector, which was defined to cover state-owned and co-operative enterprises. In 1989 the socialised sector accounted for two-thirds of the labour force. (The employment data referred to in this paragraph were supplied by the Central Statistical Office (GUS).) The remaining one-third, excluded from coverage of the survey, represented private-sector employment and self-employment; 70 percent of persons in these two excluded categories were working in agriculture (the vast bulk being self-employment on small farms). (The 10 percent of the labour force in private sector non-agricultural work represented mainly small family craft businesses.) The bulk of agriculture has always been in the private sector: in 1989 there were 760,000 persons employed in agriculture in the socialised sector compared with some 3.6 million in private sector agricultural employment and self-employment. The armed forces, police, senior government officials and employees in the sector 'Political Organisations, trade unions and other' were excluded from the earnings survey.

Since the survey referred only to full-time workers and it was legally impossible to have more than one full-time job, individuals cannot enter the survey more than once. Evidence from the 1988 Census indicated that some 10 percent of the workforce – socialised and private sectors – had a second job, this definition including self-employment on a private agricultural plot provided it was at least half a hectare in size. Those employees not working a full month were excluded, for example those who joined or left the enterprise at some time during the month. Those on paid leave or those absent for reason of sickness are included provided they received full earnings, or the equivalent in sickness pay, for the month.

Definition of earnings. Gross earnings for the month in question are defined to include basic pay, overtime, compensation for hazardous work conditions, additional payments related to job tenure or the holding of a managerial position, profit shares, bonuses and premia. All payments which are not monthly are included in the form of a monthly equivalent.

Published tabulations of the distribution from 1970 referred to 'net' earnings, although employees did not from this date pay any deductions from their earnings (neither income tax nor social security contributions). This is the basis of the distributions shown in Tables PE1–PE3. These earnings figures thus refer to payments that are both net and gross to individuals. Persons with high annual total incomes were subject to an 'equalization tax' but this was not deducted at source from earnings (we were told that the threshold for the tax in the mid 1980s was about three times average earnings). Prior to 1970 the earnings distribution was published on a 'gross' basis and these results are shown in Table PE4. Figures are available for 1970 on both the old and the new 'net' definitions. The latter show less dispersion as indicated by the following results for 1970 taken from Tables PE1 and PE4:

	Gross	Net
P10 (bottom decile as % median)	56.3	58.3
P90 (top decile as % median)	177.3	165.7
Gini coefficient (%)	26.2	23.1

Presentation of results. The results of the September earnings enquiry were published in detail in a GUS publication (e.g. *Zatrudnienie W Sektorze Uspołecznionym Według Wysokości Wynagrodzenia Za Wrzesień 1989 R*). In this source the data were reported for twenty-seven earnings bands (and unpublished tabulations show the data in forty-eight bands). Tables of the distribution with about eight to ten earnings bands were published in the annual statistical yearbook (RS). From 1970 GUS also published the decile values of the distribution in both these sources. Our tables (PE1–PE4) draw exclusively on the statistical yearbook, since the publication of decile values much reduces the need for interpolation.

(b) Income (PI1–PI7)

Survey design. The Polish household Budget Survey has been held annually from 1957. The survey has always been based on random sampling but the sampling frame and other aspects of survey design underwent a substantial number of changes. (The survey methodology, and its development, is discussed in Kordos, 1985, and Kordos and Kubiczek, 1990.)

From 1957 to 1972 the Budget Survey was restricted to the households of employees in the socialised sector (excluding agriculture), samples being drawn of enterprises and then individuals being sampled within these enterprises. Indeed, up to and including 1962 the survey focused solely on households of industrial workers, with a sample size of about 2,000. From 1963, households of employees in other sectors were included (with the exception of agriculture and forestry) and the sample size was increased to over 4,000.

From 1973 the Budget Survey was radically changed, being conducted on a territorial basis, i.e. with a sampling frame of addresses rather than of enterprises, and with a sample size of about 10,000 households. However, certain types of households continued to be excluded from the survey (see below). Until 1982 the sample was fixed for four to five years, households being asked to co-operate throughout this period. In 1982 a rotating design was adopted with quarterly sampling according to the following method. First, a master sample of addresses was drawn with a multi-stage selection process, and a brief survey of the households in this sample conducted to establish approximate household income and a range of socio-demographic characteristics. Second, every quarter for the next four years households were randomly drawn from this master-sample (again with a multi-stage process), two-thirds being asked to take part in the Budget Survey for four years (these forming a panel element in the survey design), one third being asked to take part in the survey for one year only. (The master sample was also used as the basis for drawing other Polish household surveys.) Master samples were again drawn in 1986 and 1989, with the process described above continuing as before. The 1982 and 1986 master samples contained about 100,000 households and the Budget Surveys based on them had samples of about 30,000 households. An important feature to note about the Budget Survey design is that each non-responding household was substituted using another household with similar characteristics, including income level, drawn from the master sample survey. (Response rates are discussed below.)

From 1973 onwards the Budget Survey was designed to provide information on four types of households:

households of workers,

'mixed' households, defined as households where at least one member is a worker and the household draws income from a plot of land over 0.5 hectares,

households of farmers,

households of pensioners (defined to include retired persons receiving no pension).

Households in which the principal income was from either employment or self-employment in the private non-agricultural sector were excluded from the Budget Survey, constituting about 10 percent of the labour force in 1989; also excluded were households containing members of the police or armed forces. The exclusion of the designated household types was achieved from 1982 onwards by using information collected in the master sample surveys, these households not being approached to take part in the Budget Survey.

Starting with 1986, households in rural areas have been over-represented in the survey. To allow for this, the tables in the published reports are based on re-weighted data which correct for the under-representation of urban households. For example, those in urban areas have a weight of 1.5 in 1986 and 2 in 1988 and 1989. The number of households (unweighted) by household type in 1989 was:

workers	12,991
mixed workers/farmers	3,717
farmers	3,504
pensioners	8,073

(*Budżety Gospodarstw Domowych W 1989 R*, Tables 1, 1(18), 1(30) and 1(41)).

Each household participating in the Budget Survey was surveyed throughout one quarter, during which period the household kept a daily diary of flows of income and expenditure. (The diary was for the whole household rather than for each individual within the household; however, the identity of the recipient was requested for each income entry.) The GUS interviewers returned to the household twice a month during the quarter to collect completed diaries (the diaries covered a half-month), to issue fresh diaries and to monitor and advise the households on the task of recording the required information. A household which had been drawn for the panel part of the survey was approached for data for the same quarter in the following three years. In addition to the information provided in the diaries and through interview during the relevant quarter, all households (whether in the panel part of the survey or not) were interviewed again at the end of the (calendar) year to obtain information on, amongst other things, annual incomes and occasional incomes not recorded during the household's survey quarter.

Response. The complicated design of the Budget Survey means that calculation of the rate of response has a number of dimensions. First, there is the issue of response to the master sample survey from which the Budget Survey sample was drawn. Secondly, there is the response at first selection for the Budget Survey. Thirdly, households could provide information for the requested quarter but not for the end-of-year interview. Fourthly, the households in the panel part of the

Table S3 *Response to the Polish Budget Survey 1982–1989*

Household type	Response rate (%)							
	1982	1983	1984	1985	1986	1987	1988	1989
Worker	62.8	71.7	67.2	60.8	68.9	70.5	62.3	57.9
Mixed	68.7	77.8	79.8	73.2	77.5	75.4	62.5	61.0
Farmer	64.5	74.6	72.9	65.6	71.4	69.6	67.6	57.8
Pensioner	51.7	65.4	60.1	59.9	63.1	63.9	58.2	58.8
Total	60.8	71.0	67.2	62.1	68.5	69.0	61.7	58.4

Source: Kordos and Kubiczek, 1990, Table 4.

survey (two-thirds of households sampled) could drop out without giving data for a full four years. In interpreting the information about response it has moreover to be remembered that non-participating households were replaced by others from the master sample as described above.

We understand that non-response (for whatever reason) to the first stage master sample survey was about 5–6 percent in 1982, 8 percent in 1986 and about 10 percent in 1990. Non-response at the third stage, failure to provide end-of-year data, was low. In the 1988 survey, 29,664 households provided quarterly data but the survey tables in the published report are based on 28,482 households (*Budżety Gospodarstw Domowych W 1988 R*, p. xiv). The 4 percent of households which did not enter the tabulated results were missing for a variety of reasons which appear to have extended beyond non-response at the third stage. These included the breakdown of a household through divorce, a move to a private sector non-agricultural job (excluded from the coverage of the survey), and 'incomplete' or 'doubtful' data.

We have most information about response at the second and fourth stages: at the time of first selection for the Budget Survey and in ensuing years for households in the panel part of the survey. The figures in Table S3 show for 1982–1989 the response rates at the second stage, i.e. the proportion of households selected from the master sample who were successfully contacted and who agreed to take part in the survey. The response rates prior to the introduction of the rotation design in 1982 were apparently markedly lower: Kordos (1985) reports a response rate in the pre-1982 period of only 40 percent or less. The lower response before 1982 was apparently due to the continuous nature of the survey, participation requiring a household to co-operate throughout the year and for a period of several years. The marked difference between the response rates before and after 1982 is a reason for caution when considering results spanning the two periods. The causes of non-response at the stage of first selection for the Budget Survey are shown in Table S4 for two years during 1982–1989, the years of highest (1983) and lowest (1989) response.

The figures in Table S5 give partial information on the fourth stage of response for the years 1984–1989. They show the response rate of households who had participated in the Budget Survey for three years and who were due to participate for a fourth and final year. There was evidently a sizeable rate of attrition.

Table S4 *Reasons for non-response in Polish Budget Survey 1983 and 1989 (%)*

Household type	Refusal	Household moved	Illness or household collapsed	No contact	Other reason	Total non-response
1983						
Worker	14.3	2.3	2.8	4.4	4.5	28.3
Mixed	15.4	0.0	2.1	1.4	3.3	22.2
Farmer	16.4	0.3	4.2	2.1	2.4	25.4
Pensioner	10.7	1.7	13.0	5.0	4.2	34.6
Total	13.7	1.7	5.5	4.0	4.1	29.0
1989						
Worker	22.0	3.4	2.5	9.3	3.5	42.1
Mixed	26.1	1.7	2.4	5.3	3.5	39.0
Farmer	26.8	1.5	5.4	5.5	3.0	42.2
Pensioner	15.6	2.4	11.2	7.6	4.4	41.2
Total	21.0	2.8	5.2	8.1	4.5	41.6

Source: 1983: Kordos, 1985, Table 1 and 1989: Kordos and Kubiczek, 1990, Table 3.

Income concept. From the description of the surveying method of the Budget Survey, it can be seen that information collected on incomes related to a variety of periods. The published tabulations on which we have based our Tables PI1–PI7 refer to monthly net household income, which we understand represents an estimate of the annual incomes of the households divided by twelve. The estimate of annual income for each household has been made by GUS using a combination of the diary data collected for the quarter of intensive survey and the information collected in the end-of-year interview. The latter, for example, provides information on annual bonuses or profit shares not recorded in the reference quarter.

The definition of included income has been wide-ranging, embracing income from a variety of sources and some income in kind in addition to income in cash. It included income from employment, from agriculture (including small plots), from social benefits and from property. Employment income included regular, periodical and occasional payments; a residual category of other income from work distinguished between the state and non-state sectors, but there have been no explicit questions on tips and gratuities. The income from agriculture included both the cash sales of produce and the value of produce consumed within the household or given to others, taking for this purpose the market prices in the region for fruits and vegetables and the state prices for meat. (Agricultural income was taken as net of outflows on current expenditure and investment during the reference quarter.)

Income from social benefits included in addition to cash benefits the value of free or subsidised holidays, creches and infant schools, and railway tickets. Part of the

Table S5 *Attrition in the Polish Budget Survey*

Response rates of households in their fourth year (%)

Household type	1984	1985	1986	1987	1988	1989
Worker	83.0	85.3	86.0	74.6	74.7	78.4
Mixed	88.8	91.2	91.1	80.2	79.3	83.2
Farmer	88.1	89.7	89.4	77.3	81.2	84.5
Pensioner	83.4	85.8	86.4	72.3	72.6	78.0
Total	84.2	86.4	86.9	74.7	75.1	79.2

Source: Kordos and Kubiczek, 1990, Table 5.

value of subsidised medicines was included; for example, pensioners do not have to pay the 30 percent charge for the cost of medicines and the value of this additional subsidy was treated as income in the Budget Survey.

Substantiation of data. All data on incomes from work provided by respondents to the Budget Survey in the diaries for the reference quarter were substantiated by checks with employers. The same applies to information provided in the end-of-year interview. Information on incomes from farms was checked by inspection of respondents' bank accounts, a practice aided by the monopoly of the state on the purchase of much of private agricultural production. In the case of discrepancies, the information provided by the employers and banks were taken as definitive.

In the case of income from work, the discrepancies in the Budget Survey between information provided by respondents and employers were found to be large and to vary systematically with individual characterstics. In the fourth quarter of 1989, respondents on average understated their income from work when compared with that reported by employers by 20.9 percent (Kordos and Kubiczek, 1990, Table 1). The amount rose significantly with income level; persons in the bottom 5 percent of the distribution of income from work *overstated* income by 14 percent, persons in the middle of the distribution understated by about 15–20 percent and those in the top decile by nearly 30 percent. The rate of underestimation decreased with educational level. Checking of the information on incomes from farms in the Budget Survey by inspection of respondents' bank accounts showed that the average amount of this type of income understated by respondents in 1989 was 14.6 percent, although this figure apparently varied considerably with farm size (Kordos and Kubiczek, 1990, p.10).

Presentation of results. Results of the Budget Survey were published in a number of GUS publications, but none give directly the information reproduced here in Tables PI1 and PI2. The annual statistical yearbook (RS) provides information in the 1980s for the four household types (worker, mixed, farmer and pensioner households), but not for all households together. (The information for these household types is not sufficient to combine the results to arrive at a total distribution.)

Information on the size distribution of income in the form of the number of persons and of households in eight income bands is contained in the annual Budget Survey report, e.g. *Budżety Gospodarstw Domowych W 1988 R*, and it is this source that we have used to derive Tables PI1, PI2 and PI7. The relatively small number of income bands in this source is to some extent compensated by the availability of the mean income levels within each band. The published tables provide the data in the form of distributions of *households* for different household sizes and the four household types (workers, peasants, worker-peasants and pensioners). We have recovered information on the distribution of individuals using the information published on average household size within each income band. These distributions of individuals have then been combined across different household sizes and types, to give the total number of individuals in different ranges of household per capita income. The mean income in each range is calculated in the same way. This is the basis for Tables PI1 and PI2, which cover the period 1983–1989. For the earlier years, Table PI3 presents the information available from the annual statistical yearbooks (RS) on the two largest of the household types: workers' households and pensioners' households.

As we noted above, starting in 1986, tables in the annual Budget Survey report refer to re-weighted data which correct the under-representation of households in urban areas. (The 'number of budgets', the unweighted number of households in the survey, is also given in the report.) Our Tables PI1–PI7 are based on these weighted data. (We note, however, that certain tables in the statistical yearbook (RS) appear to be be based on unweighted data.) Other GUS publications contain income distributions based on adjusted Budget Survey data e.g. *Warunki życia ludności w 1989 r* (GUS 1990).

(c) Poverty lines (PP1–PP2)

The Institute of Labour and Social Affairs (ILSA), part of the Ministry of Labour, first calculated the social minimum level of income in 1980 and has done so every year from 1982 onwards. The social minima were first made available outside the government and the Communist Party at the end of 1988. They have not to date been published in the statistical yearbook.

S.4 The USSR

(a) Earnings (UE1–UE8)

Source. For the distribution of earnings, we have drawn on two sources of data. The first is a Goskomstat 100 percent census of enterprises which we refer to as the 'March Census'. The census has been held periodically since 1956, and from 1976 was held every five years. Enterprises were obliged to provide information on earnings for all their employees. (Braithwaite and Heleniak claim that the March Census was a sample survey and question the method of sampling which they report as having been used (1989, p. 65); our information from Goskomstat, which accords with that given by previous authors, is that this source was indeed a 100 percent census, as we have described.)

The information requested from enterprises in the March Census was the number of persons in a number of discrete earnings bands. The information published for a reduced number of bands is the basis for Tables UE1, UE2, UE5 and UE7–8, with the exception of data for 1984 and 1989 in Table UE1 (see below). Table UE2 contains calculations made by Rabkina and Rimashevskaia (1978) of the decile ratio using March Census data from 1956–1976; they include the ratios for the Censuses held during 1959–1966 which are not included in Table UE1.

The second source of information about the size distribution of earnings relates to data for 1984 and 1989 used in Table UE1 and 1989 in Tables UE3 and UE6. These data come from a sample survey of 310,000 households carried out in March of those years by Goskomstat. We refer to this source as the 'March Household Survey'. This is a survey of households of state sector and collective farm employees, a similar survey having been carried out in 1957, 1972, 1974, 1978 and 1981. We understand from Goskomstat officials that they believe the information on the earnings distribution from this source to be comparable with that from the March Census. Shenfield (1984, pp. 94–95) reports that the methodology of the March Household Survey is similar to that of the Family Budget Survey described below, although, unlike that survey, it apparently covers all branches of the economy. Given that we use the March Household Survey to study the earnings of individuals, the problems of the Family Budget Survey design for the study of incomes of households, described below, are less important. (According to Shenfield, the March Household Survey actually includes the households from the Family Budget Survey as a subset; the remaining households being selected for 'one-off' participation).

It should be noted that the published information on *average* earnings in the USSR comes from a different source, as described in Chapman (1977, p. 262–264). This is the basis for Table UE4.

Coverage. The March Census covered only persons working in state enterprises. Those working on collective farms or private agricultural plots, about 10 percent of the labour force, were excluded (although state farm workers, another 10 percent of the labour force, *are* included). Those employed by 'social organisations', usually taken to mean the Communist Party and its close affiliates, were also excluded. It should be noted that our data extend only to 1986 and therefore the issue of workers in co-operatives and small legal private enterprises does not arise for the March Census; in the case of the 1989 March Household Survey, employees in both are excluded. When using earnings data from the 1989 March Household Survey, we have restricted the sample to the 250,000 persons in the survey employed in state enterprises and farms (i.e. we exclude the collective farm workers).

Employees not working a full month are excluded from the March Census. Persons were only included in the enquiry in respect of their first job unless they did two jobs for the same enterprise in which case their total earnings were included. According to Chapman (1991, p. 196), 2 percent of the state sector labour force held a second job in their own enterprise, and a similar number held second jobs in another enterprise. If part-time workers work a full month, and it is their main job, they are included in the coverage of the enquiry. However, they are identified separately in the results and our tables drawing on the March Census refer to full-time workers only. Tables showing the distribution of earnings from the March Household Survey are restricted to those full-time persons working a full month, as in the March Census.

Definition of earnings. The definition in the March Census was gross earnings for the month in question. The monthly bonus and the monthly value of any quarterly bonuses were included but annual bonuses or any other rewards based on a period of more than three months were excluded. No account was taken of the value of income in kind provided by enterprises such as meals, transport, holiday homes, etc.

Presentation of results. Information on the size distribution in the March Census was published for the first time in the late 1980s and has appeared in a number of official sources including the statistical yearbook (NK) and the compendium of labour statistics published in 1988, *Trud v SSSR*. All these sources have exactly the same amount of detail. The results we use from the March Household Survey for 1989 are taken from the survey report and those for 1984 from Chapman (1991).

(b) Income (UI1–UI5)

Survey design. Russia was one of the pioneers of family budget studies. According to Matthews, 'by the time the Bolsheviks came to power, Russia had already acquired quite a respectable history of investigations into people's living standards' (1986, p. 13–14). After the Revolution, family budget studies continued, and the All-Russian Statistical Conference of November 1922 concerned itself specifically with this subject. There were increasingly restrictions on the publication of such economic information, and analyses ceased to be published after 1928 (Matthews, 1986, p. 18).

After the Second World War, the Family Budget Survey (FBS) was established on a regular basis in 1951, and this provides the source of our tables on the distribution of per capita income (Tables UI1–UI5). Besides the information provided to us by Goskomstat, the sources we have drawn on when describing the FBS include McAuley (1979, Chapter 3), Shenfield (1983, 1984) and Boldyreva (1989). The serious student of the survey is encouraged to consult Shenfield's 700 page Ph.D. thesis on the subject (Shenfield, 1984). This contains far more detail on the design and conduct of the FBS than we can do justice to here.

The FBS has been a survey of families of persons employed in the state sector and of families of collective farmers (these two groups forming separate sub-surveys). Families have been selected by sampling individuals at their place of work.

Sampling appears to have operated principally on a quota basis, with quotas for economic sectors, industrial branches and, within these, republics and oblasts (large territorial units within republics). Beneath this level, enterprises were selected on the basis of average wage level and within each enterprise individuals were chosen according to their skill level and wage. Once included in the sample, an individual (and his or her family) was asked to participate in the FBS until they left the enterprise or retired; retirement did not lead to automatic exclusion from the sample but according to Goskomstat it was usually associated with a family dropping out from the survey. (We return below to the issue of the coverage of pensioners.) Shenfield (1983) reports that about one-third of the sample was replaced every five years; the information we were given by Goskomstat implies a much higher figure: it was claimed that 20 percent of the sample was replaced each year. Irrespective of which figure is closer to the mark, it seems clear that there has been no planned rotation; replacement occurred only when a household dropped out from the survey. Participating households were monitored by the survey throughout the year. There were interviews with the whole household twice every month (Shenfield, 1984, p. 218), with diary records being maintained continuously.

At inception in its post-war form in 1951, the sample size of the FBS was about 51,000 'families', defined as relatives who share a common budget; in 1969 the sample size was raised to around 62,000 families, and then in 1988 to 90,000. We report below in Table S6 figures for the planned sample size in each republic at the time of the increase in size of the survey in 1988.

Drawing partly on claims by Soviet writers, Shenfield (1983) reports that more than one-third of oblasts (or territories of equivalent status) were not represented in the survey, that high wage heavy industrial branches were over-represented in the selection of enterprises, and that less-skilled workers and those outside the direct production process were less likely to be selected at the final stage of drawing the sample. McAuley (1979, p. 51) describes the changes in coverage in the 1960s and 1970s, and suggests that (in the late 1970s) state farm workers were 'grossly under-represented' compared with collective farm workers, although the over-sampling of the latter means that the rural population as a whole has been over-represented (Shenfield, 1984, Chapter B2). (The increase in sample size in 1988 may have rectified this problem since it appears to have been concentrated entirely on worker/employee households (Braithwaite and Heleniak, 1989, Appendix Table 10).) It has been argued that Goskomstat deliberately under-sample single persons for fear that 'they do not maintain a regular household' (Boldyreva, 1989, p. 92).

These criticisms of the FBS appear to have been well known to those responsible for the survey. When announcing the decision to expand the sample size of the FBS from 62,000 to 90,000 households in 1988, Goskomstat specifically cited the problems of regional and branch representation, mentioning 'Siberia, the Far East and the extreme North' as being problematic (*Vestnik statistiki*, 1987, no. 9, p. 7). Boldyreva (1989, p. 91) reports that this expansion of the sample led to persons working in 'science and art, trade, public catering, material-technical supply, and the management apparatus' being covered for the first time.

From the above description of the survey design, it appears that the FBS sample was unrepresentative of the Soviet population for several reasons:

Table S6 *Planned numbers of families in USSR 1988 Family Budget Survey sample*

	Worker/employee families	Collective farm families	Total
Russia	36,422	10,898	47,320
Ukraine	9,818	6,008	15,826
Belarus	1,850	1,495	3,345
Uzbekistan	2,000	1,005	3,005
Kazakhstan	3,607	418	4,025
Georgia	1,331	724	2,055
Azerbaidzhan	1,165	420	1,585
Lithuania	849	396	1,245
Moldavia	881	399	1,280
Latvia	854	396	1,250
Kirgizia	736	449	1,185
Tadzhikistan	853	357	1,210
Armenia	798	332	1,130
Turkmenia	843	462	1,305
Estonia	793	292	1,085
Total	62,800	24,051	86,851

Source: Braithwaite and Heleniak, 1989, Appendix Table 10. This source also gives sample sizes in earlier years.

(1)   The families of those employed in the co-operative or private sectors and those not employed (e.g. students) were in general excluded from the sample.

(2)   Old-age pensioners were originally excluded. Officials at Goskomstat told us that their inclusion started in 1979 and maintained that their numbers in the FBS had increased in line with their importance in the USSR population. Shenfield reports 2,300 pensioner households in the sample in 1981 (1984, p. 127); Goskomstat officials reported to us that some 2 percent of families in the FBS in 1989 were pure pensioner families containing no wage earners, which suggests that their numbers had not in fact increased since the early 1980s. In the 1988 FBS, 4.3 percent of persons in worker/employee households were 'non-working pensioners' and 11.3 percent of persons in the families of collective farm workers were over normal pension age (sixty for men and fifty-five for women) Goskomstat (1989, p. 15 and p. 195). In the USSR as a whole, old-age pensioners in 1989 (including those working) represented 15.5 percent of the total population and persons above working age 17.1 percent (Goskomstat, 1991, p. 107, and NK, 1989, p. 27). It is difficult to compare the population with the survey figures and the proportion of pensioners living on their own in the USSR may be expected to be less than in a Western country. Nevertheless, the data suggest that pensioners in the FBS are still under-

represented in the FBS although perhaps not so severely as some commentators have stated. (We believe that they are included in the income distibution data under the 'worker/employee' or 'collective farm' household headings according to their previous employment.) However, Shenfield argues that 'the sample of pensioners has been built up by retaining participants in the survey after their retirement ... thus biases of the survey of workers and employees are carried over into the survey of pensioners' (1984, p. 189).

(3)   Among families with members working in the state sector, the probability of selection has been proportional to the number of working members since the sampling unit is the worker e.g. families with two working members have twice the chance of being selected.

(4)   The panel nature of the FBS biased the sample towards families of elder persons with long service records, something associated with higher wages and bonuses. This was only partially offset by adjusting the quotas for different types of individuals who replaced those who left the survey.

Response. Goskomstat have consistently claimed that the level of response in the FBS was very high. In common with earlier authors, we are unable to produce concrete figures. A small financial payment was made to participating families but Goskomstat told us that more reliance was placed on using moral pressure exerted through trades unions to persuade families to respond. This accords with Shenfield's conclusion that 'material and moral incentives, and propaganda and . supervisory pressures, have to be applied to recruit those selected into the survey and to retain them in the sample thereafter' (1984, p. 239). (There appear to have been no overt sanctions for refusal to take part.) Boldyreva reports the payment for participation to have been 2 rubles per month and notes that 'it is difficult to get 'deviant' families to participate' (1989, pp. 90–91). Where non-response did occur, the household concerned was substituted with another household with similar observable characteristics.

Income concept. The FBS has collected information on annual *gross* family income, including all money income from employment and from social security benefits. Reported cash income from sales of agricultural produce was included, as was the value at state prices (rather than collective farm or private market prices) of agricultural production for self-consumption (from both collective farms and private plots). The value of benefits in kind from the employer such as meals and transport, was included. In the case of *average incomes* in the survey, which were published in earlier years (the distribution was not published until 1988), the 1985 statistical yearbook (NK) reports (p. 417) that the value of benefits in kind from the state, such as education, medical services and housing ('paid' from the social consumption fund), was included in the definition of average income. On the other hand, the 1987 (p. 404) and subsequent yearbooks indicate that the value of these goods was *not* included. In the case of the *distributional data*, we were told by Goskomstat that, in the 1988 and 1989 yearbook tables on the size distribution in earlier years, the definition of income excludes the value of the social consumption funds. (Boldyreva, 1989, pp. 92–93, also notes that data on the distribution include only cash income from the consumption funds.)

Substantiation of data. Information given by respondents on earnings and pensions was substantiated with employer records.

Presentation of results. Prior to 1988, there had been no publication of the information on the distribution of income from the FBS in official sources. A basic tabulation from the FBS showing the individual distribution of gross family per capita income by percentages in ruble class intervals was published for the first time in the 1988 statistical yearbook (NK) and was repeated in the 1989 yearbook. (The table has also appeared in a number of other sources.) The table provides a series of results from 1981. Results are presented grossed-up to the population level of the USSR. The same applies to tables by republic. The grossing-up at the republic level appears to adjust for the over-sampling of collective farm households. The grossing-up to the all-Union level appears to allow for the different sampling fractions in each republic, since the proportion of the all-Union population in any income group may be obtained from the republic figures by using the true (overall) population figures in each republic as weights.

Detailed results of the survey are contained in a lengthy annual report which is not widely available. We were supplied by Goskomstat with one of what was apparently only 250 copies printed of the report for the 1989 survey (Goskomstat, 1990a). In some cases the 1989 survey report gives more detail on the distribution of income than other available sources. For example, in the case of the distribution of income by republic the FBS report for 1989 gives eight income classes compared with the five in the yearbook (NK, 1989, p. 91) and we have drawn on the more detailed source in Table UI2.

(c) Poverty lines (UP1 and UP2)

As described in Chapter 7, there has been a long series of official minimum budget studies. The recent figure of 78 rubles per month per capita calculated by Goskomstat for 1988 was publicly announced by the government, and, for example, was given at the foot of a table giving the size distribution of income published in a 1989 issue of *Ekonomicheskaia gazeta*.

S.5 BRITAIN

(a) Earnings (BE1–BE4)

Source. An annual enquiry on the distribution of gross earnings and hours of work in Britain – the New Earnings Survey (NES) – has been carried out by the Department of Employment each April since 1970. We have made use of the NES for Great Britain; there is also a similar, but separate, survey for Northern Ireland, to which we do not refer here. The NES collects information on a 1 percent sample of employees; since 1975 this sample has been formed by taking all those persons with National Insurance numbers ending in the digits '14'. The NES collects information on earnings paid, and hours worked, in the pay period (typically a week or month) including a specified date in April of each year. (An initial survey, with a 0.5 percent sample, had been held in September 1968.) Our description draws in part on Micklewright and Trinder (1981) where further details may be found. See also Adams and Owen (1989) and Part A of the annual NES reports.

Although the unit of analysis is the individual, it is employers who provide the information and they are obliged by law to do so. About three-quarters of the sample of individuals are identified from lists supplied by the Inland Revenue of the names and addresses of all employers shown in the Revenue's records to have workers with relevant National Insurance numbers; the remaining quarter is obtained from lists supplied directly by large employers (Adams and Owen, 1989, p. 17). Employers are then asked to provide detailed information on earnings and hours of work for each individual, a separate questionnaire relating to each relevant employee being sent out by the Department.

Employers thus supply micro-data on individuals to the Department rather than just the number of persons employed in a number of discrete earnings bands. It should also be noted that the survey covers only selected employees within the enterprise; the NES is not a survey of all workers in an enterprise. It is also possible that a person with more than one employment appears more than once in the sample, the records not being linked to give total earnings.

Coverage. In principle the NES covers all employees, but there are certain exceptions. Employers are not required to return forms for those in private domestic service, non-salaried directors, persons working for their spouses, clergymen holding pastoral appointments, and those employed outside Great Britain (New Earnings Survey 1990, Part A, para. 3.6). Also excluded are the armed forces, employees of the Royal Household, persons working in the Pall Mall offices of the Royal Automobile Club and the Army and Navy Club, and employees of embassies, high commissions, consulates or other official foreign or international organisations. Since 1982, establishments or paypoints located inside Enterprise Zones have not been covered in the survey (Adams and Owen, 1989, p. 17). From the same source it may be noted that there are other omissions which are not by design. A number of employers cannot be identified because local tax office records are not up-to-date; in other instances the employer is identified but the individual leaves the firm before the survey reference week. Due to the time taken to draw the sample, those persons who have recently changed job or who have become unemployed may be excluded, even if they are working in the April reference week. If an employer fails to comply with the legal obligation to provide information, then individuals with the relevant National Insurance number for inclusion in the NES will be missing from the survey.

The employer is required to indicate if an employee's earnings for the pay period in question have been affected by holidays, sickness, other absence, short-time working or because the employment lasted for only part of the period. Employees

Table S7 *Response to British New Earnings Survey 1990*

	Thousands	%
Questionnaires issued	229.1	100.0
Questionnaires returned	219.7	95.9
Questionnaires not used		
Out of scope	7.0	3.1
Employer not traced	1.4	0.6
No trace of employee	5.3	2.3
Left employer	24.7	10.8
Other reasons	4.1	1.8
Questionnaires used for tabulations	177.2	77.3

Source: NES Report 1990, Part A, para 11.1.

whose earnings have been affected in this way are excluded from many of the published tables; and the statistics used here refer to employees whose earnings were not affected by absence. In 1990, out of 136,917 full-time employees on adult rates, 1,632 (1.2 percent) received no pay and 9,042 (6.6 percent) had pay affected by absence (New Earnings Survey 1990, Part A, Table 21).

Response. The earnings information in the NES tables is typically based on rather less than 80 percent of the original sample (see Table S7). There are a number of reasons, as already indicated. The first is employer non-compliance, which Micklewright and Trinder (1981) estimate to have been 6 percent in 1980. In 1990, some 4 percent of forms issued by the Department of Employment were not returned in time for the deadline – see the figures in Table S7. Secondly, there are those out of scope, such as non-salaried directors. Thirdly, there are those who have left the employer or could not be traced. The resulting 'response' rate in 1990 was 77.3 percent.

For *full-time employees*, the overall response rate is higher. The rate for 1980 was estimated by Micklewright and Trinder (1981) to have been 81.4 percent for full-time workers and 61.9 percent for part-time workers. The figures for full-time employees in three recent years are shown in Table S8.

Definition of earnings. The employer is requested to report the employee's total gross earnings for the pay-period (week or month) in question. Data for a pay-period longer than a week are converted to a weekly basis. Gross earnings are defined to be the total payments to the employee before any statutory or other deductions, and they include overtime, shift premia, payments by results and bonuses. Where bonus or other payments are not paid in each pay period, a proportionate amount is included. Arrears of pay are excluded, as are repayments of travelling or other expenses.

Information is not collected about fringe benefits, payments in kind (except for agricultural and catering workers, where amounts may be taken into account for

Table S8 *Response rate to British New Earnings
Survey for full-time workers 1988–1990*

	Males	%	Females
1988	85.6		85.8
1989	85.8		82.7
1990	85.6		77.8

Sources: NES Report 1988, Part B, p. B(xvi), NES
Report 1989, Part A, para 11.3 and NES Report
1990, Part A, para 11.3.

employer-provided meals or accommodation), or employer contributions to pension schemes. Tips and gratuities received directly by the employee are not included (NES Report 1990, Appendix 1).

Information is collected on hours worked, which allows hourly earnings to be calculated, although in a significant minority of cases employers are not able to specify hours of work (for example for managers).

Presentation of results. The results of the NES are published in a detailed multi-volume survey report: in 1990 Parts A (published in September 1990) to F (published in December 1990). Preliminary results have also been published in the monthly Department of Employment *Employment Gazette*. The main information excludes those not paid in the pay period or whose pay was affected by absence, and all statistics in the Statistical Appendix exclude this group. The published information is classified by male/female and adult/juvenile, and prior to 1983 only separate distributions for these groups were given. In Table BE1, in search of comparability with the Eastern European information, we have combined the figures to provide a series covering all workers for the full run of surveys since 1968. (As such, it avoids the discontinuity in 1983 when the definition was changed from 'adult' to 'those paid on adult rates'.)

(b) Income (BI1–BI7)

Basic sources. There are two main sources from which income distribution statistics in the United Kingdom are derived. The first is the Survey of Personal Incomes (SPI) carried out by the Inland Revenue. This survey is based on information contained in the income tax records for a sample of taxpayers. The SPI began in 1937/8. From 1949/50 to 1969/70 there were surveys with a sample size of about 1 million cases every five years, supplemented by smaller surveys with a sample size of around 125,000 in other years. Since 1970 there have been annual surveys of this latter size (Stark, 1978). The survey assembles information entirely from the Inland Revenue records – there is no contact with the individual taxpayer. The records provide information on the size and composition of income in the relevant tax year. The main unit of analysis is the 'tax unit', which in the period in question was either a single person or a married couple.

The SPI is restricted to those people for whom income tax records are held by the Inland Revenue (see below) and many pensioners and others not in work are therefore not covered. The tax records relate to taxable income and do not cover non-taxable income, particularly certain social security benefits (such as child benefit). For these reasons, the SPI needs to be supplemented by other sources to obtain a picture of the full distribution.

The second major source is the Family Expenditure Survey (FES). This household budget survey, which began as a continuous survey in 1957, collects information on the income and expenditure of a representative sample of households in the United Kingdom (the survey's methodology is described in detail in Kemsley *et al.*, 1980). It collects information on about 7,000 households per year, the sample being drawn afresh each time (there is no panel element). Interviewing takes place continually through the year, the interviews being evenly distributed and the households being observed only once. Sampling uses a multi-stage stratified design, using the electoral register up until 1985 and a master list of post codes in 1986 and subsequent years.

The FES covers all types of private households. A household is defined as a set of persons at the same address having meals prepared together and with common housekeeping. The members of the household are not necessarily related by blood or marriage, and there may be several family units in one household. The original purpose of the FES was to provide spending weights for the index of retail prices, and respondents are asked to keep detailed expenditure diaries for fourteen days, but the income questions form an important part of the questionnaire. Information is collected on a wide range of types of income, including social security benefits received and taxes paid, which allow both net and gross income to be calculated. (The Income Schedule in 1985 was 39 pages long and contained 91 questions.) The income information includes items of household expenditure paid for by the employer, and luncheon vouchers and other free food, but not other items of income in kind. The information is collected on an individual basis, which allows total income to be calculated for sub-units within the household. This may be particularly relevant where more than one family live in the same household.

Estimates of the income distribution. The most extensive estimates of the distribution of income in the United Kingdom is the series published for many years annually in the *United Kingdom National Accounts* (referred to as the 'Blue Book' series). This series is shown in Tables BI1 and BI2. The Blue Book series 'seeks to combine the best features of the available sources' (*Economic Trends*, November 1987, p. 100). It takes the SPI as its starting point but supplements this with information from the FES. Data from the latter are used to add in non-taxable income not covered by the SPI and to augment the SPI sample for those tax units which are not included in the tax records (*Economic Trends*, November 1987, p. 100). The methods by which the sources are combined are described in detail by Ramprakash (1975) and Stark (1972 and 1978).

In Table BI1 (which covers four pages), we have assembled the full run of Blue

K

Book estimates for the post-war period, from 1949 to 1984/5. The following should be noted:

(1) even though the SPI only became an annual survey in 1962/3, distributions have been published for all years since 1949, with those for intervening years being extrapolations of a previous survey; we have not included the latter on the grounds that 'only those which corresponded to the Inland Revenue surveys, namely for 1949, 1954, 1959 and 1962 onwards can be considered reliable' (Stark, 1978, p. 49);

(2) estimates from 1975/6 (with an overlap in this year and 1976/7) have been published on a 'New Basis', where interest payments on mortgages (and certain other deductions, such as for retirement annutities) are not deducted from income;

(3) we have given the interpolations made by the Royal Commission on the Distribution of Income and Wealth (RCDIW); in the case of the median and relative percentiles, these differ significantly in a number of cases from our own interpolations, and the latter are also shown.

There are in addition estimates of the income distribution based solely on the information from the FES. These include:

(1) the summary results published in the annual report of the FES (referred to as the 'FES Report');

(2) the series published in *Economic Trends* each year (referred to as the ET series) on 'The effects of taxes and benefits on household income';

(3) the Department of Social Security series on 'Households Below Average Income' (referred to as HBAI), which replaced the earlier 'Low Income Families' tables.

The second of these is the source for Table BI4 and the third for Table BI5. We have in addition made use of the micro-data tapes of the FES to construct Tables BI3, BI6 and BI7. All of these tables relate to the United Kingdom, except for Table BI5, where the HBAI series is confined to Great Britain.

Coverage. As already explained, the SPI is limited to those people for whom income tax records are held by the Inland Revenue. Where income falls short of the threshold for the operation of Pay-As-You-Earn (collection of tax at source), there may be no tax record. In 1990/1 the threshold for inclusion was a rate of weekly or monthly pay equal to some 20 percent of the average gross earnings of full-time employees paid at adult rates. Very few of those in employment were therefore not covered. On the other hand, 'there are several million pensioners and others not in work who are [not covered and] who are heavily concentrated in the lower ranges of the income distribution' (*Economic Trends*, November 1987, p. 100).

The main exclusion from the FES is that of the institutional population, the survey being limited to the household population. The Blue Book series attempts to cover the institutional population, although, as is noted in *Economic Trends*, 'there are no satisfactory income data for the institutional population as a whole' (August 1975, p. 85). Of the 1.2 million tax units in institutions at that time, 38 percent were pensioners and assumed to be in the lower income ranges, and for a further 17 percent (inmates of prisons, psychiatric hospitals, etc.) there was assumed to be no income. The inclusion of the institutional population is likely therefore to have increased measured inequality.

Response. Non-response has been a recurrent problem with household surveys such as the FES. In 1985, the year to which data in Tables BI3, BI6 and BI7 relate, co-operating households represented 67 percent of the effective UK sample (FES Report 1985, p. iv). This was rather lower than in subsequent years, but the rate has been below 75 percent: 69 percent in 1986, 72 percent in 1987 and 71 percent in 1988. The great majority of the non-response is due to refusals to take part. In 1985, in only about 2 percent of the sample was the interviewer unable to make contact; the remaining 31 percent were refusals. It may be noted that response to the FES varies geographically. In the second half of the 1970s, when the overall response rate was 68-70 percent (in 1976–1978), the response rate to the FES in Greater London was 61 percent (Kemsley *et al.*, 1980, p. 30).

The Office of Population Censuses and Surveys, which is responsible for the FES fieldwork, has carried out investigations of the characteristics of non-respondents to the FES, by making use of the information provided on the (compulsory) returns to the Census of Population. These checks can only be made for Census years; the study by Kemsley (1975) relates to the 1971 Census and that of Redpath (1986) to the 1981 Census. The 1981 comparison indicated that response was lower among households without children and where the head was, or had been, self-employed. There was a fall in the rate of response with the age of the household head: in 1971, response by age of head of household fell from 88 percent in the range 21–25 to 62 percent above age 71.

Evidence of differential non-response to the FES has led to the development of differential grossing-up factors. The Department of Social Security has for a number of years applied factors differentiated by family composition and age, which are designed to bring the grossed-up figures in line with national population estimates. The grossing-up procedure has been extended to further dimensions in the work of Atkinson *et al.* (1988) and Gomulka (1991). In the case of the figures given in our tables, no adjustment has been made by the Central Statistical Office in constructing the ET series shown in Table BI4. The HBAI series in Table BI5 makes use of the DSS differential factors by family type. The same is applied in our own analysis of FES (Tables BI3, BI6 and BI7), where we have taken a simple average of the grossing-up factors where there is more than one family unit in the household.

Time period. The Blue Book estimates (Tables BI1 and BI2) relate to annual income. At the same time, the underlying tax records refer to anyone receiving income at any point in the tax year in question. This includes people who die during the course of the year and people who enter the relevant population, such as school-leavers. In the case of women marrying, or becoming widowed or divorced, they appear twice (once single and once as part of the couple) – see Stark (1978, p. 53). This problem of 'part-year units' was examined by the Royal Commission on the Distribution of Income and Wealth (1979, p. 36). Adjustments to the distribution of *before tax* income indicated that the exclusion of such units would reduce the share of the top 10 percent by 0.3 percentage points in 1975/6 and increase that of the bottom 50 percent from 23.8 percent to 25.7 percent. The Gini coefficient fell from 0.373 to 0.347.

In contrast to the income tax data, the FES makes no attempt to measure households' annual income. The survey collects data for a range of periods, depending on the source of income. Respondents are asked to supply information on earnings in the most recent pay period (week or month), all amounts being converted to a weekly basis, and on 'normal' earnings. In the case of different types of social security benefits, respondents are asked about current receipt and about the last amount (where benefit has been received in the preceding twelve months). The questions about investment income relate to the last twelve months and those concerning self-employment income to 'the last 12 months for which information is available'. As a result, 'the information does not relate to a common or fixed time period' (FES Report, 1985, p. 103). The published FES Report figures are on this hybrid basis. Two kinds of adjustment can be made:

(1) to bring all amounts to a common date (so that the self-employment income, for instance, recorded for a previous accounting period, is up-dated to the date of interview), as has been done with the series used here;

(2) to adjust from a current income basis to an annual income measure, as is done in the ET series in Table BI4, with for example the FES employment data being adjusted for periods of absence from work in the preceding twelve months (see Nolan, 1987, Sections 5.2 and 5.3.)

The FES data adjusted to an annual income basis may still be expected to depart from the Blue Book series. The period covered is twelve months preceding the interview; hence the figures are an average of twelve month periods ranging from the previous year to the current year.

Income concept. In general, the definition of income is based on the sum of different elements:

> earnings + self-employment income + investment income + private transfers + state benefits + other income = *gross income*

from which are subtracted

> income tax + National Insurance contributions
> to give *net income*.

Certain of these items may be negative: for example where there are losses in self-employment, or where interest paid exceeds interest received. The deductions taken into account above are limited to income tax and social security contributions.

The treatment of housing costs and related benefit payments differs in the different estimates of the size distribution:

(1) the definition stated does not allow for interest paid on mortgages by owner-occupiers, which was deducted in the earlier years of the Blue Book series. As noted, the 'new' Blue Book series, introduced in 1975/6, shows income gross of mortgage interest. The effect of this change was to increase the share of the top

10 percent by 0.8 of a percentage point and to reduce that of the bottom 50 percent by 0.7 (*Economic Trends*, May 1978, p. 92). This change made the Blue Book series comparable in this respect with the other series.

(2) imputed rent on owner-occupied property and rent-free accommodation is calculated by the OPCS and included in gross income as defined in the published FES Report. However, it is not included in any of the estimates in the Appendix.

(3) rent rebates (applying to tenants) are included by the Blue Book as part of state benefits, but rate rebates (applying to both owner-occupiers and tenants) are excluded. The same treatment is followed in the ET series, whereas the HBAI series 'before housing costs' includes both. In the FES calculations made here (Tables BI3, BI6 and BI7) both rent and rate rebates are included when calculating disposable income.

Substantiation of data. In the FES, no enquiries are made to employers to substantiate earnings data (the name of the employer is not sought), but OPCS asks respondents to substantiate their reported last weekly or monthly earnings data with wage-slips and around 70–80 percent do so (Kemsley *et al.*, 1980, p. 71). Similarly, interviewers are instructed to ask that respondents confirm their answers for other income headings with documentary evidence. The income interviews take place at the beginning of the two-week expenditure diary period and respondents may produce evidence to substantiate their answers when the interviewer returns to collect the expenditure diaries.

The accuracy of the FES information has been assessed by comparisons of the aggregate totals of different types of income (earnings, investment income, etc.) with the totals in the national accounts. Atkinson and Micklewright (1983) made such a comparison for the years 1970–1977. The figures in Table S9 show for 1977 the income totals recorded in the FES as a percentage of those in national accounts, where the FES totals have been grossed-up to national levels allowing for the sampling fraction and the average level of non-response to the survey. The FES totals were also adjusted to allow for the non-institutional population which is excluded from the survey. It should be noted that we found considerable year to year variation in some of the figures; one of our conclusions was that results for a single year need to be treated with care.

It is important in a comparison of this sort to establish suitable control totals. The national accounts figures may be based on somewhat different definitions (in the figures above we have adjusted the national accounts figures as far as we could to put them on a comparable basis). Moreover, the national accounts figures themselves are only estimates and are surrounded by considerable uncertainties. Taking account of these points, the conclusions that we reached were that the shortfall in the FES below the national accounts totals was considerably less important than had been suggested by earlier investigators, such as Sawyer (1976). At the same time, there is a major deficiency in investment income, no doubt in part on account of differentially high non-response among top income receivers, and in self-employment income, again reflecting differential non-response but also likely to arise on account of under-statement by respondents.

Table S9 *Comparison of total income in UK Family Expenditure Survey with national accounts total 1977*

Income type	FES total as % of adjusted national accounts
Earnings	93.7
Self-employment income	75.7
Occupational pensions	74.5
Social security benefits	90.9
Investment income	50.6
All income types	89.0

Source: Atkinson and Micklewright (1983) Table 2 columns 1–2, Table 3 columns 2, 5 and 7, Table 4 columns 2, 3 and 6, Table 5 columns 1–2, Table 7 columns 2, 3 and 6.

Presentation of results. The Blue Book series was published for many years annually in the *United Kingdom National Accounts*, but has in recent years been published in *Economic Trends*, that for 1984/5 published in November 1987. The results of the underlying Survey of Personal Incomes are now published in *Inland Revenue Statistics* (having previously been a separate publication of the Inland Revenue) and a selection of results are published in the statistical yearbook (the *Annual Abstract of Statistics*). The results of the FES are published by the Department of Employment in an annual volume. The ET income distribution series based on the FES is published in *Economic Trends*, and the HBAI series in *Households Below Average Income*, a publication of the Department of Social Security.

(c) Poverty lines (BP1)

Britain has no official poverty line, but since the publication of *The Poor and the Poorest* by Abel-Smith and Townsend (1965), the social assistance scale has been used by academic researchers for this purpose; and in 1974 the government began a series of estimates of 'Low Income Families' (see Atkinson, 1983, pp. 232–235). Families were considered to have low incomes if their income fell below the point at which they became entitled to social assistance or if they had income less than 40 percent above this cut-off. The social assistance scale for 1970–1987 is shown in Table BP1. At this time the assistance scheme was known as Supplementary Benefit; it has subsequently been re-christened Income Support.

Method. The extent to which there is any relation between the social assistance scale and minimum subsistence budgets is highly ambiguous. The function of the assistance benefit is to provide for minimum needs, and the scale is the successor of the original National Assistance introduced in 1948, which in turn can be traced back to the poverty lines set by Rowntree (and others) on the basis of minimum household budgets. But the determination of assistance standards has been heavily influenced by considerations of cost and of ensuring that benefits remain below the level of wages. In its Green Paper on the *Reform of Social Security*, the Department of Health and Social Security (1985) concluded that:

it is doubtful whether an attempt to establish an objective standard of adequacy would be fruitful. This is for two reasons. First, all such assessments would themselves include judgements on the standards to be achieved. Second, the level of help for those on supplementary benefit cannot be isolated from consideration ... of the returns ... that are available to people in society generally. (1985, p. 21)

In view of the ambiguity surrounding the interpretation of the assistance scale, there has been considerable interest outside government in the examination of underlying budgets – see Bradshaw and Parker (1991).

S.6 Interpolation

The basic data on which we are drawing for Eastern Europe are in the form of grouped distributions, showing the number of people or households in each of a number of income ranges. This may be accompanied by information on the overall mean income or on the mean income of each of the ranges.

As a result, we have to interpolate in order to arrive at values for summary statistics such as the median, the bottom decile or the Gini coefficient. (This would not be necessary if we had access to the micro-data.) A number of earlier writers have used graphical methods. Lydall (1968) made a graphical interpolation of the cumulated frequencies, using natural, semi-log or double-log paper, depending on the shape of the distribution in the range being estimated. Michal felt that 'the graphical method of laying a smooth ogive through the available points, on large-size paper, to be of sufficient accuracy' (1973, p. 412n.). However, while a satisfactory level of accuracy may be obtained, it is impossible for subsequent authors to reproduce the results with confidence. We decided that it was essential that the interpolation method used here should be one that could be readily reproduced by others. In this we have been greatly assisted by the availability of the micro-computer program 'INEQ' written by F. A. Cowell. This package, which may be obtained from him at the London School of Economics, computes summary statistics and inequality measures for income distributions under a wide range of assumptions. Our results were calculated using this program. Readers who wish to reproduce the results may do so by creating the necessary input files (these may be readily created from the machine-readable version of the Statistical Appendix tables, by writing a print file in LOTUS-123).

A Hypothetical Example

The basic method may be illustrated by reference to the following hypothetical data with a small number of ranges:

proportion of the population

£1 – £49	6
£50 – £99	14
£100 – £149	21
£150 – £199	23
£200 – £249	19
£250 – £299	10
£300 –	7
TOTAL	100

In terms of INEQ data types, these are 'grouped, population mean unknown'. The data are entered into INEQ in the form of pairs $(d_1, f_1), \ldots, (d_n, f_n)$, where d_i denotes the starting value of the i-th range from the bottom and f_i denotes the frequency in that range. The top range is denoted by n, so that in our example $n = 7$. The cumulative frequency up to and including range i is denoted by F_i, where this is expressed here in percentage points.

The first assumption concerns the open upper interval. In all our calculations this is assumed to be Paretian in form: i.e. the cumulative frequency in the interval $[d_n, \infty]$ is assumed to be such that:

$$100 - F = (\beta/\alpha)\, x^{-\alpha}$$

where α and β are constants. The Pareto exponent α is calculated from the top two intervals:

$$(100 - F_{n-1})/(100 - F_{n-2}) = (d_n/d_{n-1})^{-\alpha}$$

or (using the fact that $100 - F_{n-1} = f_n$ and $100 - F_{n-2} = f_n + f_{n-1}$) we can solve for:

$$\alpha = \log\{1 + f_{n-1}/f_n\}/\log\{d_n/d_{n-1}\}$$

In the present case this procedure gives a value of:

$$\log\{17/7\}/\log\{300/250\} = 4.867$$

Using this, we can calculate the top decile. We know from the top interval that:

$$7 = (\beta/\alpha)\, 300^{-\alpha}$$

Denoting the top decile by z, this must satisfy:

$$10 = (\beta/\alpha)\, z^{-\alpha}$$

Hence z is given by:

$$£300\,(0.7)^{1/\alpha} = £278.8$$

It may also be seen that the frequency at x is:

$$\beta\, x^{-\alpha-1}$$

which (substituting for β from the expression for the cumulative frequency up to d_{n-1}) is equal to:

$$a\,(f_n+f_{n-1})\,d_{n-1}^a\,x^{-a-1}$$

Evaluating at the starting point of interval $(n-1)$, we have a frequency of:

$$4.867\,(17)\,(250)^{-1}=0.331$$

This approach assumes that the Pareto distribution fits the top two intervals. The second assumption concerns the interpolation within the remaining intervals. The Pareto interpolation made in most of our work assumes that the density of x in the interval $[d_i,d_{i+1}]$ is:

$$b\,x^{-a-1}$$

where the constants a and b vary from one range to the next, and are calculated from the fact that the value of the frequency integrated over the range is equal to f_i and the assumption that the density at d_{i+1} is equal to that calculated from the range above. The procedure involves therefore working successively down from the top interval. With the alternative linear interpolation the assumption about the density is instead that it takes the form:

$$a+bx$$

Again, the constants a and b for each range are calculated from the value of f_i and the assumption that the density at d_{i+1} is equal to that calculated from the range above.

Applying the Pareto interpolation procedure to the data above, we have already calculated the frequency at the value of £250 as 0.331, so that:

$$b\,(250)^{-a-1}=0.331$$

The integral over the range is:

$$(b/a)\,(250)^{-a}\,\{(250/200)^a-1\}=19$$

INEQ uses the Newton–Raphson method to solve for a as 0.2565 and b as 340.9. Using these values we may calculate the upper quartile as £227.2.

Working back, we arrive at the lowest interval, £1 to £49. This is typically open-ended, in the sense that it includes all observations less than £50 (in our example). INEQ fits a frequency distribution to the whole range, which in the present case involves a frequency of 0.203 at $x=$ £50 and 0.014 at $x=$ £1. We may however feel that income is unlikely to fall below some minimum level, and replace the bottom interval by, say, £30–£49. This does not affect the quantiles above this point, but does affect those below and summary measures of inequality, such as the Gini coefficient, and the mean. In our example, it would raise the fifth percentile from £44.9 to £45.4, reduce the Gini coefficient from 27.7 percent to 27.4 percent, and increase the mean from £175.4 to £175.8.

Sensitivity in practice

The sensitivity of the results to different methods of interpolation may be illustrated by reference to the Hungarian income data for 1987 (we use here data with fewer

Table S10 *Sensitivity of results to interpolation method: application to Hungarian income data for 1987*

Amounts in forints

	1	2	3	Known values
Mean	5,283	5,262	5,312	5,262
Median	4,693	4,705	4,708	4,702
P_{10}	61.2	61.1	61.6	61.2
P_{90}	173.3	172.2	175.0	172.9
Var. coef	0.534	0.513	0.525	0.504
Gini coef	0.244	0.242	0.240	n/a
Decile shares:				
1 (lowest)	4.5	4.5	4.9	4.5
2	6.0	6.0	6.0	6.0
3	6.9	6.9	6.8	6.9
4	7.7	7.7	7.6	7.7
5	8.5	8.5	8.4	8.5
6	9.4	9.4	9.3	9.4
7	10.4	10.4	10.3	10.5
8	11.7	11.8	11.7	11.8
9	13.8	13.9	13.8	13.8
10	21.2	20.9	21.1	20.9
Share of top 5%	12.8	12.5	12.7	12.5

Note:

Column 1: Pareto upper tail and Pareto interpolation within ranges, information on neither overall mean nor class means used.

Column 2: Pareto upper tail and Pareto interpolation within ranges, information used on class means.

Column 3: Pareto upper tail and linear interpolation within ranges, information on neither overall mean nor class means used.

The data used in obtaining the results were as follows:

Forints per month	percent	mean
up to 2,600	6.4	2,130
2,600–3,400	13.4	3,047
3,401–4,200	18.9	3,801
4,201–5,000	17.5	4,592
5,001–5,800	13.6	5,382
5,801–6,600	9.6	6,174
6,601–7,400	6.5	6,963
7,401–10,000	9.4	8,378
above 10,000	4.7	13,417
	100.0	

Sources: HI1 (frequencies) and HI5 (means)

ranges than in Table HI1). We take this example since we have information from the micro-data on the following statistics:

median, tenth and ninetieth percentiles expressed relative to the median (referred to as P10 and P90), the decile shares and the share of the top 5 percent, and the coefficient of variation.

We also have information for this year on the mean income in different ranges, so that we can assess the contribution made by this additional information to improving the accuracy of the interpolation.

We show in Table S10 three sets of results, together with the known values. The first set of results are produced with an assumed Pareto upper tail, with Pareto interpolation within ranges, and a value of 1 for the bottom of the lowest range. It may be seen that the median, which has to be interpolated between percentiles of 38.7 percent and 56.2 percent, is 9 forints different (4,693 compared with 4,702), which seems an acceptable margin of error. The bottom decile is out by the same relative amount, so that P10 agrees with the known value. It is at the top that the main differences appear, with P90 being overstated. The same applies to the decile shares, which are identical up to the sixth decile, but where the share of the top decile is overstated (21.2 percent compared with 20.9 percent), as is that of the top 5 percent.

Information on the overall mean does not affect the interpolated percentiles, but does allow the interpolation routine to correct the overstatement of the shares of the top decile. The incorporation of the known mean (results not shown in Table S10) has the effect of reducing the share of the top 10 percent to 20.9 percent and that of the top 5 percent to 12.5 percent. Use of the further information on class means (column 2 in Table S10) produces an estimate of the median that is within 3 forints of the known value. The decile shares are all estimated exactly, except for two which differ by 0.1 percent. P90 is now too low, and in fact the percentage error is larger. Column 3 shows the results with linear interpolation, where the frequency in each range is assumed to be a linear (rather than iso-elastic) function. It may be seen that the value of P10 is now overstated, as is the share of the bottom decile. The share of the top groups, and P90, are overstated.

Finally, it may be seen that the value of the coefficient of variation is noticeably affected: the value with Pareto interpolation being some 6 percent too high. The incorporation of class mean information reduces the coefficient to closer to the known value, but it appears to be more sensitive than the Gini coefficient.

Statistical Appendix

TABLES IN STATISTICAL APPENDIX

The tables in the Statistical Appendix use the numbering system described at the beginning of Sources and Methods.

The data in each table are available as LOTUS-123 (release 3) spreadsheets for micro-computers. The name of the spreadsheet file corresponding to each table is given in the list below. A set of discs (3.5 inch) containing these spreadsheet files are available at a price of £50 (inclusive of postage and packing, payable in advance) from:

A B Atkinson
Faculty of Economics and Politics
Austin Robinson Building
Sidgwick Avenue
Cambridge CB3 9DE
United Kingdom

General Notes

1 The ranges in the tables are indicated by the lowest value in the range: for example, in Table CSE1 (continued) the first range for 1968 is that from 1–600 Crowns.

2 By convention, the starting point of the initial ranges is taken as 1, except where otherwise indicated as greater than 1 in the original source.

3 The top range is typically unbounded. For example, in Table CSE1 (continued) in 1968 there are 11,594 in the range 5,001 Crowns and upwards.

4 Where ranges are combined, we show dashes for the ranges included in the earlier figure. For example, in Table CSE1 (continued) in 1985 there are 5,620 in the range 1–1,000 Crowns (i.e. combining the ranges 1–600, 601–800 and 801–1,000).

5 The dashes do *not* indicate zero (see Note 4); where a range is empty this is indicated explicitly by zero. There are, for example, in Table CSE1 (continued) in 1977 no recorded earnings in the range 1–600 Crowns.

6 P5 denotes the fifth percentile *from the bottom*, expressed as a percentage of the median, with similar definitions for P10 etc. Var coef denotes the coefficient of variation, i.e. the standard deviaton divided by the mean.

284

7 All figures in the summary statistics that we have interpolated ourselves from the original sources *are set in italics.*

8 Where a percentile is interpolated in an open upper interval (assuming a Pareto distribution), this is indicated by an asterisk. In the case of the lowest interval commencing at 1, we have not in general attempted to interpolate percentiles and the entry is indicated by a dash.

Czechoslovakia

CSE1 Distribution of gross monthly EARNINGS in Crowns for ALL WORKERS 1959–1966
    CSE1.WK3

CSE1(continued) Distribution of gross monthly EARNINGS in Crowns for ALL WORKERS 1968–1989
    CSE1CONT.WK3

CSE2 Distribution of gross monthly EARNINGS in Crowns for MALES 1959–1966
    CSE2.WK3

CSE2(continued) Distribution of gross monthly EARNINGS in Crowns for MALES 1968–1989
    CSE2CONT.WK3

CSE3 Distribution of gross monthly EARNINGS in Crowns for FEMALES 1959–1966
    CSE3.WK3

CSE3(continued) Distribution of gross monthly EARNINGS in Crowns for FEMALES 1968–1989
    CSE3CONT.WK3

CSE4 AVERAGE gross monthly earnings in Crowns by REPUBLIC 1959–1989
    CSE4.WK3

CSE5 Distribution of gross monthly EARNINGS in Crowns by REPUBLIC 1989
    CSE5.WK3

CSI1 Individual distribution of household net per capita INCOME in Crowns (annual income) 1958—1973
    CSI1.WK3

CSI1(continued) Individual distribution of household net per capita INCOME in Crowns (annual income) 1976—1988
    CSI1CONT.WK3

CSI2 Individual distribution of household net per capita INCOME in DECILE SHARES (annual income) 1958—1988
    CSI2.WK3

CSI3 HOUSEHOLD and INDIVIDUAL distribution of net per capita income in Crowns (annual income) 1988
    CSI3.WK3

CSI4 MEAN individual net per capita income in Crowns (annual income) by REPUBLICS 1958—1988
    CSI4.WK3

CSI5 Individual distribution of household net per capita INCOME in Crowns (annual income) 1958 and 1988
   CSI5.WK3
CSI6 Household distribution of household net per capita income in Crowns (annual income divided by 12) by NUMBER OF CHILDREN 1980, 1985 and 1988
   CSI6.WK3
CSP1 SUBSISTENCE and SOCIAL MINIMA per capita monthly income in Crowns for households of different types
   CSP1.WK3

Hungary

HE1 Distribution of gross monthly EARNINGS in Forints for ALL WORKERS in SOCIALISED sector 1970–1988
   HE1.WK3
HE2 Distribution of gross monthly EARNINGS in Forints for MALES in SOCIALISED sector 1970–1988
   HE2.WK3
HE3 Distribution of gross monthly EARNINGS in Forints for FEMALES in SOCIALISED sector 1970–1988
   HE3.WK3
HE4 Distribution of gross monthly EARNINGS in Forints for ALL WORKERS in STATE sector 1951–1970
   HE4.WK3
HI1 Individual distribution of household net per capita INCOME in Forints (annual income divided by 12) 1962–1987
   HI1.WK3
HI2 Individual distribution of household net per capita income in DECILE SHARES (annual income divided by 12) 1962–1987
   HI2.WK3
HI3 Distribution of household net income adjusted in different ways for HOUSE-HOLD SIZE (annual income divided by 12) 1977–1987
   HI3.WK3
HI4 Distribution of household net income adjusted in different ways for HOUSE-HOLD SIZE in QUANTILE SHARES (annual income divided by 12) 1987
   HI4.WK3
HI5 Value of per capita SOCIAL INCOME IN KIND by household net per capita income in Forints (annual income divided by 12) 1987
   HI5.WK3
HI6 Individual distribution of household net per capita income in Forints (annual income divided by 12) by ACTIVITY STATUS and HOUSEHOLD SIZE 1987
   HI6.WK3
HP1 MINIMUM SUBSISTENCE and SOCIAL MINIMUM per capita monthly income in Forints for households of different types 1982—1989
   HP1.WK3

Poland

PE1 Distribution of monthly EARNINGS in Zloty for ALL WORKERS 1970–1982
  PE1.WK3

PE1(continued) Distribution of monthly EARNINGS in Zloty for ALL WORKERS 1983–1989
  PE1CONT.WK3

PE2 PUBLISHED DECILES and INEQUALITY MEASURES for distribution of monthly EARNINGS in Zloty for ALL WORKERS 1970–1989
  PE2.WK3

PE3 Distribution of monthly EARNINGS in Zloty for MALES and FEMALES 1972 and 1985
  PE3.WK3

PE4 Distribution of GROSS monthly EARNINGS in Zloty for ALL WORKERS 1956–1972
  PE4.WK3

PI1 Individual distribution of household net per capita INCOME for all households in Zloty (annual income divided by 12) 1983–1986
  PI1.WK3

PI1(continued) Individual distribution of household net per capita INCOME for all households in Zloty (annual income divided by 12) 1987–1989
  PI1CONT.WK3

PI2 Individual distribution of household net per capita INCOME in DECILE SHARES (annual income divided by 12) 1983–1989
  PI2.WK3

PI3 Individual distribution of household net per capita INCOME by HOUSE-HOLD TYPE in decile shares (annual income divided by 12) 1983–1989
  PI3.WK3

PI4 Individual distribution of household net per capita INCOME for WORKER HOUSEHOLDS in Zloty (annual income) 1974–1983
  PI4.WK3

PI5 Individual distribution of household net per capita INCOME for all households in Zloty (annual income divided by 12) by HOUSEHOLD SIZE 1985
  PI5.WK3

PP1 SOCIAL MINIMUM per capita monthly income in Zloty for households of different types 1981—1989
  PP1.WK3

PP2 COMPOSITION of SOCIAL MINIMUM basket for households of different types 1983 and 1989
  PP2.WK3

USSR

UE1 Distribution of gross monthly EARNINGS in Rubles for ALL WORKERS 1956–1989
  UE1.WK3

UE2 DECILE RATIOS of gross monthly EARNINGS in Rubles for ALL
WORKERS 1956–1976
UE2.WK3

UE3 Distribution of gross monthly EARNINGS in Rubles for MALES and
FEMALES 1989
UE3.WK3

UE4 AVERAGE gross monthly EARNINGS in Rubles by REPUBLICS
1940–1982
UE4.WK3

UE4(continued) AVERAGE gross monthly EARNINGS in Rubles by
REPUBLICS 1983–1989
UE4CONT.WK3

UE5 Distribution of gross monthly EARNINGS in Rubles by REPUBLICS 1981
and 1986
UE5.WK3

UE6(pages A–D) Distribution of gross monthly EARNINGS in rubles for
MALES and FEMALES by REPUBLICS 1989
UE6A.WK3
UE6B.WK3
UE6C.WK3
UE6D.WK3

UE6(continued) SUMMARY STATISTICS for distribution of gross monthly
EARNINGS for MALES and FEMALES by REPUBLICS 1989
UE6CONT.WK3

UE7 Distribution of gross monthly EARNINGS in Rubles for the UKRAINE
1968–1986
UE7.WK3

UE8 Distribution of gross monthly EARNINGS in Rubles for AZERBAIDZ-
HAN 1972–1986
UE8.WK3

UI1 Individual distribution of household gross per capita INCOME in Rubles
(annual income divided by 12) 1980–1989
UI1.WK3

UI2 Individual distribution of household gross per capita INCOME in DECILE
SHARES (annual income divided by 12) 1980–1989
UI2.WK3

UI3 Individual distribution of household gross per capita INCOME in Rubles
(annual income divided by 12) by REPUBLICS and for WORKERS and
COLLECTIVE FARM WORKERS 1989
UI3.WK3

UI3(continued) SUMMARY STATISTICS for individual distribution of household gross per capita INCOME (annual income divided by 12) by REPUBLICS
(and USSR) for WORKERS and COLLECTIVE FARM WORKERS 1989
UI3CONT.WK3

UI4 Individual distribution of household gross per capita INCOME in DECILE
SHARES (annual income divided by 12) 1980–1989 for USSR, RSFSR and

Ukraine for WORKERS and COLLECTIVE FARM WORKERS
   UI4.WK3
UI5 Distribution of household gross per capita INCOME (annual income divided
   by 12) by NUMBER of CHILDREN 1989
   UI5.WK3
UI6 Average per capita income by REPUBLIC relative to RSFSR 1960–1988
   UI6.WK3
UP1 Khrushchev minimum budgets c.1965
   UP1.WK3
UP2 Average SUBSISTENCE MINIMUM per capita monthly income in Rubles
   1988 and 1989
   UP2.WK3

Britain

BE1 Distribution of gross weekly EARNINGS in Pounds for ALL WORKERS
   1968–1979
   BE1.WK3
BE1(continued) Distribution of gross weekly EARNINGS in Pounds for ALL
   WORKERS 1980–1990
   BE1CONT.WK3
BE2 Distribution of gross weekly EARNINGS in Pounds for MALES and
   FEMALES April 1990
   BE2.WK3
BE3 Distribution of gross weekly EARNINGS in Pounds for MALES and
   FEMALES (adult workers) SUMMARY STATISTICS 1968–1990
   BE3.WK3
BE4 Distribution of gross weekly EARNINGS in Pounds by COUNTRY (Eng-
   land, Wales and Scotland) April 1990
   BE4.WK3
BI1 Tax unit distribution of tax unit net INCOME in Pounds (annual income)
   OLD BASIS 1949–1964
   BI1.WK3
BI1(continued) Tax unit distribution of tax unit net INCOME in Pounds (annual
   income) OLD BASIS 1965–1970/1
   BI1CONT.WK3
BI1(further continued) Tax unit distribution of tax unit net INCOME in Pounds
   (annual income) OLD BASIS 1971/2–1976/7
   BI1FURTH.WK3
BI1(new) Tax unit distribution of tax unit net INCOME in Pounds (annual
   income) NEW BASIS 1975/6–1984/5
   BI1NEW.WK3
BI2 Tax unit distribution of tax unit net INCOME in DECILE SHARES (annual
   income) 1949–1984/5
   BI2.WK3

BI3 Distribution of household net income adjusted in different ways for HOUSE-HOLD SIZE Pounds per week (current income) 1985
    BI3.WK3
BI4 HOUSEHOLD distribution of HOUSEHOLD EQUIVALISED net income in QUINTILE SHARES (annual income) 1977–1989
    B4.WK3
BI5 INDIVIDUAL distribution of HOUSEHOLD EQUIVALISED net income in DECILE SHARES (current income) 1979–1987
    BI5.WK3
BI6 Individual distribution of household net per capita income Pounds per week (current income) by COUNTRY 1985
    BI6.WK3
BI7 Individual distribution of household net per capita income by HOUSEHOLD SIZE Pounds per week (current income) 1985
    BI7.WK3
BP1 SOCIAL ASSISTANCE total weekly income in Pounds for households of different types 1970–1988
    BP1.WK3

Tables

Table CSE1. Distribution of gross monthly EARNINGS in crowns for ALL WORKERS 1959-1966

Lower value of range	1959	1961	1962	1963	1964	1966
1	65,429	20,907	15,271	12,156	13,779	11,272
601	92,732	48,972	39,925	31,824	31,171	20,993
701	154,167	114,134	101,893	89,645	92,213	70,415
801	224,568	180,827	165,629	169,018	176,382	140,309
901	292,210	249,347	240,953	250,318	257,224	219,234
1,001	656,242	639,741	637,780	655,590	673,366	613,461
1,201	644,372	653,068	669,420	682,991	690,557	675,854
1,401	580,977	612,123	623,421	639,568	651,072	639,590
1,601	442,128	526,316	550,156	570,045	580,325	609,256
1,801	287,149	378,699	409,506	417,260	431,376	492,517
2,001	303,092	439,621	491,380	481,737	509,696	615,343
2,501	83,010	128,637	147,074	135,164	152,475	188,948
3,001	24,738	38,823	44,173	39,298	44,781	57,171
3,501	8,283	12,764	14,553	12,719	14,634	19,065
4,001	3,218	4,757	5,371	4,472	4,910	6,913
4,501	1,219	1,822	2,091	1,692	1,861	2,759
5,001	883	1,281	1,452	1,039	1,154	2,106
Total	3,864,417	4,051,839	4,160,048	4,194,536	4,326,976	4,385,206

Mean	1,410	1,519	1,550	1,542	1,552	1,619
Median	1,338	1,440	1,468	1,466	1,470	1,539
P5	54.4	56.5	57.0	58.2	57.8	57.7
P10	62.6	63.9	64.3	64.9	64.9	64.4
P25	78.0	78.5	78.7	78.9	78.6	78.4
P75	125.2	124.9	124.9	124.1	124.6	124.1
P90	152.1	151.4	151.5	149.6	151.3	149.9
P95	172.5	171.6	171.3	168.6	170.6	168.8
P90/P10	2.43	2.37	2.36	2.30	2.33	2.33
Var coef	0.368	0.357	0.354	0.345	0.348	0.347
Gini coef	0.196	0.191	0.190	0.185	0.188	0.187

Sources:

FSU (1990), Table 26, p. 140; SR 1967, Table 4-18, p. 117.
Further information supplied by FSU was used to split the
ranges 601-800 and 801-1,000. This source gave frequencies
in percent form to two decimal places which we used to
apportion the absolute frequencies as above.

Table CSE1 (continued) Distribution of gross monthly EARNINGS in crowns for ALL WORKERS 1968-1989

Lower value of range	1968	1970	1973	1975	1977	1979	1981	1983	1985	1987	1989
1	4,294	2,974	1,354	728	0	0	0	0	5,620	4,988	3,891
601	48,656	28,029	14,317	11,754	3,430	2,442	16,587	8,274	-	-	-
801	222,488	125,312	59,511	37,400	24,051	19,510	-	-	291,566	270,893	195,968
1,001	454,665	310,447	182,787	124,134	78,975	54,852	50,979	28,203	-	-	-
1,201	619,501	494,192	329,435	265,538	190,748	139,124	133,484	121,958	-	-	-
1,401	624,269	566,664	482,159	426,768	341,564	254,819	251,091	217,694	578,164	538,696	396,838
1,601	611,183	556,641	523,823	510,896	460,050	376,992	375,866	322,603	-	-	-
1,801	567,848	563,630	534,105	520,182	495,241	450,564	451,645	363,185	1,165,431	1,153,811	1,004,957
2,001	448,258	510,181	534,685	523,198	496,132	464,046	1,237,173	1,206,109	-	-	-
2,201	334,997	417,267	502,266	525,403	506,855	472,637	-	-	-	-	-
2,401	160,794	207,771	251,353	266,445	259,541	291,408	1,079,211	1,033,578	1,001,504	1,011,057	946,172
2,501	75,860	117,342	176,242	206,440	231,075	178,013	-	-	-	-	-
2,601	157,495	234,139	347,871	399,348	441,907	458,446	-	-	-	-	-
2,801	108,671	173,741	273,661	319,967	373,385	421,703	809,852	869,198	927,690	957,720	947,818
3,001	71,054	123,138	208,829	249,062	302,776	363,862	-	-	-	-	-
3,201	47,359	86,756	155,957	185,547	240,698	307,513	-	-	-	-	-
3,401	22,209	41,128	75,734	92,772	118,387	111,844	522,873	637,062	718,769	755,225	839,818
3,501	10,430	20,251	40,732	52,671	71,787	141,754	-	-	-	-	-
3,601	22,238	42,695	83,854	106,883	145,774	200,976	-	-	-	-	-
3,801	15,499	31,404	61,510	79,511	111,470	157,940	-	-	-	-	-
4,001	21,331	42,589	85,713	114,850	174,162	253,814	270,963	361,808	439,139	464,083	574,505
4,501	9,682	20,503	41,456	56,982	86,252	129,329	137,685	200,050	270,223	298,069	399,162
5,001	11,594	25,415	21,076	28,950	44,726	68,087	169,263	223,492	176,525	191,512	285,029
5,501	-	-	11,542	16,026	25,257	37,826	-	-	-	-	-
6,001	-	-	17,564	24,297	37,359	54,578	-	-	109,447	124,743	194,208
Total	4,670,375	4,742,209	5,017,536	5,148,752	5,261,602	5,412,079	5,506,672	5,593,214	5,684,078	5,770,797	5,788,366

Mean	1,814	2,012	2,265	2,384	2,553	2,738	2,762	2,906	3,039	3,086	3,296
Median	1,704	1,920	2,124	2,277	2,411	2,602	2,597	2,734	2,875	2,945	3,225
P5	54.6	57.9	56.7	54.3	55.2	56.6	56.7	56.3	55.2	54.9	53.5
P10	65.7	62.7	63.2	64.2	64.7	62.6	63.9	62.4	63.4	63.5	61.7
P25	78.0	78.1	78.0	76.4	80.1	77.6	78.6	78.4	78.4	77.6	75.7
P75	124.9	124.2	126.8	124.1	125.3	124.7	127.7	128.6	127.0	126.0	124.3
P90	154.4	154.1	157.2	151.6	154.8	153.9	155.5	156.7	156.1	154.4	149.6
P95	176.5	175.3	178.3	173.0	176.8	175.1	176.7	176.3	174.2	172.9	171.7
P90/P10	2.35	2.46	2.49	2.36	2.39	2.46	2.43	2.51	2.44	2.43	2.43
Var coef	0.363	0.368	0.364	0.361	0.359	0.357	0.355	0.354	0.350	0.347	0.343
Gini coef	0.194	0.198	0.197	0.195	0.195	0.196	0.197	0.198	0.198	0.198	0.198

Note: the grouping assumption is linear from 1968 to 1975.

Sources:
all years: FSU (1990) Table 26, pp. 140-142;
1968-1975: SR 1976, Table 4-17, p. 129;
1977-1979: SR 1980, Table 7-19, p. 209.

Further information supplied by J. Vecernik was used to split the range 5,001 plus for 1973-1979. This source gave frequencies in percent form to two decimal places which we used to apportion the absolute frequencies as above.

Table CSE2. Distribution of gross monthly EARNINGS in crowns for MALES 1959-1966

Lower value of range	1959	1961	1962	1963	1964	1966
1	17,269	5,406	4,138	3,021	3,223	2,508
601	55,255	29,107	23,756	19,690	20,068	14,055
801	126,406	78,786	69,846	68,083	65,077	53,084
1,001	264,849	171,909	151,592	147,530	140,788	106,547
1,201	429,634	330,970	307,248	305,697	303,410	233,253
1,401	495,428	468,457	454,136	467,738	472,318	407,560
1,601	409,242	469,056	480,432	500,758	505,765	506,307
1,801	274,602	356,712	382,788	390,514	401,096	449,055
2,001	295,085	425,454	474,601	464,444	488,505	582,667
2,501	81,786	126,667	144,902	132,877	149,584	183,783
3,001	24,495	38,458	43,800	38,987	44,336	56,332
3,501	8,229	12,701	14,491	12,665	14,566	18,891
4,001	3,200	4,742	5,357	4,461	4,889	6,873
4,501	1,214	1,817	2,083	1,689	1,859	2,747
5,001	874	1,278	1,450	1,037	1,153	2,095
Total	2,487,568	2,521,520	2,560,620	2,559,191	2,616,637	2,625,757

Mean	1,607	1,747	1,788	1,778	1,796	1,877
Median	1,542	1,671	1,710	1,704	1,720	1,797
P5	58.6	61.3	61.9	62.9	62.8	63.2
P10	68.1	70.2	70.6	71.4	71.6	72.0
P25	83.2	84.2	84.4	84.9	84.7	85.2
P75	119.5	119.0	118.8	118.0	118.2	117.8
P90	142.7	141.9	141.7	140.0	141.0	139.9
P95	161.2	159.5	158.8	156.4	157.2	156.5
P90/P10	2.09	2.02	2.01	1.96	1.97	1.94
Var coef	0.317	0.304	0.299	0.289	0.292	0.289
Gini coef	0.168	0.161	0.159	0.154	0.153	0.153

Sources:
FSU (1990), Table 27, p. 149, and SR 1967, Tables 4-18 and 4-19, pp. 117-118.

Table CSE2 (continued) Distribution of gross monthly EARNINGS in crowns for MALES 1968-1989

Lower value of range	1968	1970	1973	1975	1977	1979	1987	1989
1	737	622	351	256	0	0	1,612	1,278
601	8,861	6,272	3,392	9,673	6,350	5,368	-	-
801	33,532	18,464	9,326	-	-	-	-	-
1,001	71,632	47,921	27,389	20,006	13,686	9,459	55,458	41,532
1,201	138,566	87,515	52,256	41,804	31,129	21,997	-	-
1,401	253,681	156,793	92,962	75,575	57,968	42,116	-	-
1,601	395,798	255,134	154,113	125,620	92,232	64,064	86,772	62,730
1,801	454,700	367,489	248,030	195,327	143,006	96,651	-	-
2,001	391,063	394,900	332,053	281,869	214,695	141,548	267,529	197,501
2,201	302,725	350,324	368,021	354,561	294,750	208,141	-	-
2,401	146,642	177,222	189,791	187,950	158,083	161,629	-	-
2,501	71,299	106,972	150,904	171,952	181,244	107,219	497,405	367,730
2,601	147,093	211,413	292,621	324,001	337,204	313,760	-	-
2,801	102,639	159,646	237,875	270,891	303,241	321,503	-	-
3,001	67,741	115,228	185,441	216,885	255,114	295,839	690,092	594,547
3,201	45,424	81,688	140,978	167,337	208,399	261,453	-	-
3,401	21,358	38,784	68,549	83,019	102,859	90,381	-	-
3,501	10,101	19,282	37,460	48,121	64,588	131,730	634,494	664,735
3,601	21,483	40,599	77,033	97,317	130,136	179,362	-	-
3,801	15,023	29,864	56,768	72,691	100,408	142,808	-	-
4,001	20,777	40,505	79,308	105,806	158,739	232,295	405,878	484,975
4,501	9,438	19,512	38,271	52,501	79,167	119,893	270,639	354,023
5,001	11,358	24,167	19,485	26,722	41,252	63,542	171,445	249,558

	5,501	6,001		Total

5,501	-	-	10,760	14,549	23,052	35,026	-	-
6,001	-	-	16,577	22,863	35,488	51,453	114,768	175,969
Total	2,741,671	2,750,316	2,889,714	2,967,296	3,032,790	3,097,237	3,196,092	3,194,578
Mean	2,105	2,336	2,615	2,742	2,933	3,166	3,562	3,796
Median	2,005	2,246	2,474	2,611	2,806	3,043	3,501	3,694
P5	61.5	60.0	63.5	61.4	60.4	60.1	59.6	61.2
P10	73.5	70.4	68.2	70.6	69.8	69.5	68.9	68.2
P25	83.4	84.8	83.3	83.3	83.3	82.7	82.0	85.9
P75	119.9	118.9	121.5	120.3	119.6	120.3	120.6	121.4
P90	145.0	145.6	146.4	145.1	145.5	144.3	139.9	143.6
P95	164.9	163.9	165.6	165.0	165.3	163.4	160.5	165.7*
P90/P10	1.97	2.07	2.15	2.05	2.09	2.08	2.03	2.11
Var coef	0.307	0.312	0.312	0.310	0.309	0.300	0.291	0.287
Gini coef	0.161	0.166	0.166	0.167	0.168	0.167	0.162	0.162

Note: the grouping assumption is linear for 1968-1975.

Sources:

All years: FSU (1990) Table 27, pp. 149-151;

1968-1970: SR 1971, Table 5-14, p. 146; 1973: SR 1974, Table 5-14, p. 144.
Further information supplied by J. Vecernik was used to split the
ranges between 2,001 and 4,000 for 1975-1979 and the
range 5,001 plus for 1973-1979. This source gave frequencies
in percent form to two decimal places which we used to
apportion the absolute frequencies as above.

Table CSE3. Distribution of gross monthly EARNINGS in crowns for FEMALES 1959-1966

Lower value of range	1959	1961	1962	1963	1964	1966
1	48,160	15,501	11,133	9,135	10,556	8,764
601	191,644	133,999	118,062	101,779	103,316	77,353
801	390,372	351,388	336,736	351,253	368,529	306,459
1,001	391,393	467,832	486,188	508,060	532,578	506,914
1,201	214,738	322,098	362,172	377,294	387,147	442,601
1,401	85,549	143,666	169,285	171,830	178,754	232,030
1,601	32,886	57,260	69,724	69,287	74,560	102,949
1,801	12,547	21,987	26,718	26,746	30,280	43,462
2,001	8,007	14,167	16,779	17,293	21,191	32,676
2,501	1,224	1,970	2,172	2,287	2,891	5,165
3,001	243	365	373	311	445	839
3,501	54	63	62	54	68	174
4,001	18	15	14	11	21	40
4,501	5	5	8	3	2	12
5,001	9	3	2	2	1	11
Total	1,376,849	1,530,319	1,599,428	1,635,345	1,710,339	1,759,449

Mean	1,056	1,144	1,170	1,174	1,178	1,233
Median	1,027	1,115	1,141	1,143	1,146	1,194
P5	62.3	65.3	65.8	67.7	67.9	64.7
P10	70.5	72.1	72.5	73.6	73.3	72.6
P25	83.8	84.8	85.1	85.5	85.3	85.6
P75	117.5	115.9	115.8	115.4	115.0	116.2
P90	136.8	134.7	134.3	133.5	134.6	135.1
P95	151.4	147.8	147.3	146.6	147.4	149.4
P90/P10	1.94	1.87	1.85	1.82	1.84	1.86
Var coef	0.278	0.257	0.254	0.248	0.252	0.259
Gini coef	0.149	0.139	0.137	0.133	0.135	0.140

Sources:
FSU (1990), Table 27, p. 158, and SR 1967, Table 4-19, p. 118.

Table CSE3 (continued) Distribution of gross monthly EARNINGS in crowns for FEMALES 1968-1989

Lower value of range	1968	1970	1973	1975	1977	1979	1987	1989
1	3,557	2,352	1,003	472	0	0	3,376	2,613
601	39,795	21,757	10,925	39,481	21,131	16,584	-	-
801	188,956	106,848	50,185	-	-	-	-	-
1,001	383,033	262,526	155,398	104,128	65,289	45,393	215,435	154,436
1,201	480,935	406,677	277,179	223,734	159,619	117,127	-	-
1,401	370,588	409,871	389,197	351,193	283,596	212,703	-	-
1,601	215,385	301,507	369,710	385,276	367,818	312,928	451,924	334,108
1,801	113,148	196,141	286,075	324,855	352,235	353,913	-	-
2,001	57,195	115,281	202,632	241,247	281,325	322,396	886,282	807,456
2,201	32,272	66,943	134,245	171,010	212,220	264,536	-	-
2,401	14,152	30,549	61,562	78,409	101,455	129,841	513,652	578,442
2,501	4,561	10,370	25,338	34,580	50,131	70,817	-	-
2,601	10,402	22,726	55,250	75,253	104,550	144,650	-	-
2,801	6,032	14,095	35,786	49,078	69,997	100,213	267,628	353,271
3,001	3,313	7,910	23,388	32,320	47,740	68,021	-	-
3,201	1,935	5,068	14,979	21,183	32,347	46,042	-	-
3,401	851	2,344	7,185	9,637	15,402	21,483	120,731	175,083
3,501	329	969	3,272	4,557	7,352	9,983	-	-
3,601	755	2,096	6,821	9,609	15,616	21,517	-	-
3,801	476	1,540	4,742	6,770	10,931	15,270	-	-
4,001	554	2,084	6,405	9,044	15,423	21,519	58,205	89,530
4,501	244	991	3,185	4,481	7,085	9,436	27,430	45,139
5,001	236	1,248	3,360	5,139	7,550	10,470	20,067	35,471

	Total							
5,501	'	'	'	'	'	'	'	18,239
6,001	'	'	'	'	'	'	9,975	
Total	1,928,704	1,991,893	2,127,822	2,181,456	2,228,812	2,314,842	2,574,705	2,593,788
Mean	1,400	1,565	1,789	1,896	2,035	2,166	2,495	2,679
Median	1,328	1,498	1,678	1,793	1,934	2,044	2,315	2,500
P5	64.1	63.1	65.9	64.5	63.6	62.7	58.7	59.3
P10	71.9	72.1	71.4	71.3	70.8	72.5	72.7	73.0
P25	87.2	83.6	85.1	84.3	83.4	83.6	85.9	83.4
P75	119.9	119.0	121.2	120.1	117.9	120.1	122.6	122.9
P90	143.6	140.8	145.6	145.3	146.3	146.1	148.7	150.3
P95	156.7	160.6	167.9	165.6	164.4	163.0	169.6	171.5
P90/P10	2.00	1.95	2.04	2.04	2.07	2.01	2.05	2.06
Var coef	0.286	0.303	0.315	0.315	0.314	0.308	0.312	0.312
Gini coef	0.150	0.157	0.164	0.163	0.164	0.164	0.172	0.166

Note: the grouping assumption is linear for 1970-1975.

Sources:

All years: FSU (1990), Table 27, pp. 158-160;

1968-1970: SR 1971, Table 5-14, p. 146; 1973: SR 1974, Table 5-14, p. 144.
Further information supplied by J. Vecernik was used to split the
ranges between 2,001 and 4,000 for 1975-1979. This source
gave frequencies in percent form to two decimal places which
we used to apportion the absolute frequencies as above. The
range 5,001 plus can be split for 1973-1979 by subtracting
the frequencies for males in Table CSE2 from those for all
workers in Table CSE1.

Table CSE4. AVERAGE gross monthly EARNINGS in crowns by REPUBLIC 1959-1989

	Czech Republic			Slovak Republic			Ratio Czech/Slovak (%)		
	Males	Females	All	Males	Females	All	Males	Females	All
1959	1,645	1,060	1,429	1,482	1,038	1,344	111.0	102.1	106.3
1961	1,789	1,151	1,539	1,619	1,113	1,452	110.5	103.4	106.0
1962	1,830	1,178	1,570	1,660	1,138	1,484	110.2	103.5	105.8
1963	1,818	1,182	1,562	1,656	1,142	1,478	109.8	103.5	105.7
1964	1,834	1,184	1,568	1,683	1,153	1,498	109.0	102.7	104.7
1966	1,913	1,241	1,634	1,780	1,205	1,572	107.5	103.0	103.9
1968	2,135	1,408	1,828	2,020	1,375	1,770	105.7	102.4	103.3
1970	2,370	1,575	2,030	2,246	1,535	1,963	105.5	102.6	103.4
1973	2,650	1,805	2,288	2,526	1,747	2,206	104.9	103.3	103.7
1975	2,780	1,913	2,411	2,649	1,855	2,316	104.9	103.1	104.1
1977	2,979	2,060	2,590	2,822	1,976	2,463	105.6	104.3	105.2
1979	3,213	2,190	2,777	3,054	2,112	2,648	105.2	103.7	104.9
1981	-	-	2,799	-	-	2,680	-	-	104.4
1983	-	-	2,953	-	-	2,803	-	-	105.4
1985	-	-	3,082	-	-	2,944	-	-	104.7
1987	3,613	2,518	3,130	3,450	2,449	2,992	104.7	102.8	104.6
1989	3,844	2,711	3,342	3,693	2,614	3,198	104.1	103.7	104.5

Source:
FSU (1990), Table 26, pp. 143-148, and Table 27, pp. 152-157 and pp. 161-166.

Table CSE5. Distribution of gross monthly EARNINGS in crowns by REPUBLIC 1989

Lower value of range	Czech Republic			Slovak Republic		
	Male	Female	All	Male	Female	All
1	707	1,544	2,251	571	1,069	1,640
1,001	27,510	98,300	125,810	14,022	56,136	70,158
1,601	39,570	213,139	252,709	23,160	120,969	144,129
2,001	134,055	524,383	658,438	63,446	283,073	346,519
2,501	228,112	396,912	625,024	139,618	181,530	321,148
3,001	386,894	245,580	632,474	207,653	107,691	315,344
3,501	457,728	126,761	584,489	207,007	48,322	255,329
4,001	348,081	65,327	413,408	136,894	24,203	161,097
4,501	256,402	32,515	288,917	97,621	12,624	110,245
5,001	178,484	24,714	203,198	71,074	10,757	81,831
6,001	132,523	12,990	145,513	43,446	5,249	48,695
Total	2,190,066	1,742,165	3,932,231	1,004,512	851,623	1,856,135
Mean	3,844	2,711	3,342	3,693	2,614	3,198
Median	3,749	2,538	3,287	3,592	2,415	3,088
P5	60.6	60.0	53.0	62.1	57.6	54.7
P10	67.5	72.2	61.3	69.6	74.8	62.9
P25	86.3	83.0	75.1	84.7	84.7	77.0
P75	120.7	122.8	124.5	121.6	123.7	124.1
P90	143.8	150.2	148.6	142.7	150.5	152.2
P95	166.7*	170.9	171.5	162.6	172.5	172.5
P90/P10	2.13	2.08	2.42	2.05	2.01	2.42
Var coef	0.285	0.311	0.342	0.285	0.310	0.341
Gini coef	0.162	0.168	0.198	0.160	0.160	0.196

Sources:
FSU (1990), Table 26, pp. 145, 148, and Table 27, pp. 154, 157, 163, 166.

L

Table CSI1. Individual distribution of household net per capita INCOME in crowns (annual income) 1958-1973

Lower value of range	1958 Persons	Mean	1965 Persons	Mean	1970 Persons	Mean	1973 Persons	Mean
1	7,487	1,549	2,090	1,637	1,023,769	4,897	24,025	1,451
2,401	10,690	3,080	3,891	3,121	-	-	33,296	3,081
3,601	17,709	4,220	11,289	4,297	-	-	79,889	4,288
4,801	18,567	5,397	17,397	5,414	-	-	283,808	5,495
6,001	15,474	6,586	19,119	6,602	946,834	6,642	637,299	6,654
7,201	11,691	7,764	18,481	7,797	1,168,079	7,817	893,566	7,822
8,401	8,279	8,962	16,569	8,973	1,380,183	9,020	1,161,858	9,008
9,601	5,677	10,148	12,858	10,158	1,557,196	10,209	1,367,671	10,205
10,801	3,439	11,375	8,897	11,369	1,576,841	11,403	1,487,130	11,396
12,001	2,338	12,560	6,089	12,557	1,437,271	12,586	1,526,164	12,590
13,201	1,408	13,742	3,924	13,755	1,185,724	13,786	1,418,393	13,779
14,401	913	14,929	2,636	14,948	942,160	14,972	1,161,918	14,989
15,601	448	16,150	1,621	16,160	724,430	16,181	953,724	16,171
16,801	272	17,340	1,008	17,371	556,947	17,358	757,760	17,376
18,001	133	18,484	570	18,494	432,803	18,592	594,715	18,561
19,201	106	19,653	313	19,724	1,232,506	23,981	485,564	19,772
20,401	44	21,059	162	21,007	-	-	376,391	20,971
21,601	43	22,119	100	22,126	-	-	287,773	22,164
22,801	26	23,414	77	23,417	-	-	218,376	23,379
24,001	59	32,728	157	28,552	-	-	157,704	24,571
25,201	-	-	-	-	-	-	119,217	25,755
26,401	-	-	-	-	-	-	351,022	31,074
Total	104,803		127,248		14,164,743		14,377,263	

Mean	6,358	8,261	12,231	13,705
Median	5,866	7,834	11,570	12,950
P5	-	46.8	47.7	51.3
P10	48.5	56.7	56.7	59.8
P25	71.1	74.2	75.8	77.4
P75	137.2	129.6	128.0	127.1
P90	178.6	162.3	161.4	159.1
P95	208.7	185.1	185.3	181.2
P90/P10	3.68	2.86	2.85	2.66
Var coef	0.504	0.415	0.433	0.391
Gini coef	0.271	0.226	0.225	0.210

Note: the numbers for 1958 and 1965 are the survey numbers, those for later years are grossed-up to population level.

Sources:

1958: Peněžní příjmy domácností v roce 1958 (Mikrocensus 1959). Československá statistika č. 29, Státní statistický úřad 1960, Table 1, pp. 56-57;

1965: Peněžní příjmy domácností v roce 1965 (Mikrocensus 1966). Československá statistika č. 42, Státní statistický úřad 1969, Table 1, p. 65;

1970: Sčítání lidu, domů a bytů ČSSR 1970. Předběžné výsledky. 2% výběrové šetření - příjmová část, FSÚ 1972, Table 4, p. 154;

1973: Mikrocensus 1973, Československá statistika č. 101, FSÚ 1975, Table 2, pp. 54-55.

Table CSI1 (continued) Individual distribution of household net per capita INCOME in crowns (annual income) 1976-1988

Lower value of range	1976		1980		1985		1988	
	Persons	Mean	Persons	Mean	Persons	Mean	Persons	Mean
1	550,304	6,025	451,491	7,267	364,449	5,223	176,693	8,421
7,201	633,289	7,862	-	-	-	-	-	-
8,401	931,022	9,055	611,894	9,101	341,101	10,273	-	-
9,601	1,195,374	10,228	787,345	10,226	672,535	11,456	237,593	10,290
10,801	1,362,003	11,423	1,023,975	11,431	816,714	12,642	472,988	11,545
12,001	1,458,839	12,614	1,188,704	12,617	1,036,893	13,831	640,711	12,638
13,201	1,418,596	13,809	1,367,561	13,828	1,218,805	15,035	800,156	13,845
14,401	1,309,718	14,997	1,399,069	15,020	1,364,012	16,217	1,003,174	15,036
15,601	1,109,802	16,195	1,272,478	16,190	1,331,520	17,406	1,160,966	16,277
16,801	934,549	17,405	1,147,129	17,406	1,232,349	18,601	1,257,160	17,420
18,001	750,906	18,604	969,470	18,597	1,058,048	19,807	1,277,633	18,610
19,201	635,912	19,807	819,612	19,798	881,445	21,007	1,104,486	19,814
20,401	503,697	21,006	682,370	20,997	766,868	22,204	974,158	21,008
21,601	434,732	22,190	579,195	22,211	639,556	23,416	871,624	22,203
22,801	353,547	23,396	492,083	23,393	549,221	24,589	738,219	23,406
24,001	289,373	24,602	418,887	24,606	486,867	25,815	665,495	24,603
25,201	221,495	25,793	368,673	25,793	400,401	27,002	579,495	25,810
26,401	167,750	27,004	295,298	26,993	349,042	28,205	490,502	26,998
27,601	121,780	28,187	242,769	28,209	300,791	29,411	434,652	28,217
28,801	101,989	29,391	188,964	29,417	246,243	30,598	367,593	29,419
30,001	69,247	30,606	163,083	30,595	211,832	31,813	315,519	30,616
31,201	227,200	35,941	125,749	31,805	178,017	33,010	280,371	31,804
32,401	-	-	103,877	33,010	-	-	245,630	32,976

	33,601	–	417,538	39,387	146,504	34,203	206,728	34,176
	34,801	–	–	–	121,721	35,382	163,851	35,418
	36,001	–	–	–	511,159	42,306	257,475	37,154
	38,401	–	–	–	–	–	605,074	48,338
Total	14,781,124		15,117,213		15,226,093		15,327,957	
Mean	15,278		17,603		19,865		21,735	
Median	14,271		16,272		18,456		19,912	
P5	53.5		56.2		59.2		59.4	
P10	62.1		63.4		66.4		66.3	
P25	78.3		79.5		81.4		81.1	
P75	128.2		128.6		127.1		127.8	
P90	161.5		162.9		160.3		161.6	
P95	183.0		186.8		182.9		185.0	
P90/P10	2.60		2.57		2.41		2.44	
Var coef	0.383		0.386		0.376		0.398	
Gini coef	0.207		0.205		0.199		0.201	

Sources:

1976: Mikrocensus 1977, Československá statistika č. 40, FSU 1978, Table 2, pp. 52-53;
1980: Mikrocensus 1981, Československá statistika č. 46, FSU 1982, Table 2, pp. 2-3;
1985: Mikrocensus 1986, Československá statistika č. 41, FSU 1987, Table 2, pp. 2-3;
1988: Mikrocensus 1989, Československá statistika č. 9, 10, 11, FSU 1990, Table 2, pp. 2-3.

Table CSI2. Individual distribution of household net per capita INCOME
in DECILE SHARES (annual income) 1958-1988

Decile	1958	1965	1970	1973	1976	1980	1985	1988
				Percent				
1	2.9	4.1	4.3	4.6	4.8	5.0	4.9	5.3
2	5.3	6.0	6.0	6.3	6.4	6.4	6.7	6.6
3	6.6	7.0	7.1	7.3	7.3	7.3	7.5	7.4
4	7.6	8.0	8.1	8.2	8.1	8.1	8.3	8.1
5	8.7	9.0	9.0	9.0	8.9	8.9	8.9	8.8
6	9.8	10.0	9.8	9.9	9.8	9.7	9.7	9.6
7	11.1	11.0	10.8	10.8	10.8	10.6	10.6	10.5
8	12.7	12.3	12.1	12.0	12.0	11.9	11.8	11.7
9	14.9	14.1	13.9	13.8	13.8	13.8	13.6	13.5
10	20.4	18.4	19.0	18.1	18.0	18.3	17.9	18.5
Top 5%	11.5	10.2	10.9	10.1	10.0	10.2	10.0	10.6
HIM	2.18	1.91	1.89	1.81	1.81	1.80	1.76	1.78

Note: HIM denotes the ratio of average income above the mean to average income
             below the mean.

Source:
interpolated from Table CSI1.

Table CSI3. HOUSEHOLD and INDIVIDUAL distribution of net
per capita income in crowns (annual income) 1988

Lower value of range	Households	Persons	Average household size
1	45,552	176,693	3.88
9,601	74,219	237,593	3.20
10,801	199,899	472,988	2.37
12,001	232,386	640,711	2.76
13,201	270,494	800,156	2.96
14,401	320,642	1,003,174	3.13
15,601	369,444	1,160,966	3.14
16,801	399,619	1,257,160	3.15
18,001	402,577	1,277,633	3.17
19,201	350,383	1,104,486	3.15
20,401	316,231	974,158	3.08
21,601	286,044	871,624	3.05
22,801	249,669	738,219	2.96
24,001	231,202	665,506	2.88
25,201	209,720	579,495	2.76
26,401	186,176	490,502	2.63
27,601	171,004	434,652	2.54
28,801	151,918	367,593	2.42
30,001	137,058	315,519	2.30
31,201	124,149	280,371	2.26
32,401	112,512	245,630	2.18
33,601	98,560	206,728	2.10
34,801	81,296	163,851	2.02

Table CSI3 (continued) HOUSEHOLD and INDIVIDUAL distribution of net
per capita income in crowns (annual income) 1988

Lower value of range	Households	Persons	Average household size
36,001	131,764	257,475	1.95
38,401	351,000	605,074	1.72
Total	5,503,518	15,327,957	2.79

Mean	22,960	21,660
Median	20,736	19,846
P5	56.7	59.2
P10	63.6	66.6
P25	79.0	81.3
P75	132.5	128.1
P90	168.8	162.0
P95	194.5*	185.3
P90/P10	2.65	2.43
Var coef	0.429	0.386
Gini coef	0.219	0.199

Notes: (a) interpolations made without using information on class means
in both cases, and taking the lowest range as 101-. This accounts
for the differences between the second column of summary statistics
and those for the individual distribution in Table CSI1(continued).
(b) the mean for persons is the published overall mean; this
differs slightly from the figure implied by the class means and
shown in Table CSI1(continued).

Source:

Table CSI4. MEAN individual net per capita income in crowns (annual income) by REPUBLICS 1958-1988

	Czech Republic	Slovak Republic	Ratio Czech/Slovak
1958	7,029	4,085	1.72
1965	6,348	4,642	1.37
1970	12,936	10,701	1.21
1973	14,463	12,102	1.20
1976	15,297	13,840	1.11
1980	18,204	16,365	1.11
1985	20,607	18,607	1.11
1988	22,314	20,392	1.09

Source:

1958: Microcensus Report 1959, Table 1, p. 56;
1965: Microcensus Report 1966, Table 1, p. 65;
1970: Microcensus Report 1970, Table 5, p. 155 and Table 6, p. 156;
1973: Microcensus Report 1973, Table 157, p. 222 and Table 208, p. 282;
1976: Microcensus Report 1977, Table 42, p. 99 and Table 82, p. 146;
1980: Microcensus Report 1981, Table 102, p. 104 and Table 202, p. 206;
1985: Microcensus Report 1986, Table 102, p. 131 and Table 202, p. 260;
1988: Microcensus Report 1989, Table 2, p. 2 (CSR and SSR tables);
(see Tables CSI1 and CSI1(continued) for full citations).

Table CSI5. Individual distribution of household net per capita INCOME in crowns (annual income) by REPUBLIC 1958 and 1988

	1958				1988			
Lower value of range	Czech Republic Persons	Mean	Slovak Republic Persons	Mean	Czech Republic Persons	Mean	Slovak Republic Persons	Mean
1	1,954	1,800	5,533	1,460	66,349	8,500	110,344	8,374
2,401	5,143	3,120	5,547	3,043	-	-	-	-
3,601	10,757	4,244	6,952	4,184	-	-	-	-
4,801	13,400	5,410	5,167	5,361	-	-	-	-
6,001	12,197	6,599	3,277	6,539	-	-	-	-
7,201	9,570	7,773	2,121	7,726	-	-	-	-
8,401	6,998	8,968	1,281	8,933	120,233	10,292	117,360	10,288
9,601	4,918	10,148	759	10,162	265,974	11,558	207,014	11,528
10,801	3,033	11,378	406	11,352	399,708	12,634	241,003	12,644
12,001	2,064	12,555	274	12,601	496,805	13,849	303,351	13,837
13,201	1,287	13,742	121	13,753	620,746	15,040	382,428	15,029
14,401	827	14,916	86	15,048	726,500	16,230	434,466	16,222
15,601	401	16,149	47	16,158	791,436	17,424	465,724	17,414
16,801	240	17,350	32	17,265	845,494	18,612	432,139	18,607
18,001	123	18,491	10	18,404	740,846	19,613	363,640	19,816
19,201	99	19,674	7	19,364	643,677	21,009	330,481	21,007
20,401	36	21,009	8	21,288	585,166	22,207	286,458	22,196
21,601	41	22,141	2	21,667	493,822	23,414	244,397	23,392
22,801	23	23,399	3	23,523	452,897	24,604	212,609	24,601
24,001	49	30,764	10	39,081	409,083	25,821	170,412	25,786
25,201	-	-	-	-	350,922	27,001	139,580	26,991
26,401	-	-	-	-	305,478	28,216	129,174	28,222
27,601	-	-	-	-	266,333	29,427	101,260	29,396
28,801	-	-	-	-	231,306	30,623	84,213	30,598
30,001	-							

	1958				1988			
31,201	–	–	–	–	204,680	31,805	75,691	31,802
32,401	–	–	–	–	187,154	32,981	58,476	32,961
33,601	–	–	–	–	155,813	34,205	50,915	34,089
34,801	–	–	–	–	128,540	35,419	35,311	35,415
36,001	–	–	–	–	195,539	37,154	61,936	37,154
38,401	–	–	–	–	470,245	46,150	134,829	46,992
Total	73,160	7,029	31,643	4,805	10,154,726		5,173,211	
Mean	7,029		4,805		22,314		20,392	
Median	6,522		4,397		20,407		18,910	
P5	45.6		–		59.7		58.8	
P10	55.7		–		66.9		66.0	
P25	74.2		67.7		81.2		81.5	
P75	133.1		139.9		128.8		125.9	
P90	170.7		188.9		162.5		157.6	
P95	196.8		224.0		185.7		179.9	
P90/P10	3.07		–		2.43		2.39	
Var coef	0.445		0.578		0.379		0.376	
Gini coef	0.239		0.306		0.198		0.194	

Notes: (a) the 1958 figures are sample numbers: the 1988 figures are grossed-up to population levels;
              (b) in interpolating the Slovak Republic figures for 1958, ranges above 18,001 have been combined.

Sources:
1958: Microcensus Report 1959, Table 1, pp. 56-57;
1988: Microcensus Report 1989, Table 2, pp. 2-3 (CSR and SSR tables);
(see Tables CSI1 and CSI1(continued) for full citations).

Table CSI6. Household distribution of household net per capita income in crowns (annual income divided by 12) by NUMBER OF CHILDREN 1980, 1985 and 1988

1980

Lower value of range	Number of Children in Household				
	None	1	2	3	4+
			Percent		
1	21.0	10.4	16.9	36.3	68.6
1,001	9.4	10.7	24.1	35.1	23.0
1,201	8.2	16.8	29.3	19.5	6.9
1,401	8.2	21.2	18.0	6.7	1.5
1,601	8.9	17.9	7.5	1.8	0.0
1,801	9.3	11.3	2.8	0.4	0.0
2,001	9.1	6.0	0.9	0.2	0.0
2,201	7.6	2.8	0.3	0.0	0.0
2,401	18.3	2.9	0.2	0.0	0.0
Total	100.0	100.0	100.0	100.0	100.0
number of households ('000s)	2,857	953	1,133	319	86

1985

Lower value of range	Number of Children in Household				
	None	1	2	3	4+
			Percent		
1	10.5	5.0	6.7	16.2	46.3
1,001	9.0	6.6	14.1	27.4	30.5
1,201	10.1	11.0	24.2	31.9	15.8
1,401	9.1	16.2	26.5	16.4	6.1
1,601	8.4	18.7	16.3	5.5	1.2
1,801	8.2	16.9	7.4	1.8	0.1
2,001	8.6	12.0	2.9	0.5	0.0
2,201	8.2	6.6	1.1	0.2	0.0
2,401	27.9	7.0	0.8	0.1	0.0
Total	100.0	100.0	100.0	100.0	100.0
number of households ('000s)	2,766	907	1,194	339	82

1988

Lower value of range	Number of Children in Household				
	None	1	2	3	4+
			Percent		
1	5.7	3.5	4.7	10.8	39.7
1,001	7.9	5.5	10.5	21.9	30.2
1,201	9.0	8.4	19.4	31.5	18.8
1,401	9.9	12.6	26.4	21.9	7.7
					2.8

1,801	7.7	17.4	11.1	3.3	0.4
2,001	8.0	14.5	5.1	1.2	0.4
2,201	9.0	9.6	2.1	0.4	0.0
2,401	35.5	11.6	1.5	0.4	0.0
Total	101.0	100.0	100.0	100.0	100.0
number of households ('000s)	2,987	947	1,193	311	66

Source:
information provided by A. Kroupova, Federal Ministry of Labour and Social Affairs, Prague.

Table CSP1. SUBSISTENCE and SOCIAL MINIMA per capita monthly income in crowns for households of different types 1970-1988

	Year				
Household type	1970	1976	1980	1985	1988
(a) Subsistence Minimum					
Single Pensioner	472	596	663	766	843
Productive age head:					
One adult	682	862	958	1,107	1,219
Two adults, two children	478	605	671	776	854
Two adults, five children	404	510	567	655	722
(b) Social Minimum					
Single Pensioner	629	795	884	1,021	1,125
Productive age head:					
One adult	909	1,149	1,277	1,475	1,625
Two adults, two children	637	806	895	1,034	1,139
Two adults, five children	538	680	756	873	962

Source:
information provided by M. Hirsl, Research Institute of Social Development and Labour (VUSRP), Prague.

Table HE1. Distribution of gross monthly EARNINGS in forints for ALL WORKERS in SOCIALISED Sector 1970-1988

Percent

Lower value of range	1970	1972	1974	1976	1978	1978	1980	1982	1980	1982	1984	1986	1988
1	1.2	0.9	0.5	1.1	1.6	0.7	0.4	0.5	0.0	1.1	2.6	1.1	1.0
801	1.5	1.0	0.6	-	-	-	-	-	-	-	-	-	-
1,001	13.5	10.3	5.1	2.5	-	-	-	-	-	-	-	-	-
1,501	14.5	12.7	8.1	5.0	4.4	4.1	2.1	1.2	1.3	-	-	-	-
1,801	10.8	10.2	8.1	5.3	11.1	11.1	7.4	4.1	4.3	8.5	-	-	-
2,001	14.1	13.3	12.0	9.4	-	-	-	-	-	-	-	-	-
2,301	9.0	9.2	9.0	7.3	14.5	14.6	12.0	8.3	9.3	-	-	-	-
2,501	14.6	16.9	17.9	17.3	15.4	15.7	14.0	10.8	12.9	-	4.4	1.7	-
3,001	9.0	10.9	14.1	15.9	14.6	14.7	14.2	12.2	14.1	20.8	8.0	3.9	14.3
3,501	5.0	6.2	9.7	12.6	12.0	12.2	13.0	12.2	13.7	-	10.1	6.2	-
4,001	2.8	3.4	5.7	8.6	8.7	8.9	10.7	11.3	12.0	23.9	11.1	7.7	-
4,501	1.6	1.9	3.4	5.5	-	-	-	-	-	-	11.6	8.8	-
4,801	-	-	-	-	-	-	-	-	-	-	-	-	-
5,001	0.9	1.2	2.1	3.4	5.8	5.9	7.9	9.6	9.5	19.3	10.4	9.4	12.5
5,501	0.6	0.7	1.3	2.1	3.8	3.9	5.6	7.7	7.0	-	9.0	9.1	-
6,001	0.5	0.7	1.4	2.2	4.1	4.2	6.4	5.9	8.1	12.0	7.4	8.6	12.8
6,501	-	-	-	-	-	-	-	4.3	-	-	5.9	7.7	-
7,001	0.4	0.5	0.9	1.0	1.9	1.9	3.0	3.1	3.8	6.6	4.6	6.6	6.3
7,501	-	-	-	-	-	-	-	2.3	-	-	3.5	5.6	5.9
8,001	-	-	-	0.6	1.5	1.5	2.3	2.8	2.8	3.3	4.6	8.2	5.5
8,501	-	-	-	-	-	-	-	-	-	-	-	-	5.0
9,001	-	-	-	-	-	-	-	1.5	-	1.9	2.7	5.3	8.4
10,001	-	-	0.1	0.2	0.6	0.6	1.0	0.9	1.2	1.1	1.5	3.4	11.4
11,001	-	-	-	-	-	-	-	0.5	-	0.6	0.9	2.1	-
12,001	-	-	-	-	-	-	-	0.8	-	0.9	1.7	2.3	6.5
14,001	-	-	-	-	-	-	-	-	-	-	-	2.3	3.7

													16,001
16,001	-	-	-	-	-	-	-	-	-	-	-	-	2.2
18,001	-	-	-	-	-	-	-	-	-	-	-	-	1.4
20,001	-	-	-	-	-	-	-	-	-	-	-	-	0.9
22,001	-	-	-	-	-	-	-	-	-	-	-	-	0.8
25,001	-	-	-	-	-	-	-	-	-	-	-	-	0.7
30,001	-	-	-	-	-	-	-	-	-	-	-	-	0.5
40,001	-	-	-	-	-	-	-	-	-	-	-	-	0.3
Total	100.0	100.0	100.0	100.0	100.0	100.0	100.0	100.0	100.0	100.0	100.0	100.0	100.1
mean	2,373	2,524	2,905	3,280	3,847	3,885	4,285	4,868	4,577	5,145	5,529	6,664	8,920
median	2,187	2,330	2,672	3,066	3,601	3,628	3,998	4,531	4,290	4,826	5,106	6,117	7,766
P5	50.5	49.3	52.0	52.8	53.9	55.4	55.3	53.8	57.2	55.5	54.9	54.2	50.0
P10	59.4	59.8	63.5	60.5	61.1	62.1	62.7	61.3	64.6	62.6	63.2	62.0	58.3
P25	78.0	77.3	77.8	76.6	77.3	77.9	77.9	77.4	79.2	78.0	78.3	77.9	74.4
P75	129.0	129.5	130.4	128.3	126.9	126.7	126.7	128.0	125.3	126.3	127.9	128.7	135.1
P90	166.1	165.3	165.1	161.2	159.2	158.6	158.1	160.8	154.7	157.0	161.8	163.9	183.0
P95	197.2	193.1	193.2	186.8	184.7	183.4	184.2	186.3	178.7	182.5	187.8	192.5	225.9
P90/P10	2.80	2.76	2.60	2.67	2.60	2.55	2.52	2.62	2.39	2.51	2.56	2.64	3.14
Var coef	0.446	0.436	0.423	0.415	0.412	0.402	0.401	0.413	0.380	0.393	0.420	0.445	0.605
Gini coef	0.229	0.226	0.221	0.219	0.214	0.208	0.207	0.214	0.197	0.205	0.213	0.221	0.268

Notes: (a) the figures from 1978 (second column) to 1988 relate only to those in full-time occupations;
(b) the figures from 1980 (second column) include wage supplements.

Sources:

1970: FKA 1970 Table 9 pp. 198-9. (The definition of earnings in 1970 appears to be different from that
in subsequent years. We conjecture that this may account for the difference from SY 1980 Table 24 p. 143.)

1972: FKA 1972 Table 11 pp. 236-7; 1974: FKA 1974 Table 9 pp. 136-7; 1976: FKA 1976 Table 20 pp. 78-9;

1978 (first column): FKA 1984 Table 9, pp. 18-19, line 28; 1978 (second column): FKA 1984 Table 9, pp. 18-19, line 23;

1980(column 1): FKA 1984 Table 9, pp. 18-19, line 18;

1980(column 2): FKA 1980 Table 20, p. 26, lower table;

1982(column 1): FKA 1982 Table 15 p. 210-1; 1982(column 2): SY 1984 Table 5.13, p. 72;

1984: FKA 1986 Table 11, pp. 22-23, line 30; 1986: FKA 1986 Table 21 p. 100-1; 1988: FKA 1988, Table 11 pp. 64-5;

Table HE2. Distribution of gross monthly EARNINGS in forints for MALES in SOCIALISED sector 1970-1988

Percent

Lower value of range	1970	1972	1974	1976	1978	1978	1980	1982	1982	1984	1986	1988
1	0.4	0.3	0.2	0.4	0.5	0.3	0.2	0.3	0.1	1.3	0.7	0.8
801	0.4	0.3	0.2	-	-	-	-	-	-	-	-	-
1,001	4.4	3.3	1.6	0.9	-	1.1	0.5	0.5	0.2	-	-	-
1,501	7.6	6.0	3.1	1.3	1.2	-	-	-	-	-	-	-
1,801	8.3	6.7	3.9	1.8	-	4.0	2.1	1.4	0.7	-	-	-
2,001	14.5	12.2	7.7	4.2	4.0	-	-	-	-	-	-	-
2,301	11.3	10.3	7.6	4.6	-	-	-	-	-	-	-	-
2,501	20.7	22.1	19.5	14.6	8.5	8.5	5.4	3.4	2.0	1.8	0.8	7.0
3,001	13.7	15.8	18.8	18.6	13.7	13.7	9.5	5.8	4.1	3.7	1.6	-
3,501	7.8	9.4	13.9	17.3	17.0	16.8	13.6	9.0	6.8	6.0	2.8	-
4,001	4.4	5.4	8.8	12.7	15.7	15.8	15.2	11.8	9.9	8.6	4.2	-
4,501	2.5	3.1	5.3	8.4	12.3	12.4	14.1	12.8	12.2	10.7	5.9	-
4,801	-	-	-	-	-	-	-	-	-	-	-	-
5,001	1.5	1.9	3.3	5.3	8.5	8.6	11.2	12.1	12.7	11.4	7.6	8.4
5,501	0.9	1.2	2.1	3.3	5.8	5.8	8.2	10.3	11.5	10.7	8.7	-
6,001	0.9	1.1	2.2	3.5	6.4	6.5	9.8	8.2	17.0	9.4	9.2	11.1
6,501	-	-	-	-	-	-	-	6.2	-	7.8	9.0	-
7,001	0.7	0.9	1.6	1.6	3.0	3.1	4.8	4.6	9.9	6.3	8.2	6.2
7,501	-	-	-	-	-	-	-	3.4	-	4.9	7.3	6.2
8,001	-	-	-	1.1	2.4	2.4	3.7	4.3	5.2	6.7	11.1	6.1
8,501	-	-	-	-	-	-	-	-	-	-	-	5.8
9,001	-	-	-	-	-	-	-	2.4	3.1	4.0	7.5	10.2
10,001	-	-	0.2	0.4	1.0	1.0	1.7	1.4	1.8	2.4	5.0	14.4
11,001	-	-	-	-	-	-	-	0.8	1.1	1.5	3.2	-
12,001	-	-	-	-	-	-	-	1.3	1.7	2.8	3.5	8.7
14,001	-	-	-	-	-	-	-	-	-	-	3.7	5.1

16,001	-	-	-	-	-	-	-	-	-	-	-	3.1
18,001	-	-	-	-	-	-	-	-	-	-	-	2.0
20,001	-	-	-	-	-	-	-	-	-	-	-	1.3
22,001	-	-	-	-	-	-	-	-	-	-	-	1.2
25,001	-	-	-	-	-	-	-	-	-	-	-	1.1
30,001	-	-	-	-	-	-	-	-	-	-	-	1.1
40,001	-	-	-	-	-	-	-	-	-	-	-	0.9
												0.5
Total	100.0	100.0	100.0	100.0	100.0	100.0	100.0	100.0	100.0	100.0	100.0	100.1
mean	2,783	2,944	3,373	3,820	4,434	4,452	4,928	5,549	5,928	6,251	7,561	10,199
median	2,569	2,732	3,161	3,596	4,151	4,166	4,620	5,200	5,550	5,798	6,972	8,863
P5	57.6	58.5	56.8	57.6	58.8	59.2	59.5	56.4	59.4	56.8	55.4	51.1
P10	67.7	66.0	65.1	65.7	67.2	67.5	67.4	65.4	67.2	65.4	64.4	59.8
P25	82.0	81.4	79.7	81.2	82.1	82.0	82.0	80.9	82.0	80.7	80.1	76.8
P75	125.8	125.4	124.4	123.3	122.9	122.9	123.0	124.2	123.5	125.5	125.9	133.1
P90	158.8	157.7	155.8	152.6	152.4	152.6	152.2	154.5	153.3	157.6	159.3	181.1
P95	185.8	183.9	181.1	176.8	178.4	178.0	175.8	179.2	177.1	183.9	187.3	225.6
P90/P10	2.35	2.39	2.39	2.32	2.27	2.26	2.26	2.36	2.28	2.41	2.47	3.03
Var coef	0.397	0.394	0.383	0.370	0.370	0.367	0.367	0.379	0.363	0.401	0.432	0.600
Gini coef	0.201	0.200	0.199	0.191	0.188	0.187	0.186	0.195	0.186	0.202	0.210	0.264

Notes: (a) the figures from 1978 (second column) to 1988 relate only to those in full-time occupations;
(b) the figures from 1982 (second column) include wage supplements.

Sources:

1970: FKA 1970 Table 9 pp. 198-9. (The definition of earnings in 1970 appears to be different from that
in subsequent years. We conjecture that this may account for the difference from SY 1980 Table 24 p. 143.)
1972: FKA 1972 Table 11 pp. 236-7; 1974: FKA 1974 Table 9 pp. 136-7; 1976: FKA 1976 Table 20 pp. 78-9;
1978 (first column): FKA 1984 Table 9, pp. 18-19, line 29; 1978 (second column): FKA 1984 Table 9, pp. 18-19, line 24;
1980: FKA 1984 Table 9, pp. 18-19, line 19;
1982(first column): FKA 1982 Table 15 pp. 210-1; 1982(second column): FKA 1984 Table 9, pp. 18-19, line 9;
1984: FKA 1986 Table 11, pp. 22-23, line 33; 1986: FKA 1986 Table 21 pp. 100-1; 1988: FKA 1988, Table 11 pp. 64-5;

Table HE3. Distribution of gross monthly EARNINGS in forints for FEMALES in SOCIALISED sector 1970-1988

Lower value of range	1970	1972	1974	1976	1978	1978	1980	1982	1982	1984	1986	1988
					Percent							
1	2.4	1.6	0.8	1.9	3.0	1.3	0.8	0.9	0.2	4.2	1.6	1.3
801	3.0	1.8	1.0	-	-	-	-	-	-	-	-	-
1,001	25.7	19.4	9.6	4.5	-	-	-	-	-	-	-	-
1,501	23.8	21.5	14.5	9.7	8.3	8.1	4.1	2.2	1.0	-	-	-
1,801	14.1	14.7	13.5	9.8	-	-	-	-	-	-	-	-
2,001	13.5	14.7	17.6	15.9	20.0	20.3	13.9	7.7	4.0	-	-	-
2,301	5.9	7.8	10.7	10.8	-	-	-	-	-	-	-	-
2,501	6.4	10.1	16.0	20.5	21.8	22.3	20.0	14.6	10.2	7.6	2.8	23.0
3,001	2.7	4.5	8.1	12.5	17.7	18.1	19.4	17.3	15.5	13.3	6.8	-
3,501	1.2	1.9	4.3	6.8	11.8	12.1	14.9	16.2	17.0	15.2	10.3	-
4,001	0.6	0.9	1.8	3.5	7.3	7.5	10.1	12.7	15.0	14.2	11.9	-
4,501	0.3	0.5	0.9	1.8	4.2	4.3	6.6	9.2	11.5	12.0	12.2	-
4,801	-	-	-	-	-	-	-	-	-	-	-	-
5,001	0.2	0.3	0.5	1.0	2.4	2.4	4.0	6.3	8.3	9.2	11.2	17.3
5,501	0.1	0.1	0.3	0.5	1.2	1.4	2.4	4.3	5.7	6.9	9.6	-
6,001	0.1	0.1	0.3	0.5	1.3	1.3	2.2	2.9	6.4	5.0	7.8	14.8
6,501	-	-	-	-	-	-	-	1.9	-	3.6	6.2	-
7,001	0.0	0.1	0.1	0.2	0.5	0.5	0.8	1.3	2.8	2.6	4.8	6.3
7,501	-	-	-	-	-	-	-	0.8	-	1.8	3.6	5.4
8,001	-	-	-	0.1	0.3	0.3	0.6	0.9	1.2	2.1	4.8	4.7
8,501	-	-	-	-	-	-	-	0.4	0.6	1.1	-	4.1
9,001	-	-	-	0.0	0.1	0.1	0.2	0.2	0.3	0.5	2.7	6.3
10,001	-	-	0.0	-	-	-	-	0.1	0.1	0.3	1.5	7.8
11,001	-	-	-	-	-	-	-	0.1	0.2	0.4	0.8	-
12,001	-	-	-	-	-	-	-	-	-	-	0.8	4.0
14,001	-	-	-	-	-	-	-	-	-	-	0.6	2.1

16,001	-	-	-	-	-	-	-	-	-	-	-	1.1
18,001	-	-	-	-	-	-	-	-	-	-	-	0.6
20,001	-	-	-	-	-	-	-	-	-	-	-	0.4
22,001	-	-	-	-	-	-	-	-	-	-	-	0.3
25,001	-	-	-	-	-	-	-	-	-	-	-	0.2
30,001	-	-	-	-	-	-	-	-	-	-	-	0.1
40,001	-	-	-	-	-	-	-	-	-	-	-	0.1
Total	100.0	100.0	100.0	100.0	99.9	100.0	100.0	100.0	100.0	100.0	100.0	99.9
mean	1,821	1,991	2,315	2,609	3,109	3,159	3,502	3,974	4,332	4,664	5,590	7,430
median	1,754	1,854	2,184	2,449	2,936	2,954	3,273	3,723	4,059	4,350	5,183	6,566
P5	56.6	56.0	55.1	57.7	59.8	62.1	61.3	58.3	61.2	59.0	59.0	54.5
P10	62.4	62.4	66.1	67.4	67.0	68.3	67.7	66.2	68.8	66.7	66.2	62.3
P25	79.1	84.0	81.9	80.9	79.6	81.1	81.5	80.3	81.6	80.4	80.0	76.7
P75	121.9	125.3	122.8	124.9	125.0	124.4	124.5	125.6	123.9	125.6	126.6	133.5
P90	148.2	156.9	154.0	154.8	153.3	153.2	153.3	156.6	151.9	156.3	158.1	177.8
P95	172.4	178.2	175.5	176.8	174.3	175.3	175.2	179.3	173.9	179.0	182.7	212.0
P90/P10	2.37	2.51	2.33	2.30	2.29	2.24	2.26	2.36	2.21	2.34	2.39	2.85
Var coef	0.382	0.395	0.363	0.368	0.370	0.353	0.355	0.365	0.350	0.368	0.385	0.609
Gini coef	0.200	0.200	0.190	0.190	0.194	0.184	0.184	0.190	0.181	0.192	0.200	0.243

Notes: (a) the figures from 1978 (second column) to 1988 relate only to those in full-time occupations;

(b) the figures from 1982 (second column) include wage supplements.

Sources:

1970: FKA 1970 Table 9 pp. 198-9. (The definition of earnings in 1970 appears to be different from that in subsequent years. We conjecture that this may account for the difference from SY 1980 Table 24 p. 143.)

1972: FKA 1972 Table 11 pp. 236-7; 1974: FKA 1974 Table 9 pp. 136-7; 1976: FKA 1976 Table 20 pp. 78-9;

1978 (first column): FKA 1984 Table 9, pp. 18-19, line 30; 1978 (second column): FKA 1984 Table 9, pp. 18-19, line 25;

1980: FKA 1984 Table 9, pp. 18-19, line 19;

1982(first column): FKA 1982 Table 15 pp. 210-1; 1982(second column): FKA 1984 Table 9, pp. 18-19, line 10;

1984: FKA 1986 Table 11, pp. 22-23, line 34; 1986: FKA 1986 Table 21 pp. 100-1; 1988: FKA 1988, Table 11 pp. 64-5;

HE4. Distribution of gross monthly EARNINGS in forints for ALL WORKERS in STATE sector, 1951-1970

Lower value of range	1951	1955	1956	1957	1958	1960	1961	1962	1964	1966	1968	1970
						Percent						
1	54.5	29.9	25.5	7.3	6.0	4.4	3.5	4.0	2.5	1.7	1.7	1.0
801	18.2	23.0	22.5	14.6	12.6	10.6	10.0	8.4	6.6	4.9	3.9	1.4
1,001	20.4	17.8	18.6	19.1	17.9	15.1	39.2	39.4	33.0	11.2	25.8	13.4
1,201	-	15.6	17.5	23.9	24.1	24.1	-	-	-	17.2	-	-
1,501	4.9	9.9	11.5	22.6	25.5	27.7	28.5	29.0	31.4	32.5	19.7	14.6
1,801	-	-	-	-	-	-	-	-	-	-	12.0	10.9
2,001	1.4	2.7	3.1	8.2	9.4	11.6	11.9	12.1	15.9	18.8	13.4	14.2
2,301	-	-	-	-	-	-	-	-	-	-	6.6	9.2
2,501	0.4	0.7	0.9	2.8	3.0	4.0	4.2	4.4	6.2	7.7	9.1	14.7
3,001	0.2	0.4	0.4	1.5	1.5	2.5	2.7	2.7	4.4	6.0	4.1	9.0
3,501	-	-	-	-	-	-	-	-	-	-	1.9	5.0
4,001	-	-	-	-	-	-	-	-	-	-	0.9	2.7
4,501	-	-	-	-	-	-	-	-	-	-	0.4	1.5
5,001	-	-	-	-	-	-	-	-	-	-	0.5	1.0
5,501	-	-	-	-	-	-	-	-	-	-	-	0.5
6,001	-	-	-	-	-	-	-	-	-	-	-	0.5
7,001	-	-	-	-	-	-	-	-	-	-	-	0.4
Total	100.0	100.0	100.0	100.0	100.0	100.0	100.0	100.0	100.0	100.0	100.0	100.0
Mean	-	1,056	1,101	1,411	1,456	1,553	1,576	1,584	1,727	1,833	1,908	2,372
Median	-	974	1,019	1,310	1,370	1,449	1,469	1,480	1,603	1,712	1,786	2,208
P5	-	-	-	-	-	56.4	57.5	56.8	56.1	57.0	55.3	49.1
P10	-	-	-	65.5	65.0	63.6	64.5	65.0	63.5	61.3	61.3	57.2
P25	-	-	-	79.0	77.9	78.4	78.7	79.3	79.3	78.9	77.6	78.3
P75	-	129.7	130.1	127.5	125.8	126.8	126.3	125.8	126.8	125.9	126.8	128.9
P90	-	167.0	164.1	161.7	156.9	158.2	157.8	157.7	157.9	156.6	159.2	165.3
P95	-	195.1	195.1	186.7	179.3	181.5	181.3	180.5	182.3	182.5	184.2	191.5

P90/P10	-	-	2.47	2.41	2.49	2.45	2.42	2.48	2.55	2.60	2.89
Var coef	0.435	0.421	0.394	0.379	0.394	0.393	0.390	0.404	0.421	0.403	0.445
Gini coef	0.227	0.222	0.205	0.200	0.204	0.201	0.201	0.205	0.210	0.210	0.228

Notes: (a) in view of the heavy concentration in the lowest range in 1951, we have not calculated any summary statistics;

    (b) when interpolating the distribution for 1960 and 1961 the lowest value of the bottom range was set at 5 (rather than 1).

Sources:

1951: SY 1971, Table 15, p. 106;

1955-1957: SY 1957, Table 16, p. 69;

1958: SE 1958, Table 20, p. 73;

1960: SY 1966, Table 9, p. 55;

1961-1966: SY 1968, Table 15, p. 85 (for 1966 the range 1,001-1,500 has been divided in the proportions

indicated by SY 1966 Table 9, p. 55);

1968: FKA 1968 Table 7, pp. 122-123;

1970: FKA 1970 Table 9, pp. 200-201.

Table HI1. Individual distribution of household net per capita INCOME in forints (annual income divided by 12) 1962-1987

Lower value of range	1962	1967	1972	1977 Percent	1982	1987
1	10.2	9.8	3.6	1.5	1.9	1.3
401	21.1	-	-	-	-	-
601	24.0	14.8	5.4	1.9	-	-
801	17.9	19.1	9.2	3.4	-	-
1,001	12.1	18.4	12.8	5.4	-	-
1,201	6.8	13.8	13.8	8.1	4.5	-
1,401	3.4	9.7	13.7	9.9	-	-
1,601	2.0	5.9	11.2	10.7	-	-
1,801	1.1	3.6	8.8	10.1	9.7	1.7
2,001	1.4	3.0	6.4	10.1	-	-
2,201	-	-	4.4	9.4	13.9	3.4
2,401	-	1.9	3.1	8.6	-	13.4
2,601	-	-	2.1	6.7	7.8	-
2,801	-	-	1.6	5.4	7.2	-
3,001	-	-	1.9	4.0	7.2	-
3,201	-	-	-	3.5	6.8	-
3,401	-	-	2.0	2.7	5.7	9.3
3,601	-	-	-	2.0	5.1	-
3,801	-	-	-	1.6	4.7	9.6
4,001	-	-	-	4.5	3.7	-
4,201	-	-	-	-	3.7	9.1
4,401	-	-	-	-	2.8	-
4,601	-	-	-	-	4.5	8.4
5,001	-	-	-	-	1.7	7.3
5,201	-	-	-	-	1.5	-
5,401	-	-	-	0.6	2.3	-
5,801	-	-	-	-	0.8	6.2
6,001	-	-	-	-	1.9	9.7

6,601					1.5	6.5
7,401					-	2.5
7,801					1.1	6.9
10,001					-	4.7
Total	100.0	100.0	100.0	100.0	100.0	100.0
Mean	823	1,138	1,586	2,333	3,385	5,262
Median	754	1,059	1,476	2,176	3,133	4,709
P5	-	48.7	44.9	51.5	55.6	52.2
P10	73.0	57.0	56.2	60.7	62.0	61.3
P25		76.1	75.2	77.6	79.5	76.9
P75	136.2	131.0	130.0	127.8	128.6	131.3
P90	175.1	164.6	165.2	160.7	162.1	172.6
P95	207.5	188.2	193.7	184.5	187.8	208.8
P90/P10	-	2.89	2.94	2.65	2.61	2.81
Var coef	- (0.499)	- (0.438)	0.474 (0.441)	0.415 (0.396)	0.402 (0.417)	0.504 (0.545)
Gini coef	0.257	0.227	0.236	0.214	0.209	0.244

Notes:

(a) for 1987, we have information on the mean income per range for a less detailed set of ranges. This information is given in Table HI5 under the heading "Total personal income";

(b) the first value of the coefficient of variation is taken from SY Table 35.8, p.441; the coefficient in brackets is interpolated from our data;

(c) values of P10, P90 and the median supplied by KSH for 1977, 1982 and 1987 are given in Table HI3.

Sources:

1962: SE 1964 Table 4.2 p. 296 and Table 4.5 p. 299;
1967: SY 1968 Tables 8 and 9 p. 326;
1972: SY 1978 Table 30 p. 380 and Table 33 p. 382;
1977: SY 1978 Table 30 p. 380 and Table 33 p. 382;
1982: SY 1982 Table 19.19 p. 298 and Table 19.23 pp. 304-5 and Andorka (1989), Table 1, p. 146.
1987: SY 1988 Table 35.3 p. 432 Table 35.5 pp. 434-5 and Andorka (1989), Table 1, p. 146.

Data from the yearbook tables listed above were combined for all years years with data in Andorka et al (1990), p. 99. Data for 1982 were also taken from Elteto and Vita (1989, Table 3).

Table HI2. Individual distribution of household net per capita INCOME in DECILE SHARES (annual income divided by 12) 1962-1987

Decile	1962	1967	1972	1977	1982	1987
				Percent		
1	3.6	4.1	4.0	4.5	4.9	4.5
2	5.6	6.0	5.9	6.3	6.4	6.0
3	6.6	7.2	7.0	7.3	7.3	6.9
4	7.8	8.0	7.9	8.1	8.1	7.7
5	8.6	8.7	8.8	8.9	8.9	8.5
6	9.4	10.0	9.8	9.8	9.7	9.4
7	11.2	11.0	10.8	10.7	10.7	10.5
8	12.4	12.0	12.1	12.0	11.9	11.8
9	14.1	13.9	14.0	13.7	13.7	13.8
10	20.8	19.1	19.7	18.6	18.6	20.9
Top 5%	12.1	11.0	11.5	10.6	10.6	12.5
HIM	2.09	1.92	1.96	1.84	1.82	2.00

Note: HIM denotes the ratio of average income above the mean to average income below the mean.

Sources:
1962: Jovedelemeloszlas Magyarorszagon (KSH 1967), p. 279;
1967: Jovedelmi Szinvonal-Jovedelmi Kulonbsegek (KSH 1969), p. 155;
1972-1987: SY 1988, Table 35.8, p. 441.

Table HI3. Distribution of household net income adjusted in different ways
for HOUSEHOLD SIZE (annual income divided by 12) 1977-1987

	1. Household distribution of household income			2. Individual distribution of household per capita income			3. Individual distribution of household equivalent income		
	1977	1982	1987	1977	1982	1987	1977	1982	1987
Q10	2,158	3,407	4,674	1,330	1,992	2,878	1,397	2,101	3,273
median	6,547	9,401	13,185	2,186	3,140	4,701	2,219	3,188	5,032
Q90	11,429	16,402	25,386	3,497	5,083	8,129	3,142	4,759	8,329
P10	33.0	36.2	35.4	60.8	63.4	61.2	63.0	65.9	65.0
P90	174.6	174.5	192.5	160.0	161.9	172.9	141.6	149.3	165.5
P90/P10	5.30	4.81	5.43	2.63	2.55	2.82	2.25	2.27	2.54

Notes: (a) Q10, Q90 are the forint values of the tenth and ninetieth percentiles;
(b) distribution 3 is labelled "per consumption unit" in the Hungarian literature.
The equivalence scale for this distribution is given below.

i) 1977 and 1982

child under 4	0.4
child aged 4-6	0.5
child at school aged 6-10	0.6
child not at school aged 7-13	0.7
dependents above retirement age	0.7
child at school aged 11-13	0.8
retired persons	0.8
all other persons	1
addition for head of household	0.4

ii) 1987

child under 3	0.45
child aged 3-5	0.5
child aged 6-10	0.6
child aged 11-14	0.7
child aged 15-18	0.95
economically active person	1
inactive man aged 19-59	0.9
inactive woman aged 19-54	0.9
inactive man aged 60+	0.8
inactive woman aged 55+	0.8
addition for head of household	0.2

Source:
the forint values of the quantiles for the distributions in this table are
not published and were kindly supplied to us by KSH. The equivalence scales
for Distribution 3 are from A Csaladi Jovedelmek Szinvonala Es Szorodasa 1982,
p. 181 (KSH 1985), and Jovedelemeloszlas Magyarorszagon, p. 185 (KSH 1990).

Table HI4. Distribution of household net income adjusted in different ways
for HOUSEHOLD SIZE in QUANTILE SHARES (annual income divided by 12) 1987

Share of:	1. Household distribution of household income	2. Individual distribution of household per capita income	3. Individual distribution of household equivalent income
Bottom 5%	1.0	1.9	2.0
Decile 1	2.4	4.5	4.6
Decile 2	4.0	6.0	6.1
Deciles 3 and 4	12.5	14.6	14.7
Deciles 5 and 6	18.0	17.9	17.9
Deciles 7 and 8	24.2	22.3	22.2
Decile 9	15.5	13.9	13.7
Decile 10	23.4	20.9	20.7
Top 5%	13.9	12.5	12.3
HIM	2.58	2.00	1.95
RHI	23.1	17.1	16.6

Notes: (a) see Table HI3 for equivalence scale used in column 3;

               (b) HIM denotes the ratio of the average income above the mean to average income below the mean;

               (c) RHI denotes the Robin Hood Index (see Chapter 5), calculated from the information above.

Source:

Jovedelemeloszlas Magyarorszagon (KSH 1990), pp. 117, 123, 125.

Table HI5. Value of per capita SOCIAL INCOME IN KIND by household net per capita income in forints (annual income divided by 12) 1987

Lower value of range of per capita monthly personal income	Mean values in forints per month in each range of personal income								
	Public health	Educa-tion	Social welfare	Culture, sports, recrea-tion	Contrib-ution to meals	Other allot-ments	Total social income	Total personal income	Social income as percent of personal income
1	256	478	66	60	10	23	893	2,130	41.9
2,601	296	419	80	77	18	28	918	3,047	30.1
3,401	288	397	56	93	24	26	882	3,801	23.2
4,201	264	358	49	103	28	23	825	4,592	18.0
5,001	252	317	47	115	34	28	793	5,382	14.7
5,801	252	288	38	118	36	37	767	6,174	12.4
6,601	254	272	37	132	41	40	776	6,963	11.1
7,401	234	254	32	142	43	39	744	7,773	9.6
8,201	228	238	38	139	46	45	733	8,934	8.2
10,001	218	254	35	165	45	57	774	13,417	5.8
All persons	264	348	51	106	29	31	829	5,262	15.8

Note: the number of persons in each range of per capita personal income may be calculated from Table HI1.

Source: SY 1988, Table 35.10 p. 442-3 (this source gives annual amounts of social income which we have divided by 12, rounding to the nearest forint).

Table HI6. Individual distribution of household net per capita income in forints (annual income divided by 12) by ACTIVITY STATUS and HOUSEHOLD SIZE 1987

Lower value of range	Active Head					Inactive Head	
	Number of Dependants aged under 19 years					Single person	2+
	None	1	2	3	4		
			Percent				
1	1.1	2.3	6.9	20.8	58.3	4.3	9.3
2,601	2.5	9.3	19.3	30.5	24.4	20.8	17.7
3,401	7.2	19.2	26.8	22.7	9.8	25.0	22.5
4,201	13.7	23.4	17.9	11.6	3.5	17.4	18.8
5,001	17.4	16.9	10.7	7.4	2.2	12.4	11.3
5,801	16.0	8.8	7.3	2.3	0.9	7.9	7.8
6,601	12.8	6.5	3.2	1.5	0.3	3.5	5.0
7,401	18.8	9.3	5.3	2.1	0.0	6.1	5.4
10,001	10.5	4.4	2.5	1.0	0.5	2.7	2.3
Total	100.0	100.1	99.9	99.9	99.9	100.1	100.1
Percentage of number of persons	25.5	22.2	27.1	6.0	2.0	15.8	0.5

Source:
SY 1988, Table 35.5 pp. 434-5 and Table 35.2, p. 430.

Table HP1. MINIMUM SUBSISTENCE and SOCIAL MINIMUM per capita monthly income in forints for households of different types 1982-1989

Type of household	1982	1983	1984	1985	1986	1987	1988	1989
MINIMUM SUBSISTENCE level								
Households with active earners of which:	2,010	2,160	2,330	2,510	2,620	2,850	3,310	3,940
One parent, one child	2,230	2,400	2,590	2,790	2,920	3,170	3,680	4,310
Married couple, no children	2,360	2,530	2,730	2,940	3,080	3,350	3,840	4,540
of which: in towns	2,710	2,920	3,150	3,390	3,540	3,850	4,410	5,080
in villages	2,120	2,270	2,460	2,650	2,780	3,020	3,460	4,190
Married couple, one child	2,190	2,350	2,440	2,730	2,860	3,110	3,610	4,230
of which: in towns	2,410	2,590	2,790	3,000	3,150	3,420	3,970	4,540
in villages	1,910	2,050	2,210	2,380	2,490	2,710	3,150	3,800
Married couple, two children	1,920	2,060	2,220	2,390	2,500	2,720	3,180	3,760
of which: in towns	2,120	2,280	2,460	2,640	2,770	3,010	3,520	4,120
in villages	1,680	1,800	1,950	2,090	2,190	2,380	2,780	3,310
Married couple, three children	1,660	1,780	1,920	2,060	2,160	2,350	2,780	3,310
Households with no active earners of which:	1,840	1,950	2,130	2,320	2,430	2,640	3,010	3,640
Single persons	2,090	2,230	2,420	2,650	2,800	3,040	3,470	4,100
in towns	2,240	2,390	2,600	2,850	3,010	3,270	3,730	4,330
in villages	1,800	1,910	2,070	2,270	2,400	2,600	2,970	3,600
Married couple	1,760	1,870	2,040	2,210	2,330	2,530	2,890	3,460
of which: in towns	1,940	2,070	2,260	2,450	2,570	2,790	3,190	3,760
in villages	1,610	1,710	1,860	2,020	2,120	2,300	2,630	3,210
All Households	1,??0	2,120	2,2?0	2,4?0	2,5?0	2,8?0	3,2?0	3,8?0

SOCIAL MINIMUM level

Households with active earners of which:	2,470	2,640	2,850	3,050	3,200	3,480	4,040	4,730
One parent, one child	2,750	2,940	3,170	3,400	3,570	3,880	4,500	5,160
Married couple, no children	2,900	3,100	3,340	3,590	3,760	4,090	4,680	5,430
of which: in towns	3,260	3,490	3,760	4,030	4,220	4,590	5,260	5,940
in villages	2,670	2,850	3,070	3,300	3,480	3,780	4,330	5,120
Married couple, one child	2,680	2,870	3,100	3,320	3,490	3,790	4,400	5,080
of which: in towns	2,880	3,090	3,330	3,560	3,750	4,080	4,740	5,370
in villages	2,400	2,560	2,770	2,970	3,120	3,390	3,940	4,690
Married couple, two children	2,340	2,510	2,710	2,890	3,040	3,300	3,860	4,470
of which: in towns	2,540	2,720	2,930	3,130	3,290	3,580	4,190	4,790
in villages	2,110	2,250	2,430	2,600	2,730	2,970	3,470	4,060
Married couple, three children	2,050	2,190	2,370	2,530	2,660	2,890	3,420	4,020
Households with no active earners of which:	2,210	2,330	2,550	2,760	2,910	3,160	3,610	4,360
Single persons	2,430	2,580	2,810	3,060	3,240	3,520	4,020	4,760
of which: in towns	2,590	2,760	3,000	3,280	3,470	3,760	4,290	4,990
in villages	2,200	2,330	2,530	2,760	2,920	3,170	3,620	4,410
Married couple	2,130	2,260	2,460	2,660	2,800	3,040	3,470	4,160
of which: in towns	2,260	2,400	2,620	2,830	2,970	3,220	3,680	4,340
in villages	1,980	2,100	2,280	2,470	2,590	2,810	3,210	3,930
All Households	2,430	2,590	2,800	3,000	3,140	3,410	3,960	4,650

Sources:
SY 1988, Tables 19.15 and 19.16, pp. 312-313, and SY 1989, Tables 19.15 and 19.16, pp. 308-309.

Table PE1. Distribution of monthly EARNINGS in zloty for ALL WORKERS 1970-1982

Lower value of range	1970	1972	1976	1978	1980	1981	1982
				Percent			
1	9.2	4.8	1.9	3.1	2.7	0.7	4.8
1,201	7.3	4.4	-	-	-	-	-
1,401	4.4	3.1	-	-	-	-	-
1,501	25.0	20.6	5.9	-	-	-	-
2,001	22.2	23.0	10.6	6.7	-	-	-
2,501	14.6	17.2	13.8	9.0	4.6	-	-
3,001	11.7	16.8	27.4	23.0	15.8	4.3	-
4,001	3.5	6.0	18.1	21.3	19.4	11.7	-
5,001	1.4	2.3	9.9	14.4	18.0	16.1	-
6,001	0.5	1.0	5.4	8.9	23.1	32.0	16.2
7,001	0.2	0.4	3.0	5.4	-	-	-
8,001	0.1	0.3	2.7	4.9	9.4	18.7	25.1
10,001	0.0	0.1	0.9	2.0	3.9	8.5	22.4
12,000	-	-	0.3	0.8	1.8	3.7	13.9
14,000	-	-	0.1	0.3	0.8	1.8	7.5
16,000	-	-	0.0	0.2	0.4	1.6	5.9
20,001	-	-	-	-	0.1	0.6	2.0
24,001	-	-	-	-	-	0.5	1.4
28,001	-	-	-	-	-	-	-
30,001	-	-	-	-	-	-	0.8
Total	100.1	100.0	100.0	100.0	100.0	100.2	100.0

mean	*2,261*	*2,597*	*4,012*	*4,816*	*5,890*	*7,697*	*11,175*
median	*2,097*	*2,374*	*3,628*	*4,366*	*5,395*	*6,997*	*10,317*
P5	*-*	*51.0*	*49.9*	*49.2*	*51.4*	*57.2*	*58.6*
P10	*58.3*	*60.3*	*58.0*	*57.5*	*59.1*	*64.3*	*66.4*
P25	*76.0*	*76.7*	*75.7*	*75.0*	*75.8*	*79.6*	*80.6*
P75	*129.7*	*129.7*	*132.2*	*132.3*	*130.2*	*127.6*	*123.5*
P90	*165.7*	*168.9*	*177.3*	*175.6*	*170.1*	*163.0*	*155.7*
P95	*198.1*	*199.7*	*210.2*	*208.3*	*200.2*	*194.6*	*183.4*
P90/P10	*2.84*	*2.80*	*3.05*	*3.05*	*2.88*	*2.53*	*2.35*
Var coef	*0.446*	*0.455*	*0.463*	*0.466*	*0.437*	*0.456*	*0.423*
Gini coef	*0.232*	*0.232*	*0.241*	*0.242*	*0.229*	*0.218*	*0.202*

Note: (a) the values of the median, P10 and P90, are calculated for all years except 1972 using the deciles in Table PE2; the other summary statistics are based solely on interpolating the range data above.

Sources:

1970: RS 1974 Table 6(149), p. 167 and RS 1982 Table 8(164), p. 127, including footnote;
1972: RS 1974 Table 6(149), p. 167 and RS 1980 Table 6(154), p. 112, including footnote;
1976: RS 1980 Table 6(154), p. 112 and RS 1982 Table 8(164), p. 127 and footnote;
1978: RS 1980 Table 6(154), p. 112 and RS 1982 Table 8(164), p. 127;
1980: RS 1982 Table 8(164), p. 127 and RS 1986 Table 7(163), p. 279;
1981: RS 1982 Table 8(164), p. 127 and RS 1986 Table 7(163), p. 279;
1982: RS 1986 Table 7(163), p. 279.

M

Table PE1(continued) Distribution of monthly EARNINGS in zloty for ALL WORKERS 1983-1989

Lower value of range	1983	1984	1985	1986	1987	1988	1989
				Percent			
1	1.6	0.7	0.2	2.2	0.5	0.3	0.6
6,001	7.8	3.2	1.2	-	-	-	-
8,001	14.3	8.8	3.9	-	-	-	-
10,001	18.2	13.9	7.4	9.8	8.1	-	-
12,000	17.6	16.2	10.4	-	-	-	-
14,000	13.7	15.0	12.4	7.9	-	-	-
16,000	15.2	20.9	24.1	9.6	5.6	-	-
18,001	-	-	-	20.5	15.1	8.1	-
20,001	6.0	10.6	9.3	-	-	-	-
22,001	-	-	7.4	17.2	24.9	-	-
24,001	2.5	4.9	9.8	-	-	-	-
26,001	-	-	-	6.5	-	-	-
28,001	0.7	1.4	3.1	5.3	7.2	-	-
30,001	2.4	4.4	4.1	7.3	11.6	23.9	-
34,001	-	-	3.2	6.0	11.2	-	-
40,001	-	-	1.6	2.9	2.5	-	-
42,001	-	-	-	-	3.7	27.8	-
46,001	-	-	1.0	1.6	3.4	-	-
52,001	-	-	0.9	3.2	0.8	-	-
54,001	-	-	-	-	2.8	18.8	-
66,001	-	-	-	-	1.5	9.9	-
78,001	-	-	-	-	0.7	5.0	-
90,001	-	-	-	-	0.4	2.6	4.2
102,001	-	-	-	-	-	1.6	-
114,001	-	-	-	-	-	0.9	-
126,001	-	-	-	-	-	0.5	-
130,001	-	-	-	-	-	-	13.6

	1983	1984	1985	1986	1987	1988	1989
138,001	-	-	-	-	-	0.6	-
170,001	-	-	-	-	-	-	21.8
210,001	-	-	-	-	-	-	21.1
250,001	-	-	-	-	-	-	15.0
290,001	-	-	-	-	-	-	9.3
330,001	-	-	-	-	-	-	5.4
370,001	-	-	-	-	-	-	3.2
410,001	-	-	-	-	-	-	1.8
450,001	-	-	-	-	-	-	1.2
490,001	-	-	-	-	-	-	2.8
Total	100.0	100.0	100.0	100.0	100.0	100.0	100.0
mean	14,099	16,410	20,081	24,636	29,712	53,471	247,508
median	12,875	14,915	18,299	21,996	26,938	49,389	227,800
P5	55.2	55.9	54.3	51.9	52.5	55.4	57.8
P10	62.9	63.5	61.9	60.9	61.3	62.7	65.4
P25	7.9	79.1	79.2	77.6	77.7	78.2	81.2
P75	126.7	128.1	129.9	129.3	129.0	126.3	126.3
P90	161.9	164.4	167.5	169.1	168.8	163.3	159.0
P95	191.9	194.8	200.1	206.5	204.7	191.6	188.1
P90/P10	2.58	2.59	2.70	2.77	2.76	2.60	2.43
Var coef	0.478	0.465	0.440	0.563	0.453	0.408	0.433
Gini coef	0.220	0.220	0.224	0.242	0.230	0.212	0.207

Note: (a) the values of the median, P10 and P90, are calculated using the deciles in Table PE2; the other summary statistics are based solely on interpolating the range data above.

Sources:

1983: RS 1986 Table 7(163), p. 279;
1984: RS 1986 Table 7(163), p. 279;
1985: RS 1986 Table 7(163), p. 279 and RS 1988 Table 5(222), p. 161;
1986: RS 1988 Table 5(222), p. 161 and RS 1987 Table 7(227), p. 172;
1987: RS 1988 Table 5(222), p. 161 and RS 1989 Table 5(247), p. 184;
1988: RS 1989 Table 5(247), p. 184;
1989: RS 1990 Table 5(332), p. 224.

Table PE2. PUBLISHED DECILES and INEQUALITY MEASURES for distribution of monthly EARNINGS in zloty for ALL WORKERS 1970-1989

Deciles	1970	1976	1978	1980	1981	1982	1983	1984	1985	1986	1987	1988	1989
1	1,223	2,106	2,511	3,186	4,501	6,849	8,092	9,469	11,336	13,404	16,503	30,961	148,900
2	1,481	2,558	3,055	3,820	5,217	7,912	9,527	11,102	13,427	16,027	19,644	36,511	173,200
3	1,696	2,920	3,512	4,362	5,834	8,739	10,711	12,413	15,118	18,120	22,171	41,005	192,200
4	1,890	3,269	3,926	4,870	6,412	9,526	11,791	13,647	16,688	20,049	24,524	45,153	209,800
5	2,097	3,628	4,366	5,395	6,997	10,317	12,875	14,915	18,299	21,996	26,93?	49,389	227,800
6	2,322	4,019	4,847	5,968	7,657	11,164	14,064	16,353	20,082	24,175	29,611	54,020	247,600
7	2,571	4,516	5,479	6,658	8,439	12,185	15,490	18,055	22,261	26,826	32,868	59,648	271,400
8	2,912	5,228	6,281	7,570	9,534	13,592	17,467	20,427	25,270	30,495	37,331	67,210	304,500
9	3,474	6,433	7,667	9,179	11,403	16,068	20,840	24,523	30,645	37,187	45,481	80,642	362,100
Deciles as % median													
P10	58.3	58.0	57.5	59.1	64.3	66.4	62.9	63.5	61.9	60.9	61.3	62.7	65.4
P20	70.6	70.5	70.0	70.8	74.6	76.7	74.0	74.4	73.4	72.9	72.9	73.9	76.0
P30	80.9	80.5	80.4	80.9	83.4	84.7	83.2	83.2	82.6	82.4	82.3	83.0	84.4
P40	90.1	90.1	89.9	90.3	91.6	92.3	91.6	91.5	91.2	91.1	91.0	91.4	92.1
P60	110.7	110.8	111.0	110.6	109.4	108.2	109.2	109.6	109.7	109.9	109.9	109.4	108.7
P70	122.6	124.5	125.5	123.4	120.6	118.1	120.3	121.1	121.7	122.0	122.0	120.8	119.1
P80	138.9	144.1	143.9	140.3	136.3	131.7	135.7	137.0	138.1	138.6	138.6	136.1	133.7
P90	165.7	177.3	175.6	170.1	163.0	155.7	161.9	164.4	167.5	169.1	168.8	163.3	159.0
Inequality measures													
Gini coef	0.231	0.244	-	0.231	0.213	0.201	0.215	0.226	0.233	-	-	-	-
RHI	16.5	17.5	-	16.6	15.2	14.2	15.2	16.0	16.4	18.4	16.4	15.2	14.5

Note: RHI denotes the Robin Hood Index (see Chapter 5), referred to in the original source as the "maximum equalisation" indicator.

Sources:
1970, 1976, 1980-1985: RS 1986 Table 8(164), p. 283 and inequality measures from Table 9(165), p. 287;
1978: RS 1985 Table 8(224), p. 163;
1986-1988: RS 1989 Table 6(248), p. 185;
1989: RS 1990 Table 6(333), p. 225.

Table PE3. Distribution of monthly EARNINGS in zloty for MALES and FEMALES 1972 and 1985

Lower value of range	1972 Males	1972 Females	1972 All	1985 Males	1985 Females	1985 All
			Percent			
1	1.5	9.5	4.8	0.1	0.3	0.2
1,201	2.1	7.7	4.4	-	-	-
1,401	14.5	36.5	23.7	-	-	-
2,001	20.9	25.9	23.0	-	-	-
2,501	20.8	12.1	17.2	-	-	-
3,001	24.2	6.6	16.8	-	-	-
4,001	9.3	1.3	6.0	-	-	-
5,001	5.4	0.4	3.3	-	-	-
6,001	-	-	-	0.6	1.9	1.2
7,001	1.2	0.0	0.7	-	-	-
8,001	-	-	-	1.9	6.7	3.9
10,001	0.1	0.0	0.1	3.8	12.4	7.4
12,001	-	-	-	6.4	15.9	10.4
14,001	-	-	-	9.0	17.0	12.4
16,001	-	-	-	22.4	26.0	24.1
20,001	-	-	-	19.8	12.4	16.7
24,001	-	-	-	13.6	4.8	9.8
28,001	-	-	-	4.6	1.1	3.1
30,001	-	-	-	17.8	1.5	10.8
Total	100.0	100.0	100.0	100.0	100.0	100.0

Table PE3 (continued) Distribution of monthly EARNINGS in zloty for MALES and FEMALES 1972 and 1985

Lower value of range	1972			1985		
	Males	Females	All	Males	Females	All
			Percent			
mean	2,997	2,021	2,595	23,685	16,147	20,344
median	2,748	1,945	2,364	21,036	15,506	18,299
P5	54.2	-	51.3	54.4	58.5	54.0
P10	63.0	62.7	60.4	62.9	65.8	61.9
P25	79.5	79.2	77.6	78.8	80.5	78.3
P75	128.5	122.9	129.9	128.7	122.6	129.0
P90	164.0	148.6	169.7	166.8	147.3	167.5
P95	196.1	170.4	201.9	208.8*	164.8	202.4*
P90/P10	2.60	2.37	2.81	2.65	2.24	2.70
Var coef	0.415	0.365	0.455	0.560	0.321	0.512
Gini coef	0.215	0.194	0.232	0.239	0.175	0.233

Notes:

(a) in the interpolations the lowest range is taken to start at 25 in 1972 and 3,000 in 1985.

(b) the statistics for the median, P10 and P90 in 1985 make use of the decile data for all workers in Table PE2 and the following deciles for males and females (source: RS 1986 Table 8(164), p. 283):

decile:	1	2	3	4	5	6	7	8	9
males	13,228	15,640	17,524	19,259	21,036	23,049	25,521	28,937	35,090
females	10,196	11,812	13,125	14,331	15,506	16,738	18,152	19,970	22,836
ratio	1.30	1.32	1.34	1.34	1.36	1.38	1.41	1.45	1.54

(c) the other summary statistics for 1985 are interpolated using the range data above and do not use information on the deciles.

Sources:

1972: RS 1974 Table 6(149), p. 167;

Table PE4. Distribution of GROSS monthly EARNINGS in zloty for ALL WORKERS 1956-1970

Lower value of range	1956	1957	1958	1959	1960	1961	1962	1963	1964	1965	1967	1970
					Percent							
1	3.3	2.6	1.5	0.0	2.2	0.0	0.0	0.0	0.0	0.0	3.3	4.2
501	5.1	3.8	2.7	2.7	·	0.0	0.0	0.0	0.0	0.0	·	·
601	6.8	4.6	2.9	2.2	2.0	3.1	2.7	0.0	0.0	0.0	·	·
701	8.4	5.9	4.1	3.0	2.7	2.6	2.6	4.2	3.7	3.2	·	·
801	9.3	7.0	5.1	3.9	3.8	3.7	3.3	3.0	2.7	2.4		
901	9.6	7.4	6.1	4.9	4.6	4.2	4.0	3.7	3.2	2.9	2.6	
1,001	16.3	15.4	14.0	12.1	11.7	11.0	10.4	9.2	8.1	7.3	6.1	4.5
1,201	17.0	18.5	19.4	19.2	13.0	12.5	12.1	10.9	10.1	9.4	7.9	6.1
1,401	·	·	·	·	6.3	6.3	6.3	5.9	5.7	5.3	29.4	25.4
1,501	14.3	18.8	22.2	24.4	25.4	26.0	25.8	26.1	26.4	25.8	19.0	19.7
2,001	5.6	8.4	11.3	13.4	14.2	14.9	15.3	16.6	17.7	18.3	12.9	14.5
2,501	2.3	3.9	5.4	6.9	7.1	7.8	8.3	9.4	10.2	11.2	16.4	21.4
3,001	1.8	3.4	4.8	6.5	6.3	7.1	8.2	9.8	10.9	12.5	2.4	4.2
5,001	0.2	0.3	0.5	0.8	0.7	0.8	1.0	1.2	1.3	1.7		
Total	100.0	100.0	100.0	100.0	100.0	100.0	100.0	100.0	100.0	100.0	100.0	100.0
mean	1,236	1,410	1,573	1,717	1,730	1,786	1,841	1,931	1,993	2,079	2,251	2,510
median	1,086	1,247	1,403	1,534	1,562	1,610	1,651	1,742	1,812	1,879	2,014	2,207
P5	49.4	45.6	45.2	45.9	47.2	48.5	48.0	47.5	46.7	46.7	48.0	47.5
P10	57.8	54.5	55.2	55.9	56.6	57.0	57.0	56.2	55.8	55.6	56.7	56.3
P25	75.2	73.5	74.1	74.5	74.9	75.0	74.9	74.5	74.7	74.4	75.2	76.4
P75	136.6	138.0	136.7	135.0	133.6	133.3	133.8	133.1	132.3	133.9	136.9	136.9
P90	183.7	184.5	181.9	180.7	176.3	176.3	178.2	176.1	173.3	173.8	174.3	177.3
P95	221.5	224.9	216.6	213.5	207.0	206.4	209.1	206.6	202.9	205.3	207.0	215.7
P90/P10	3.18	3.39	3.30	3.23	3.11	3.09	3.13	3.13	3.11	3.12	3.07	3.15
Var coef	0.525	0.525	0.516	0.519	0.496	0.492	0.505	0.501	0.492	0.508	0.513	0.568
Gini coef	0.259	0.266	0.260	0.258	0.250	0.247	0.251	0.249	0.247	0.250	0.251	0.262

Sources:

1956-1959: RS 1961, Table 6(566), p. 373;

1960: RS 1967, Table 9(815), p. 550 and RS 1969, Table 9 (845), p. 540;

1961-1965: RS 1967, Table 9 (815), p. 550 and RS 1972, Table 8 (827), p. 559;

1967: RS 1969, Table 9 (845), p. 540 and RS 1972, Table 8 (827), p. 559;

1970: RS 1972, Table 8 (827), p. 559.

Table PI1. Individual distribution of household net per capita INCOME for all households in zloty (annual income divided by 12) 1983-1986

Lower value of range	1983		1984		1985		1986	
	Persons	Mean	Persons	Mean	Persons	Mean	Persons	Mean
1	5,585	3,215	7,251	3,970	3,748	4,054	5,763	4,905
4,001	7,819	4,559	-	-	-	-	-	-
5,001	9,700	5,519	6,751	5,514	4,281	5,547	-	-
6,001	9,493	6,500	7,984	6,506	12,217	7,042	11,422	7,096
7,001	8,624	7,506	7,668	7,516	-	-	-	-
8,001	12,542	8,909	13,704	8,966	13,555	9,010	15,483	9,032
10,001	7,172	10,882	9,792	10,927	11,045	10,950	16,132	10,973
12,001	7,742	15,954	6,034	12,891	7,658	12,937	13,991	12,983
14,001	-	-	8,226	19,551	5,313	14,869	10,785	14,950
16,001	-	-	-	-	9,485	21,524	13,111	17,786
18,001	-	-	-	-	-	-	-	-
20,001	-	-	-	-	-	-	12,420	26,248
Total	68,677		67,410		67,302		99,107	
Mean	7,963		9,554		11,148		13,402	
Median	7,208		8,549		9,979		12,103	
P5	49.3		47.9		48.9		47.9	
P10	58.6		57.4		57.6		56.7	
P25	75.1		74.5		75.0		74.6	
P75	132.5		133.1		134.2		133.6	
P90	171.5		173.3		175.1		174.4	
P95	203.7		211.0		209.2		205.6	
P90/P10	2.93		3.02		3.04		3.07	
Var coef	0.506		0.564		0.527		0.506	
Gini coef	0.246		0.258		0.253		0.250	

Source:

the data are derived from the annual reports of the Polish Budget Survey, Budzety Gospodarstw Domowych, which gives information separately for 4 groups:

worker households

mixed worker/farmer households

farmer households

pensioner households.

They are combined using the following information provided for each type:

weighted numbers in each income range/household size group from Tables 2, 2(19), 1(30), and 2(42).

total number of persons in household size groups, using for the 6+ group Tables 1, 1(18), 1(30) and, for the 3+ group in the case of pensioners, Table 1(41).

average income per person from Tables 6, 5(22), 4(33) and 5(45).

The table numbers are the same for each of the years.

Table PI1(continued) Individual distribution of household net per capita INCOME for all households in zloty (annual income divided by 12) 1987-1989

Lower value of range	1987 Persons	1987 Mean	1988 Persons	1988 Mean	1989 Persons	1989 Mean
1	10,519	6,496	3,988	9,583	1,313	23,482
8,001	13,143	9,035	-	-	-	-
10,001	33,782	12,060	-	-	-	-
12,001	-	-	26,673	16,760	-	-
14,001	30,665	15,877	-	-	-	-
16,001	-	-	-	-	-	-
18,001	18,734	19,794	-	-	-	-
20,001	-	-	39,686	23,946	-	-
22,001	11,075	23,846	-	-	-	-
26,001	5,991	27,802	-	-	-	-
28,001	-	-	27,407	31,651	-	-
30,001	7,426	38,894	-	-	15,931	48,943
36,001	-	-	15,073	39,606	-	-
44,001	-	-	7,665	47,587	-	-
52,001	-	-	3,927	55,504	-	-
60,001	-	-	4,579	78,810	33,255	75,218
90,001	-	-	-	-	31,250	104,166
120,001	-	-	-	-	20,196	133,644
150,001	-	-	-	-	11,108	163,519
180,001	-	-	-	-	5,606	193,210
210,001	-	-	-	-	7,464	278,961
Total	131,335		128,998		126,123	
Mean	16,535		29,796		112,968	
Median	14,933		26,782		100,872	

P5	48.0	49.7	44.9
P10	56.5	59.0	54.5
P25	74.7	75.8	72.6
P75	133.3	133.0	135.9
P90	175.1	174.8	180.2
P95	206.6	207.0	217.0
P90/P10	3.10	2.96	3.31
Var coef	0.500	0.502	0.548
Gini coef	0.250	0.246	0.268

Source:
see Table PI1.

Table PI2. Individual distribution of household net per capita INCOME in DECILE SHARES (annual income divided by 12) 1983-1989

Decile	1983	1984	1985	1986	1987	1988	1989
				Percent			
1	4.2	4.1	4.2	4.1	4.1	4.3	3.8
2	5.9	5.7	5.7	5.7	5.7	5.9	5.4
3	6.8	6.7	6.7	6.7	6.7	6.8	6.5
4	7.7	7.6	7.6	7.6	7.7	7.7	7.5
5	8.5	8.5	8.5	8.5	8.6	8.5	8.4
6	9.6	9.5	9.4	9.5	9.5	9.5	9.5
7	10.6	10.6	10.6	10.7	10.6	10.6	10.7
8	12.0	11.9	12.0	12.1	12.1	12.0	12.2
9	14.1	13.9	14.1	14.3	14.3	14.1	14.4
10	20.6	21.7	21.1	20.7	20.6	20.7	21.6
Top 5%	12.3	13.2	12.6	12.2	12.1	12.2	12.9
HIM	2.01	2.08	2.06	2.04	2.04	2.02	2.15

Note: HIM denotes the ratio of average income above the mean to average income below the mean.
Source:
interpolated from Table PI1.

Table PI3. Individual distribution of household net per capita INCOME
by HOUSEHOLD TYPE in decile shares (annual income divided by 12) 1975-1989

	1975	1980	1983	1984	1985	1986	1987	1988	1989
					Percent				
Worker Households									
Decile:									
1	4.6	4.5	4.7	4.5	4.5	4.4	4.3	4.7	4.3
2	6.1	6.0	6.0	5.9	5.9	5.8	5.8	6.1	5.8
3	7.1	7.0	7.0	6.9	6.8	6.8	6.8	7.0	6.8
4	8.0	7.9	7.9	7.7	7.8	7.7	7.8	7.8	7.8
5	8.9	8.8	8.8	8.7	8.6	8.7	8.7	8.7	8.7
6	9.8	9.7	9.7	9.6	9.6	9.7	9.6	9.6	9.7
7	10.8	10.9	10.7	10.6	10.6	10.8	10.8	10.7	10.8
8	12.0	12.1	12.0	11.9	12.1	12.2	12.2	12.0	12.1
9	13.8	13.9	13.9	13.8	14.1	14.3	14.4	14.0	14.1
10	18.9	19.2	19.3	20.4	20.0	19.6	19.6	19.4	19.9
RHI	15.5	16.1	15.9	16.7	16.8	16.9	17.0	16.1	16.9
Mixed Households									
Decile:									
1	4.4	4.3	4.4	4.0	4.2	4.4	4.3	4.3	4.1
2	5.8	5.7	5.9	5.7	5.7	5.9	5.9	5.8	5.6
3	6.7	6.7	6.9	6.8	6.8	6.8	6.8	6.8	6.7
4	7.7	7.7	7.7	7.6	7.7	7.8	7.8	7.7	7.6
5	8.7	8.6	8.6	8.5	8.6	8.6	8.7	8.7	8.6
6	9.7	9.5	9.6	9.5	9.5	9.6	9.5	9.6	9.7
7	10.8	10.6	10.7	10.7	10.6	10.7	10.6	10.7	10.9
8	12.1	12.2	12.1	12.0	12.0	12.2	12.0	12.1	12.3
9	14.4	14.3	14.0	13.9	13.9	14.3	14.2	14.2	14.4
10	19.7	20.4	20.1	21.3	21.0	19.7	20.2	20.1	20.1
RHI	17.0	17.5	16.9	17.9	17.5	16.9	17.0	17.1	17.7

Farmer Households

Decile:									
1	3.1	3.2	2.3	2.4	2.4	2.9	2.9	2.8	2.4
2	4.9	4.6	4.1	4.2	4.3	4.4	4.5	4.3	4.0
3	5.9	5.8	5.4	5.3	5.5	5.4	5.5	5.5	5.1
4	7.1	7.0	6.5	6.3	6.6	6.5	6.5	6.6	6.4
5	7.9	7.9	7.6	7.5	7.7	7.5	7.5	7.6	7.6
6	9.0	8.8	8.8	8.7	8.8	8.8	8.7	8.9	8.8
7	10.6	10.1	10.2	10.2	10.3	10.2	10.2	10.5	10.4
8	12.4	12.0	12.2	12.2	12.2	12.1	12.3	12.5	12.5
9	15.1	15.0	15.9	15.5	15.6	15.3	15.3	15.6	16.1
10	24.0	25.6	27.0	27.7	26.6	26.9	26.6	25.7	26.7
RHI	22.1	22.7	25.3	25.6	24.7	24.5	24.4	24.3	25.7

Pensioner Households

Decile:									
1	4.9	4.4	4.6	4.3	4.4	4.4	4.3	4.4	4.3
2	6.3	5.9	6.3	6.0	6.2	6.4	6.3	6.3	6.0
3	7.1	7.0	7.4	7.0	7.2	7.4	7.3	7.3	7.0
4	8.0	7.9	8.1	7.8	8.0	8.2	8.2	8.2	8.0
5	8.7	8.7	8.8	8.5	8.8	9.0	9.0	9.1	8.9
6	9.7	9.6	9.6	9.4	9.7	9.8	9.8	9.9	9.7
7	10.7	10.8	10.6	10.3	10.6	10.7	10.7	10.8	10.8
8	11.8	12.1	11.8	11.5	11.7	11.8	11.8	11.8	12.0
9	13.8	13.8	13.5	13.3	13.7	13.6	13.6	13.6	13.9
10	19.0	19.8	19.3	21.9	19.7	18.7	19.0	18.6	19.4
RHI	15.3	16.5	15.2	17.0	15.7	14.8	15.1	14.8	16.1

Note: RHI denotes Robin Hood Index (see Chapter 5).

Sources:

1975 from RS 1981 Tables 19(162) and 20(163), p. 129; 1983: RS 1984 Tables 19(188) and 20(189), p. 127; 1984: RS 1985 Tables 19(202) and 20(203), p. 133; 1986: RS 1987 Table 19(211), p. 149; 1980, 1985 and 1987: RS 1988 Table 19(208), p. 139; 1988: RS 1989 Table 19(233), p. 162; 1989: RS 1990 Table 21(317), p. 204.

Table PI4. Individual distribution of household net per capita INCOME for WORKER HOUSEHOLDS in zloty (annual income) 1974-1983

Lower value of range	1974	1975	1976	1978 Percent	1979	1980	1981	1982	1983
1	5.9	3.3	2.3	0.6	0.3	3.3	4.6	5.8	3.8
12,001	9.6	7.0	4.8	7.1	4.5	-	-	-	-
15,001	12.9	9.7	8.0	-	-	-	-	-	-
18,001	26.8	24.2	21.1	15.9	11.2	8.6	16.8	-	-
24,001	20.0	22.6	22.4	19.8	17.1	13.4	-	-	-
30,001	12.0	15.3	16.8	17.6	17.6	16.4	-	-	-
36,001	12.8	17.9	24.6	22.5	26.2	26.6	25.2	-	-
48,001	-	-	-	16.5	23.1	16.3	21.8	15.1	8.7
60,001	-	-	-	-	-	15.4	14.0	17.8	11.3
72,001	-	-	-	-	-	-	8.0	17.8	12.4
84,001	-	-	-	-	-	-	9.6	14.4	12.8
96,001	-	-	-	-	-	-	-	10.2	20.9
108,001	-	-	-	-	-	-	-	6.9	-
120,001	-	-	-	-	-	-	-	12.0	13.8
144,001	-	-	-	-	-	-	-	-	16.3
Total	100.0	100.0	100.0	100.0	100.0	100.0	100.0	100.0	100.0

	1974	1975	1976	1978	1979	1980	1981	1982	1983
Mean	25,281	28,213	31,833	36,792	42,175	44,565	54,553	86,187	108,894
Median	22,654	25,535	27,776	32,400	35,806	39,646	49,513	79,639	97,113
P10	58.7	58.2	58.7	59.7	61.0	57.2	58.1	65.1	59.2
P25	76.5	75.1	74.9	75.1	75.0	75.4	76.5	78.8	75.6
P75	132.1	127.7	128.9	128.9	130.1	130.3	131.4	126.2	130.6
P90	170.1*	167.4*	177.7*	175.2*	184.2*	172.9*	167.9	157.2*	171.5*
P90/P10	2.90*	2.87*	3.03*	2.93*	3.02*	3.03*	2.89	2.42*	2.90*
Var coef	0.531	0.559	0.718	0.666	0.840	0.603	0.500	0.421	0.572
Gini coef	0.244	0.246	0.272	0.264	0.284	0.258	0.240	0.204	0.251

Sources:

1974: RS 1976 Table 16(136), p. 88;
1975: RS 1977 Table 14(113), p. 75;
1976: RS 1978 Table 14(112), p. 70;
1978: RS 1979 Table 14(121), p. 84;
1979: RS 1980 Table 14(133), p. 90;
1980: RS 1981 Table 18(161), p. 128;
1981: RS 1982 Table 17(141), p. 96;
1982: RS 1983 Table 18(185), p. 113;
1983: RS 1984 Table 18(187), p. 126.

Table P15. Individual distribution of household net per capita INCOME
for all households in zloty (annual income divided by 12) by HOUSEHOLD SIZE 1985

Lower value of range	Number of persons in household											
	1		2		3		4		5		6	
	Persons	Mean	Persons	Mean	Persons	Mean	Persons	Mean	Persons	Mean	Persons	Mean
1	43	3,732	258	4,211	917	3,985	460	3,960	725	4,152	1,346	4,067
5,001	72	5,672	438	5,590	645	5,556	844	5,547	1,080	5,524	1,202	5,535
6,001	583	7,156	1,526	7,084	1,740	7,022	3,200	7,093	2,660	7,017	2,509	6,961
8,001	742	8,911	1,874	8,995	2,021	9,026	4,368	9,036	2,510	8,965	2,041	9,032
10,001	401	10,818	1,560	10,945	2,297	11,011	3,960	10,964	1,680	10,923	1,148	10,892
12,001	226	12,894	1,222	12,938	2,135	13,004	2,620	12,910	905	12,893	551	12,879
14,001	149	14,960	976	14,968	1,742	14,935	1,660	14,912	490	14,888	296	14,847
16,001	618	23,138	2,808	22,338	2,995	20,601	1,908	20,446	630	22,039	526	24,066
Total	2,834		10,662		14,492		19,020		10,680		9,618	
Mean	12,397		13,264		12,315		11,024		9,489		8,804	
Median	9,920		11,526		11,683		10,294		8,650		7,782	
P5	62.0		49.8		-		54.9		-		-	
P10	68.5		57.1		50.2		62.9		61.8		-	
P25	80.9		73.5		71.4		79.0		77.1		75.8	
P75	148.5		140.9*		130.0		125.9		128.6		130.5	
P90	205.1*		182.7*		161.1*		155.5*		163.7		171.4	
P95	254.0*		222.4*		188.0*		180.8*		193.6*		211.9*	
P90/P10	2.99*		3.20*		3.21*		2.47*		2.65		0.641	
Var coef	0.657		0.586		0.479		0.411		0.495		0.641	
Gini coef	0.275		0.270		0.247		0.206		0.228		0.258	

Note: size 3 includes pensioner households with 3 or more members.

Source:

see Table P1.

Table PP1. SOCIAL MINIMUM per capita monthly income in zloty for households of different types 1981-1989

Household type	1981	1982	1983	1984	1985	1986	1987	1988	1989
(a) September									
Pensioner:									
One person	-	5,835	6,330	7,502	8,239	9,590	12,897	22,550	75,030
Two persons	-	-	5,415	6,446	7,051	-	11,357	-	67,335
Worker:									
One person	-	6,315	7,025	8,327	9,476	10,710	14,564	25,090	84,905
Four person	-	5,275	5,725	6,941	7,826	8,720	12,061	19,350	71,250
(b) December									
Pensioner:									
One person	3,096	6,045	6,655	7,491	9,080	10,741	14,674	24,310	155,990
Two persons	-	-	5,670	6,413	7,859	9,504	12,980	-	138,370
Worker:									
One person	3,322	6,415	7,490	8,635	10,219	12,012	16,406	26,875	179,900
Four person	3,014	5,325	6,120	7,205	8,525	9,828	13,656	21,710	147,875
c) Average for the year									
Pensioner:									
One person	3,000	6,100	6,400	7,300	8,100	9,600	12,700	19,800	64,400
Two persons	2,700	5,600	5,800	6,200	7,000	8,300	11,200	17,200	57,100
Worker:									
One person	3,200	6,400	7,000	8,300	9,300	10,700	14,200	22,500	73,100
Four person	2,700	5,400	5,700	6,900	7,700	8,900	11,800	18,200	60,100

Note: the social minimum is calculated four times a year, typically in March, June, September and December. In addition, a calculation is made of the average value during the year which, during the period in question, involved taking a weighted average of the minima applying in different months. We present the September (August in 1986) and December figures together with the annual figure. In this table a dash indicates either that the calculation of the minimum was not made for that household type or that we do not have information for the relevant figure.

Source: information provided by the Institute for Labour and Social Affairs, Warsaw, and by I. Topinska.

Table PP2. COMPOSITION of SOCIAL MINIMUM basket for households of different types 1983 and 1989

	1983				1989			
	Pensioner		Worker		Pensioner		Worker	
Item:	Single person	Two persons	Single person	Four persons	Single person	Two persons	Single person	Four persons
				Percent				
Food	50.8	54.8	52.3	57.6	56.6	61.3	57.8	62.4
Clothing and shoes	14.0	15.7	12.5	14.5	11.5	12.3	9.9	11.4
Housing	17.4	13.1	15.5	10.2	13.5	9.7	11.7	8.2
Hygiene and health	3.1	3.6	2.8	2.7	2.7	3.0	2.4	2.3
Culture and education	4.7	2.7	4.2	2.4	5.1	2.9	4.4	2.1
Transport and communications	0.7	0.9	3.6	3.4	1.5	1.7	4.7	4.5
Other expenditures	9.3	9.2	9.1	9.2	9.1	9.1	9.1	9.1
Total	100.0	100.0	100.0	100.0	100.0	100.0	100.0	100.0
Per capita monthly zloty value of the basket	5,670	6,655	7,490	6,120	155,990	138,370	179,900	147,875

Note: the figures refer to calculations of the basket for December of each year.
Source:
information provided by the Institute of Labour and Social Affairs, Warsaw.

Table UE1. Distribution of gross monthly EARNINGS in rubles for ALL WORKERS 1956-1989

Lower value of range	1956	1968	1972	1976	1981	1986	1984	1989
			Percent					
1	71.0	32.7	23.6	15.2	6.4	4.9	4.8	2.8
80	13.2	21.3	18.5	14.6	13.6	11.3	8.3	4.9
91	-	-	-	-	-	-	5.9	3.8
101	6.6	15.1	14.7	13.2	12.3	10.3	12.6	8.8
121	3.6	10.7	12.1	12.9	12.5	11.0	11.6	8.7
141	2.0	7.3	9.5	11.6	11.7	11.4	12.4	10.4
161	1.9	7.4	11.9	16.2	19.2	18.4	10.9	10.2
181	-	-	-	-	-	-	8.7	9.3
201	-	3.1	5.6	9.0	12.5	15.3	5.7	6.9
221	-	-	-	-	-	-	6.7	9.5
251	-	1.3	2.1	3.8	5.6	7.7	6.1	10.6
301	0.4	1.1	2.0	3.4	6.2	9.6	2.8	5.6
351	-	-	-	-	-	-	1.5	3.3
401	-	-	-	-	-	-	2.0	5.2
Total	100	100	100	100	100	100	100	100
Mean	-	107.65	124.43	144.22	167.37	186.34	168.90	206.88
Median	-	96.59	111.05	130.07	149.25	162.07	150.91	181.70
P5	-					49.5	53.1	45.8
P10	-				57.0	55.7	56.3	54.1
P25	-		73.3	72.0	73.2	72.1	72.0	73.5
P75	-	134.1	137.5	134.1	132.8	136.4	132.8	137.6
P90	-	176.2	178.7	176.7	175.6	182.8	175.9	184.5

Table UE1 (continued) Distribution of gross monthly EARNINGS in rubles for ALL WORKERS 1956-1989

Lower value of range	1956	1968	1972	1976	1981	1986	1984	1989
			Percent					
P95	-	213.0	214.0	210.1	213.6*	226.6*	212.5	223.1
P90/P10	-	-	-	-	3.08	3.28	3.12	3.41
Var coef	-	0.532	0.546	0.527	0.567	0.638	0.514	0.580
Gini coef	-	0.262	0.265	0.260	0.258	0.276	0.249	0.272

Note: (a) in the original source the lower bounds of ranges from 101 rubles upwards in 1956-1981 and 1986 are 101.01, 120.01, 140.01, 160.01, 200.01, and 300. These were used when interpolating summary statistics. (For the interpolation of statistics for 1984 and 1989 all lower bounds are as in the tables above.)
(b) the data in 1956-1981 and 1986 are drawn from the March Census of state enterprises and organisations; the data for 1984 and 1989 are drawn from the March Household Survey in those years of 310,000 families.

Sources:
1956-1981 and 1986: NK 1988, p. 79 (recalculated to exclude part-time workers and apprentices).
1984: Chapman (1991), Table A.2, p. 200;
1989: Goskomstat (1990b), p. 274.

Table UE2. DECILE RATIOS of gross monthly EARNINGS in rubles
for ALL WORKERS 1956-1976

	P90/P10
1956	4.44
1959	4.21
1961	4.02
1964	3.69
1966	3.26
1968	2.83
1972	3.10
1976	3.35

Source:
N E Rabkina and N M Rimashevskaia (1978), p. 20.
(The decile ratios are given by the authors to two decimal places.)

Table UE3. Distribution of gross monthly EARNINGS in rubles
for MALES and FEMALES 1989

Lower value of range	Males	Females	All
		Percent	
1	1.6	4.1	2.8
80	2.1	7.8	4.9
91	2.0	5.7	3.8
101	5.0	12.8	8.8
121	5.7	11.9	8.7
141	8.3	12.5	10.4
161	9.7	10.7	10.2
181	10.1	8.5	9.3
201	7.8	5.9	6.9
221	11.9	7.1	9.5
251	14.2	6.7	10.6
301	8.1	3.0	5.6
351	5.0	1.5	3.3
401	8.5	1.8	5.2
Total	100.0	100.0	100.0

Mean	242.48	170.18	206.88
Median	215.11	152.44	181.70
P5	46.0	52.9	45.8
P10	54.2	56.9	54.1
P25	75.2	72.8	73.5
P75	132.7	133.9	137.6
P90	177.9	175.8	184.5
P95	217.2*	209.1	223.1*
P90/P10	3.28	3.09	3.41
Var coef	0.585	0.490	0.580
Gini coef	0.265	0.244	0.272

Source:
Goskomstat (1990b), pp. 275-276 (data from
March 1989 survey of 310,000 families).

Table UE4. AVERAGE gross monthly EARNINGS in rubles by REPUBLICS 1940-1982

	1940	1950	1960	1970	1975	1980	1981	1982
(a) Earnings level								
USSR	33.1	64.1	80.6	122.0	145.8	168.9	172.5	177.3
RSFSR	33.9	65.7	83.1	126.1	153.2	177.7	181.8	187.3
Ukraine	32.2	62.7	78.3	115.2	133.5	155.1	157.9	163.1
Belarus	28.6	53.7	63.2	106.4	125.5	150.0	153.2	157.3
Uzbekistan	29.7	59.6	70.1	114.8	136.6	155.5	158.9	159.4
Kazakhstan	29.8	62.0	81.5	123.7	147.6	167.1	170.4	173.8
Georgia	33.3	63.6	74.8	106.1	118.9	145.2	148.5	152.8
Azerbaidzhan	35.4	66.0	77.3	109.6	125.1	148.4	152.7	154.9
Lithuania	30.4	54.0	72.4	119.6	142.3	166.1	169.6	174.5
Moldavia	26.7	50.8	67.4	102.8	117.0	138.3	140.5	146.0
Latvia	31.4	62.3	78.5	125.6	146.4	171.4	175.0	180.4
Kirgizia	30.2	57.8	74.9	112.6	134.2	147.9	150.3	152.2
Tadzhikistan	36.5	62.6	78.3	117.6	136.2	145.5	147.9	149.5
Armenia	34.3	59.6	75.9	123.0	138.6	163.1	166.3	169.7
Turkmenia	35.2	66.3	84.9	130.0	162.6	176.2	178.8	181.6
Estonia	32.2	63.8	81.9	135.3	159.8	188.7	192.8	196.4

b) Ratio to average earnings in RSFSR

USSR	0.98	0.98	0.97	0.97	0.95	0.95	0.95	0.95
RSFSR	1.00	1.00	1.00	1.00	1.00	1.00	1.00	1.00
Ukraine	0.95	0.95	0.94	0.91	0.87	0.87	0.87	0.87
Belarus	0.84	0.82	0.76	0.84	0.82	0.84	0.84	0.84
Uzbekistan	0.88	0.91	0.84	0.91	0.89	0.88	0.87	0.85
Kazakhstan	0.88	0.94	0.98	0.98	0.96	0.94	0.94	0.93
Georgia	0.98	0.97	0.90	0.84	0.78	0.82	0.82	0.82
Azerbaidzhan	1.04	1.00	0.93	0.87	0.82	0.84	0.84	0.83
Lithuania	0.90	0.82	0.87	0.95	0.93	0.93	0.93	0.93
Moldavia	0.79	0.77	0.81	0.82	0.76	0.78	0.77	0.78
Latvia	0.93	0.95	0.94	1.00	0.96	0.96	0.96	0.96
Kirgizia	0.89	0.88	0.90	0.89	0.88	0.83	0.83	0.81
Tadzhikistan	1.08	0.95	0.94	0.93	0.89	0.82	0.81	0.80
Armenia	1.01	0.91	0.91	0.98	0.90	0.92	0.91	0.91
Turkmenia	1.04	1.01	1.02	1.03	1.06	0.99	0.98	0.97
Estonia	0.95	0.97	0.99	1.07	1.04	1.06	1.06	1.05

Note: the 1940-1960 figures are converted to new rubles (in 1961, 1 new ruble replaced 10 old rubles - see McAuley, 1979, p. 361, footnote 15).

Source:
Trud v SSSR 1988, p. 154-155.

Table UE4 (continued) AVERAGE gross monthly EARNINGS in rubles by REPUBLICS 1983-1989

	1983	1984	1985	1986	1987	1988	1989
(a) Earnings level							
USSR	180.5	184.8	190.1	195.6	202.9	219.8	240.4
RSFSR	190.8	195.5	201.4	207.8	216.1	235.2	258.6
Ukraine	165.8	169.6	173.9	179.0	185.0	199.8	217.7
Belarus	160.6	167.2	173.7	180.5	190.0	207.6	227.8
Uzbekistan	161.9	161.6	164.2	165.9	169.7	182.0	193.8
Kazakhstan	178.3	181.3	186.5	192.7	199.3	214.6	233.6
Georgia	156.4	161.6	167.6	170.6	177.2	186.9	197.7
Azerbaidzhan	155.5	159.7	162.6	161.7	164.9	171.0	179.0
Lithuania	177.9	183.9	190.0	194.7	204.1	222.6	244.1
Moldavia	150.6	155.2	157.7	161.8	166.7	181.5	200.6
Latvia	183.6	190.3	195.9	201.4	208.9	227.0	249.9
Kirgizia	154.6	158.0	162.6	166.4	171.4	183.6	197.5
Tadzhikistan	150.6	153.8	157.8	162.0	165.9	177.1	188.3
Armenia	172.0	176.8	180.3	184.5	191.0	196.8	219.9
Turkmenia	183.4	186.8	191.1	193.1	198.4	208.4	221.3
Estonia	200.6	208.3	215.1	221.0	229.0	249.2	270.1

b) Ratio to average earnings in RSFSR

USSR	0.95	0.95	0.94	0.94	0.94	0.94	0.93
RSFSR	1.00	1.00	1.00	1.00	1.00	1.00	1.00
Ukraine	0.87	0.87	0.86	0.86	0.86	0.85	0.84
Belarus	0.84	0.86	0.86	0.87	0.88	0.88	0.88
Uzbekistan	0.85	0.83	0.82	0.80	0.79	0.77	0.75
Kazakhstan	0.93	0.93	0.93	0.93	0.92	0.91	0.90
Georgia	0.82	0.83	0.83	0.82	0.82	0.79	0.76
Azerbaidzhan	0.81	0.82	0.81	0.78	0.76	0.73	0.69
Lithuania	0.93	0.94	0.94	0.94	0.94	0.95	0.94
Moldavia	0.79	0.79	0.78	0.78	0.77	0.77	0.78
Latvia	0.96	0.97	0.97	0.97	0.97	0.97	0.97
Kirgizia	0.81	0.81	0.81	0.80	0.79	0.78	0.76
Tadzhikistan	0.79	0.79	0.78	0.78	0.77	0.75	0.73
Armenia	0.90	0.90	0.90	0.89	0.88	0.84	0.85
Turkmenia	0.96	0.96	0.95	0.93	0.92	0.89	0.86
Estonia	1.05	1.07	1.07	1.06	1.06	1.06	1.04

Sources:
Trud v SSSR 1988, p. 154-155;
NK 1988, p. 81;
NK 1989, p. 78.

Table UE5. Distribution of gross monthly EARNINGS in rubles by REPUBLICS 1981 and 1986

	1	80	121	161	201	251	301	Total	Mean	Median	P10	P90	P90/P10
				Rubles							Percent		
(a) 1981													
USSR	6.4	26.0	24.2	19.2	12.5	5.6	6.2	100	167.29	149.45	56.9	175.3	3.08
RSFSR	4.8	23.1	23.7	20.1	13.9	6.4	7.9	100	178.31	157.35	56.4	177.4	3.14
Ukraine	7.2	29.6	26.3	18.4	10.7	4.1	3.7	100	153.58	139.35	60.0	168.6	2.81
Belarus	7.8	28.2	26.9	19.5	11.3	4.0	2.3	100	150.19	140.73	59.0	162.1	2.75
Uzbekistan	10.9	32.3	24.2	16.4	8.8	3.7	3.6	100	146.60	131.31	60.3**	175.0	2.90**
Kazakhstan	8.1	29.3	23.2	17.3	11.1	5.2	5.9	100	161.43	141.97	57.8	181.4	3.14
Georgia	11.2	35.8	22.6	14.8	7.6	3.7	4.3	100	145.82	125.79	62.9**	185.6	2.95**
Azerbaidzhan	13.0	36.2	21.4	14.2	7.5	3.6	4.2	100	143.56	121.72	64.0**	190.2	2.97
Lithuania	6.6	23.8	24.5	21.0	14.3	5.8	4.1	100	163.05	152.56	56.0	163.5	2.92
Moldavia	10.4	34.6	26.8	15.7	8.0	2.7	1.8	100	138.49	126.47	62.9**	166.5	2.65**
Latvia	6.3	22.9	24.0	20.9	14.2	6.4	5.4	100	168.15	155.37	55.2	167.2	3.03
Kirgizia	9.9	33.5	24.0	16.2	9.4	3.7	3.2	100	145.89	130.28	61.5	175.1	2.85
Tadzhikistan	11.8	31.0	23.9	16.7	10.0	3.7	2.8	100	144.85	131.17	59.4**	172.8	2.91**
Armenia	9.5	29.2	22.4	16.7	10.2	5.2	6.7	100	162.88	141.14	57.0	187.2	3.28
Turkmenia	5.9	25.4	21.6	18.8	13.3	7.0	8.1	100	175.96	155.47	54.5	181.4	3.33
Estonia	4.7	19.0	21.9	21.1	16.8	8.5	8.0	100	183.51	167.08	54.3	169.8	3.13

(b) 1986

USSR	4.9	21.7	22.5	18.4	15.3	7.7	9.6	100	186.21	161.88	56.0	182.9	3.27
RSFSR	3.7	18.5	21.2	19.2	16.5	8.8	12.0	100	200.18	172.70	54.9	184.6*	3.36*
Ukraine	5.5	24.9	24.9	18.5	14.1	6.3	5.9	100	168.65	150.50	58.7	174.6	2.97
Belarus	5.4	22.6	24.6	20.3	15.9	6.9	4.4	100	167.52	155.78	57.1	164.3	2.88
Uzbekistan	8.6	29.8	25.9	15.1	11.1	4.8	4.6	100	155.03	134.18	61.5	183.4	2.98
Kazakhstan	5.7	25.1	22.9	16.6	13.9	7.1	8.7	100	178.67	152.35	57.5	188.7	3.28
Georgia	9.2	32.0	23.9	12.7	9.6	5.0	7.6	100	164.70	131.07	61.9	207.3	3.35
Azerbaidzhan	10.7	34.6	22.2	12.7	9.3	4.6	5.9	100	154.19	126.42	62.7**	200.8	3.20**
Lithuania	4.8	19.7	21.5	19.9	18.0	8.9	7.2	100	181.21	167.48	54.4	166.3	3.05
Moldavia	7.6	29.5	26.0	17.6	11.3	4.7	3.3	100	152.68	138.93	59.9	171.4	2.86
Latvia	4.8	18.5	21.4	19.7	17.1	9.3	9.1	100	187.74	169.33	54.1	172.9	3.20
Kirgizia	7.5	31.0	24.2	15.5	11.6	5.4	4.9	100	157.29	136.67	60.9	184.2	3.02
Tadzhikistan	10.5	28.4	23.3	16.2	11.9	5.3	4.4	100	154.74	137.41	57.7**	180.7	3.13**
Armenia	5.8	27.3	22.5	15.0	12.7	6.6	10.1	100	183.36	147.46	59.0	204.2*	3.46*
Turkmenia	4.7	23.4	22.5	16.8	14.9	7.9	9.9	100	185.96	158.82	57.0	188.3	3.30
Estonia	3.7	15.4	19.4	19.4	18.2	11.3	12.6	100	204.51	181.73	53.0	176.3*	3.33*

Note: in the case of certain republics, the lowest range contains more than 10 percent of the population; in this table, we have interpolated in the bottom range to estimate P10, in contrast to our standard practice. These values are marked with a double asterisk.

Source:
NK 1988, p. 82.

Table UE6 (page A) Distribution of gross monthly EARNINGS in rubles
for MALES and FEMALES by REPUBLICS 1989

| Lower value of range | RSFSR | | |
	Males	Females Percent	All
1	0.9	2.3	1.6
80	1.3	5.6	3.4
91	1.3	4.7	3.0
101	3.4	11.1	7.2
121	4.4	11.2	7.8
141	7.0	12.8	9.8
161	8.8	11.3	10.1
181	10.0	9.4	9.7
201	7.9	6.7	7.3
221	12.5	8.3	10.4
251	15.5	8.1	11.9
301	9.4	3.9	6.6
351	6.1	2.0	4.1
401	11.5	2.6	7.1
Total	100	100	100

Lower value of range	Ukraine Males Percent	Females Percent	All	Belarus Males Percent	Females Percent	All
1	1.2	4.2	2.7	1.2	4.1	2.6
80	1.9	9.8	5.8	1.3	7.0	4.1
91	2.0	7.4	4.7	1.4	4.9	3.1
101	5.6	16.0	10.9	4.2	13.2	8.6
121	6.9	14.2	10.5	5.1	12.8	8.9
141	10.1	13.2	11.7	8.3	12.9	10.5
161	11.7	10.6	11.2	11.0	11.4	11.2
181	11.4	7.4	9.4	11.5	9.3	10.4
201	8.7	5.0	6.9	9.7	6.4	8.1
221	12.4	5.3	8.8	13.6	7.7	10.7
251	13.4	4.3	8.8	15.8	6.3	11.1
301	6.8	1.6	4.2	8.2	2.2	5.3
351	3.4	0.6	2.0	4.4	1.1	2.8
401	4.5	0.4	2.4	4.3	0.7	2.6
Total	100	100	100	100	100	100

Source:
Goskomstat (1990b), pp. 277-285 (data are from March 1989 survey of 310,000 families).

Table UE6 (page B) Distribution of gross monthly EARNINGS in rubles for MALES and FEMALES by REPUBLICS 1989

Lower value of range	Uzbekistan			Kazakhstan		
	Males	Females Percent	All	Males	Females Percent	All
1	5.6	13.7	9.2	1.7	4.1	2.9
80	6.3	16.1	10.7	2.4	10.6	6.3
91	5.7	8.1	6.8	2.4	7.3	4.7
101	11.9	15.1	13.2	6.1	14.6	10.2
121	9.9	10.8	10.3	6.4	12.3	9.2
141	11.9	11.0	11.6	8.9	11.5	10.1
161	10.8	7.7	9.4	8.8	9.4	9.1
181	9.4	5.1	7.5	9.7	7.5	8.7
201	5.7	3.3	4.6	7.4	5.5	6.5
221	7.8	3.8	6.0	11.2	6.0	8.7
251	7.4	3.4	5.6	13.7	5.9	10.0
301	3.6	1.1	2.5	8.4	3.0	5.8
351	1.8	0.4	1.2	4.9	1.4	3.2
401	2.2	0.4	1.4	8.0	0.9	4.6
Total	100	100	100	100	100	100

Lower value of range	Georgia Males Percent	Georgia Females Percent	Georgia All	Azerbaidzhan Males Percent	Azerbaidzhan Females Percent	Azerbaidzhan All
1	3.8	10.0	6.7	6.4	15.9	10.5
80	6.0	15.0	10.2	7.3	16.7	11.4
91	4.5	8.4	6.3	5.4	8.7	6.9
101	9.7	17.4	13.3	12.2	16.5	14.1
121	8.7	12.9	10.6	9.6	12.3	10.7
141	11.7	10.2	11.1	10.1	9.5	9.8
161	10.7	7.3	9.1	11.0	7.1	9.3
181	8.8	5.9	7.4	8.6	4.1	6.7
201	5.6	3.5	4.6	5.3	2.2	3.9
221	8.5	3.6	6.2	7.2	2.8	5.3
251	9.4	3.6	6.7	7.5	2.3	5.2
301	5.0	1.1	3.2	3.8	1.1	2.7
351	2.7	0.7	1.8	2.2	0.3	1.4
401	4.9	0.4	2.8	3.4	0.5	2.1
Total	100	100	100	100	100	100

Source:
Goskomstat (1990b), pp. 286-297 (data are from March 1989 survey of 310,000 families).

Table UE6 (page C) Distribution of gross monthly EARNINGS in rubles
for MALES and FEMALES by REPUBLICS 1989

| Lower value of range | Lithuania | | | Moldavia | | |
	Males	Females Percent	All	Males	Females Percent	All
1	0.9	4.8	2.9	3.5	6.1	4.8
80	1.7	7.2	4.4	3.6	10.4	6.9
91	1.1	4.8	3.0	3.0	7.4	5.2
101	3.8	13.6	8.7	9.4	13.7	11.4
121	4.5	9.8	7.2	9.9	13.2	11.5
141	7.2	12.2	9.7	11.1	11.1	11.1
161	10.0	10.6	10.3	10.4	9.8	10.1
181	11.0	10.1	10.5	9.2	7.0	8.1
201	9.1	4.6	6.8	7.6	6.0	6.8
221	12.8	7.3	10.0	9.8	6.3	8.1
251	15.7	8.3	12.1	10.4	5.4	8.0
301	9.2	3.2	6.2	5.7	2.3	4.1
351	5.5	1.6	3.5	3.3	0.7	2.0
401	7.5	1.9	4.7	3.1	0.6	1.9
Total	100	100	100	100	100	100

Lower value of range	Latvia			Kirgizia		
	Males	Females Percent	All	Males	Females Percent	All
1	1.0	3.3	2.2	5.5	10.4	7.8
80	1.4	6.2	3.9	6.6	12.5	9.4
91	1.5	3.9	2.7	4.5	7.3	5.8
101	3.7	11.7	7.8	10.5	14.9	12.5
121	3.7	10.0	7.0	9.0	12.6	10.7
141	6.5	11.2	8.9	11.3	11.9	11.6
161	9.0	12.8	11.0	9.6	8.3	9.0
181	9.7	9.1	9.4	9.6	7.7	8.7
201	8.6	7.3	7.9	5.3	3.9	4.6
221	13.9	8.7	11.2	9.3	4.1	6.9
251	16.6	8.3	12.4	9.8	3.6	6.9
301	11.3	4.0	7.5	4.0	1.7	2.9
351	6.3	2.1	4.1	2.2	0.5	1.4
401	6.8	1.4	4.0	2.8	0.6	1.8
Total	100	100	100	100	100	100

Source:
Goskomstat (1990b), pp. 289-309 (data are from March 1989 survey of 310,000 families).

Table UE6 (page D) Distribution of gross monthly EARNINGS in rubles
for MALES and FEMALES by REPUBLICS 1989

| Lower value of range | Tadzhikistan | | | Armenia | | |
	Males	Females Percent	All	Males	Females Percent	All
1	8.4	20.6	13.3	2.5	7.9	5.1
80	6.4	12.7	8.9	4.6	11.7	8.0
91	5.6	7.9	6.5	3.5	6.9	5.2
101	10.5	11.1	10.7	9.3	14.3	11.8
121	10.3	10.3	10.3	9.4	12.1	10.7
141	11.6	8.9	10.6	12.9	12.2	12.6
161	10.2	6.7	8.8	12.3	10.8	11.6
181	8.0	6.2	7.3	9.7	7.5	8.6
201	5.6	4.4	5.1	5.9	5.2	5.6
221	7.8	4.1	6.3	9.4	4.8	7.1
251	8.2	4.3	6.6	9.8	4.4	7.2
301	3.2	1.7	2.6	4.4	1.6	3.0
351	1.8	0.5	1.3	2.1	0.4	1.2
401	2.4	0.6	1.7	4.2	0.2	2.3
Total	100	100	100	100	100	100

Lower value of range	Turkmenia Males	Females Percent	All	Estonia Males	Females Percent	All
1	2.4	7.7	4.7	0.9	2.7	1.8
80	2.8	10.6	6.2	1.1	4.3	2.7
91	3.1	6.3	4.5	1.0	3.7	2.4
101	7.0	16.7	11.2	2.9	9.5	6.2
121	8.0	11.2	9.4	2.5	10.4	6.5
141	10.8	13.0	11.9	4.1	11.0	7.6
161	11.6	10.3	11.0	8.4	12.1	10.3
181	9.2	6.6	8.1	8.3	9.4	8.8
201	8.3	5.3	7.0	7.7	7.1	7.4
221	10.2	4.5	7.7	14.3	10.0	12.1
251	13.0	5.1	9.5	19.3	10.4	14.9
301	6.3	1.7	4.3	11.3	4.3	7.7
351	3.2	0.6	2.0	7.5	2.5	5.0
401	4.1	0.4	2.5	10.7	2.6	6.6
Total	100	100	100	100	100	100

Source:
Goskomstat (1990b), pp. 310-321 (data are from March 1989 survey of 310,000 families).

Table UB6 (continued) SUMMARY STATISTICS for distribution of gross monthly EARNINGS for MALES and FEMALES by REPUBLICS 1989

	Mean	Median	P5	P10	P25	P75	P90	P95	P90/P10	Var coef	Gini coef
(a) Males											
USSR	242.48	215.11	46.0	54.2	75.2	132.7	177.9	217.2*	3.28	0.585	0.265
RSFSR	266.31	233.21	45.9	59.0	76.1	133.1	179.6*	223.2*	3.04*	0.632	0.268
Ukraine	219.22	199.10	50.6	58.9	77.8	130.5	166.5	196.4	2.83	0.467	0.229
Belarus	227.94	212.83	49.6	61.1	78.9	127.0	160.4	183.1	2.63	0.407	0.212
Uzbekistan	175.60	157.53	-	53.8	69.1	135.7	177.9	211.7	3.31	0.506	0.254
Kazakhstan	237.27	211.10	46.3	51.1	72.1	134.9	178.5	216.5*	3.49	0.577	0.268
Georgia	199.03	173.08	46.7	53.4	72.7	138.5	186.6	230.3	3.49	0.644	0.284
Azerbaidzhan	180.31	158.87	-	52.6	68.5	136.9	185.7	227.7	3.53	0.592	0.277
Lithuania	244.71	222.69	48.0	60.1	77.9	129.9	168.0	198.6*	2.79	0.483	0.235
Moldavia	197.52	179.19	46.3	56.3	74.1	135.7	177.4	205.0	3.15	0.469	0.246
Latvia	246.89	230.56	45.1	59.5	77.3	129.6	160.8	185.1*	2.71	0.430	0.223
Kirgizia	184.52	169.21	-	49.1	65.7	137.0	172.7	207.4	3.52	0.520	0.261
Tadzhikistan	174.10	156.10	-	52.8	69.8	137.3	177.7	215.3	3.36	0.539	0.267
Armenia	199.11	175.27	47.1	57.3	77.3	134.5	174.8	216.1	3.05	0.642	0.265
Turkmenia	209.70	191.37	47.3	56.3	76.3	133.4	170.1	200.2	3.02	0.488	0.245
Estonia	270.28	248.91	46.5	61.3	76.6	128.5	163.9*	195.0*	2.67*	0.485	0.233
(b) Females											
USSR	170.18	152.44	52.9	56.9	72.8	133.9	175.8	209.1	3.09	0.490	0.244
RSFSR	183.92	165.39	50.5	58.6	75.1	133.4	174.3	208.1	2.97	0.498	0.245
Ukraine	150.92	138.83	58.1	61.5	75.6	129.8	167.0	192.4	2.72	0.407	0.214
Belarus	164.93	153.02	52.8	57.4	74.5	130.4	164.8	186.9	2.87	0.411	0.220
Uzbekistan	133.98	114.92	-	68.5**	74.1	140.5	187.0	220.8	2.73**	0.461	0.233
Kazakhstan	159.97	142.74	56.5	59.4	73.2	136.1	181.0	213.7	3.05	0.457	0.240
Georgia	137.06	120.06	-	66.6	75.8	135.9	178.7	213.1	2.68	0.446	0.228
Azerbaidzhan	127.76	108.52	-	71.9**	76.8	136.7	177.6	218.9	2.47**	0.497	0.229
Lithuania	173.22	154.25	51.9	53.7	69.4	135.2	177.5	209.7	3.31	0.494	0.249
Moldavia	154.86	139.56	-	60.3	73.7	135.7	175.0	204.8	2.90	0.442	0.233
Latvia	179.55	165.69	49.5	55.8	72.9	132.4	168.8	199.4	3.02	0.434	0.232

Kirgizia	143.06	133.42	-	59.9**	72.6	132.4	167.3	202.3	2.79**	0.465	0.234
Tadzhikistan	135.88	115.99	-	60.9**	71.7	148.0	196.9	235.1	3.23**	0.527	0.269
Armenia	147.03	135.89	-	59.8	72.9	131.7	167.9	195.4	2.81	0.411	0.222
Turkmenia	148.95	134.78	-	60.4	75.3	131.8	176.2	201.4	2.92	0.428	0.226
Estonia	191.67	174.08	49.5	56.8	74.1	135.9	169.7	202.4	2.99	0.462	0.238
(c) All Workers											
USSR	206.88	181.70	45.8	54.1	73.5	137.6	184.5	223.1*	3.41	0.580	0.272
RSFSR	225.12	194.69	46.7	54.0	74.2	136.8	186.4	228.2*	3.45	0.612	0.275
Ukraine	184.65	168.11	49.3	56.8	73.3	133.6	172.6	203.0	3.04	0.484	0.244
Belarus	197.35	182.71	46.3	55.5	74.7	132.4	167.7	194.8	3.02	0.444	0.234
Uzbekistan	157.07	140.77	-	57.1	70.8	134.1	181.3	214.8	3.18	0.513	0.257
Kazakhstan	199.69	176.35	46.5	53.3	70.3	139.4	186.4	222.7	3.50	0.568	0.276
Georgia	169.62	145.08	-	56.3	70.7	139.4	192.4	236.5	3.42	0.598	0.277
Azerbaidzhan	157.30	135.19	-	59.0**	71.6	137.2	193.5	236.1	3.28**	0.590	0.275
Lithuania	208.95	186.87	43.8	53.9	74.4	136.6	178.7	211.4	3.32	0.524	0.260
Moldavia	176.87	159.40	50.4	55.1	72.4	136.9	178.7	209.8	3.24	0.479	0.250
Latvia	211.92	193.78	44.2	53.5	74.6	134.5	173.6	198.4	3.25	0.462	0.244
Kirgizia	165.23	144.62	-	55.9	70.7	137.5	184.7	218.4	3.31	0.524	0.260
Tadzhikistan	158.86	141.51	-	53.9**	67.3	139.1	185.3	218.9	3.44**	0.552	0.276
Armenia	173.69	154.80	-	54.4	71.0	133.1	176.2	206.0	3.24	0.591	0.258
Turkmenia	183.18	163.53	49.2	54.3	72.3	137.7	178.6	209.6	3.29	0.505	0.255
Estonia	230.35	210.33	44.1	53.7	74.6	130.9	172.8	203.6*	3.22	0.508	0.253

Note: in the case of certain republics, the lowest range contains more than 10 percent of the population; in this table, we have interpolated in the bottom range to estimate P10, in contrast to our standard practice. These values are marked with a double asterisk. Where the bottom range contains more than 5 percent of the population, we have not interpolated P5.

Source:
interpolated from Table UE6 (pages A-D) and Table UE3 (for USSR).

Table UE7. Distribution of gross monthly EARNINGS in rubles for the UKRAINE 1968-1986

Lower value of range	1968	1972	1976 Percent	1981	1986
1	35.5	26.3	17.0	7.2	5.5
80	22.2	20.0	16.1	15.5	12.8
101	14.8	15.3	14.5	14.1	12.1
121	10.1	11.9	13.8	13.9	12.6
141	6.5	8.9	11.6	12.3	12.2
161	6.5	10.3	15.0	18.4	18.5
201	2.6	4.4	7.4	10.7	14.1
251	1.0	1.5	2.7	4.1	6.3
300	0.8	1.3	2.0	3.7	6.0
Total	100	100	100	100	100

Mean	103.79	117.23	134.59	153.50	168.92
Median	91.45	104.64	123.11	138.80	150.90
P5	-	-	-	55.7	52.5
P10	-	-	-	59.8	57.8
P25	-	-	72.2	74.6	73.4
P75	135.4	136.7	133.0	132.0	134.9
P90	178.5	176.6	170.4	169.4	174.6
P95	211.4	208.3	200.3	200.8	-
P90/P10	-	-	-	2.83	3.02
Var coef	0.501	0.507	0.475	0.486	0.518
Gini coef	0.246	0.250	0.242	0.236	0.249

Notes: (a) the lower bounds used for the interpolations are as in the original table: 80, 101.01, 120.01, 140.01, 160.01, 200, 250.01, 300;
(b) linear interpolation.

Source:
Narodnoe khoziaistvo Ukrainskoi SSR v 1988g, Kiev 1989, p. 45.

Table UE8. Distribution of gross monthly EARNINGS
in rubles for AZERBAIDZHAN 1972-1986

Lower value of range	1972	1976	1981	1986
			Percent	
1	27.7	15.2	2.6	2.3
70	14.2	14.3	11.8	9.6
80	7.7	7.8	10.2	11.2
90	6.8	7.9	11.5	10.2
101	6.0	6.6	7.3	6.6
111	5.3	6.2	6.7	6.2
121	4.5	5.6	6.1	6.0
131	4.1	5.4	5.4	5.8
141	3.6	4.6	5.1	5.2
151	3.1	4.0	4.4	4.8
161	5.2	5.9	7.7	6.8
181	3.9	4.9	6.2	5.7
201	4.7	6.2	7.4	9.2
251	1.9	3.1	3.5	4.5
301	1.1	1.9	3.3	4.7
401	0.2	0.4	0.8	1.2
Total	100	100	100	100

Mean	110.05	125.63	140.2	148.77
Median	90.53	107.96	119.88	126.17
P5	-	-	59.5	57.7
P10	-	-	62.6	61.8
P25	-	68.8	75.3	72.5
P75	151.0	141.5	141.1	143.9
P90	208.1	194.0	187.1	202.4
P95	247.1	236.3	240.3	245.0
P90/P10	-	-	2.99	3.27
Var coef	0.535	0.515	0.505	0.530
Gini coef	0.271	0.261	0.252	0.266

Notes: (a) the data include part-time workers and apprentices;
(b) the lower bounds used for the interpolation are as in the original table: 70, 80, 101.01, 110.01, 120.01, 130.01, 140.01, 150.01, 160.01, 180.01, 200.01, 250.01, 300.01, 400.01;
(c) linear interpolation.

Source: Narodnoe khoziaistvo Azerbaidzhanskoi SSR v 1988g, Baku 1990, p. 48.

Table U11. Individual distribution of household gross per capita INCOME in rubles (annual income divided by 12) 1980-1989

Lower value of range	1980	1985	1988	1989
		millions		
1	19.3	11.8	8.3	7.9
50.1	49.3	37.8	27.7	23.8
75.1	61.6	54.8	44.7	39.2
100.1	51.8	53.6	50.2	46.3
125.1	35.0	41.7	44.9	43.5
150.1	21.7	28.9	35.0	36.1
175.1	12.5	18.6	25.7	27.4
200.1	10.9	19.0	28.8	33.8
250.1	3.4	11.0	20.2	28.7
Total	265.5	277.2	285.5	286.7
Mean	109.68	127.4	145.18	156.99
Median	101.00	114.84	131.68	140.58
P5	45.9	45.0	43.0	40.9
P10	53.4	53.7	52.7	51.4
P25	73.3	74.3	72.7	71.5
P75	135.6	135.5	135.3	136.4
P90	173.8	177.3	174.1	178.0
P95	200.4	206.9	207.3	217.1
P90/P10	3.25	3.30	3.30	3.46
Var coef	0.454	0.503	0.535	0.600
Gini coef	0.245	0.256	0.262	0.277

Sources:
NK 1988, p. 92; NK 1989, p. 89.

Table UI2. Individual distribution of household gross per capita
INCOME in DECILE SHARES (annual income divided by 12) 1980

Decile	1980	1985	1988	1989
		Percent		
1	4.0	3.9	3.8	3.6
2	5.5	5.5	5.5	5.3
3	6.7	6.7	6.6	6.4
4	7.8	7.6	7.5	7.3
5	8.8	8.5	8.5	8.4
6	9.7	9.6	9.6	9.5
7	10.9	10.8	10.8	10.6
8	12.5	12.3	12.3	12.2
9	14.5	14.5	14.3	14.3
10	19.5	20.6	21.1	22.3
Top 5%	10.9	12.0	12.6	13.6
HIM	2.02	2.08	2.11	2.20

Note: HIM denotes the ratio of average income above the
mean to average income below the mean.

Source:
interpolated from Table UI1.

Table UI3. Individual distribution of household gross per capita INCOME in rubles (annual income divided by 12)
by REPUBLICS and for WORKERS and COLLECTIVE FARM WORKERS 1989

Ranges	1	75.1	100.1	125.1	150.1	175.1	200.1	250.1	Total	Absolute total (millions)
					Percent					
USSR										
workers	9.7	13.3	16.2	15.5	12.9	9.8	12.2	10.4	100.0	249.09
coll.farm	20.0	16.2	15.7	13.5	10.5	7.8	9.1	7.2	100.0	37.63
total	11.1	13.7	16.1	15.2	12.6	9.5	11.8	10.0	100.0	286.72
RSFSR										
workers	4.8	10.8	15.3	15.7	14.0	11.2	14.6	13.6	100.0	136.26
coll.farm	7.6	13.5	16.7	15.9	13.2	10.2	12.4	10.5	100.0	11.09
total	5.0	11.0	15.4	15.7	13.9	11.1	14.4	13.4	100.0	147.35
Ukraine										
workers	6.2	14.5	19.2	18.2	14.3	9.9	11.0	6.7	100.0	41.36
coll.farm	5.2	13.0	18.2	18.1	14.8	10.8	12.1	7.8	100.0	10.14
total	6.0	14.2	19.0	18.2	14.4	10.1	11.2	6.9	100.0	51.50
Belarus										
workers	3.3	10.3	16.7	17.9	15.7	11.9	14.4	9.8	100.0	8.55
coll.farm	3.5	9.9	15.2	16.5	14.8	11.9	15.4	12.8	100.0	1.63
total	3.3	10.2	16.5	17.7	15.6	11.9	14.6	10.3	100.0	10.18
Uzbekistan										
workers	38.5	22.5	15.1	9.7	5.7	3.4	3.2	1.9	100.0	14.35
coll.farm	56.7	23.2	11.5	4.9	2.1	0.9	0.7	-	100.0	5.66
total	43.6	22.7	14.1	8.3	4.7	2.7	2.5	1.4	100.0	20.01
Kazakhstan										
workers	14.5	17.6	17.4	15.0	10.9	8.1	9.0	7.5	100.0	15.65
coll.farm	32.6	21.0	16.0	10.8	7.1	4.5	4.7	3.3	100.0	0.90
total	15.5	17.8	17.3	14.8	10.7	7.9	8.8	7.3	100.0	16.55
Georgia										
workers	13.2	16.8	17.9	14.7	11.5	8.3	9.7	7.9	100.0	4.42
coll.farm	12.1	14.8	15.5	14.1	11.3	9.0	11.4	11.8	100.0	1.00
total	13.0	16.4	17.5	14.6	11.5	8.4	10.0	8.6	100.0	5.42
Azerbaidzhan										
workers	34.4	20.4	15.2	10.4	6.9	4.4	4.8	3.5	100.0	5.90
coll.farm	29.5	19.5	15.4	11.2	7.8	5.3	6.1	5.2	100.0	1.17
total	33.6	20.3	15.2	10.5	7.0	4.5	5.0	3.8	100.0	7.07

Lithuania	workers	2.5	7.5	12.7	15.3	14.4	12.7	17.6	17.3	100.0	3.14
	coll.farm	1.1	4.5	9.5	12.8	14.2	13.0	20.8	24.1	100.0	0.55
	total	2.3	7.1	12.2	14.9	14.4	12.7	18.1	18.3	100.0	3.69
Moldavia	workers	11.0	17.2	19.2	16.1	12.2	8.7	9.2	6.4	100.0	3.38
	coll.farm	14.7	20.2	20.4	15.7	10.7	7.1	7.1	4.1	100.0	0.97
	total	11.8	17.9	19.5	16.0	11.9	8.3	8.7	5.9	100.0	4.35
Latvia	workers	2.2	7.3	12.6	15.1	14.7	13.1	17.8	17.2	100.0	2.36
	coll.farm	3.7	8.4	12.3	13.9	12.9	11.4	17.2	20.2	100.0	0.31
	total	2.4	7.4	12.6	15.0	14.5	12.9	17.7	17.5	100.0	2.67
Kirgizia	workers	31.2	22.4	17.0	11.4	7.0	4.3	4.2	2.5	100.0	3.41
	coll.farm	39.3	25.1	16.1	9.3	4.9	2.5	2.8	-	100.0	0.88
	total	32.9	23.0	16.8	11.0	6.6	3.9	3.9	2.0	100.0	4.29
Tadzhikistan	workers	46.6	21.0	13.4	8.1	4.5	2.6	2.4	1.4	100.0	3.65
	coll.farm	62.2	23.6	9.4	3.2	1.1	0.4	0.1	-	100.0	1.52
	total	51.2	21.8	12.2	6.7	3.5	2.0	1.7	1.0	100.0	5.17
Armenia	workers	13.8	19.3	19.8	15.7	11.3	7.6	7.8	4.7	100.0	3.00
	coll.farm	18.5	18.4	17.0	13.5	10.1	7.2	8.3	7.0	100.0	0.34
	total	14.3	19.2	19.5	15.5	11.2	7.6	7.9	4.9	100.0	3.34
Turkmenia	workers	28.1	21.2	17.1	11.7	8.1	5.0	5.2	3.6	100.0	2.25
	coll.farm	46.8	25.1	14.3	7.2	3.5	1.6	1.5	-	100.0	1.31
	total	35.0	22.6	16.1	10.0	6.4	3.7	3.8	2.3	100.0	3.56
Estonia	workers	1.9	6.2	11.0	13.9	14.1	12.6	19.2	21.1	100.0	1.41
	coll.farm	1.5	4.5	8.2	10.6	11.7	11.6	19.6	32.3	100.0	0.16
	total	1.9	6.0	10.7	13.6	13.9	12.5	19.2	22.2	100.0	1.57

Source:
Goskomstat (1990a) Vol I, p. 13, vol II, p. 3.

Table U13(continued) SUMMARY STATISTICS for individual distribution of household gross per capita INCOME
(annual income divided by 12) by REPUBLICS (and USSR) for WORKERS and COLLECTIVE FARM WORKERS 1989

	Mean	Median	P5	P10	P25	P75	P90	P95	P90/P10	Var coef	Gini coef
Workers											
USSR	161.86	142.55	-	53.2	72.3	135.8	181.2*	225.0*	3.40*	0.653	0.284
RSFSR	179.65	155.45	48.8	57.7	74.2	134.0	181.8*	229.0*	3.15*	0.685	0.277
Ukraine	152.22	139.01	-	60.2	75.8	130.3	166.0	197.4*	2.76	0.488	0.235
Belarus	168.69	152.46	53.7	61.8	76.8	130.1	166.4	200.5*	2.69	0.506	0.234
Uzbekistan	98.62	86.44	-	.	.	142.3	193.4	232.6	.	0.601	0.298
Kazhakhstan	144.71	125.78	-	54.3**	71.2	138.4	185.6	229.8*	3.42**	0.652	0.286
Georgia	147.21	128.50	-	53.3**	72.9	138.1	184.8	228.1*	3.47**	0.643	0.287
Azerbaidzhan	108.44	93.93	-	.	.	145.0	201.6	245.7	.	0.687	0.327
Lithuania	197.70	170.51	50.5	58.7	75.7	131.7	180.9*	229.9*	3.08*	0.712	0.274
Moldavia	144.34	128.71	-	56.9**	74.6	134.8	175.5	212.0*	3.08**	0.553	0.259
Latvia	197.83	171.60	51.1	59.0	75.9	130.8	178.9*	226.8*	3.03*	0.694	0.270
Kirgizia	107.80	95.71	-	.	.	139.4	188.0	224.7	.	0.582	0.289
Tadzhikistan	88.62	78.35	-	.	.	143.8	196.7	238.4	.	0.637	0.320
Armenia	134.60	121.09	-	56.7**	74.7	134.6	174.7	207.5	3.08**	0.521	0.255
Turkmenia	114.68	100.89	-	.	.	141.7	191.4	231.3	.	0.631	0.303
Estonia	213.98	181.15	50.4	57.7	75.6	132.1	186.4*	241.7*	3.23*	0.832	0.290
Collective farm workers											
USSR	138.90	121.90	-	45.8**	68.1	141.6	189.8	233.2*	4.14**	0.671	0.310
RSFSR	164.21	144.13	-	55.9	73.5	135.0	179.7*	223.0*	3.21*	0.635	0.274
Ukraine	158.14	143.85	-	60.2	76.1	130.4	166.3	199.0*	2.76	0.498	0.236
Belarus	178.66	157.42	51.4	59.6	75.7	131.9	174.8*	216.3*	2.93*	0.600	0.257
Uzbekistan	72.82	69.67**	-	.	.	134.1	173.4	202.3	.	0.530	0.288
Kazhakhstan	109.39	95.61	-	.	.	142.8	196.3	238.1	.	0.655	0.314
Georgia	164.47	137.93	-	51.6**	70.3	141.1	196.3*	251.8*	3.80**	0.822	0.316
Azerbaidzhan	120.06	101.47	-	.	.	146.4	204.9	254.5*	.	0.743	0.332
Lithuania	227.99	190.90	51.6	58.3	76.3	131.7	188.4*	246.9*	3.23*	0.903	0.293
Moldavia	130.97	118.18	-	57.2**	74.9	133.9	174.0	205.7	3.04**	0.510	0.251

Latvia	208.63	172.40	46.7	55.3	73.2	136.0	195.2*	256.6*	3.53*	0.955	0.313
Kirgizia	92.92	84.38	-	-	-	136.7	178.8	210.1	-	0.516	0.267
Tadzhikistan	68.20	66.92**	-	-	-	127.6	162.9	185.8	-	0.465	0.257
Armenia	138.21	118.82	-	50.9***	70.9	141.4	192.2	238.3*	3.77**	0.685	0.303
Turkmenia	83.36	77.67	-	-	-	134.2	175.2	205.2	-	0.510	0.271
Estonia	282.50	77.67	32.5	45.6	71.2	134.2*	175.2*	205.2*	3.84*	0.510	0.271
Workers and collective farm workers											
USSR	158.83	140.11	-	51.6***	71.6	136.5	182.1	226.0*	3.53**	0.659	0.289
RSFSR	178.65	154.60	48.6	57.5	74.1	134.1	181.9*	229.1*	3.16*	0.685	0.278
Ukraine	153.35	139.91	-	60.2	75.9	130.4	166.1	197.7*	2.76	0.489	0.235
Belarus	170.29	153.23	53.5	61.5	76.6	130.4	167.8*	203.0*	2.73*	0.520	0.238
Uzbekistan	91.29	81.04	-	-	-	140.7	192.1	232.3	-	0.605	0.304
Kazakhstan	142.92	124.34	-	53.8***	70.7	138.7	186.2	230.4*	3.46**	0.654	0.289
Georgia	150.15	130.17	-	52.9***	72.5	138.7	186.9	232.5*	3.53***	0.673	0.292
Azerbaidzhan	110.33	94.98	-	-	-	145.4	202.8	248.2	-	0.701	0.328
Lithuania	201.93	173.32	50.6	58.5	75.8	131.8	182.2*	232.7*	3.11*	0.738	0.278
Moldavia	141.33	126.20	-	57.0***	74.7	134.7	175.5	211.3*	3.08***	0.547	0.258
Latvia	198.72	171.54	50.6	58.6	75.6	131.4	180.6*	229.8*	3.08*	0.716	0.274
Kirgizia	104.06	93.40	-	-	-	139.0	186.3	222.3	-	0.564	0.287
Tadzhikistan	82.94	74.19**	-	-	-	139.8	190.1	232.5	-	0.618	0.308
Armenia	134.85	120.96	-	56.1**	74.3	135.2	176.0	209.8	3.14**	0.532	0.259
Turkmenia	102.26	91.70	-	-	-	139.5	189.8	229.3	-	0.617	0.307
Estonia	219.18	183.24	50.0	57.4	75.4	132.9	190.0*	248.9*	3.31*	0.909	0.299

Note: in the case of certain republics, the lowest range contains more than 10 percent of the population; in this table, we have interpolated P10 - in contrast to our standard practice - where the bottom range contains 20 percent or fewer. These values are marked with a double asterisk. A double asterisk is also used where the median is interpolated in the lowest range.

Source: interpolated from Table UI3.

Table UI4. Individual distribution of household gross per capita
INCOME in DECILE SHARES (annual income divided by 12) 1980-1989
for USSR, RSFSR and UKRAINE for WORKERS and COLLECTIVE FARM WORKERS

Decile	RSFSR			Ukraine			USSR		
	Workers	Collective farm workers	Total	Workers	Collective farm workers	Total	Workers	Collective farm workers	Total
					Percent				
1	4.0	3.9	4.0	4.5	4.5	4.5	3.5	2.8	3.4
2	5.5	5.5	5.5	6.0	6.0	6.0	5.3	4.8	5.2
3	6.4	6.4	6.4	6.9	6.9	6.9	6.4	6.0	6.3
4	7.3	7.4	7.3	7.8	7.8	7.8	7.3	7.1	7.3
5	8.2	8.3	8.2	8.7	8.7	8.7	8.3	8.2	8.3
6	9.1	9.3	9.1	9.6	9.5	9.6	9.3	9.4	9.3
7	10.3	10.4	10.3	10.6	10.6	10.6	10.5	10.8	10.5
8	11.6	11.9	11.6	11.9	11.9	11.9	12.0	12.5	12.1
9	13.9	14.0	13.9	13.8	13.7	13.8	14.2	14.9	14.3
10	23.6	22.9	23.6	20.2	20.4	20.3	23.2	23.7	23.3

Note: based on less detailed ranges than Table UI2, which accounts for the difference in the Total USSR figures.

Source:
interpolated from Table UI3.

Table UI5. Household distribution of household gross per capita INCOME
(annual income divided by 12) by NUMBER of CHILDREN 1989

Range (rubles)	0	75.1	100	125	150	175	200	Total
					Percent			
All worker and employee families with children	18.3	20.4	22.5	17.1	9.8	5.2	6.7	100.0
of which with 1 child	8.2	15.5	23.2	21.5	13.8	7.8	10	100.0
2	17.8	26.3	25.7	15.5	7.2	3.3	4.2	100.0
3	48.2	27.1	13.9	6.1	2.4	1.2	1.1	100.0
4	75.2	16.7	5.6	1.5	0.6	0.2	0.2	100.0
more than 5	90.2	7.5	1.6	0.3	0.3	0.1	0	100.0
All collective farm families with children	48.5	23.5	14.7	7.4	3.1	1.4	1.4	100.0

Table UI5 (continued) Household distribution of household gross per capita INCOME
(annual income divided by 12) by NUMBER of CHILDREN 1989

Range (rubles)	0	75.1	100	125	150	175	200	Total
					Percent			
of which								
with 1 child	24.6	26.9	22.5	13.5	6.2	3.2	3.1	100.0
2	42.9	29.7	16.5	6.7	2.5	0.7	1	100.0
3	69.9	19.4	7.1	2.5	0.8	0.3	0	100.0
4	88.3	8.9	1.7	0.8	0.2	0.1	0	100.0
more than 5	96	3	0.8	0.2	0	0	0	100.0

Source:
NK 1989, p. 90.

Table UI6. Average per capita income by REPUBLIC relative to RSFSR 1960-1988

RSFSR = 100	1960	1965	1970	1975	1980	1985	1988
Ukraine	87.7	93.3	89.9	95.3	94.1	96.2	94.4
Belarus	75.3	83.3	86.9	87.8	93.4	97.6	99.1
Uzbekistan	71.8	68.4	68.7	64.4	65.0	61.2	60.9
Kazakhstan	88.2	84.2	81.0	80.4	83.7	85.2	88.9
Georgia	87.4	82.3	82.8	84.0	86.3	84.8	81.5
Azerbaijan	67.7	63.8	61.1	66.7	66.5	70.4	64.7
Lithuania	100.0	103.4	109.0	98.0	104.0	109.8	110.0
Moldavia	64.8	80.3	79.6	81.4	82.7	85.1	87.5
Latvia	115.9	115.0	115.8	109.3	109.1	109.6	109.3
Kirgizia	66.6	72.7	67.1	66.4	63.5	62.7	64.0
Tadzhikistan	61.4	68.1	58.3	58.8	54.7	53.3	48.9
Armenia	78.8	77.8	80.6	64.6	70.0	69.2	67.8
Turkmenistan	68.6	72.5	73.0	76.3	68.0	65.3	63.7
Estonia	119.7	121.8	123.3	114.6	107.7	111.1	107.8

Note: the figures relate to personal income.
Sources:
1960-1970: McAuley (1979), Table 5.1, p. 109;
1975-1988: Goskomstat (1989), p. 47.

Table UP1. Khrushchev minimum budgets c.1965

	'Current minimum' Rubles	%	'Prospective minimum' Rubles	%	'Rational minimum' Rubles	%
Food	28.8	55.9	34.0	51.0	52.5	34.3
Clothing, footwear	10.8	20.9	13.4	20.1	33.3	21.7
Furniture, household goods	1.2	2.6	2.5	3.8	7.0	4.6
Toiletries, medicines	0.7	2.2	1.2	1.7	4.3	2.8
Cultural goods and sportswear	1.1	1.3	1.2	1.8	5.6	3.6
Tobacco	1.4	2.7	0.4	0.6	0.9	0.6
Alcoholic drinks	(a)	(a)	2.2	3.4	5.1	3.3
Other goods and savings	-	-	0.2	0.3	7.0	4.5
Housing, communal services	2.8	5.4	3.4	5.1	6.8	4.5
Holidays, various services	0.7	1.4	3.3	4.9	8.7	5.7
Cinema, theatre, other cultural	0.9	1.7	1.4	2.1	5.2	3.4
Hairdressing, baths, laundry	1.2	2.3	-	-	-	-
Transport, post, telegraph	1.2	2.3	2.5	3.7	12.0	7.7
Membership fees	0.6	1.2	0.7	1.0	5.0	3.3
Other services	(b)	(b)	0.3	0.5	(b)	(b)
Total	51.4	100.0	66.6	100.0	153.3	100.0

Note: (a) alcoholic drinks are combined with tobacco in the 'Current minimum';
(b) other services are combined with 'Membership fees' except for the 'Prospective minimum';
(c) the budgets relate to an urban family of 4 and give per capita amounts.

Source:
Matthews (1986), Table 1.1, p. 20.

Table UP2. Average SUBSISTENCE MINIMUM per capita monthly income in rubles 1988 and 1989

	Amount At state trade prices	At state trade and collective farm prices
1988	78	84
1989	81	87

Sources:
Sotsial'noe razvitie SSSR 1989, Goskomstat, 1991, p. 117;
Ekonomichestaya gazeta, 1989, no 25, p. 11;
Gur'ev and Zaitseva (1990).

Table BE1. Distribution of gross weekly EARNINGS in pounds for ALL WORKERS 1968-1979

Lower value of range	1968	1970	1971	1972	1973	1974	1975	1976	1977	1978	1979
1	1,213	812	333	3,915	1,981	395	17	17	104	341	155
6	1,039	1,175	669	.	.	.	.	.	.	.	.
7	1,518	1,624	1,141	.	.	.	.	.	.	.	.
8	1,906	2,314	1,462	.	.	.	.	.	.	.	.
9	2,253	2,904	1,908	.	.	.	.	.	.	.	.
10	2,365	3,651	2,514	1,771	1,086	907	76	33	.	.	.
11	2,279	3,645	2,750	2,126	1,319	.	.	.	.	.	.
12	2,356	4,058	3,502	2,642	1,618	2,886	370	131	.	.	.
13	2,612	4,092	3,634	2,798	1,789	.	.	.	.	.	.
14	2,532	4,464	3,830	3,298	2,309	.	.	.	.	.	.
15	2,772	4,627	3,930	3,422	2,746	9,462	2,673	1,124	495	.	.
16	2,724	4,734	4,297	3,681	2,840	.	.	.	.	.	.
17	2,767	4,481	4,192	3,591	2,960	.	.	.	.	.	.
18	2,759	4,736	4,620	3,820	3,207	.	.	.	.	.	.
19	2,639	4,927	4,788	4,093	3,165	.	.	.	.	.	.
20	5,323	9,638	9,329	8,294	6,628	5,172	2,102	999	1,706	942	398
22	4,815	9,245	9,077	8,625	6,804	7,927	3,867	2,099	.	.	.
24	4,363	9,202	9,518	.	6,862	.	.	.	.	.	.
25	.	.	.	.	.	.	.	.	.	.	.
26	3,459	8,230	8,759	8,673	7,004	5,613	3,256	1,899	1,161	2,067	996
27	.	.	.	.	.	8,573	5,459	3,358	2,008	.	.
28	2,980	7,273	8,052	8,382	7,005	6,270	4,328	2,851	2,002	3,527	2,026
30	4,922	14,026	16,827	8,373	8,892	8,959	6,734	4,400	3,485	.	.
32	.	.	.	9,618	8,217	.	.	.	.	.	.
32.5	.	.	.	.	8,197	.	.	.	.	.	.
35	2,542	8,581	11,546	8,929	7,365	6,418	4,766	3,547	2,840	1,979	1,217
37	.	.	.	7,658	6,928	.	7,096	5,841	4,324	3,341	1,910
37.5	.	.	.	.	.	.	.	.	.	.	.
40	1,299	4,756	6,776	6,689	.	8,694	5,288	10,724	9,270	2,711	1,821
42	.	.	.	5,617	.	5,681	7,042	.	.	4,407	3,078
42.5	.	.	.	.	5,693	7,453	.	.	.	.	.
45	709	2,852	4,122	4,378	5,155	4,903	4,891	11,335	10,548	3,291	2,327
47	.	.	.	3,559	.	6,419	7,146	.	.	4,980	3,576
47.5	.	.	.	.	4,360	.	.	.	.	.	.
50	773	2,564	4,007	2,892	6,207	3,737	11,097	11,828	11,077	4,124	2,764
52	.	.	.	3,824	.	4,870	.	.	.	5,218	3,904

	1968	1970	1971	1972	1973	1974	1975	1976	1977	1978	1979
60	327	1,071	1,691	2,887	4,476	3,938	8,034	10,211	10,475	9,288	7,725
65	170	568	839	1,259	2,186	2,920	6,569	8,782	9,412	8,918	7,545
70						3,323	5,246	7,538	8,628	8,550	7,179
75							3,725	6,373	7,441	7,851	7,158
80	180	520	692	1,151	1,660	1,706	2,803	5,175	6,684	7,603	6,780
85							2,174	4,135	4,931	6,709	6,620
90						954	1,656	3,115	4,615	5,696	5,953
95							1,343	2,558	3,551	5,051	5,952
100	130	458	615	865	1,268	561	1,592	3,887	5,302	7,215	9,286
110						390	1,026	2,415	3,319	5,464	7,205
120						231	635	1,491	2,115	3,412	5,153
130						257	676	931	1,305	2,409	3,690
140								674	923	1,678	2,744
150						167	317	821	682	1,096	1,817
160									848	1,367	2,291
170						116	218	486			
180									412	725	1,259
200						79	130	319	223	444	676
220									235	382	563
250						47	94	94	138	245	451
300								78	68	155	245
400									32	70	61
Total	65,726	131,228	135,420	139,435	134,082	125,065	121,846	130,513	131,358	130,675	121,950
mean	21.50	25.06	27.63	30.83	35.12	40.10	52.33	62.23	68.15	76.67	86.72
median	19.71	22.66	25.17	28.13	32.34	37.49	48.26	57.20	62.35	70.47	79.80
P5	39.1	40.8	41.1	41.4	41.0	44.1	47.0	47.9	49.3	49.1	48.9
P10	47.8	49.3	50.5	50.2	50.4	52.2	55.4	56.7	58.2	57.3	56.8
P25	69.0	70.0	71.3	70.9	69.2	71.0	73.6	75.1	76.9	74.7	74.1
P75	135.0	135.9	134.4	134.4	133.5	130.9	131.6	131.0	130.8	131.3	131.6
P90	174.4	175.3	173.3	173.1	171.0	167.2	167.5	168.4	166.9	166.8	168.1
P95	207.6	208.1	206.4	206.9	203.3	197.2	196.5	197.2	195.1	196.2	196.2
P90/P10	3.65	3.56	3.42	3.45	3.39	3.20	3.02	2.97	2.87	2.91	2.96
Var coef	0.577	0.582	0.570	0.552	0.544	0.519	0.482	0.472	0.463	0.478	0.465
Gini coef	0.280	0.275	0.268	0.269	0.267	0.257	0.241	0.238	0.232	0.238	0.238

Notes: (a) numbers refer to NES sample numbers; (b) linear interpolation; (c) all full-time workers whose pay was not affected by absence.

Sources:
1968: NES 1968, Table 14, p. 36; 1970: NES 1970, Table 2, p. 33; 1971: NES 1971, Table 7, p. 36;
1972: NES 1972, Table 8, p. 31; 1973: NES 1973, Table 8, p. 7; 1974: NES 1974, Table 19, p. A26;
1975: NES 1975, Table 19, p. A27; 1976: NES 1976, Table 19, p. A27; 1977: NES 1977, Table 19, p. A27;
1978: NES 1978, Table 19, p. A28; 1979: NES 1979, Table 19, p. A34.

Table BEI(continued) Distribution of gross weekly EARNINGS in pounds for ALL WORKERS 1980-1990

Lower value of range	1980	1981	1982	1983	1984	1985	1986	1987	1988	1989	1990
1	2,669	1,424	2,896	2,024	1,509	979	701	1,285	756	2,488	1,557
40	954	510	-	-	-	-	-	-	-	-	-
42	1,279	766	-	-	-	-	-	-	-	-	-
45	1,165	725	-	-	-	-	-	-	-	-	-
47	1,975	1,129	1,757	1,107	775	557	490	-	-	-	-
50	1,646	1,041	-	-	-	-	-	-	-	-	-
52	2,696	1,438	2,266	1,515	1,014	810	552	-	-	-	-
55	1,946	1,278	-	-	-	-	-	-	-	-	-
57	3,072	2,282	3,365	2,128	1,649	1,190	837	660	463	-	-
60	5,706	4,314	3,935	2,917	2,022	1,468	1,108	797	544	-	-
65	6,202	4,697	4,246	3,507	2,998	1,972	1,533	1,172	806	-	-
70	6,463	5,430	4,666	3,575	3,188	2,591	1,950	1,433	1,118	-	-
75	6,467	5,535	4,922	4,308	3,344	2,991	2,629	1,971	1,377	2,055	1,329
80	6,564	5,827	5,144	4,343	3,839	3,126	2,712	2,262	1,698	-	-
85	6,549	5,686	5,329	4,548	3,780	3,541	2,910	2,660	2,148	-	-
90	6,425	5,904	5,203	4,715	4,122	3,497	3,309	2,676	2,503	3,117	2,049
95	6,014	5,787	-	-	-	-	-	-	-	-	-
100	11,487	11,119	10,449	9,833	8,484	7,251	6,916	5,909	5,146	4,268	2,953
110	10,223	10,419	9,984	9,270	8,597	7,984	7,075	6,403	5,716	4,971	3,880
120	8,110	9,025	9,116	8,900	8,005	7,640	7,658	6,537	6,041	5,295	4,437
130	6,926	7,608	8,215	8,200	7,727	7,181	6,880	6,942	6,336	5,582	4,751
140	5,304	6,307	7,211	7,929	7,162	7,145	7,217	6,594	6,416	5,780	4,932
150	3,931	5,580	6,692	6,837	7,002	6,477	6,627	6,448	6,330	6,347	5,763
160	3,024	4,359	5,072	6,027	6,372	6,297	6,277	5,847	6,297	5,812	5,446
170	2,375	3,541	4,314	5,203	5,663	5,938	6,162	5,941	5,760	5,536	5,342
180	2,979	5,164	3,912	4,095	4,734	5,607	5,420	5,659	5,536	5,167	5,011
190	-	-	2,842	3,740	4,053	4,638	5,452	4,826	5,397	5,476	5,123

Income	1980	1981	1982	1983	1984	1985	1986	1987	1988	1989	1990
200	1,932	3,528	4,636	5,423	6,718	7,398	8,887	9,650	9,776	10,063	10,035
220	1,663	3,046	4,143	5,402	6,566	7,798	9,809	11,121	12,672	13,295	13,424
250	1,291	2,296	2,294	3,194	4,110	4,920	6,323	7,198	9,630	10,775	11,290
280	-	-	1,084	1,318	1,852	2,308	3,015	3,618	4,635	6,256	6,702
300	815	1,504	1,482	2,108	2,738	3,518	4,698	5,889	8,249	4,758	6,161
320	-	-	-	-	-	-	-	-	-	5,565	7,208
350	-	-	715	946	1,321	1,709	2,385	3,165	4,457	6,020	7,778
400	273	513	905	1,361	1,912	2,577	3,785	1,751	2,543	3,446	4,665
450	-	-	-	-	-	-	-	1,109	1,676	2,277	3,251
500	-	-	-	-	-	-	-	2,316	3,519	2,317	3,221
600	-	-	-	-	-	-	-	-	-	2,773	3,857
Total	128,125	127,782	126,795	124,473	121,256	119,108	123,317	121,839	127,545	129,439	130,165
mean	*106.09*	*121.00*	*132.57*	*144.36*	*156.03*	*167.71*	*181.43*	*195.01*	*213.99*	*235.03*	*258.63*
median	*96.77*	*109.16*	*119.18*	*129.48*	*139.40*	*149.41*	*161.08*	*172.43*	*187.81*	*205.80*	*225.35*
P5	*49.2*	*49.4*	*49.5*	*48.8*	*48.4*	*48.3*	*48.4*	*47.5*	*47.3*	*46.2*	*47.3*
P10	*57.3*	*57.2*	*57.1*	*56.9*	*55.9*	*56.0*	*55.7*	*55.0*	*54.7*	*54.2*	*54.8*
P25	*74.6*	*74.4*	*74.3*	*74.4*	*73.7*	*73.4*	*72.9*	*72.6*	*72.3*	*72.1*	*71.7*
P75	*132.4*	*134.0*	*133.9*	*133.4*	*134.5*	*134.6*	*135.3*	*135.3*	*137.1*	*137.5*	*138.0*
P90	*170.6*	*175.8*	*176.4*	*176.9*	*178.5*	*179.2*	*179.7*	*182.3*	*183.9*	*183.6*	*186.5*
P95	*203.1*	*208.6*	*211.2*	*211.5*	*214.3*	*215.3*	*217.3*	*221.4*	*225.9*	*226.5*	*228.0*
P90/P10	*2.98*	*3.07*	*3.09*	*3.11*	*3.19*	*3.20*	*3.23*	*3.31*	*3.36*	*3.39*	*3.40*
Var coef	*0.493*	*0.500*	*0.519*	*0.533*	*0.543*	*0.552*	*0.571*	*0.582*	*0.589*	*0.633*	*0.634*
Gini coef	*0.247*	*0.251*	*0.256*	*0.257*	*0.261*	*0.263*	*0.267*	*0.273*	*0.276*	*0.283*	*0.283*

Note: see Table BE1.

Sources:

1980: NES 1980, Table 19, p. A33; 1981: NES 1981, Table 19, p. A74; 1982: NES 1982, Table 34, p. B18;
1983: NES 1983, Table 34, p. B16; 1984: NES 1984, Table 34, p. B33; 1985: NES 1985, Table 34, p. B32;
1986: NES 1986, Table 34, p. B35; 1987: NES 1987, Table 34, p. B36; 1988: NES 1988 Table 34, p. B34.1;
1989: NES 1989, Table 19, p. A19.1; 1990: NES 1990, Table 19, p. A19.1.

Table BE2. Distribution of gross weekly EARNINGS in pounds for MALES and FEMALES
April 1990

Lower value of range	Male Number	%	Female Number	%	% female in range
1	714	0.8	843	1.9	54.1
80	505	0.6	824	1.8	62.0
90	688	0.8	1,361	3.0	66.4
100	1,002	1.2	1,951	4.3	66.1
110	1,357	1.6	2,523	5.6	65.0
120	1,712	2.0	2,725	6.1	61.4
130	1,932	2.3	2,819	6.3	59.3
140	2,220	2.6	2,712	6.0	55.0
150	2,758	3.2	3,005	6.7	52.1
160	2,799	3.3	2,647	5.9	48.6
170	2,997	3.5	2,345	5.2	43.9
180	3,054	3.6	1,957	4.3	39.1
190	3,234	3.8	1,889	4.2	36.9
200	6,816	8.0	3,219	7.2	32.1
220	9,573	11.2	3,851	8.6	28.7
250	8,441	9.9	2,849	6.3	25.2
280	4,978	5.8	1,724	3.8	25.7
300	4,595	5.4	1,566	3.5	25.4
320	5,680	6.7	1,528	3.4	21.2
350	6,513	7.6	1,265	2.8	16.3
400	4,089	4.8	576	1.3	12.3
450	2,947	3.5	304	0.7	9.4

					female as % male
500	2,951	3.5	270	0.6	8.4
600	3,599	4.2	258	0.6	6.7
Total	85,154	100.0	45,011	100.0	34.6
mean	290.82		198.51		68.3
median	253.49		174.21		68.7
P5	47.3		53.6		77.9
P10	56.3		62.3		76.0
P25	74.3		76.3		70.6
P75	135.6		139.1		70.5
P90	182.8		181.1		68.1
P95	224.9		207.7		63.5
P90/P10	3.25		2.91		
Var coef	0.625		0.498		
Gini coef	0.274		0.245		

Notes: (a) numbers refer to NES sample numbers; (b) Paretian interpolation; (c) all full-time workers whose pay was not affected by absence.

Source:

NES 1990, Table 19, p. A19.1.

Table BE3. Distribution of gross weekly EARNINGS in pounds for MALES and FEMALES (adult workers) SUMMARY STATISTICS 1968-1990

Year	Female median as % male median	Male percent of median					Female percent of median				
		P10	P25	P75	P90	P90/P10	P10	P25	P75	P90	P90/P10
1968	53.0	65.7	80.0	126.7	161.4	2.46	67.0	80.0	129.7	171.2	2.56
1970	53.7	65.4	79.7	126.7	160.6	2.46	66.4	79.8	129.3	170.4	2.57
1971	55.7	66.1	80.3	126.5	160.7	2.43	66.6	80.2	127.3	165.8	2.49
1972	55.7	65.5	79.7	126.4	160.9	2.46	65.6	79.6	128.6	167.1	2.55
1973	54.4	65.6	79.9	125.3	158.5	2.42	67.4	80.7	127.6	164.7	2.44
1974	56.4	66.8	80.7	124.6	157.0	2.35	67.7	81.0	126.4	159.1	2.35
1975	61.0	67.0	81.0	125.3	157.6	2.35	67.4	81.5	125.2	164.5	2.44
1976	64.4	67.6	81.3	125.6	159.5	2.36	66.1	80.2	125.9	165.9	2.51
1977	64.9	68.1	81.4	125.6	157.7	2.32	68.6	82.1	124.7	162.1	2.36
1978	63.2	66.8	80.6	125.1	157.9	2.36	69.1	82.2	125.3	161.4	2.34
1979	62.2	66.0	80.3	125.1	156.9	2.38	69.4	82.1	124.7	158.6	2.29
1980	63.9	65.9	80.1	126.5	161.6	2.45	68.4	81.3	126.1	161.3	2.36
1981	65.0	65.6	79.8	129.5	167.7	2.56	68.0	80.6	129.8	172.6	2.54
1982	64.7	64.5	79.0	129.8	168.1	2.61	66.9	79.7	129.4	169.0	2.53
1983	65.7	64.1	78.8	129.8	169.7	2.65	66.4	79.7	129.9	168.3	2.53
1983	67.2	62.7	78.2	130.2	170.4	2.72	66.5	79.9	129.9	167.4	2.52
1984	66.5	61.6	77.2	130.6	171.5	2.78	66.2	79.2	130.2	166.3	2.51
1985	66.7	60.8	76.9	131.0	171.5	2.82	65.8	78.7	130.9	164.5	2.50
1986	66.7	60.2	76.6	131.6	173.3	2.88	65.1	78.6	132.7	170.0	2.61
1987	67.0	59.4	75.7	132.5	176.2	2.97	64.2	78.1	133.5	171.7	2.67
1988	67.4	59.0	75.5	134.0	178.3	3.02	63.4	77.2	136.6	177.5	2.80
1989	68.0	58.5	75.1	134.0	179.9	3.08	63.1	77.1	138.0	180.5	2.86
1990	68.7	58.3	74.9	134.6	181.1	3.11	62.5	76.7	137.9	178.6	2.86

Notes: (a) the statistics below the line refer to workers on adult rates; those above the line refer to men aged 21 and over and women aged 18 and over;
(b) full-time workers whose pay was not affected by absence.

Sources::
1968: NES 1970, p. 21;
1970-1975: RCDIW, Report No 7, Table 2.16, pp. 46-47;
1976-1979: NES 1986, Table 30, pp. B29-B30;
1980-1990: NES 1990, Table 15, pp. A15.1-2.

Table BE4. Distribution of gross weekly EARNINGS in pounds by COUNTRY (England, Wales and Scotland) April 1990

Lower range of range	England		Wales		Scotland		Great Britain	
	Males	Females	Males	Females Percent	Males	Females	Males	Females
1	4.9	5.1	7.5	8.4	6.6	7.3	5.2	5.4
100	-	9.0	-	12.2	-	13.0	-	9.6
120	-	6.0	-	7.1	-	6.1	-	6.0
130	4.5	6.1	6.1	7.3	6.1	7.0	4.6	6.3
140	-	5.9	-	7.2	-	6.6	-	6.0
150	6.2	6.7	8.4	7.8	7.5	7.8	6.5	6.8
160	-	6.0	-	6.4	-	5.8	-	6.0
170	3.5	14.1	4.1	13.3	4.1	13.5	3.5	14.1
180	7.3	-	8.8	-	8.3	-	7.5	-
200	8.1	7.5	8.9	6.3	8.5	6.4	8.2	7.3
220	11.6	9.1	11.4	6.2	11.1	7.2	11.5	8.8
250	16.3	11.0	17.4	9.0	14.8	7.2	16.2	10.5
300	5.6	7.1	5.4	5.7	5.4	7.4	5.6	7.1
320	7.0	-	5.9	-	6.2	-	6.9	-
350	8.0	6.4	6.9	3.1	7.0	4.7	7.9	6.1
400	5.0	-	3.0	-	4.8	-	4.9	-
450	3.7	-	2.5	-	3.3	-	3.6	-
500	8.3	-	3.7	-	6.3	-	7.9	-
Total	100	100	100	100	100	100	100	100

mean	299.50	204.10	258.60	180.30	276.40	187.20	295.60	201.50
median	261.00	179.90	237.70	160.00	243.30	163.50	258.20	177.50
P10	58.3	62.4	58.1	64.4	58.5	63.9	58.3	62.5
P25	75.1	76.7	74.8	78.8	74.7	77.9	74.9	76.7
P75	134.2	138.0	129.4	135.0	136.0	137.2	134.6	137.9
P90	182.0	178.0	165.5	182.0	182.2	191.7	181.1	178.6
P90/P10	3.12	2.85	2.85	2.82	3.11	3.00	3.11	2.86

Note: all full-time workers on adult rates whose pay was not affected by absence.

Source:

NES 1990, Part E, Table 110, p. E110.1, Table 113, p. E113.1;
Table 114, pp. E114.2-3, and Table 116, pp. E116.2-3.

Table B1. Tax unit distribution of tax unit net INCOME in pounds (annual income) OLD BASIS 1949-1964

Lower value of range	1949		1954		1959		1962		1963		1964	
	Number of tax units and total income in range											
	'000s	£ m	'000s	£ m	'000s	£ m	'000s	£ m	'000s	£ m	'000s	£ m
50	12,840	2,054	8,980	1,481	6,200	1,049	5,070	990	4,330	815	4,054	805
250	10,140	3,529	9,040	3,379	7,440	2,792	6,570	2,486	7,075	2,706	6,884	2,604
500	2,020	1,190	5,770	3,511	6,630	4,108	6,155	3,844	5,895	3,725	5,750	3,520
750	442	375	1,600	1,347	3,880	3,324	4,830	4,168	5,045	4,420	4,608	3,924
1,000	368.4	498	721	941	1,731	1,955	4,145	5,113	4,540	5,757	4,797	5,935
1,500					321	595					844	1,476
2,000	84.4	222	131	340	206	493	353	940	428	1,098	355	830
3,000					61	208					110	368
4,000	5.14	21.5	7.8	34.4	20	89	59	281	72	351	50	223
5,000					8	42					25	140
6,000	0.06	0.5	0.2	1.6	3	23	18	129	15	113	22	148
10,000											1	14
Total	25,900	7,890	26,250	11,035	26,500	14,678	27,200	17,951	27,400	18,985	27,500	19,987
Mean	303	(251)	420	(363)	553	(487)	664	(579)	692	(607)	726	(603)
Median	250		323		477		561		573		596	
P5												
P10												
P25	138	(148.2)	47	(152.6)	54	(54.3)	54	(55.3)	54	(57.6)	54	(59.2)
P75	208	(206.7)	167	(203.8)	152	(150.6)	152	(149.7)	154	(150.2)	159	(156.2)
P90	260.8		227		202	(199.4)	207	(196.4)	210	(197.4)	212	(222.9)
P95			242.9		230.5		235.5		243.1		251.9	
P90/P10												
Var coef	0.835		0.750		0.757		0.758		0.755		0.764	
Gini coef	0.355	(0.353)	0.358	(0.358)	0.360	(0.360)	0.356	(0.353)	0.356	(0.354)	0.366	(0.362)

Note: in the lower part of the table, there are in some cases two figures for each year; the first is from the original source, the second, in brackets, is our interpolation, as are other figures in italics.

Sources:

(a) the mean, median, Gini coefficient and the summary statistics given without decimal places are from RCDIW, Report 7, Table A.4, p. 167;

(b) data for individual years:

1949: National Income and Expenditure 1958, Table 31, p. 28;

1954: National Income and Expenditure 1965, Table 21, p. 30 and 1958, Table 31, p. 29 (for total income in top two ranges);

1959: National Income and Expenditure 1969, Table 23, p. 27 and 1965, Table 21, p. 30;

1962: National Income and Expenditure 1965, Table 21, p. 31;

1963: National Income and Expenditure 1967, Table 26, p. 32;

1964: National Income and Expenditure 1969, Table 23, p. 27 and 1967, Table 26, p. 33 (information to divide ranges above £2,000).

Table B1(continued) Tax unit distribution of tax unit net INCOME in pounds (annual income) OLD BASIS 1965-1970/1

Lower value of range	1965		1966		1967		1968/9		1969/70		1970/1	
	Number of tax units and total income in range											
	'000s	£ m	'000s	£ m	'000s	£ m	'000s	£ m	'000s	£ m	'000s	£ m
1	0	0	0	0	0	0	2,387	561	3,214	814	4,389	1,443
50	3,006	616	2,603	549	2,338	493	-	-	-	-	-	-
250	6,841	2,535	6,338	2,545	5,906	2,372	2,521	856	-	-	-	-
275	-	-	-	-	-	-	-	-	-	-	-	-
330	-	-	-	-	-	-	-	-	1,426	526	-	-
400	-	-	-	-	-	-	2,360	1,065	1,964	888	1,505	700
420	-	-	-	-	-	-	-	-	-	-	-	-
500	5,431	3,358	5,523	3,514	5,418	3,471	2,185	1,202	2,140	1,181	2,001	1,111
600	-	-	-	-	-	-	2,058	1,343	1,956	1,275	2,013	1,318
700	-	-	-	-	-	-	2,154	1,618	2,011	1,511	1,845	1,392
750	5,153	4,408	4,765	4,133	4,822	4,203	-	-	-	-	-	-
800	-	-	-	-	-	-	1,823	1,551	1,878	1,596	1,908	1,623
900	-	-	-	-	-	-	1,751	1,663	1,656	1,572	1,672	1,586
1,000	6,460	8,386	6,116	7,319	6,466	7,790	4,104	4,611	3,916	4,388	3,424	3,842
1,250	-	-	-	-	-	-	3,093	4,224	3,390	4,645	2,925	4,009
1,500	-	-	1,488	2,527	1,832	3,132	1,877	3,015	2,172	3,505	2,561	4,145
1,750	-	-	-	-	-	-	737	1,374	1,071	1,991	1,727	3,221
2,000	595	1,510	595	1,366	730	1,664	507	1,117	722	1,583	853	1,797
2,250	-	-	-	-	-	-	-	-	-	-	428	1,010
2,500	-	-	-	-	-	-	210	601	254	691	261	681
2,750	-	-	-	-	-	-	-	-	-	-	160	457
3,000	-	-	211	770	224	814	181	589	221	751	313	1,065
4,000	84	401	-	-	-	-	76	341	93	413	124	544
5,000	-	-	60	366	63	385	35	192	41	225	53	288
6,000	30	215	-	-	-	-	28	192	32	219	27	178
7,000	-	-	-	-	-	-	-	-	-	-	11	80
8,000	-	-	1	22	1	21	3	24	3	27	5	39
10,000	-	-	-	-	-	-	1	7	1	11	1	8
Total	27,600	21,429	27,700	23,111	27,800	24,345	28,091	26,146	28,161	27,812	28,206	30,537

Mean	776	834	875	931	988	1,083
Median	661 (673)	711 (728)	758 (761)	819 (822)	870 (873)	924 (926)
P5	–	–	–	–	–	–
P10	–	36.4	37.8	36.3	–	–
P25	55 (57.4)	55 (61.7)	56 (61.2)	60 (59.6)	60 (59.9)	60 (61.0)
P75	153 (150.5)	150 (147.9)	146 (147.8)	150 (150.0)	150 (150.6)	156 (156.8)
P90	201 (204.0)	200 (197.6)	199 (198.6)	194 (192.9)	194 (194.3)	205 (205.5)
P95	250.9	240.3	243.3	226.3	227.5	241.7
P90/P10	–	5.40	5.25	5.32	–	–
Var coef	0.743	0.708	0.684	0.671	0.672	0.668
Gini coef	0.354 (0.352)	0.337 (0.336)	0.335 (0.334)	0.332 (0.332)	0.335 (0.335)	0.339 (0.338)

Notes: (a) see note to Table B1;

(b) in interpolating, the following ranges have been combined: in 1966, £5,000 and above, in 1968/9, £6,000 and above, and in 1970/1, £7,000 and above.

Sources:

(a) the mean, median, Gini coefficient and the summary statistics given without decimal places are from RCDIW, Report 7, Table A.4, p. 167;

(b) data for individual years:

1965: National Income and Expenditure 1967, Table 26, p. 33;

1966 and 1967: National Income and Expenditure 1969, Table 23, p. 28;

1968/9 - 1970/1: Economic Trends, May 1978, Tables 1-3, pp. 82-84.

Table B11(further continued) Tax unit distribution of tax unit net INCOME in pounds (annual income) OLD BASIS 1971/2-1976/7

Lower value of range	1971/2 '000s	1971/2 £ m	1972/3 '000s	1972/3 £ m	1973/4 '000s	1973/4 £ m	1974/5 '000s	1974/5 £ m	1975/6 '000s	1975/6 £ m	1976/7 '000s	1976/7 £ m
						Number of tax units and total income in range						
1	3,367	1,126	4,871	2,105	3,589	1,803	2,077	1,122	1,881	1,199	1,414	963
420	1,548	733	-	-	-	-	-	-	-	-	-	-
500	1,838	1,018	2,594	1,797	-	-	-	-	-	-	-	-
595	-	-	-	-	2,364	1,674	-	-	-	-	-	-
600	1,865	1,213	-	-	-	-	-	-	-	-	-	-
625	-	-	-	-	-	-	1,706	1,219	-	-	-	-
700	1,671	1,253	4,164	3,688	3,964	3,499	3,489	3,092	2,776	2,460	2,025	1,805
750	-	-	-	-	-	-	-	-	-	-	-	-
800	1,785	1,519	-	-	-	-	-	-	-	-	-	-
900	1,542	1,468	-	-	-	-	-	-	-	-	-	-
1,000	3,290	3,701	3,227	3,647	2,981	3,351	3,304	3,723	3,018	3,414	5,047	6,433
1,250	2,876	3,953	2,945	4,057	2,657	3,642	2,506	3,447	2,840	3,902	4,495	7,853
1,500	2,704	4,379	2,686	4,366	2,524	4,101	2,322	3,779	2,253	3,663	3,465	7,776
1,750	2,080	3,888	2,280	4,264	2,417	4,524	2,126	3,982	1,907	3,581	2,956	8,121
2,000	1,351	2,846	3,154	7,018	3,755	8,370	3,874	8,680	3,624	8,130	-	-
2,250	791	1,867	1,273	3,466	2,035	5,539	2,865	7,833	3,213	8,855	2,676	8,668
2,500	484	1,259	-	-	-	-	-	-	-	-	-	-
2,750	284	810	769	2,611	1,229	4,181	2,806	9,528	4,366	15,079	2,262	8,447
3,000	453	1,542	-	-	-	-	-	-	-	-	1,551	6,576
3,500	159	711	183	813	288	1,280	658	2,905	1,560	6,841	1,003	4,755
4,000	-	-	-	-	-	-	-	-	-	-	-	-
4,500	81	442	95	517	133	726	285	1,538	484	2,616	919	4,979
5,000	31	201	81	553	125	858	177	1,204	320	2,159	370	2,381
6,000	18	127	-	-	-	-	-	-	-	-	188	1,396
7,000	17	145	20	178	41	365	55	487	67	591	128	1,118
8,000	-	-	-	-	-	-	-	-	-	-	-	-
9,000	5	62	5	53	13	137	16	172	21	231	34	366
10,000	-	-	-	-	-	-	-	-	-	-	-	-

12,000	-	-	3	36	5	72	5	69	7	88	12	155
12,500	-	-	-	-	-	-	-	-	-	-	-	-
15,000	-	-	0.5	8	2	32	2	32	3	43	3	51
17,500	-	-	-	-	-	-	-	-	-	-	-	-
20,000	-	-	0.5	15	1	18	1	16	1	14	1	29
Total	28,240	34,263	28,351	39,192	28,123	44,172	28,274	52,828	28,341	62,866	28,549	71,872
Mean	1,213	-	1,383	-	1,571	-	1,868	-	2,218	-	2,517	-
Median	1,031	*(1,038)*	1,187	*(1,202)*	1,348	*(1,354)*	1,604	*(1,617)*	1,927	*(1,937)*	2,160	*(2,178)*
P5	-	-	-	-	-	-	-	-	-	-	34.5	-
P10	-	-	-	-	-	-	44.4	-	44.0	-	43.4	-
P25	60	*(59.4)*	61	*(61.4)*	60	*(61.2)*	61	*(61.1)*	62	*(62.3)*	62	*(63.9)*
P75	156	*(156.0)*	153	*(152.1)*	152	*(152.5)*	154	*(152.9)*	153	*(152.9)*	155	*(154.4)*
P90	208	*(205.2)*	202	*(201.1)*	201	*(200.8)*	203	*(202.9)*	199	*(200.8)*	205	*(203.4)*
P95	244.6	-	238.6	-	238.8	-	238.9	-	232.3	-	237.3	-
P90/P10	-	-	-	-	-	-	4.57	-	4.57	-	4.69	-
Var coef	0.682	-	0.660	-	0.660	-	0.630	-	0.596	-	0.595	-
Gini coef	0.342	*(0.342)*	0.331	*(0.333)*	0.328	*(0.327)*	0.324	*(0.324)*	0.315	*(0.315)*	0.315	*(0.315)*

Notes: (a) see note to Table B11;
(b) in interpolating for 1973/4, 1974/5 and 1975/6, the ranges £10,000 and above have been combined.

Sources:

(a) the mean, median, Gini coefficient and the summary statistics given without decimal places are from RCDIW, Report 7, Table A.4, p. 167;

(b) data for individual years:

1971/2: Economic Trends, May 1978, Table 4, p. 85;
1972/3: Economic Trends, August 1975, Table 1, p. 91;
1973/4: Economic Trends, June 1976, Table 1, p. 100
1974/5: National Income and Expenditure 1966-76, Table 4.8, p. 33;
1975/6: Economic Trends, May 1978, Table 1, p. 93;
1976/7: Economic Trends, February 1979, Table 2, p. 89.

Table B11(new) Tax unit distribution of tax unit net INCOME in pounds (annual income) NEW BASIS 1975/6-1984/5

Lower value of range	1975/6 '000s	1975/6 £ m	1976/7 '000s	1976/7 £ m	1977/8 '000s	1977/8 £ m	1978/9 '000s	1978/9 £ m	1981/2 '000s	1981/2 £ m	1984/5 '000s	1984/5 £ m
				Number of tax units and total income in range								
1	1,862	1,181	1,399	963	2,427	1,985	1,446	1,014	1,141	634	2,778	4,630
750	2,738	2,436	2,016	1,806	-	-	-	-	-	-	-	-
1,000	2,979	3,389	4,975	6,364	4,709	6,191	3,895	5,134	3,662	5,999	-	-
1,250	2,793	3,839	-	-	-	-	-	-	-	-	-	-
1,500	2,149	3,483	4,363	7,636	4,029	7,111	3,685	6,445	-	-	-	-
1,750	1,817	3,413	-	-	-	-	-	-	-	-	-	-
2,000	3,405	7,645	3,277	7,359	3,288	7,431	3,320	7,462	5,207	13,567	5,013	13,708
2,500	3,101	8,546	2,760	7,594	2,740	7,539	2,691	7,391	-	-	-	-
3,000	4,465	15,515	2,585	8,385	2,376	7,727	2,340	7,602	4,583	15,977	4,750	17,343
3,500	-	-	2,279	8,537	2,131	7,990	2,090	7,834	-	-	-	-
4,000	1,849	8,141	1,623	6,895	1,954	8,295	1,961	8,331	3,536	15,587	3,652	16,675
4,500	-	-	1,133	5,365	1,548	7,339	1,714	8,136	-	-	-	-
5,000	612	3,312	1,136	6,154	1,915	10,408	2,593	14,124	2,915	15,885	2,908	15,989
6,000	414	2,807	484	3,116	863	5,549	1,602	10,298	2,269	14,659	2,309	15,022
7,000	-	-	237	1,764	419	3,112	791	5,877	1,907	14,259	1,866	13,957
8,000	97	849	185	1,619	304	2,678	595	5,305	1,431	12,155	1,542	13,116
9,000	-	-	-	-	-	-	-	-	1,009	9,565	1,351	12,809
10,000	38	414	59	646	104	1,133	199	2,167	1,320	14,794	2,381	26,482
12,500	15	194	26	341	58	761	94	1,212	531	7,301	1,354	18,440
15,000	5	88	8	128	22	364	47	774	242	3,914	632	10,142
17,500	-	-	-	-	-	-	-	-	113	2,108	349	6,514
20,000	2	63	4	104	5	131	11	262	91	2,041	309	6,806
25,000	-	-	-	-	-	-	-	-	30	826	116	3,141
30,000	-	-	-	-	-	-	2	57	15	499	48	1,547
35,000	-	-	-	-	-	-	-	-	6	223	22	827
40,000	-	-	-	-	-	-	-	-	5	235	19	831
50,000	-	-	-	-	-	-	-	-	5	384	17	1,211
Total	28,341	65,315	28,549	74,776	28,892	85,744	29,076	99,425	30,018	150,612	31,416	199,190

	1975/6		1976/7		1977/8		1978/9		1981/2		1984/5	
Mean	2,305	(1,978)	2,619	(2,226)	2,970	(2,499)	3,420	(2,905)	5,020	(4,073)	6,340	(4,904)
Median	1,974		2,204		2,500		2,890		4,090		4,990	
P5	-		34.0		-		34.5		30.2		-	
P10	43.5		42.8		44.3		44.4		41.6		47.6	
P25	61	(61.6)	61	(63.0)	60.5		60.6		65.5		62.0	
P75	159	(155.7)	159	(157.6)	159.8		158.6		161.9		167.0	
P90	205.4		211	(209.5)	213.2		213.3		229.2		247.2	
P95	242.1		247.2		251.7		250.3		284.0		302.9	
P90/P10	4.72		4.90		4.81		4.80		5.50		5.19	
Var coef	0.636		0.628		0.635		0.641		0.740		0.764	
Gini coef	0.326	(0.326)	0.326	(0.326)	0.330	(0.330)	0.335	(0.335)	0.360	(0.359)	0.360	(0.362)

Notes: (a) see note to Table B1;
(b) in interpolating, the starting point of the lowest range is taken as £50; and for 1978/9 the ranges above £20,000 have been combined;
(c) the NEW BASIS differs from the OLD BASIS in that in this table income is gross of amounts spent on mortgage interest; in the previous tables, mortgage interest is deducted in calculating net income.

Sources:

1975/6: Economic Trends, May 1978, Table 2, p. 94 and Table E, p. 92, P25, P75, Gini from RCDIW, Report No 7, Table A.3, p. 167.

1976/7: National Income and Expenditure 1979, Table 4.8, p. 37 and mean/median, P25, P75, P90 and Gini from RCDIW, Report No 7, Tables A.3 and A.4, p. 167.

1977/8: National Income and Expenditure 1980, Table 4.9, p. 37 and notes, p. 113.

1978/9: National Income and Expenditure 1982, Table 4.9, p. 37 and notes, p. 110.

1981/2: Economic Trends, July 1984, Table A, p. 97 and Table 1, p. 105.

1984/5: Economic Trends, November 1987, Table A, p. 94 and Table 1, p. 103.

Table BI2. Tax unit distribution of tax unit net INCOME in DECILE SHARES (annual income) 1949-1984/5

Deciles	1	2	3	4	5 Percent	6	7	8	9	10	Top 5%	Top 1%
1949	-	-	-	-	26.5	9.5	10.5	11.9	14.5	27.1	17.7	6.4
1954	-	-	11.6	6.4	8.3	9.1	10.3	13.3	15.7	25.3	15.9	5.3
1959	-	6.0	5.2	6.6	7.2	9.9	11.2	12.9	15.7	25.2	15.8	5.3
1962	-	5.9	5.6	6.0	8.3	9.6	11.2	13.1	14.9	25.6	16.3	5.7
1963	-	6.5	5.3	5.8	8.2	9.3	11.2	13.0	15.3	25.4	15.9	5.3
1964	-	6.5	5.1	5.6	8.0	8.8	11.1	12.9	16.1	25.9	16.0	5.3
1965	-	6.9	4.8	6.2	7.9	9.3	11.0	12.9	15.6	25.4	15.7	5.2
1966	-	7.2	5.0	6.8	7.8	9.6	10.8	13.0	15.3	24.5	15.1	5.1
1967	-	7.1	4.9	7.1	7.7	9.7	11.0	13.0	15.2	24.3	14.8	4.9
1968/9	-	6.6	5.3	6.6	8.1	9.7	11.5	13.1	15.5	23.6	14.4	4.6
1969/70	-	6.4	5.2	6.7	8.1	9.7	11.4	13.3	15.6	23.6	14.4	4.7
1970/1	-	6.6	5.2	6.5	7.8	9.5	11.2	13.3	15.9	23.9	14.5	4.5
1971/2	-	6.6	5.1	6.4	7.8	9.4	11.3	13.4	15.9	24.1	14.6	4.6
1972/3	-	6.8	5.5	6.5	8.0	9.5	11.2	13.2	15.8	23.6	14.2	4.4
1973/4	3.2	4.2	5.4	6.4	7.8	9.5	11.2	13.2	15.5	23.6	14.3	4.5
1974/5	3.1	4.4	5.3	6.4	7.8	9.4	11.4	13.2	15.8	23.2	13.7	4.0
1975/6	3.2	4.4	5.4	6.5	7.9	9.7	11.4	13.4	15.8	22.3	13.0	3.6
1976/7	3.1	4.6	5.2	6.8	7.9	9.4	11.3	13.4	15.9	22.4	12.9	3.5
1975/6	3.1	4.3	5.3	6.3	7.7	9.6	11.3	13.5	15.8	23.1	13.6	3.9
1976/7	3.0	4.5	5.1	6.6	7.7	9.3	11.3	13.3	16.0	23.2	13.6	3.9
1977/8	3.0	4.4	5.2	6.2	7.7	9.3	11.3	13.4	16.2	23.3	13.7	3.9
1978/9	2.9	4.1	5.1	6.4	7.7	9.3	11.3	13.5	16.3	23.4	13.7	3.9
1981/2	2.4	4.0	5.2	6.3	7.3	8.8	10.8	13.2	16.4	25.6	15.3	4.6
1984/5	2.7	4.2	4.9	6.0	7.1	8.6	10.4	13.0	16.6	26.5	16.0	4.9

Notes: (a) the shares do not necessarily add to 100% on account of rounding (in original data);

(b) the figures below the line are the "new" series, including mortgage interest payments (see Table B1(new));

(c) the lowest decile shares are not shown separately in earlier years, the figure under 5 for 1949 is the share of the bottom 50%, that under 3 for 1954 is the share of the bottom 30%, and that under 2 for 1959-1972/3 is the share of the bottom 20%.

Sources:

1949 to 1976/7: RCDIW Report No 7, Table A.3, p. 167.

1977/8: National Income and Expenditure 1980, p. 113.

1978/9, 1981/2 and 1984/5: Economic Trends, November 1987, Table A, p. 94.

Table B13. Distribution of household net income adjusted in different ways
for HOUSEHOLD SIZE pounds per week (current income) 1985

Lower value of range	1. Household distribution of household income (thousands)	%	2. Individual distribution of household per capita income (thousands)	%	3. Individual distribution of household equivalent income (thousands)	%
1	387.7	1.8	1,521.6	2.8	1,027.6	1.9
20	-	-	922.5	1.7	-	-
22.5	-	-	1,101.8	2.0	-	-
25	-	-	1,341.6	2.4	-	-
27.5	-	-	1,464.8	2.7	-	-
30	-	-	1,712.1	3.1	-	-
32.5	-	-	1,668.5	3.0	-	-
33	-	-	-	-	349.9	0.6
35	-	-	2,306.8	4.2	1,226.6	2.2
37.5	-	-	2,652.4	4.8	-	-
39	-	-	-	-	352.1	0.6
40	379.8	1.7	2,508.3	4.5	2,640.7	4.8
42.5	-	-	2,175.7	3.9	-	-
45	388.4	1.8	1,998.5	3.6	3,480.5	6.3
47.5	-	-	2,098.9	3.8	-	-
50	603.0	2.8	2,180.3	3.9	1,552.4	2.8
52	-	-	-	-	2,266.0	4.1
52.5	-	-	2,222.4	4.0	-	-
55	733.5	3.3	1,747.1	3.2	3,690.6	6.7
57.5	-	-	1,948.5	3.5	-	-
60	707.9	3.2	3,202.1	5.8	3,385.5	6.1
65	620.9	2.8	2,643.4	4.8	3,425.8	6.2
70	613.1	2.8	2,248.7	4.1	3,024.9	5.5
75	571.2	2.6	2,107.0	3.8	2,709.6	4.9
80	661.0	3.0	1,975.7	3.6	3,030.4	5.5
85	553.2	2.5	1,581.0	2.9	2,367.0	4.3
90	543.4	2.5	1,229.6	2.2	2,397.2	4.3
95	560.2	2.6	1,155.8	2.1	1,233.3	2.2
98	-	-	-	-	780.9	1.4
100	521.4	2.4	2,036.9	3.7	3,681.1	6.7
105	545.1	2.5	-	-	-	-

	(1)	%	(2)	%	(3)	%
110	483.8	2.2	1,250.4	2.3	3,005.3	5.4
115	491.9	2.2				
120	854.6	3.9	1,786.9	3.2	2,020.3	3.7
130	875.1	4.0			1,873.4	3.4
140	916.3	4.2	869.6	1.6	1,253.8	2.3
150	902.3	4.1			985.6	1.8
160	757.2	3.5	638.9	1.2		
170	747.0	3.4			1,247.2	2.3
180	654.4	3.0	308.8	0.6	626.3	1.1
190	674.9	3.1				
200	1150.5	5.3	433.2	0.8	1,302.2	2.4
220	963.1	4.4				
240	809.8	3.7				
250			225.7	0.4		
260	712.8	3.3				
280	450.7	2.1				
300	373.0	1.7			328.8	0.6
320	385.0	1.8				
340	246.8	1.1				
360	199.9	0.9				
380	137.7	0.6				
400	405.3	1.9				
500	154.0	0.7				
600	163.2	0.7				
Total	21,898.9	100.0	55,265.5	100.0	55,265.0	100.0
Mean	162.94		64.57		88.18	
Median	138.29		54.71		77.24	
P5	35.6		42.6		51.4	
P10	41.8		52.0		58.1	
P25	60.4		71.8		73.0	
P75	153.0		144.5		138.4	
P90	212.5		200.9		182.6	
P95	258.3		248.7		221.1	
P90/P10	5.09		3.86		3.14	
Var coef	0.691		0.624		0.562	
Gini coef	0.342		0.297		0.265	

Note: Income is net of income tax and National Insurance contributions; self-employment income is indexed to mid-1985; a proportionate correction of 19.5 percent is made for the under-reporting of self-employment income; where individual total net income is negative, it is set to zero; earned income is 'normal earnings'; state benefits are included when in current receipt (including housing benefit).

Source: calculations from FES Base Tapes.

Table BI4. HOUSEHOLD distribution of HOUSEHOLD EQUIVALISED net income in QUINTILE SHARES (annual income) 1977-1989

Quintile group	Share of total income % 1977	1979	1981	1983	1985	1987	1988	1989
Bottom	9.7	9.4	9.3	9.5	9.2	8.2	7.6	7.6
2nd	14	13	13	13	13	12	11	12
3rd	18	18	17	17	17	16	16	17
4th	23	23	23	23	23	23	23	23
Top	36	36	38	38	38	41	42	41
Gini coef	0.27	0.27	0.28	0.28	0.29	0.33	0.35	0.34

Sources:

Economic Trends, March 1991, Table N, p. 118 and Economic Trends, January 1992, Table 1 (Appendix 4), p. 164 and Table 2 (Appendix 4), p. 165.

Table BI5. INDIVIDUAL distribution of HOUSEHOLD EQUIVALISED net income in DECILE SHARES (current income) 1979-1987

Decile	Percent 1979	1981	1983	1985	1987
1	4.3	4.1	4.1	4.2	3.8
2	5.8	5.7	5.7	5.5	5.1
3	6.8	6.5	6.6	6.4	5.9
4	7.6	7.4	7.4	7.3	6.9
5	8.6	8.4	8.4	8.3	8.0
6	9.6	9.3	9.3	9.3	8.9
7/8	23.0	22.6	22.6	22.8	22.2
9/10	34.3	36.0	35.9	36.2	39.1
Total	100	100	100	100	100

Notes: (a) the shares do not necessarily add to 100% on account of rounding (in original data);
(b) the figures relate to income before the deduction of housing costs.

Sources:
Social Trends, 1991, Table 5.16, p. 93 and Households Below Average Income 1981-87, Table A1, pp. 10-11 and Annex, p. 46.

Table BI6. Individual distribution of household net per capita income pounds per week (current income) by COUNTRY 1985

Range	ENGLAND thousands	%	WALES thousands	%	SCOTLAND thousands	%
1	1,307.9	2.8	53.2	1.8	63.4	1.3
20	640.8	1.4	64.8	2.2	133.8	2.7
22.5	884.5	1.9	61.7	2.1	121.3	2.4
25	1,097.6	2.4	64.5	2.2	100.0	2.0
27.5	1,175.1	2.5	97.0	3.3	167.2	3.3
30	1,491.5	3.2	36.9	1.3	163.8	3.3
32.5	1,361.9	2.9	59.6	2.0	217.5	4.4
35	2,033.7	4.4	85.3	2.9	149.5	3.0
37.5	2,244.2	4.9	204.4	7.0	133.3	2.7
40	2,216.1	4.8	106.1	3.6	118.9	2.4
42.5	1,790.5	3.9	159.8	5.5	181.4	3.6
45	1,567.7	3.4	142.5	4.9	242.4	4.9
47.5	1,709.4	3.7	107.6	3.7	210.7	4.2
50	1,736.1	3.8	163.0	5.6	252.2	5.0
52.5	1,818.1	3.9	70.8	2.4	279.7	5.6
55	1,502.6	3.2	80.7	2.8	154.9	3.1
57.5	1,582.1	3.4	70.0	2.4	271.7	5.4
60	2,639.5	5.7	189.3	6.5	332.9	6.7
65	2,217.4	4.8	161.1	5.5	249.5	5.0
70	1,938.7	4.2	127.8	4.4	162.3	3.3
75	1,801.5	3.9	131.4	4.5	126.2	2.5
80	1,683.4	3.6	114.0	3.9	178.4	3.6
85	1,341.9	2.9	87.1	3.0	127.9	2.6

90	955.0	2.1	65.1	2.2	181.9	3.6
95	1,022.8	2.2	26.6	0.9	95.1	1.9
100	1,721.2	3.7	143.7	4.9	157.5	3.2
110	1,074.0	2.3	46.7	1.6	107.5	2.2
120	1,573.2	3.4	83.1	2.8	96.5	1.9
140	785.3	1.7	25.9	0.9	58.4	1.2
160	523.6	1.1	13.3	0.5	96.5	1.9
180	243.8	0.5	46.1	1.6	18.8	0.4
200	381.0	0.8	14.5	0.5	28.7	0.6
250	196.3	0.4	14.9	0.5	14.5	0.3
Total	46,258.2	100.0	2,918.3	100.0	4,994.3	100.0
Mean	65.06		64.53		63.05	
Median	55.09		54.52		54.98	
P5	43.00		43.1		43.3	
P10	52.3		52.5		51.8	
P25	71.4		73.4		72.6	
P75	145.0		142.1		138.3	
P90	201.5		196.6		190.5	
P95	248.6		243.2		245.7	
P90/P10	3.85		3.75		3.67	
Var coef	0.629		0.613		0.559	
Gini coef	0.303		0.295		0.286	

Note: see note to Table B13.

Source: calculations from FES Base Tapes.

Table B17. Individual distribution of household net per capita income by HOUSEHOLD SIZE pounds per week (current income) 1985

Lower value of range	Household size 1 thousands	%	2 thousands	%	3 thousands	%	4 thousands	%	5 thousands	%	6+ thousands	%
1	35.8	0.6	39.8	0.3	17.8	0.2	33.0	0.2	0.0	0.0	17.0	0.4
5	11.9	0.2	16.8	0.1	17.8	0.2	22.0	0.2	28.3	0.4	0.0	0.0
10	8.1	0.1	52.0	0.4	101.6	0.9	200.1	1.4	284.5	4.5	635.0	16.5
20	4.3	0.1	33.2	0.2	50.8	0.5	136.7	0.9	311.4	4.9	386.2	10.0
22.5	11.9	0.2	24.4	0.2	87.2	0.8	523.8	3.6	272.1	4.3	182.3	4.7
25	8.5	0.1	79.4	0.6	179.6	1.7	476.3	3.3	361.3	5.7	236.6	6.1
27.5	16.1	0.3	102.9	0.7	357.2	3.3	501.2	3.4	327.1	5.2	160.4	4.2
30	13.3	0.2	198.6	1.4	371.6	3.5	467.9	3.2	390.4	6.2	270.2	7.0
32.5	19.0	0.3	356.7	2.5	299.0	2.8	585.6	4.0	242.3	3.8	165.9	4.3
35	54.9	0.9	539.2	3.8	404.8	3.8	815.3	5.6	347.5	5.5	145.0	3.8
37.5	112.8	1.9	660.1	4.7	497.9	4.6	787.5	5.4	403.7	6.4	190.6	5.0
40	150.1	2.6	782.6	5.6	403.8	3.8	716.4	4.9	326.5	5.2	128.8	3.3
42.5	204.8	3.5	596.2	4.2	401.0	3.7	620.0	4.3	246.5	3.9	107.2	2.8
45	157.4	2.7	518.4	3.7	419.1	3.9	623.1	4.3	188.0	3.0	92.5	2.4
47.5	209.6	3.6	465.4	3.3	364.9	3.4	589.5	4.1	264.5	4.2	205.0	5.3
50	268.7	4.6	397.8	2.8	476.5	4.4	726.4	5.0	270.4	4.3	40.5	1.1
52.5	282.7	4.9	480.4	3.4	517.4	4.8	521.7	3.6	313.3	5.0	107.0	2.8
55	355.7	6.1	321.3	2.3	284.9	2.7	515.8	3.6	164.9	2.6	104.5	2.7
57.5	307.8	5.3	349.6	2.5	426.2	4.0	571.2	3.9	199.2	3.2	94.4	2.5
60	591.8	10.2	565.6	4.0	637.7	6.0	953.9	6.6	271.5	4.3	181.6	4.7
65	422.5	7.3	554.1	3.9	560.6	5.2	791.8	5.5	223.4	3.5	91.0	2.4
70	308.9	5.3	641.0	4.6	624.8	5.8	452.7	3.1	204.1	3.2	17.2	0.4
75	176.1	3.0	621.4	4.4	517.8	4.8	547.6	3.8	187.5	3.0	56.6	1.5
80	200.5	3.4	568.1	4.0	491.2	4.6	572.7	3.9	80.3	1.3	62.8	1.6
85	145.4	2.5	601.6	4.3	368.2	3.4	360.9	2.5	36.0	0.6	69.0	1.8
90	133.0	2.3	489.5	3.5	291.1	2.7	246.2	1.7	49.1	0.8	20.8	0.5
95	131.8	2.3	450.3	3.2	267.4	2.5	240.6	1.7	65.7	1.0	0.0	0.0
100	289.8	5.0	886.5	6.3	473.5	4.4	307.2	2.1	61.4	1.0	18.6	0.5

110	251.9	4.3	610.4	4.3	213.0	2.0	130.3	0.9	44.7	0.7	0.0	0.0
120	365.7	6.3	900.8	6.4	203.8	1.9	223.2	1.5	76.4	1.2	17.0	0.4
140	228.4	3.9	379.3	2.7	199.4	1.9	48.3	0.3	14.1	0.2	0.0	0.0
160	113.8	2.0	310.7	2.2	86.5	0.8	84.9	0.6	17.4	0.3	25.6	0.7
180	57.2	1.0	132.3	0.9	40.1	0.4	63.9	0.4	15.2	0.2	0.0	0.0
200	93.3	1.6	220.9	1.6	36.7	0.3	48.3	0.3	14.1	0.2	19.8	0.5
250	79.4	1.4	97.7	0.7	26.7	0.2	22.0	0.2	0.0	0.0	0.0	0.0
Total	5,823.1	100.0	14,045.0	100.0	10,717.4	100.0	14,528.2	100.0	6,302.9	100.0	3,848.7	100.0
Mean	82.87		79.31		64.96		56.67		47.90		39.91	
Median	66.12		68.83		58.00		50.51		41.36		32.92	
P5	59.9		49.0		48.7		47.9		48.4		39.5	
P10	66.8		54.2		55.0		54.8		54.8		55.0	
P25	81.8		65.6		72.8		73.5		72.5		66.6	
P75	151.7		145.5		138.3		134.9		136.7		150.4	
P90	209.5		195.5		179.3		176.7		182.3		202.5	
P95	256.0		234.9		210.5		211.3		226.6		247.5	
P90/P10	3.13		3.61		3.26		3.22		3.33		3.68	
Var coef	0.618		0.599		0.506		0.546		0.554		0.665	
Gini coef	0.281		0.291		0.264		0.263		0.274		0.326	

Note: see note to Table BI3.
Source:
calculations from FES Base Tapes.

Table BP1. SOCIAL ASSISTANCE total weekly income in pounds for households of different types 1970-1988

Household type	1970	1972	1974	1976	1978	1980	1982	1984	1986	1988
Single pensioner	5.30	6.30	8.15	13.70	17.90	23.70	29.60	34.10	37.50	38.65
Pensioner couple	8.85	10.45	12.85	21.55	28.35	37.65	47.35	54.55	60.00	61.85
Household where head unemployed:										
Single	4.80	5.80	7.15	10.90	14.50	18.30	23.25	26.80	29.50	30.40
Couple	7.85	9.45	11.65	17.75	23.55	29.70	37.75	43.50	47.85	49.35
Couple+1 child	9.50	11.45	14.10	21.50	28.50	35.95	45.65	52.65	57.95	59.75
Couple+2 children	11.15	13.45	16.55	25.25	33.45	42.20	53.55	61.80	68.05	70.15
Couple+3 children	12.80	15.45	19.00	29.00	38.40	48.45	61.45	70.95	78.15	80.55
Couple+5 children	16.10	19.45	23.90	36.50	48.30	60.95	77.25	89.25	98.35	101.35

Notes: (a) Supplementary Benefit rate in force at 1 January;
      (b) the long-term rate (long-term addition before 1973) applies in the case of pensioners, but not for the unemployed;
      (c) children assumed to be aged 5-10.

Source:
Social Security Statistics 1989, Table 34.01, pp. 239-240.

Bibliography

Abel, I., 1990, 'Subsidy Reduction in the Hungarian Economy', *European Economy*, No. 43: 21–34.

Abel-Smith, B. and Townsend, P., 1965, *The Poor and the Poorest*, Bell, London.

Adam, J., 1984, *Employment and Wage Policies in Poland, Czechoslovakia and Hungary since 1950*, St Martin's Press, New York.

Adams, M. and Owen, J., 1989, 'The New Earnings Survey Panel Dataset' New Earnings Survey Panel Project Working Paper 1, EMRU, Department of Employment, London.

Ahmad, E., 1991, 'Social Safety Nets in Transition Economies', IMF, Washington DC.

Aleksandrova, E. and Fedorovskaia, E., 1984, 'Mekhanizm formirovaniia i povysheniia potrebnostei', *Voprosy ekonomiki*, Vol. 1: 15–25.

Alexeev, M. V. and Gaddy, C. G., 1991, 'Trends in Wage and Income Distribution under Gorbachev: Analysis of New Soviet Data', Berkeley-Duke Occasional Papers on the Second Economy in the USSR, paper 25, Duke University, Durham NC.

Andorka, R., 1989, 'Poverty in Hungary', *Research Review on Hungarian Social Sciences*, No. 3: 135–148.

Andorka, R., Kolosi, P. and Vukovich, G., 1990, *Társadalmi Riport 1990*, TARKI, Budapest.

Ashworth, M. and Dilnot, A., 1987, 'Company Cars Taxation', *Fiscal Studies*, Vol. 8: 1–14.

Atkinson, A. B., 1983, *The Economics of Inequality*, second edition, Oxford University Press, Oxford.

1989, *Poverty and Social Security*, Harvester Wheatsheaf, Hemel Hempstead.

1990, 'The Department of Social Security Report on Households Below Average Income 1981–87', Welfare State Programme Research Note 22, STICERD, London School of Economics.

1991a, 'Poverty, Statistics, and Progress in Europe', Welfare State Programme Discussion Paper 60, STICERD, London School of Economics.

1991b, 'What is Happening to the Distribution of Income in the UK?', Keynes Lecture, British Academy.

1991c, 'A National Minimum? A History of Ambiguity in the Determination of Benefit Scales in Britain', in Wilson, T. and D., editors, *The State and Social Welfare*, Longman, London.

1991d, 'The Social Safety Net', Welfare State Programme Discussion Paper 66, STICERD, London School of Economics.

1991e, 'Comparing Poverty Rates Internationally: Lessons from Recent Studies in Developed Countries', *World Bank Economic Review*, Vol. 5: 3–21.

Atkinson, A. B. and Bazen, S., 1984, 'The SMIC and Earnings in France and Britain', TIDI Research Note 8, London School of Economics.

Atkinson, A. B., Gomulka, J. and Sutherland, H., 1988, 'Grossing-up FES Data for Tax-Benefit Models', in Atkinson, A. B., and Sutherland, H., editors, *Tax-Benefit Models*, STICERD Occasional Paper 10, London School of Economics, London.

Atkinson, A. B. and Harrison, A. J., 1978, *Distribution of Personal Wealth in Britain*, Cambridge University Press.

Atkinson, A. B. and Micklewright, J., 1983, 'On the Reliability of Income Data in the Family Expenditure Survey 1970–77', *Journal of the Royal Statistical Society*, Series A, Vol. 146: 33–61.

1991, 'Economic Transformation in Eastern Europe and the Distribution of Income', in Atkinson, A. B. and Brunetta, R., editors, *Economics for the New Europe*, Macmillan, Basingstoke.

Atkinson, A. B., Micklewright, J. and Stern, N. H., 1988, 'Comparison of the FES and New Earnings Survey 1971–1977', in Atkinson, A. B. and Sutherland, H., editors, *Tax-Benefit Models*, STICERD Occasional Paper 10, London School of Economics, London.

Barreiros, M. L., 1991, 'The Use of Household Budget Surveys in Evaluating Social Consequences of Transition', paper presented at the BLS/Eurostat conference on Economic Statistics for Economies in Transition, Washington DC, 14–16 February 1991.

Beddoes, Z. M. and Lindemann, M., 1991, 'The Social Safety Net in Poland: A Brief Survey', in Williams, S., Beschel, R. and McNamara, K., editors, *Social Safety Nets in East/Central Europe*, John F. Kennedy School of Government, Harvard University.

Berend, I. T., 1990, *The Hungarian Economic Reforms 1953–1988*, Cambridge University Press, Cambridge.

Bergson, A., 1984, 'Income Inequality under Soviet Socialism', *Journal of Economic Literature*, Vol. 22: 1052–1099.

Beveridge, W., 1942, *Social Insurance and Allied Services*, Cmd. 604, HMSO, London.

Boldyreva, T., 1989, 'Columns of Figures or an Instrument of Social Policy?', *Problems of Economics*, Vol. 32: 89–102.

Bourit, F., Hernu, P. and Perrot, M., 1983, 'Les Salaires en 1982', *Economie et Statistique*, 154 (April): 17–32.

Brada, J. C., 1991, 'The Economic Transition of Czechoslovakia from Plan to Market', *Journal of Economic Perspectives*, Vol. 5: 171–177.

Bradshaw, J. and Parker, H., 1991, 'Summary Budget Standards for Three

Families', Family Budget Unit Working Paper No. 12, University of York.

Braithwaite, J. D. and Heleniak, T. E., 1989, 'Social Welfare in the USSR: The Income Recipient Distribution', Center for International Research, US Bureau of the Census, Washington DC.

Bruinooge, G., Éltető, Ö., Fajth, G. and Grubben, G., 1990, 'Income Distributions in an International Perspective – The Case of Hungary and the Netherlands', *Statistical Journal of the United Nations*, Vol. 7: 39–53.

Buettner, T., 1991, 'Pension Benefits in Three East European Countries', Luxembourg Income Study East-West Conference, August 1991.

Buhmann, B., Rainwater, L., Schmaus, G. and Smeeding, T. M., 1988, 'Equivalence Scales, Well-being, Inequality and Poverty', *Review of Income and Wealth*, Vol. 34: 115–142.

Burtless, G., 1990, editor, *A Future of Lousy Jobs?*, The Brookings Institution, Washington DC.

Bútora, A., 1969, 'Study on Minimum Pensions', Social Security Research Institute, Bratislava.

Callan, T. and Nolan, B., 1991, 'Concepts of Poverty and the Poverty Line', *Journal of Economic Surveys*, Vol. 5: 243–261.

Cazes, S. and Le Cacheux, J., 1991, 'Inégalités de revenu, pauvreté et protection sociale en Union soviétique', *Revue de l'OFCE*, No. 38: 143–205.

Central Statistical Office, 1976, 'Effects of Taxes and Benefits on Household Income 1975', *Economic Trends*, No. 278.

1979, 'Bias in the FES – Some Results', unpublished.

1990, 'The Effects of Taxes and Benefits on Household Income 1987', *Economic Trends*, No. 439.

1991, 'The Effects of Taxes and Benefits on Household Income 1988', *Economic Trends*, No. 449.

CERC (Centre d'Etude des Revenus et des Coûts), 1989, *Les Français et leur revenus: le tournant des années 80*, La Documentation Française, Paris.

Chapman, J. G., 1977, 'Soviet Wages under Socialism', in Abouchar, A., editor, *The Socialist Price Mechanism*, Duke University Press, Durham NC.

1979, 'Are Earnings More Equal under Socialism: The Soviet Case, with Some United States Comparisons', in Moroney, J. R., editor, *Income Inequality: Trends and International Comparisons*, D. C. Heath, Lexington, MA.

1983, 'Earnings Distribution in the USSR, 1968–1976', *Soviet Studies*, Vol. 35: 410–413.

1989, 'Income Distribution and Social Justice in the Soviet Union', *Comparative Economic Studies*, Vol. 31: 14–45.

1991, 'Recent and Prospective Trends in Soviet Wage Distribution', in Standing, G., editor, *In Search of Flexibility: The New Soviet Labour Market*, ILO, Geneva.

Charap, J. and Dyba, K., 1991, 'Transition to a Market Economy: The Case of Czechoslovakia', *European Economic Review*, Vol. 35: 581–590.

Coates, K. and Silburn, R., 1970, *Poverty: The Forgotten Englishmen*, Penguin, Harmondsworth.

Cornell, K., 1991, 'The Social Safety Net in the Czech and Slovak Federal Republic:

A Brief Survey', in Williams, S., Beschel, R. and McNamara, K., editors, *Social Safety Nets in East/Central Europe*, John F. Kennedy School of Government, Harvard University.

Coulter, F., Cowell, F. A. and Jenkins, S. P., 1991, 'Equivalence Scale Relativities and the Extent of Inequality and Poverty', University of Bath School of Social Sciences Discussion Papers in Economics 02/91.

Cowell, F. A., 1977, *Measuring Inequality*, Philip Allan, Oxford.

Department of Health and Human Resources, 1990, *Social Security Bulletin Annual Statistical Supplement*, Washington DC.

Department of Health and Social Security, 1985, *Reform of Social Security, Volume 2: Programme for Change*, Cmnd. 9518, HMSO, London.

1988, *Low Income Families – 1985*, London.

Department of Social Security, 1990, *Households Below Average Income 1990*, London.

Deutscher Bundestag, 1987, *Materialien zum Bericht zur Lage der Nation im geteilten Deutschland 1987*, Bonn.

Dilnot, A., Johnson, P. and Stark, G., 1991, 'Tax Policy and the 1991 Budget', *Fiscal Studies*, Vol. 12: 23–33.

Dlouhý, J., 1991, 'The Impact of Social Transfers on Income Distribution in the Czech and Slovak Federal Republic', World Bank Socialist Economies Reform Unit, Research Paper 4.

Dmitriev, V. V., 1989, 'What We Don't Know', *Problems of Economics*, Vol. 32: 59–71.

Dmoch, T., 1979, 'Wpływ społecznych funduszów spożycia na rozkłady dochodów ludności', in *Tendencje rozwoju społecznego*, GUS, Warsaw

1983, 'Fundusze społeczne w społecznoekonomicznych grupach gospodarstw domowych', GUS, Warsaw.

Ellman, M., 1980, 'A Note on the Distribution of Earnings in the USSR under Brezhnev', *Slavic Review*, Vol. 39: 669–671.

1990, 'A Note on the Distribution of Income in the USSR under Gorbachev', *Soviet Studies*, Vol. 42: 147–148.

Elster, J., 1991, 'Local Justice: How Institutions Allocate Scarce Goods and Necessary Burdens', *European Economic Review*, Vol. 35: 273–92.

Éltető, Ö., 1990, 'Econometric Methods for Computing the Minimum Income Level of Socially Justified Needs', mimeo, KSH, Budapest.

Éltető, Ö. and Frigyes, E., 1968, 'New Income Inequality Measures as Efficient Tools for Causal Analysis and Planning', *Econometrica*, Vol. 36: 383–396.

Éltető, Ö. and Láng, Gy., 1971, 'Income Level – Income Stratification in Hungary', *Acta Oeconomica*, Vol. 7: 303–324.

Éltető, Ö. and Vita, L., 1989, 'A Micro-Simulation Experiment for the Estimation of the Possible Effect of Incomes from the Underground Economy on the Income Distribution: Methods and Results', paper presented at the 47th Session of the International Statistical Institute, Paris, 29 August–6 September 1989.

Esping-Andersen, G. and Micklewright, J., 1991, 'Welfare State Models in OECD Countries: An Analysis for the Debate in Central and Eastern Europe', in

Cornia, G. A. and Sipos, S., editors, *Children and the Transition to the Market Economy*, Avebury, Aldershot.

Eurostat, 1990, *Inequality and Poverty in Europe (1980–1985)*, Rapid Report, No. 7.

Farkas, K. Z. and Pataki, J., 1984, 'Shortage of Commodities and Public Opinion in Hungary', *Acta Oeconomica*, Vol. 32: 287–301.

Feinstein, C. H., 1988, 'The Rise and Fall of the Williamson Curve', *Journal of Economic History*, Vol. 48: 699–729.

Ferge, Z., 1988, 'The Trends and Functions of Social Policy in Hungary', in Jallade, J-P., editor, *The Crisis of Distribution in European Welfare States*, Trentham Books, Stoke-on-Trent.

1991a, 'Social Security Systems in the New Democracies of Central and Eastern Europe: Past Legacies and Possible Futures', in Cornia, G. A. and Sipos, S., editors, *Children and the Transition to the Market Economy*, Avebury, Aldershot.

1991b, 'The Social Safety Net in Hungary: A Brief Survey', in Williams, S., Beschel, R. and McNamara, K., editors, *Social Safety Nets in East/Central Europe*, John F. Kennedy School of Government, Harvard University.

Fields, G. S. and Jakubson, G. H., 1990, 'The Inequality-Development Relationship in Developing Countries', Discussion Paper, Cornell University.

Flakierski, H., 1979, 'Economic Reform and Income Distribution in Hungary', *Cambridge Journal of Economics*, Vol. 3: 15–32.

1981, 'Economic Reform and Income Distribution in Poland: the Negative Evidence', *Cambridge Journal of Economics*, Vol. 5: 137–158.

1986, *Economic Reform and Income Distribution*, M. E. Sharpe, Armonk.

1991, 'Social Policies in the 1980s in Poland: A Discussion of New Approaches', in Adam, J., editor, *Economic Reforms and Welfare Systems in the USSR, Poland and Hungary*, Macmillan, London.

FSU, 1985, *Historická statistická ročenka ČSSR*, SNTL, Prague.

1990, *Časové řady základnich ukazatelů statisticky práce*, Prague.

Gardner, H. S., 1991, 'Product Quality and Price Inflation in Transitional Economies', mimeo, Baylor University.

Gelb, A. and Gray, C., 1991, *The Transformation of Economies in Central and Eastern Europe*, World Bank, Washington, D.C.

George, V., 1991, 'Social Security in the USSR', mimeo, University of Kent.

Gomulka, J., 1991, report to Department of Social Security on grossing-up.

Goskomstat, 1989, *Biudzhety rabochikh, sluzhashchikh i kolkhoznikov v 1975–1988gg*, ('Budgets of workers, employees and collective farm workers 1975–1988'), Moscow, 1989.

1990a, *Biudzhety rabochikh, sluzhashchikh i kolkhoznikov v zavisimosti ot urovnia srednedushevogo sovokupnogo dokhoda v 1989*, ('Budgets of workers, employees and collective farm workers according to level of average per capita income in 1989'), Moscow.

1990b, *Sostav sem'i, dokhody i zhilishchnve usloviia semei rabochikh sluzhashchikh i kolkhoznikov*, ('Composition of the family, incomes and living conditions of workers, employees and collective farm workers'), Moscow.

1991, *Sotsial'noe razvitie SSSR 1989*, ('Social Development in the USSR 1989'), Moscow.

Gregory, P. R. and Stuart, R. C., 1989, *Comparative Economic Systems*, third edition, Houghton Mifflin, Boston.

Grossman, G., 1987, 'Roots of Gorbachev's Problems; Private Income and Outlay in the Late 1970s', *Gorbachev's Economic Plans*, US Congress Joint Economic Committee, Washington DC.

Gunderson, M., 1989, 'Male-Female Wage Differentials and Policy Responses', *Journal of Economic Literature*, Vol. 27: 46–72.

Gur'ev, V. and Zaitseva, A., 1990, 'Stoimost' zhizni, prozhitochnyi minimum, inflatsiia', *Vestnik statistiki*, No. 6: 20–29.

GUS, 1981, *Wpływ społecznego funduszu spożycia na zmiany w rozkładach dochodów ludności*, Studia i Materialy, No. 15, GUS, Warsaw.

Haddad, L. and Kanbur, R., 1990, 'How Serious is the Neglect of Intrahousehold Inequality?', *Economic Journal*, Vol. 100: 866–881.

Hagenaars, A. J. M., 1986, *The Perception of Poverty*, North-Holland, Amsterdam.

Hayek, F. A., 1960, *The Constitution of Liberty*, Routledge and Kegan Paul, London.

Henle, P. and Ryscavage, P., 1980, 'The Distribution of Earned Income among Men and Women, 1958–77', *Monthly Labor Review*, Vol. 103 (4): 3–10.

Heston, A. and Summers, R., 1990, 'Consequences of Expanded Availability of Goods and Services for Price Collection and Measurement of Trends in Ouput and Inflation' mimeo, University of Pennsylvania.

Hills, J., 1988, *Changing Tax*, CPAG, London.

1989, 'Counting the Family Silver: The Public Sector's Balance Sheet 1957 to 1987', *Fiscal Studies*, Vol. 10: 66–85.

1991, *Unravelling Housing Finance*, Clarendon Press, Oxford.

Hiršl, M., 1971a, 'Vital Minimum, Theory and Practice of Social Policy', Volume of Studies No. 40, Social Security Research Institute, Prague.

1971b, 'Deliberations on the Contents of the Term of Vital Minimum', *Politická ekonomie*, No. 5.

1971c, 'Vital Minimum and Population Groups with Insufficient Income in the CSSR', *Politická ekonomie*, No. 6.

1973, 'The Scope and Structure of Population with Limited Possibilities of Consumption in Czechoslovakia (1970)' (in Czech), Prague

1979, 'The Analysis of the Groups of Families with Limited Consumption Possibilities in CSSR in 1976' (in Czech), Prague.

1980, 'The Relation Between Labour and Social Incomes in Different Types of Households (Czechoslovakia 1960–1976)' (in Czech), Prague.

1988, 'The Development of the Groups of Families with Limited Consumption in 1980–1985', VUSRP, Prague.

1990a, 'Recommendation of the Commission of Experts to Guarantee an Existence Minimum', 30 October 1990, Federal Ministry of Work and Social Affairs.

1990b, *Současné problémy životního minima ve vyspělých zemich*, Prognosticky Ustav CSAV, Prague.

Hiršl, M. and Kučerák, J., 1978, 'Problems of Minimum Living Standards in

Present-Day Czechoslovakia', European Social Development Programme, Expert Group on Minimum Levels of Living Working Paper No. 2, United Nations (NB the title page of this paper has the name of M. Nebeský).

Hoch, R., Kovács, J. and Timar, J., 1978, 'Standard of Living Policy and Long-Range Planning of the Living Standard', in Friss, I., editor, *Essays on Economic Policy and Planning*, Corrina Kiadó, Gyoma.

Hungarian Central Statistical Office, 1975, *Hungarian Survey on Relative Income Differences*, KSH, Budapest.

ILO, 1985, *The Cost of Social Security*, ILO, Geneva.

1989, *From Pyramid to Pillar: Population Change and Social Security in Europe*, ILO, Geneva.

IMF, The World Bank, OECD and EBRD, 1991, *A Study of the Soviet Economy*, OECD, Paris.

Johnson, P. and Webb, S., 1989, 'Counting People with Low Incomes: The Impact of Recent Changes in Official Statistics', *Fiscal Studies*, Vol. 10: 66–82.

Juhász, J., 1979, 'Impact of the Consumer Price System on the Income and Consumption Patterns in Hungary', *Acta Oeconomica*, Vol. 22: 69–86.

Kakwani, N. C., 1977, 'Applications of Lorenz Curves in Economic Analysis', *Econometrica*, Vol. 45: 719–727.

1980, *Income Inequality and Poverty*, Oxford University Press, Oxford.

Kapustin, E. I. and Kuznetsova, N. P., 1972, 'Regional'nye osobennosti povysheniia zhiznennogo urovnia naseleniia', *Ekonomicheskiye nauki*, No. 1: 49–59.

Kazmierczak, T., 1990, 'The Policy of Social Assistance Concerning the Child and the Family in the Light of the Project of the Social Assistance Bill', National Policy Paper No. 5, UNICEF Roundtable on Safety Nets for Children in Central and Eastern Europe, Warsaw, 16–18 October 1990.

Kemsley, W. F. F., 1975, 'A Study of Differential Response Based on a Comparison of the 1971 Sample with the Census', *Statistical News*, No. 31 (November): 3–21.

Kemsley, W. F. F., Redpath, R. U. and Holmes, M., 1980, *Family Expenditure Survey Handbook*, HMSO, London.

Kendall, M. G. and Stuart, A., 1969, *The Advanced Theory of Statistics*, Vol. 1, Griffin, London.

Kondor, Y., 1971, 'An Old-New Measure of Income Inequality', *Econometrica*, Vol. 39: 1041–1042.

Kopits, G., 1991, 'Social Security in Transition Economies', Fiscal Affairs Department, IMF, Washington DC.

Kordos, J., 1985, 'Towards an Integrated System of Household Surveys in Poland', *Bulletin of the International Statistical Institute*, Proceedings of the 45th Session, Vol. 51, Book 1, Amsterdam.

1990, 'Some Aspects of Living Conditions of Households of Retired Persons and Pensioners in Poland', paper presented at Third Polish–British Seminar on Social Policy, Madralin.

1991, 'Poverty Measurement in Poland', Central Statistical Office, Warsaw.

Kordos, J. and Kubiczek, A., 1990, 'Methodological Problems in the Household Budgets Surveys in Poland', mimeo, GUS.

Kornai, J., 1990, *The Road to a Free Economy*, W. W. Norton, New York.

Kroupová, A. and Huslar, O., 1991, 'Children at the Turning Point: Economic Reform and Social Policy in Czechoslovakia', in Cornia, G. A. and Sipos, S., editors, *Children and the Transition to the Market Economy*, Avebury, Aldershot.

KSH, 1989, 'Incidence Analysis: The Impact of Consumer and Housing Subsidies on the Household Income Distribution', Central Statistical Office, Budapest.

Ksiezopolski, M., 1991, 'The Labour Market in Transition and the Growth of Poverty in Poland', *Labour and Society*, Vol. 16: 175–192.

Kupa, M. and Fajth, G., 1990, 'Incidence-Study '90: The Hungarian Social-Policy Systems and Distribution of Incomes of Households', Central Statistical Office and Ministry of Finance, Budapest.

Kuznets, S., 1953, *Share of Upper Income Groups in Income and Savings*, National Bureau of Economic Research, New York.

  1955, 'Economic Growth and Income Inequality', *American Economic Review*, Vol. 45(2): 1–28.

  1989, *Economic Development, the Family, and Income Distribution*, Cambridge University Press.

Laky, T., 1984, 'Small Enterprises in Hungary – Myth and Reality', *Acta Oeconomica*, 32(1–2): 39–63.

Lansley, S., 1977, 'Changes in the Inequality of Household Incomes in the UK 1971–1975', University of Reading Discussion Paper in Economics Series A, No. 98.

Le Cacheux, J., 1990, 'L'URSS', in Fitoussi, J-P., editor, *A. L'Est, En Europe*, Presses de la Fondation Nationale des Sciences Politiques, Paris.

Le Grand, J., 1982, *The Strategy of Equality*, Allen and Unwin, London.

Levy, F. and Murnane, R. J., forthcoming, 'Earnings Levels and Earnings Inequality: A Review of Recent Trends and Proposed Explanations', *Journal of Economic Literature*.

Loznevaya, M., 1968, *Sotsialisticheski trud*, 10.

Lubin, N., 1984, *Labour and Nationality in Soviet Central Asia*, Macmillan, London.

Lydall, H. F., 1968, *The Structure of Earnings*, Oxford University Press, Oxford.

  1979, 'Some Problems in Making International Comparisons of Inequality', in Moroney, J. R., editor, *Income Inequality: Trends and International Comparisons*, D. C. Heath, Lexington, MA.

Mahalanobis, P. C., 1960, 'A Method of Fractile Graphical Analysis', *Econometrica*, Vol. 28(2): 325–351.

Marnie, S., 1990, 'Labour Market Reform in the USSR: Fact or Fiction?', paper presented at conference of European Association for Comparative Economic Studies, Verona.

  1992, *The Soviet Labour Market in Transition*, Ph. D. thesis, European University Institute, Florence.

Matthews, M., 1978, *Privilege in the Soviet Union*, Allen and Unwin, London.

  1986, *Poverty in the Soviet Union*, Cambridge University Press.

  1989, *Patterns of Deprivation in the Soviet Union Under Brezhnev and Gorbachev*, Hoover Institution Press, Stanford.

Mayhew, K., 1981, 'Incomes Policy and the Private Sector', in Fallick, J. L. and

Elliott, R. F., editors, *Incomes Policies, Inflation and Relative Pay*, Allen and Unwin, London.

McAuley, A. N. D., 1979, *Economic Welfare in the Soviet Union*, University of Wisconsin Press, Madison.

1980, 'Social Welfare under Socialism: A Study of Soviet Attitudes Towards Redistribution', in Collard, D., Lecomber, R. and Slater, M., editors, *Income Distribution: the Limits to Redistribution*, Scientechnica, Bristol.

1981, *Women's Work and Wages in the Soviet Union*, Allen and Unwin, London.

1991, 'The Welfare State in the USSR', in Wilson, T. and D., editors, *The State and Social Welfare*, Longmans, London.

Michal, J. M., 1973, 'Size-Distribution of Earnings and Household Incomes in Small Socialist Countries', *Review of Income and Wealth*, Vol. 19: 407–427.

1978, 'Size-Distribution of Household Incomes and Earnings in Developed Socialist Countries', in Krelle, W. and Shorrocks, A. F., editors, *Personal Income Distribution*, North-Holland, Amsterdam.

Micklewright, J. and Trinder, C., 1981, 'New Earnings Surveys 1968–80: Sampling Methods and Non-Response', TIDI Programme Discussion Paper 31, STI-CERD, London School of Economics.

Milanovic, B., 1990a, 'Poverty in Poland, Hungary, and Yugoslavia in the Years of Crisis, 1978–87', Background Paper for the 1990 *World Development Report*, Policy, Research and External Affairs Working Paper 507, Washington DC.

1990b, 'Poverty in Poland, 1978-88', World Bank, Washington DC.

Ministry of Finance, 1987, *Act on the Personal Income Tax*, Public Finance in Hungary 39/B, Ministry of Finance, Budapest.

Moore, B., 1987, *Authority and Inequality under Capitalism and Socialism*, Clarendon Press, Oxford.

Moravová, J., 1966, 'Construction of Economic Scales of Consumption Units', Dissertation for Faculty of Political Economy, Economic College, Prague.

Moroney, J. R., 1979, 'Do Women Earn Less Under Capitalism?', *Economic Journal*, Vol. 89, 601–613.

Morrisson, C., 1984, 'Income Distribution in East European and Western Countries', *Journal of Comparative Economics*, Vol. 8: 121–138.

1985, 'Distribution of Incomes and Rights in the West and in the East', in Kende, P. and Strmiska, Z., editors, *Equality and Inequality in Eastern Europe*, Berg.

Musgrave, R. A., 1959, *The Theory of Public Finance*, McGraw-Hill, New York.

Myant, M., 1983, 'Income inequalities in Czechoslovakia', *Co-Existence*, Vol. 20: 189–215.

1989, *The Czechoslovak Economy 1948–1988*, Cambridge University Press, Cambridge.

National Administration of Social Insurance, *Pocket Statistics 1989*, Budapest.

Newby, E., 1982, *A Traveller's Life*, Picador, London.

Nolan, B., 1987, *Income Distribution and the Macroeconomy*, Cambridge University Press, Cambridge.

Nove, A., 1972, *An Economic History of the U.S.S.R.*, Pelican Books, London.

O'Donnell, O. and Propper, C., 1991, 'Equity and the Distribution of National Health Service Resouces', *Journal of Health Economics*, Vol. 10: 1–19.

O'Higgins, M. and Jenkins S. P., 1989, 'Poverty in Europe', paper presented at seminar on Poverty Statistics in the European Community, Noordwijk, 24–26 October 1989.

Ofer, G. and Vinokur, A., 1980, 'The Distribution of Income of the Urban Population in the Soviet Union', unpublished.

1992, *The Soviet Household under the Old Regime*, Cambridge University Press, Cambridge.

Okrasa, W., 1987, 'Redistribution, Inequality and Inequity: an East-West Comparison', in Le Grand, J. and Okrasa, W., editors, *Social Welfare in Britain and Poland*, STICERD Occasional Paper 12, London School of Economics.

1988, 'Redistribution and the Two Dimensions of Inequality: an East-West Comparison', *European Economic Review*, Vol. 32: 633–643.

Okun, A. M., 1975, *Equality and Efficiency: The Big Tradeoff*, The Brookings Institution, Washington DC.

Olenski, J., 1991, 'Statistical Production Processes in Transition (Experiences of the Central Statistical Office of Poland)', paper presented at the BLS/Eurostat conference on Economic Statistics for Economies in Transition, Washington DC, 14–16 February 1991.

OPCS, 1981, *The General Household Survey 1979*, HMSO, London.

Orczyk, J., 1989, 'The Influence of Social Benefits on Personnel Turnover in Polish Enterprises', in Millard, F., editor, *Social Welfare and the Market*, STICERD Occasional Paper 15, London School of Economics.

Orshansky, M., 1965, 'Counting the Poor: Another Look at the Poverty Profile', *Social Security Bulletin*, Vol. 28: 3–29.

Oxenstierna, S., 1990, *From Labour Shortage to Unemployment? The Soviet Labour Market in the 1980s*, Swedish Institute for Social Research Dissertation Series 12, Almqvist and Wiksell International, Stockholm.

Paglin, M., 1975, 'The Measurement and Trend of Inequality: A Basic Revision', *American Economic Review*, Vol. 65: 598–609.

Pechman, J. A., 1985, *Who Paid The Taxes, 1966–85*, Brookings Institution, Washington DC.

Pekník, J. and Kučerák, J., 1974, 'Contribution to Methods of Investigating and Computing Social Minimum', *Politická ekonomie*, No. 8.

Pern, A. L., 1989, 'The Family Budget in the Mirror of Statistics', *Problems of Economics*, Vol. 32: 81–88.

Phelps Brown, H., 1977, *The Inequality of Pay*, Oxford University Press, Oxford.

1988, *Egalitarianism and the Generation of Inequality*, Oxford University Press, Oxford.

Piachaud, D., 1981, 'Peter Townsend and the Holy Grail', *New Society*, 10 September, 419–421.

Pockney, B. P., 1991, *Soviet Statistics Since 1950*, Dartmouth.

Podgórski, J., 1991, 'Subjective Poverty Lines – Some Results for Poland', paper presented at the conference on Poverty Measurement for Economies in Transition in Eastern European Countries, Warsaw, 7–9 October 1991.

Prest, A. and Barr, N., 1985, *Public Finance in Theory and Practice*, seventh edition, Weidenfeld and Nicolson, London.

Pryor, F. L., 1973, *Property and Industrial Organization in Communist and Capitalist Nations*, Indiana University Press, Bloomington.

Pudney, S., 1991, 'Tax Reform in Hungary: Analysis of Household Survey Data', mimeo, Department of Applied Economics, University of Cambridge.

Rabkina, N. E. and Rimashevskaia, N. M., 1972, *Osnovy differentsiatsii zarabotnoi platy i dokhodov naseleniia*, Moscow.

1978, 'Raspredelitel'nie otnosheniia i sotsial'nyi progress' EKO, No. 5, pp.17–32

Ramprakash, D., 1975, 'Distribution of Income Statistics for the United Kingdom, 1972/73: Sources and Methods', *Economic Trends*, No. 262 (August): 78–96.

Rawls, J., 1971, *A Theory of Justice*, Harvard University Press, Cambridge, MA.

Redor, D., 1988, *Les Inegalités de Salaires à l'Est et à l'Ouest*, Economica, Paris.

Redpath, R. U., 1986, 'A Second Study of Differential Response Comparing Census Characteristics of FES Respondents and Non-Respondents', *Statistical News*, No. 72 (February): 13–16.

Rein, M., 1970, 'Problems in the Definition and Measurement of Poverty', in Townsend, P., editor, *The Concept of Poverty*, Heinemann, London.

Rimashevskaia, N. M., 1990, 'Nash prozhitochnyi minimum', *Sotsialisticheskii trud*, No. 8.

Robinson, S., 1976, 'A Note on the U-Hypothesis Relating Income Inequality and Economic Development', *American Economic Review*, Vol. 66: 437–440.

Rogovin, V. Z., 1989, 'Social Justice and the Socialist Distribution of Vital Goods', in Yanowitch, M., editor, *New Directions in Soviet Social Thought*, M. E. Sharpe, Armonk, New York.

Rosen, H. S., 1985, *Public Finance*, Irwin, Homewood, Illinois.

Royal Commission on the Distribution of Income and Wealth, 1979, *Fifth Report on the Standing Reference*, HMSO, London.

Rutgaizer, V. M., Shmarov, A. I. and Kirichenko, N. V., 1989, 'Reforma roznichnykh tsen, mekhanizm kompensatsii i razvitie potrebitel'skogo rynka', *EKO* No. 3: 58–70.

Rutkowski, J., 1991, 'Social Expenditures in Poland: Main Programs and Recent Trends', World Bank Socialist Economies Reform Unit, Research Paper 1.

Ryan, M., 1990, *Contemporary Soviet Society: A Statistical Handbook*, Edward Elgar, Aldershot.

Saenko, G. P. and Mal'ginova, E. G., 1989, 'Property and Family Well-Being', *Problems of Economics*, Vol. 32: 72–80.

Salamin, J., 1991, 'Calculation of the Poverty Level (Hungarian Experiences)', paper presented at the conference on Poverty Measurement for Economies in Transition in Eastern European Countries, Warsaw, 7–9 October 1991.

Samuelson, P. A. and Nordhaus, W. D., 1989, *Economics*, thirteenth edition, McGraw-Hill, New York.

Sarkisyan, G. S. and Kuznetsova, N. P., 1967, *Potrebnosti i dokhod sem'i, uroven', struktura, perspektivy*, Moscow.

Sawhill, I. V., 1988, 'Poverty in the U.S.: Why is it so Persistent?', *Journal of Economic Literature*, Vol. 26: 1073–1119.

Sawyer, M., 1976, 'Income Distribution in OECD Countries', *OECD Economic Outlook*, 3–36.

Sen, A. K., 1976, 'Real National Income', *Review of Economic Studies*, Vol. 43(1): 19–39.

1977, 'On Weights and Measures', *Econometrica*, Vol. 45: 1539–1572.

1983, 'Poor, Relatively Speaking', *Oxford Economic Papers*, Vol. 35: 153–169.

Shenfield, S., 1983, 'A Note on Data Quality in the Soviet Family Budget Survey', *Soviet Studies*, Vol. 35(4): 561–568.

1984, *The Mathematical–Statistical Methodology of the Contemporary Soviet Family Budget Survey*, Ph.D. thesis, Centre for Russian and East European Studies, Faculty of Commerce and Social Science, University of Birmingham.

Shenfield, S. and Hanson, P., 1986, 'The Functioning of the Soviet System of State Statistics (Findings from Interviews with Former Soviet Statistical Personnel)', CREES Special Report SR-86-1, Centre for Russian and East European Studies, University of Birmingham.

Shorrocks, A. F, 1983, 'Ranking Income Distributions', *Economica*, Vol. 50: 3–17.

Simons, H., 1938, *Personal Income Taxation*, University of Chicago Press, Chicago.

Sipos, S., 1991, 'Current and Structural Problems Affecting Children in Central and Eastern Europe', in Cornia, G. A. and Sipos, S., editors, *Children and the Transition to the Market Economy. Safety Nets and Social Policies in Central and Eastern Europe*, Avebury, Aldershot.

Smeeding, T., 1982, *Alternative Methods for Valuing Selected In-Kind Transfer Benefits and Measuring their Effect on Poverty*, US Bureau of the Census Technical Paper 50.

Smeeding, T., O'Higgins, M. and Rainwater, L., editors, 1990, *Poverty, Inequality and Income Distribution in Comparative Perspective*, Harvester Wheatsheaf, Hemel Hempstead.

Smolensky, E., Stiefel, L., Schmundt, M. and Plotnick, R., 1977, 'Adding In-Kind Transfers to the Personal Income and Outlay Account: Implications for the Size Distribution of Income', in Juster, F. T., editor, *The Distribution of Economic Well-Being*, Ballinger, Cambridge, MA.

Stahl, D. O. and Alexeev, M., 1985, 'The Influence of Black Markets on a Queue-Rationed Centrally Planned Economy', *Journal of Economic Theory*, Vol. 35: 234–250.

Stark, T., 1972, *The Distribution of Personal Income in the United Kingdom 1949–1963*, Cambridge University Press, Cambridge.

1978, 'Personal Incomes', in Atkinson, A. B., Harrison, A. J. and Stark, T., *Wealth and Personal Incomes*, Reviews of United Kingdom Statistical Sources, Vol. VI, Pergamon Press, Oxford.

Stigler, G. J., 1945, 'The Cost of Subsistence', *Journal of Farm Economics*, Vol. 27: 303–314.

Szalai, J., 1989, 'Poverty in Hungary During the Period of Economic Crisis', Background Paper for the 1990 *World Development Report*, The World Bank.

Sziraczki, G., 1990, 'Poverty in Eastern Europe', paper presented to European Association of Labour Economists Annual Conference, Lund.

Szulc, A., 1990, 'Aggregate Poverty Measures for Poland: 1980–1989 Evidence', paper presented at Third Polish-British Seminar on Social Policy, Madralin.

1991, 'Poverty Measures for Poland in the Eighties', in Panek T. and Szulc, A., *Income Distribution and Poverty Theory and a Case Study of Poland in the Eighties*, Central Statistical Office, Warsaw.

Teichova, A., 1988, *The Czechoslovak Economy 1918–1980*, Routledge, London.

Telyukov, A., 1991, 'Social Security System in the USSR: Long-Established

Patterns and Innovative Trends', unpublished.

Thompson, A., 1991, 'The Czechoslovakian Social Safety Net Benefit Provision', mimeo.

Topińska, I., 1991, 'The Impact of Social Transfers on Income Distribution: Poland, 1989', World Bank Socialist Economies Reform Unit, Research Paper 2.

Treml, V. G., 1990, 'Note on the Unrepresentativeness of the Goskomstat Household Budget Survey' unpublished research memorandum for the Berkeley-Duke Project on the Second Economy in the USSR, Department of Economics, Duke University, Durham, NC.

United Nations, 1977, *Provisional Guidelines on Statistics of the Distribution of Income, Consumption and Accumulation of Households*, Department of Economic and Social Affairs, Studies in Methods, Series M, No. 61, United Nations, New York

1981, *A Survey of National Sources of Income Distribution Statistics*, Department of International Economic and Social Affairs, Statistical Papers, Series M, No. 72, United Nations, New York

UN Economic Commission for Europe, 1967, *Incomes in Postwar Europe: A Study of Policies, Growth and Redistribution*, Geneva.

van Praag, B., Hagenaars, A. J. M. and van Weeren, J., 1982, 'Poverty in Europe' *Review of Income and Wealth*, Vol. 28: 345–359.

Večerník, J., 1990, 'Income Differentiation in Czechoslovakia: Some Evidence and Hypotheses on Systemic Specificities', Institute of Sociology, Academy of Sciences, Prague.

1991a, 'Earnings Distribution in Czechoslovakia: Intertemporal Changes and International Comparison', *European Sociological Review*, Vol. 7(3): 237–252.

1991b, 'Poverty in Czechoslovakia – A Brief Report Based on Two Surveys', unpublished.

Vielrose, E., 1978, 'Patterns of the Distribution of Earnings in Poland', in Krelle, W. and Shorrocks, A. F., editors, *Personal Income Distribution*, North-Holland, Amsterdam.

Vienna Institute for Comparative Economic Studies, 1984, *COMECON DATA 1983*, Macmillan, London.

1991, *COMECON DATA 1990*, Macmillan, London.

Vinokur, A. and Ofer, G., 1987, 'Inequality of Earnings, Household Income, and Wealth in the Soviet Union in the 1970s', in Millar, J. R., editor, *Politics, Work, and Daily Life in the USSR*, Cambridge University Press, Cambridge.

Vita, L., 1991, 'On the Future of Household Income Surveys in Hungary', paper presented at the BLS/Eurostat conference on Economic Statistics for Economies in Transition, Washington DC. 14–16 February 1991.

Wiktorow, A. and Mierzewski, P., 1991, 'Promise or Peril? Social Policy for Children during the Transition to the Market Economy in Poland', in Cornia, G. A. and Sipos, S., editors, *Children and the Transition to the Market Economy*, Avebury, Aldershot.

Wiles, P. J. D., 1974, *Distribution of Income: East and West*, North-Holland, Amsterdam.

1977, *Economic Institutions Compared*, Basil Blackwell, Oxford.

1978, 'Our Shaky Data Base', in Krelle, W. and Shorrocks, A. F., editors, *Personal Income Distribution*, North-Holland, Amsterdam.

1987, 'The Second Economy, Its Definitional Problems', in Alessandrini, S. and Dallago, B., editors, *The Unofficial Economy*, Gower, Aldershot.

Wiles, P. J. D. and Markowski, S., 1971, 'Income Distribution under Communism and Capitalism', *Soviet Studies*, Part I, Vol. 22(3): 344–369 and Part II, Vol. 22(4): 487–511.

Williams. C. A., Turnbull, J. G. and Cheit, E. F., 1982, *Economic and Social Security*, 5th edition, Wiley, New York.

Williamson, J. G., 1985, *Did British Capitalism Breed Inequality?*, Allen and Unwin, Boston.

World Bank, 1989, *Poland: Subsidies and Income Distribution*, Report No. 7776-POL, Washington DC.

1990, *World Development Report 1990*, Oxford University Press, Oxford.

1991a, *Czechoslovakia: Transition to a Market Economy*, World Bank, Washington DC.

1991b, *Hungary: Reform of the Social Policy and Distribution System*, World Bank, Washington DC.

1991c, *Hungary: Reform of Social Policy and Expenditures*, Report No. 9349-HU, World Bank, Washington DC.

Zam, M., 1991, 'Economic Reforms and Safety Nets in Hungary: Limits to Protection', in Cornia, G. A. and Sipos, S., editors, *Children and the Transition to the Market Economy*, Avebury, Aldershot.

Zaslavskaya, T. I., 1991, 'Socioeconomic Aspects of *Perestroyka*', in Hewett, E. A. and Winston, V. H., editors, *Milestones in Glasnost and Perestroyka*, The Brookings Institution, Washington DC.

Name Index

435

Subject Index